Israel, the Diaspora and Jewish Identity

Israel, the Diaspora and Jewish Identity

EDITED BY
DANNY BEN-MOSHE AND ZOHAR SEGEV

SUSSEX
ACADEMIC
PRESS

BRIGHTON • PORTLAND

2 4 6 8 10 9 7 5 3 1

First published 2007 in Great Britain by
SUSSEX ACADEMIC PRESS
PO Box 139
Eastbourne BN24 9BP

and in the United States of America by
SUSSEX ACADEMIC PRESS
920 NE 58th Ave Suite 300
Portland, Oregon 97213-3786

British Library Cataloguing in Publication Data
A CIP catalogue record for this book is available from the British Library.

Library of Congress Cataloging-in-Publication Data
Israel, the Diaspora, and Jewish identity / edited by Danny Ben-Moshe and Zohar Segev.
p. cm.
Includes bibliographical references and index.
ISBN 978-1-84519-189-4 (h/c : alk. paper)
ISBN 978-1-84519-242-6 (pbk : alk. paper)
1. Jews—Identity. 2. Israel and the diaspora. 3. Jews—United States—Identity. 4. Jews—United States—Attitudes toward Israel. 5. Jews—Israel—Identity. I. Ben-Moshe, Danny. II. Segev, Zohar.

DS143.I73 2007
305.892'4—dc22

2006038374

Typeset and designed by SAP, Brighton & Eastbourne
Printed by TJ International, Padstow, Cornwall
This book is printed on acid-free paper.

Contents

Introduction
World Jewry, Identity and Israel

Danny Ben-Moshe and Zohar Segev

Scan any Jewish newspaper in any part of the world, pick up a calendar of Jewish communal events on any continent, examine the list of organizations housed in Jewish community centres in capital cities or regional locations, and it is clear that Israel is a central feature in Diaspora Jewish life. This is why Israel has been described, in this book and more widely, as the civil religion of Diaspora Jews.

Israel-related activity in Diaspora Jewish life is manifest in several quantifiable ways, such as Israel visits, *aliyah*, donations, educational programmes, lobbying initiatives or letters to the editor complaining of media bias. There are many books and articles describing and analysing these various phenomena. What is less clear, however, and less examined in the literature, is what this tells us about the place of Israel in Diaspora Jewish identity – a question that this book addresses.

Jewish identification is of course voluntary, and identification with Israel as a component of that identity is similarly voluntary. Jews, like everyone else, have multiple identities and Israel is only one aspect of Jewish identity that has to compete and coexist with many other Jewish and non-Jewish factors. The chapters that follow explore what it is about Israel that resonates or not with Diaspora Jews, leading them to place Israel above, alongside or below competing or complementary considerations in their identity. The purpose is to probe the way in which this identity is manifest.

The place of Israel in Diaspora Jewish identity is important for three key reasons:

- First, it has been established that those who have a stronger identification with Israel have a stronger Jewish identity and vice versa. This issue of Diaspora identification with Israel is therefore relevant to the future of the Jewish people threatened by assimilation.
- Secondly, the nature and extent of identification with Israel of Diaspora Jews is central to the process of establishing a notion of Jewish peoplehood. This issue, taken up in several contributions in this volume,[1] is now at the cutting edge of the debate about Israel–Diaspora relations. Simply put, it is only possible to speak about Jews as a people if Jews outside of Israel identify with those inside Israel, and of course, vice versa.
- Thirdly, the place of Israel in the identity of Diaspora Jews is relevant to the nature of Judaism, Zionism and indeed notions of Jewish peoplehood in the Jewish state,

> and practical issues relating to the soft power of Israel in international affairs. In the 1950s, prominent American Zionist leader Dr Emanuel Neumann explained that the involvement of Diaspora Jewry in Israel was important for their identity as Jews. However, he also said it was vital to Israel, which could otherwise become a Levantine–Middle East state with a limited future if it did not have the cultural, economic and political involvement of Diaspora Jewry in general and US Jewry in particular.[2]

Diaspora identity is traditionally influenced by language, historical memory, national religion and minority status.[3] That identity is a construct that is the result of, and a response to, social and historical change. These constructs have changed throughout Jewish history, but Israel, albeit in various forms, has always remained central to Jewish identity.

The Holocaust and the establishment of the State of Israel were the two most formative events of the twentieth century for the Jewish people and Jewish identity. In almost all the countries considered in this volume, living memory of these events explains levels of identification with Israel. The younger the age group and the further removed from these formative events, the weaker the level of identification with Israel. As several contributions in this volume document, generational factors are one clear criterion determining the level of identification with Israel.

From 1990 to the present, much has been said of the crisis of Jewish identity in the Diaspora, evident through assimilation. However, there is an equally great crisis of identity in Israel itself. Not only has Israel experienced post-Zionism on the secular left, it is now grappling with the end of the Greater Israel experiment, with theocratic post-Zionism emerging on the right.

These are some of the constructs shaping the place of Israel in Diaspora identity. Accordingly, contributors in this volume ponder what impact these phenomena have on the identity of Diaspora Jewry and whether they lead them to be closer to or further away from Israel.

When the Diaspora is mentioned, especially in Israel, the term "American Jewry" would probably be a more accurate description of what is being discussed. This Israeli focus on six-sevenths of World Jewry outside of Israel may make sense in terms of Israel's official interest in the one world superpower, but it is myopic when it comes to understanding how and why Jews identify with the Jewish state, nuances in the dynamics of Israel–Diaspora relations, and alternative models for these relations.

This book literally considers the Diaspora in the broader sense of the word. This approach better reflects the diverse Jewish world, and enables us to consider qualitative dimensions of Jewish existence that may not be present in the quantitatively dominant American sphere. Indeed, in terms of identification with Israel, American Jewry is by all measures lagging behind most other communities. Accordingly (apart from the editors), of the contributors to this book, twenty are from Israel, nine are from America, and twelve are from other Diasporas including three from England, three from Australia, two from France, and others from Canada, South Africa and Argentina.

The underlying ethos in this book is that Israel and the Diaspora need to engage each other as partners on the issue of identity. Accordingly, the volume is co-authored by academics in Israel and the Diaspora and, as noted, the range of contributors reflects the diversity of the Diaspora. Furthermore, following each chapter in **Part I: Themes and Issues** is both an Israeli- and a Diaspora-based commentary responding to the issues raised in the chapter. Both Israeli and Diaspora writers offer concluding thoughts at the end of the book.

Analysis of the place of Israel in Diaspora Jewish identity is tackled in two main ways: through transnational themes and issues **(Part I: Themes and Issues)**, and through country- or region-specific analysis **(Part II: Countries and Regions)**. These constitute the two main sections of the book.

Part I probes the way in which Israel features and coexists, or not, with other aspects of Diaspora hybrid identities through themes and issues. These include:

- *Anti-Semitism*, by Associate Professor Danny Ben-Moshe, which notes that the upsurge of (new) anti-Semitism since September 2000 has done more than a plethora of education campaigns to enhance Jewish identification with Israel.
- *Israel visits* and the extent to which they provide a sense of Jewish peoplehood as an aspect of identity, discussed by Dr David Mittelberg.
- *Religion*, including Orthodox Jewry, analyzed by Professor Chaim I. Waxman, Reform Judaism by Michael Livini, and Conservative Judaism by Dr Daniel Gordis.
- *Political orientation*, because for a number of Diaspora Jews their Jewish identification is manifest in their political stance in relation to the peace process; this is analyzed in terms of the non- and anti-Zionist left by Dr Philip Mendes, and the Zionist left and right by Dr Ofira Seliktar.
- *Israeli foreign and defence policy*, with Dr Jonathan Rynhold asking to what extent Israeli governments take into account the impact of their decisions on Diaspora identity.
- *Gender*, as Dr Elana Sztokman notes, shapes the nature of the place of Israel in Diaspora identity.
- *Israelis in the Diaspora*, as considered by Professor Steven Gold.

Each chapter in **Part I: Themes and Issues** has a respondent from Israel and the Diaspora commenting on the issues raised in that chapter. The aim is not to highlight differences or points of agreement, but rather to kick start a conversation that focuses thinking about identity around the issues raised in the specific chapters.

Part II is dedicated to specific countries and regions. Where possible the authors are from the countries being written about, so that we can hear not only academic experts, but also authentic voices from these communities. There are no respondents in this section of the book. Contributors in this section are:

- *Canada:* Dr David Goldberg of the Canada–Israel Committee.
- *Britain:* Dr Colin Shindler of the School of Oriental and African Studies at the University of London.
- *Latin America:* Dr Graciela Ben-Dror, originally from Uruguay, but now at Haifa University.
- *France:* Dr Erik Cohen, originally from Morocco, educated in France and an émigré to Israel, where he now works at Bar-Ilan University.
- *Australia:* Associate Professor Suzanne Rutland of Sydney University.

- *America:* Dr Robert Wexler, President of the University of Judaism, Los Angeles.
- *South Africa:* Professor Milton Shain and Associate Professor Richard Mendelsohn of the University of Cape Town.
- *Russia:* Professor Larissa Remennick, of Bar-Ilan University, Israel, originally from Moscow, Russia.

It has obviously not been viable to include every Diaspora community in this volume, but there has been a concerted effort to include as many communities as possible. Three additional contributions were to be included from non-English speaking countries, but for a range of reasons beyond our control the prospective authors were ultimately unable to participate in this project.

Finally, consistent with the principles of partnership, dialogue and equity, two concluding perspectives are offered: the first by Professor Gabriel Sheffer of the Hebrew University in Jerusalem, a leading international authority on diasporas, and the second by Dr Steven Bayme of the American Jewish Committee in New York, one of the most informed figures on Israel–Diaspora relations. Each tries, from their respective vantage points, to synthesise what the various contributions tell us about the place of Israel in Diaspora Jewish identity, and points to future directions in Israel–Diaspora relations, and the possible place of Israel in Diaspora identity.

The voices in this book are consciously not just those of academics, reflecting the fact that there are many stakeholders in the shaping of identity. Aside from the co-editors, twenty-five contributors are academics, while fourteen come from a range of relevant positions in the Jewish world, including two informal educators (Lazarus and Livini), a Director General of a Jewish Agency department (Hoffmann), a Hillel director (Trajtenberg), a Rabbi (Hammer), two staff members of the Madel Institute (Katzman and Gordis), two journalists, one from Israel (Barkat) and one from the UK (Freedland), a member of a political think tank in America (Lasensky), and three professionals from Diaspora Jewish community organizations (Hart, Goldberg and Bayme). These categories are somewhat misleading, as many of the contributors wear several hats, but listing their primary roles is a useful adjunct.

As this book was being compiled the flaws in a division between Israel and the Diaspora became apparent. Several contributors have lived and worked in both Israel and the Diaspora, as is the case with the two co-editors. Several of the Israel-based writers were originally from the Diaspora. Some Israeli participants spent extended periods of time in the Diaspora while preparing their contributions. Some contributors had professional appointments in both Israel and the Diaspora, where they split their time. Some of the Diaspora contributors were either Israelis now living in the Diaspora or had made *aliyah* before returning to live in the Diaspora after many years. One Diaspora contributor even made *aliyah* during the writing of this book. These circumstances made it apparent that not only is the Israel–Diaspora division a somewhat false one, but that many Jews have a transnational identity in which both Israel and the Diaspora are central parts, adding a further level of complexity to the deliberations raised herein.

This book is conceptualised as a dialogue between Israel and the Diaspora on the issue of identity. By its nature it is only the beginning of a conversation, but hopefully one that can trigger more in-depth and wider debate. There are aspects to that debate we have been unable to include in this volume, such as philanthropy, Hebrew language and culture, and media activism, which we hope will be considered in ongoing deliberations on the issue of identity. The absence of empirical information on the issue of Israel identity among Diaspora Jews meant many of the contributors could only ask questions rather than definitively answer them, but it is hoped that their discussions add to our theoretical and applied understanding of diasporas and the place of Israel in Diaspora Jewish identity.

Overall, Jews — like everyone else — have contested identities. For some, other aspects of their Jewish identity dominate, such as religion and culture, in which Israel may not be a significant feature. For others still, non-Jewish universal factors take supremacy in their identity. This is a challenge for all those concerned with Israel–Diaspora relations and the existence of a Jewish peoplehood. Evidence suggests that the old paradigms of "Israel or" no longer apply; that new models must be created to allow for these multiple identities, which need to become complementary identities. Models that have framed Israel–Diaspora relations in the past will not necessarily govern that relationship in the future which this book will play a very modest part in shaping. Assessing the place of Israel in the identity of Diaspora Jews helps enable consideration of future directions of this identity.

Of course in the debate about Jewish identity and Jewish peoplehood, the place of Israel in Diaspora identity is only half the issue. The other half is the place of the Diaspora in the identity of Israeli Jews. This is not the subject of this volume but is nevertheless an important piece of the jigsaw that requires urgent consideration.

As Israel races ahead to become the numerically largest Jewish community in the world it is timely to consider its place in the identity of Diaspora Jews. However, Israel is not, of course, a monolithic place. The identity Israel offers Diaspora Jews is a multiple one: it is Mamoona, kibbutz, Tel Aviv beach, the Kotel, the gay pride parade, settlers in Hebron and more. There are and always will be layers of identity.[4] The question is not only on which layer does Israel feature in the identity of Diaspora Jews, but which part of Israel is it that features in that identity?

We are deeply indebted to all the contributors to this volume for their efforts, to our research assistant Michelle Perl, copy-editor Iris Lauchland, and to the support of our families and the assistance of the publishers.

DANNY BEN-MOSHE
Melbourne, Australia

ZOHAR SEGEV
Haifa, Israel

May 2007

Notes

1 See particularly the contributions in this volume by Mittelberg, Grant and Marmur, and Bayme.
2 Neumann, 12 September 1957, Central Zionist Archives A-123/528.
3 William Safran, "Comparing Diasporas: A Review Essay", *Diaspora*, 8, 3 (Winter 1999).
4 Lou Drofenik, "The Filo Pastry of Identity: Lifting The Many Layers of Maltese Cultural Identity." Paper presented at the Institute for Community Engagement and Policy Alternatives seminar, Victoria University, Melbourne, 6 September 2005.

Part I

ISSUES AND THEMES

1

The New Anti-Semitism, Jewish Identity and the Question of Zionism

Danny Ben-Moshe

Anti-Semitism has been central to the development of Zionism. As a young man Theodor Herzl loved the Austrian capital Vienna, which he believed embodied all that was good about cosmopolitanism. However, it was the election of anti-Semite Karl Lueger as the mayor of Vienna in 1895 and Herzl's exclusion from elite circles in that city, not to mention the Dreyfus trial he witnessed in Paris in 1894, that turned the assimilated Jewish writer into the founder of political Zionism.

There has thus been, from the outset of Zionism, a very strong nexus between anti-Semitism and the development of Zionist identity. It was the most extreme form of anti-Semitism, the Holocaust, which placed Israel in the identity of world Jewry. It was this mass murder across Europe of a third of the Jewish people that converted the majority of world Jewry into Zionists, into believers that Jews had the need and right to a state of their own. "Never again" became the Jewish mantra — with the State of Israel being the means to ensure these words would not be hollow.

In the lead up to the Six Day War, however, genocide again seemed possible and Jews throughout the Diaspora rallied for the Jewish state in a way they had never done before. It was not only identifying Zionists that were affected by these events, but many other Jews as well. Non-Zionist French Jew Raymond Aron, for example, wrote a week after the war about how, as a second Auschwitz seemed possible, "that within him too there mounted an irresistible feeling of solidarity".[1]

More than Ben-Gurion or Begin, it was Abdul Gamal Nasser's hateful rhetoric in the lead up to the Six Day War — a language directed at the State of Israel but familiar to Jews worldwide — that turned non-Zionists into Zionists. It was the palpable fear of Israel's elimination and the pure joy at its survival that placed Israel squarely in the identity of world Jewry.

Israeli military heroism meant Jews around the world no longer had to bow down before the anti-Semite. Growing up in apartheid South Africa, Hirsh Goodman describes how he used to be taunted by an anti-Semite in his local park and how, when he became an Israeli paratrooper he thought of those taunts and what he would do if he went back to South Africa, took a walk in his old local park and that anti-Semite dared to call him a "fucking Jew".[2] As the new Jew (re)created by Israel he was in a position to confront the anti-Semites from his Diaspora past.

On a more significant level, but as part of the same mental process, Natan Sharansky described the lack of strength Jews had in the former Soviet Union as a result of anti-Semitism and then described how:

> The strength arrived, unexpectedly, from a far-off land and war. The stellar Israeli victory in the Six Day War enabled us to stand tall. People suddenly treated Jews differently. Even the anti-Semitic jokes changed. They were no longer about the cowardly, mendacious Jew. They were about the upstart, brave and victorious Jew.
>
> It was through the war that I became aware of the Jewish state, and of the language and culture it embodied. I was suddenly exposed to the existence of Jewish people, to the existence of tradition and culture. I was no longer a disconnected individual in an alienating and hostile world. I was a person with an identity and roots. I felt that I had a history, a nation, and a country behind me. That I had, at the end of the earth, a homeland. That I belonged. That feeling was my companion through years of struggle for human rights, in the framework of the Zionist movement, and through long years in prison. Even in solitary confinement I believed that the Jewish people and the State of Israel would fight for me. I was not alone. I was arrested a few months after the Entebbe operation. The operation signified that Israel was prepared to go any distance to save its citizens, and it made a huge impression on me. During my years in prison, every aircraft in Siberia's skies sounded to me like the rescue force coming to liberate me. True, I was not rescued by an airplane or bold military mission, but I was certainly released from my prison by the Jewish people and the State of Israel. I truly was not alone.[3]

Over subsequent years, starting in a more significant way with the Lebanon War in 1982, the unquestioning identification with Israel that characterised the Diaspora began to erode. This took place as the more confident and established State engaged in acts that were not about existential survival (such as settlement building in the disputed territories) with which the Diaspora did not concur. It was the attempt to get out of this political quagmire that led to even greater distancing between Israel and the Diaspora, for as Israelis experienced the economic benefits of the Oslo peace process in the 1990s the Diaspora felt free to turn inward and address its own crisis of assimilation. The collapse of that peace process after the Camp David Summit in 2000, and the subsequent outbreak of the Israeli–Palestinian war unleashed a wave of anti-Semitism worldwide which, as with the events of 1967, 1948 and Herzl's experiences, once again placed Israel squarely and strongly in the identity of the majority of world Jewry.

The New Anti-Semitism

Anti-Semitism has gone through many guises and the Jew hatred that was unleashed with the Palestinian response to Ariel Sharon's walk on the Temple Mount in September 2000 is known as the "new anti-Semitism", which has also been described as "Judeophobia". This term, coined in the book *A New AntiSemitism? Debating*

Judeophobia in 21st-Century Britain,[4] refers to anti-Semitism in the United Kingdom, but can also be applied more broadly. According to the authors Barry Kosmin and Paul Ignaski, Judeophobia is:

> a fear of, and hostility toward Jews as a collectivity, rather than the propagation of racial ideologies of the old anti-Semitism . . . It is a mindset characterized by an obsession with, and vilification of, the State of Israel, and Jews in general, in the case of Britain, as a consequence of their strong sense of attachment to Israel. Today's Judeophobia is an assault on the essence of the Jewish collectivity, both in terms of a Jewish sovereign state in its ancient homeland, and the nature of robust, emancipated, and self-aware Diaspora communities.[5]

For the new anti-Semitism there is a very clear connection between Israel and the Diaspora. As British Chief Rabbi Jonathan Sacks described it:

> By attacking Israel rather than Jews; be demonizing it and blaming it for all the troubles of the world. It is then able to turn the whole system, created to protect Jews, into a weapon with which to attack Jews. Accuse Israel (and by implication Jews everywhere) of racism, apartheid and ethnic cleansing, and you are then able to say: if you are against these things, then you must be against Israel and Jews.[6]

This Israel–Diaspora link has been evident in many anti-Semitic incidents. For example, after being arrested in October 2000 for stabbing yeshiva student Mayer David Myers 29 times at a bus stop in London, Algerian Nabil Ouldeddine told police, "Israel are the murderers. They kill women and children. So I stabbed him."[7] The link was made similarly clear to an elderly Jewish doctor beaten by three men in *kefiyah*s in Cape Town in September 2001 as they repeatedly said, "You Jews are the ones making trouble in the Middle East."[8]

The link between hatred for Israel and attacks on Diaspora Jews is clear. It is what Roger Cukierman, President of the French Jewish umbrella body *Conseil Représentatif des Institutions juives de France* (CRIF) (Representative Council of French Jewish Institutions) described in 2004 as Arab and Islamic attacks in Europe occurring "in the shadow" of the conflict on the Middle East.[9] The question is, does this increase or diminish the place of Israel in the identity of Diaspora Jews who are exposed to this hatred and vilification?

Diaspora Jews have three options in response to the threat and vulnerability posed by the new anti-Semitism:

- Distance themselves from Israel as the cause of their anti-Semitism;
- Move closer toward Israel in the realisation that they are in a common boat and need a homeland just in case; or
- Work towards securing their place in the societies in which they live based on a Bundist rather than Zionist approach.

These are the deliberations that this chapter considers.

Responding to the New Anti-Semitism: Society and the Workplace

The new anti-Semitism has led many Jews to question their acceptance in the global community. This is particularly pronounced for Jews on the left of the Jewish political spectrum, as it is the Left not the Right who lead the new anti-Semitic charge. As French philosopher Pierre-André Taguieff put it, there is a "new planetary Judeophobia" on the Left, which is an "anti-Jewish anti-racism".[10]

It was the new anti-Semitism that led American feminist, religiously progressive and politically dovish academic Phyllis Chesler to write a book on the subject. The impact of this phenomena was made clear by Chesler stating how she didn't want to write *The New Anti-Semitism* (2003), how she wanted to avoid becoming a "professional Jew" and how she did not want "to psychologically live in a ghetto".[11] She admitted:

> I find it extraordinary that I am writing a book about a new language of anti-Semitism, one that is so intimately connected to the events of 9/11. Who would ever have thought that such a work would be necessary in the twenty-first century . . . But I must speak out. Something awful is happening to the world Jews. If the daily violence and demented propaganda against them is not effectively countered, I fear that the Jews may again be sacrificed to a world gone mad and in search of a sacred scapegoat.[12]

Chesler may have thought that it was religious right-wingers who had in their imagination another Holocaust in which Jews are sacrificed, but now it had entered her own worldview.

One dimension of the significance of the new anti-Semitism is its impact on the way Jews relate to non-Jews. As Chesler wrote, "my heart is broken by the cunning and purposeful silence of progressives and academics on the subject of anti-Semitism and terrorism." She clarified that by silence she really means betrayal.[13] Chesler reached the conclusion that she could no longer trust public intellectuals, a serious consequence for an American Jewish public intellectual.[14] If Jews have less trust in the broader public, will it increase the trust they have in Jewish figures and the Jewish state?

The discrimination experienced by Chesler at an individual level relates to her engagement with Israel. She noted how it was after she started standing up for Israel that she stopped being invited to public and private events, and that her advice was no longer sought.[15] If identification with Israel is the cause for her personal exclusion, is Israel also the sanctuary, not in a physical sense, but in a spiritual, intellectual, philosophical and political way? If so, does this enhance the place of Israel in the identity of individuals who have had a similar experience to Chesler?

Mimi Schwartz, an activist in the America's left-wing Jewish Tikkun community, had a similar experience to Chesler. An American child of refugees from Germany, she wrote how she believed anti-Semitism was part of her parents' old world, not her new world. That had changed, however, when at the New Jersey College where she had taught for 22 years, anti-Semitic anti-Israel leaflets appeared with Hitler and Israeli soldiers of equal size, with a Christ-like figure crucified on a Star of David rather than a cross, with the caption "Stop the murder. Free the Palestinians." It was not so much the fliers that disturbed Schwartz, but the response to them.

Because these contentious fliers were put up without permission, a 'Rally of Harmony' was organized to try and calm the situation on campus. Schwartz, who expected her left-wing colleagues and friends of many years to readily attend, was shocked to discover that they boycotted the event. They argued that the real issue was the Israeli occupation and that taking the fliers down was a conspiracy. As one of her long-standing friends said, "All the fliers did was display Palestinian suffering. So what if they didn't get official permission, a mere technicality, an excuse meant to appease the Holocaust powers who were organizing the rally". When this history professor was asked if she found the Christ-like imagery offensive, she said it was to her the image of a Palestinian mother weeping for her son. The words 'power' and 'conspiracy' and the lack of offence that the people she knew and trusted had taken at these images struck Schwartz. Suddenly she realized, "So this is why my Dad left Germany!" because of the attitudes of people like that — leaving her over 50 years on from the Holocaust feeling "betrayed".[16]

If Israel has pushed liberal colleagues away from Schwartz because she perceives their new anti-Semitism or tolerance of it, the question that follows is whether left-wing Jewish critics of Israel like her are pulled closer to Israel in the process? Are they, like a Jew in Germany in the 1930s, in need of a new homeland, or at least knowing that the option of a Jewish homeland is there? The experience of the new anti-Semitism may lead Jews to question the very society they are in, or, as the Toronto-based Gil Troy said, "Rather than asking what Israel did to deserve such criticism, it is time to start asking, where did liberalism go wrong?"[17]

Evidence suggests two responses from the Jewish Left. One is to accept the thesis of the broad Left and move away from being critics of Israeli policy to being opponents of the Zionist idea. This has clearly been the case for some, such as left-wing American Jew Joel Kovel. Alternatively, left-wing Jews will move away from the Left to be closer to Israel. Mimi Schwartz, who believes in speaking out against Israeli policies she opposes, recounts how, when confronted with new anti-Semitism, she "wanted to yell. And what about Israeli mothers who are suffering? And don't the Israelis have the right to self-defence?"[18]

What needs to be clearly recognised is that Jews across the Diaspora are experiencing actual anti-Semitism or the fear of anti-Semitism in their day-to-day lives, in which Israel is a feature. As British Chief Rabbi Sacks put it, it is becoming "uncomfortable" to be a Jew in the UK.[19] The change is apparent in informal interactions, such as the workplace, with German Jews reporting that people now say things about Jews and Israel they would not previously have said and that it was possible to lose friends if you defended Israel.[20] Italian Jews report being much more careful about what they say as the community, "had been frightened and destabilized by the public discourse on Israel and the Jews".[21]

Responses to the new anti-Semitism will obviously have a practical impact on communal planning. For example, leaders of the French Jewish community have explained how anti-Semitism in schools and the non-action of teachers in response to such incidents is one factor that explains Jewish school numbers rising from 1,500 in the 1980s to more than 30,000 today.[22] Will this lead to a more parochial community, but one where children are more exposed to Israel than they would be in a state school?

The fact is, of course, that we do not know how the Jews of Germany, Italy, France and many other Diasporas respond to situations in which anti-Semitism is manifest. One of the contentions of this chapter is that the nature of Jewish communal data gathering on anti-Semitism counts anti-Semitic incidents, but does not probe and allow for analysis of the impacts of these incidents on the Jewish and wider communities. However, it is the impact data that is also required. There is some evidence from the UK and France to support the contention that the reliance on, and identification with, Israel amongst Diaspora Jewry is enhanced as a result of the new anti-Semitism.[23]

Political Vulnerability and Closeness to Israel — The Muslim Factor

If workplace and personal interactions are one consideration influencing the place and importance of Israel for Diaspora Jews, broader political considerations are another. In Europe this is manifest in relation to the Islamic community of 15 million whose political mobilisation threatens the political influence and sense of security of European Jewry.

Events around the new anti-Semitism suggest that the rapidly growing Islamic communities of Europe are likely to be a significant political force; far greater in numbers than European Jewry will ever be. This raises the issue of whether European policy towards Israel and Jews will be determined by the influence of the Islamic community on domestic politics. This influence could increase as the Islamic community becomes more politically sophisticated, organized and integrated into mainstream political parties. The early evidence suggests that this is happening.

In 2004 Secretary-General of the European Jewish Congress, Serge Cwajgenbaum left no room for doubt about the political impact of the Islamic electorate, asserting that the initial European responses of denying the wave of anti-Semitism was because of political concerns about the 15 million Muslims on the continent.[24] Indeed, when violent anti-Semitism became an issue of growing concern in France the Jewish community felt there was an inadequate response from the authorities. Reflecting on this, Jean-Yves Camus, head of research at the Paris-based European Center for Research and Action on Racism and Anti-Semitism, said of the non-reaction of socialist Prime Minister Lionel Jospin to anti-Semitic incidents in the lead up to the 2002 election, "He did not react. Out of ignorance? Maybe. Or maybe because part of the Socialist leadership thought that many Muslims would vote against Jospin."[25]

Representatives of Italian, Belgium and French Jewry have expressed the view that deference to the Muslim electorate could mean that Jewish communities are not listened to in the future.[26] Indeed, French Jewish representatives speak of a feeling of isolation and not being able to identify supporters, and Jewish representatives in Belgium expressed a fear that they might be abandoned by politicians looking for new voters such as Muslims. In both these countries 10 percent of the electorate are Muslims.[27] Once again the issue arises, will the growing sense of insecurity be filled by a growing closeness to Israel? Does diminished trust in your own government to protect your welfare as a Jew lead to increased reliance on the Government of Israel to protect you as a Jew? The rise in *aliyah* of French Jewry over the past few years, with a 21 percent increase in the first half of 2003, a 26 percent increase in the first half of 2004 and a 30 percent increase in 2005, suggests that for some the answer is very clear.[28] It is important to note that some of those who are seen as being engaged in the new anti-Semitism draw a distinction between supporters of Israel and Jews. For example, Ken Livingstone, the Mayor of London, supported an event which celebrated the 350 years of Jewish life in London, an event which had no Israel-specific dimension.[29]

Dealing with the manifestation and fear of anti-Semitism is not just a European concern. What does the small Venezuelan Jewish community feel when its President, Hugo Chavez, complements his warm ties with Iran and Hamas by saying in a 2005 Christmas Eve address that, "the minorities, the descendants of those who crucified

Christ, have taken over the riches of the world"?[30] Evidence suggests that a rise in *aliyah* is one, albeit minority response.

What is beyond doubt is that fear has returned as a factor in Jewish life and the nature of Jewish life has been changed as a result. Jews feel unable to identify themselves as such in public, with Rabbis in France and Belgium openly advising their community not to do so by wearing *kippot* (skullcaps) in public. In 2004, 55 percent of US Jewry believed anti-Semitism was a "very serious problem", up from 41 percent in 2003 and 26 percent in 2001. Sixty-seven percent said it would increase worldwide in years to come, including 49 percent in America.[31] As Robert Wexler describes in his chapter on American Jewry in this volume, Jewish community sentiment is that the level of anti-Semitism is likely to continue and increase.

To some extent, the impact of anti-Semitism on the place of Israel in the identity of Diaspora Jewry will depend on its actual extent or the extent of fear about anti-Semitism. In Italy, Jews have expressed fears that, since anti-Jewish stereotypes were alive in Italy and even held by intellectuals, "eventually overt anti-Semitism could arise quite easily".[32] The extent of the new anti-Semitism shows how quickly hatred of Jews can gather momentum and become a real threat. As an unpublished and controversial European Union Monitoring Commission report on anti-Semitism found:

> In the heated public debate on Israeli politics and the boundary between criticism of Israel and anti-Semitism, individuals who are not politically active and do not belong to one of the ideological camps mentioned above become motivated to voice their latent anti-Semitic attitudes (mostly in the form of telephone calls and insulting letters).[33]

In his book *The Return of Anti-Semitism*, Gabriel Schoenfeld writes:

> Great shocks, as we know from the last century, can produce political flux beyond all foresight. In recent years the world has been subjected to a series of such shocks, September 11 being the greatest of them. More may be on the way, and where their repercussions will end no one can yet know. But the concomitant and hardly coincidental revival of the ancient fear and hatred known as anti-Semitism must make one tremble. So too must the indifference and denial that have greeted its resurgence.[34]

All these events have an impact on Jewish identity and the role of Israel in being a safety net for that identity. As one French Jew who bought a holiday home in Israel, said in 2006:

> We purchased the apartment in 2001, at the height of the Intifada. We had only one reason: we wanted to inject money into the Israeli economy during its hardest period. Since owning the apartment, we come to Israel a lot, but today I can say that we came because of the war. France has Jews of European descent, and Jews of African descent. Jews who experienced the Holocaust and Jews who experienced the Arab hatred. We know what it's like to live with anti-Semitism, and we know that the only real solution is to come and live in Israel. People in their fifties can't make *aliyah* and start over, but we are still suffering from the rising Muslim power in France and the changing French demography, which works against us, and for this reason we have to show solidarity with Israel.[35]

Reinforcing the Israel 'Just in Case Syndrome'

In his 2003 book about the new anti-Semitism, Anti-Defamation League National Director Abe Foxman argues that:

> After the Holocaust Israel is also the place of last refuge for endangered Jews, the country where Jews can go when they are rejected everywhere else . . . The Holocaust deepened the Jewish sense of anxiety about depending on the goodwill of others, which two millennia of tragedy had already developed. The existence of Israel, a homeland established by Jews for Jews, serves as [a] psychological insurance policy of the Jews who are well aware that if there had been an Israel during World War II, many of the six million would have been saved.[36]

Foxman points out this is not theoretical, citing *aliyah* from the former Soviet Union and Ethiopian Jewry as communities saved by Israel, and he expresses the concern that Israel could be called upon to save additional Jewish communities experiencing the new anti-Semitism. He cites Argentina, South Africa, Morocco, Tunisia and Iran, and possibly (under extreme circumstances) France as potentially vulnerable communities to whom Israel may need to come to the rescue.[37]

Whether or not 700,000 French Jews are likely to need an emergency airlift to Tel Aviv is a moot point, but there is no doubt that the new anti-Semitism has reinforced the place of Israel as a refuge which is there for world Jewry 'just in case'. As Professor Walter Reich, former director of the US Holocaust Memorial Museum observed in 2002, the wave of global anti-Semitism is a reminder "of the core reason for the Jewish state's existence". Reich concludes, "Jews will never have secure homes anywhere unless they also have a national home in Israel — a haven to which they can escape from wherever they are if the beast of anti-Semitism is ever again given the power to put its passions in murderous gear."[38]

What I dub the 'just in case syndrome' is for many Diaspora Jews the fundamental way in which Israel features in their identity; because of, and in response to, anti-Semitism — including the most personally successful Diaspora Jews in the most successful of Diasporas, such as America. The 'just in case' syndrome runs deep in the Jewish psyche, including those not known for their affinity to Israel. For example, Ian Katz, feature editor with the anti-Israel *Guardian* newspaper in England, described how, despite his despair at Israel's political actions, "somewhere inside there is always a small persistent voice saying: these people are putting their necks on the line, making sacrifices, doing ugly things, so that there will be a sanctuary for you if you ever need one. Who are you to criticize?"[39]

A 2004 study of Melbourne Jewry identified anti-Semitism as a major issue of concern. What is significant for this chapter, however, is that the surveyed respondents not only recognised anti-Semitism as an issue of major concern, but clearly expressed the 'just in case' syndrome as a result. As one 50-year-old respondent said, "Israel just needs to be sufficiently strong to protect Jews wherever they are and to remain a true safe haven".[40]

The link between anti-Semitism in the Diaspora and the need for Israel to be there just in case was articulated in the Melbourne survey by a 30-year-old mother of two young children. She described anti-Semitism as:

> A big issue, I work in a very non-Jewish area and I'm just waiting for the day when there will be some anti-Semitic remarks directed against me, which there have been in the past in other environments. It is a problem when shuls are graffitied and there are guards at every door of every Jewish organization and communal function, it's a worry. Ten years ago you didn't see that. Guards at every school, it's a necessity.[41]

When asked what role there is for Israel in countering this anti-Semitism, the mother responded that it was not to provide guards to these vulnerable institutions but rather, "You know that you have a place to go to and when an opportunity arises and things get so bad in your country you know that there's always Israel for you".[42] Indeed, against the backdrop of the Venezuelan President Hugo Chavez's overt hostility towards Israel, a Venezuelan Jewish delegation travelled to Israel in 2006 with the specific aim of establishing optimal immigration options for the country's Jews.[43]

In practical terms the Israel–Palestinian fighting since 2000 and the concomitant new anti-Semitism has led the Diaspora to rally to Israel's defence in the face of political attacks, while Israel has increased its sense of responsibility for the Diaspora. As then Israeli Foreign Minister Silvan Shalom told the European Jewish Congress in 2004, "We are determined that Jews — whether they live in Jerusalem or Paris or Stockholm, in Jerba or Haifa or Istanbul — should be able to live their lives, free of the fear of verbal or physical attack."[44] Israel being at the forefront of countering this problem for world Jewry can increase the reliance on Israel by world Jewry and thus its place in their identity. In this respect the Israeli–Palestinian fighting has, according to Yossi Shain and Barry Bristman, 'resecuritised' the Israel–Diaspora relationship, and for these authors:

> the link between Israeli security and the diaspora has been the strongest in terms of identity formation and community mobilization . . .
>
> The new manifestations of the Middle East conflict and the September attacks on the United States have returned the question of Jewish security to the heart of Jewish communities worldwide, and to the core of diasporic relations with Israel.[45]

If this thesis is correct, and according to Shain and Bristman "the revival of an 'us versus them' conflict" has brought the two sides closer together",[46] the consequences of anti-Semitism reinforces the place of Israel in Diaspora Jewish identity.

Limited Impact on Identity and the Jewish Anti-Zionist Option

It should not be assumed that the new anti-Semitism will automatically increase the place of Israel in the identity of Diaspora Jews. This is because if Israel is perceived as being the "reason" for the anti-Semitism it can lead Jews to distinguish themselves from Israel in an attempt to avoid the anti-Semitism. Members of the Belgium Jewish community, for example, complained about the lack of distinction between Israelis and Jews in the media, saying they are blamed for situations with the Palestinians they themselves deplore. Similar views were expressed by Jews from France, Germany, Spain and Greece.[47]

It must be recognised that the rise of the new anti-Semitism does not necessarily lead to a fundamental change in identity. Writing the cover story "A dangerous time to be a Jew" in the British magazine *New Statesman*, Simon Sebag Montefiore detailed the alarming rise of anti-Semitism and the way Israel was demonised. He concluded:

> Until 9/11, Anglo Jewry had become accustomed to prejudiced (media) coverage of Israel. But if you were not a Zionist, as many Jews are not, you did not need to worry. Since 9/11, and particularly post-Iraq, we have witnessed a sea change. It is as if, in the mythical scale of 9/11, al Qaeda had unlocked a forgotten cultural capsule of anti-Semitic myths, sealed and forgotten since the Nazis, the Black Hundreds and the medieval blood libels. Just words? But words matter in a violent world. This weird and scary nonsense is an international phenomenon, not a British one. Despite it, Britain retains the easygoing tolerance and pragmatism, the sources of her greatness. It is still better to be a Jew in England than anywhere else.[48]

Sebag Montefiore's response suggests that one Jewish response to the new anti-Semitism is to reinforce commitment to the democratic and multicultural societies of which Jews are a part.

Israel clearly sees itself as a primary stakeholder in confronting anti-Semitism, evidenced by then Israeli Foreign Minister Silvan Shalom proposing in Brussels in November 2003 a joint Israel–EU ministerial council to fight anti-Semitism. However, Serge Cwajgenbaum, Secretary-General of the European Jewish Congress, did not endorse this proposal.[49] To the contrary, he argued that the fate of Jews in Europe was the responsibility of European governments. In terms of the Zionist idea, Cwajgenbaum was emphasizing the Diasporic rather than the Israel-centric approach.

At the more extreme end, for some Jews such as Oxford University Philosophy Fellow Brian Klug, the encounter with the new anti-Semitism has led them to explicitly reject Zionism. He asserts that the reason for the Israeli–Palestinian conflict is political and the manifestations of anti-Semitism are because Zionism was a colonial movement the solution is political; "the empirical evidence overwhelmingly supports the view that hostility towards Israel, at bottom, is not a new form of anti-Semitism; it is a function of a deep and bitter political conflict."[50]

In Klug's view, people who support Palestinians and the Palestinians themselves are not anti-Semitic; "they are just not being Jewish": just as being pro-Israel does not make one *ipso facto* Islamophobic.[51] Israel is opposed, Klug argues, not because of anti-Semitism but because it is a 'rule breaker' and warns that "the longer Israel is at loggerheads with the rest of the region, the more likely it is that anti-Semitism will take on a life of its own".[52] There is thus a clear political conclusion for the State of Israel and the Zionist movement.

> The goal of Zionism was to normalise the Jewish condition. The point of the Jewish state was to put the Jewish people on the same footing as other peoples. But if Israel is a lightning rod for worldwide anti-Semitism, then what Zionism has done is to reproduce, in the form of a state, the plight of the individual Jew down the centuries.[53]

Further into his article Klug adds:

> If Herzl knew about the extent to which Israel would be embroiled in conflict and controversy, and if he thought this was fundamentally due to anti-Semitism, he would be appalled. First, it would mean that his solution was itself encumbered with the very problem it was intended to solve. Second, if the predicament of the Jewish state today is equivalent to that of the individual Jew in the past, there is no equivalent solution. Israel cannot apply the same

> remedy: it cannot 'take itself off' to another corner of the globe. It has nowhere to go. Herzl's advice no longer prevails.[54]

Opening up debate about the correctness or otherwise of Herzl's thesis seems to put the entire Zionist thesis up for re-evaluation. Klug, for instance, argues that the new anti-Semitism raises questions about the assumptions on which Zionism was based, such as Jews constituting a nation, which Klug claims is as burning an issue of debate today as it was at the time of the Balfour Declaration. Arguing that the nature of Israel's establishment makes it a special case of nineteenth-century nationalism, given its clash with Palestinian nationalism he argues, "It is not anti-Semitic to reject this (nationalist) model" as the solution to the problem of the Jews may be not to embrace the ideology of which Jews have been a victim.[55]

A similar argument to Klug's is employed by American Jew, Tony Jutd, who is even more explicit in his conclusion:

> The behaviour of the self-described Jewish state affects the way everyone else looks at Jews. The increased incidence of attacks on Jews in Europe and elsewhere is primarily attributable to misdirected efforts, often by young Muslims, to get back at Israel. The depressing truth is that Israel's behaviour is not just bad for the US, although it surely is. It is not even just bad for Israelis, as many Israelis silently acknowledge. The depressing truth is that Israel today is bad for the Jews.

With this, Jutt concludes that Israel is an "anachronism" and the solution is a bi-national state.[56]

For individuals such as Klug and Jutt, the new anti-Semitism is a reason for Israel not only to be removed from Jewish identity, but to be removed *per se.*

Summary

Anti-Semitism leads to three responses in terms of Jewish identity.

First, moving closer to Israel. It is the contention of this chapter that this is the dominant response. As long as the criticism directed at Israel by the international community is seen to be predicated on anti-Semitic principles — what Sharansky describes as demonization, double standards and delegitimization[57] — moving closer to Israel will become the norm for the majority of Jews. Increased *aliyah* in response to this anti-Semitism is part of this response, and while there is clearly a trend of increased *aliyah*, specifically from France, this is likely to remain a highly symbolic but minority response.

Secondly, working to build the democratic and multicultural protection mechanisms against anti-Semitism by emphasising the identity of the country of residence based on a Bundist rather than Zionist identity. This will clearly be a way in which Jews will seek to evade and rectify the problems of anti-Semitism. The extent to which it will occur will vary from Diaspora to Diaspora, depending on local culture and conditions.

These first and second options are not mutually exclusive, as communities move closer to Israel, but also seek to address anti-Semitism in their Diaspora home.

Thirdly, moving away from Israel, and at its extreme end embracing anti-Zionism. This will be a minority response but will be more pronounced on the Left by those

Jews who are troubled by Israeli policies *vis-à-vis* the Palestinians. However, as this response is likely to have a disproportionate appeal amongst intellectuals it has the potential to become a more long-term phenomenon.

Jewish anti-Zionism and the approach of Klug and Jutt raises multiple questions. If anti-Semitism has been staved off for 50 years, in part because of Israel, how much worse could it have been up until now without the Jewish state? If anti-Semitism exists now with the Jewish state, how much worse would it be without a Jewish state? If Jews in the Diaspora feel vulnerable with Israel in existence, how much more vulnerable would they feel without a Jewish state? In a world of the beheadings of Nick Burg and murder of Daniel Pearl, would Jews be safer without Israel? When the President of a state such as Iran advocates Holocaust denial, how can we say anti-Semitism is a thing of the past? If anything, the perpetuity of anti-Semitism confirms the need for a Jewish state rather than diminishes it. These developments reinforce Zionism, for while Israel may be the immediate focus of such anti-Semitism and genocidal intent, Israel remains, in the true Zionist sense, the greatest obstacle to that genocide.

It should, however, be noted that while the belief in the need for a Jewish state may be reinforced by anti-Semitism, it does not mean that the Zionist notion of "kibbutz Galuyot" (the ingathering of the exiles), and the "negation of the Golah" (Exile) is about to occur. It is true that Jews may leave countries where anti-Semitism is on the rise. However, as the Venezuelan case demonstrates, Florida is a destination preferred to Jerusalem.[58]

Ultimately, if Israel and the Diaspora collaborate on responding to the new anti-Semitism, this hatred can be a vehicle to reinvigorate and strengthen the notion of Jewish peoplehood. The maintenance of cultural, psychological and social boundaries is deemed important in the political sphere of homeland–ethnic diaspora relations.[59] The rise in anti-Semitism, the hostility towards Israel amongst the wider societies, and the sense of embattlement Diaspora communities have felt, is likely to increase the boundaries between Diaspora communities and their host societies, thus strengthening Israel–Diaspora relations. However, the new anti-Semitism poses yet another educational challenge; that of confronting anti-Semitism while ensuring that a generation of Jews do not grow up with an identity defined by those who hate them.

Notes

1 Yossi Shain and Barry Bristman (2002) 'Diaspora kinship and loyalty: the renewal of Jewish national security', *International Affairs* 78, 1, p. 87.
2 Hirsh Goodman, *Let Me Create A Paradise, God Said to Himself: A Journey of Conscience From Johannesburg To Jerusalem* (New York: BBS Public Affairs, 2005), p. 62.
3 Natan Sharansky, in *I Am Jewish, Personal Reflections Inspired by the Last Words of Daniel Pearl,* Judea and Rith Pearl (eds) (Woodstock, Vermont: Jewish Lights Publishing, 2004), pp. 32, 33.
4 Paul Iganski and Barry Kosmin (eds), *A New Anti-Semitism? Debating Judeophobia in 21*st *Century Britain* (London: Institute for Jewish Policy Research/Profile Books, 2003).
5 *Ha'aretz*, English Internet Edition, 3 June 2003.
6 Jonathan Sacks, "The Greatest Weapon of Mass Destruction." Paper presented at the Europe against anti-Semitism for a union of diversity seminar, Brussels, 19 February 2004; European Commission, European Jewish Congress, Conference of European Rabbis, viewed online 12 October 2005 at: <http://ec.europa.eu/dgs/policy_advisers/ archives/ publications/seminar_en.htm>.

7 Phyllis Chesler *The New Anti-Semitism: The Current Crisis and What We Must Do About It* (Hoboken, New Jersey: Jossey-Bass, 2003), p. 105.
8 Ibid., p. 129.
9 Roger Cukierman, Address to the Europe against anti-Semitism for a union of diversity seminar, Brussels, 19 February 2004.
10 *Manifestations of anti-Semitism in the European Union*, Synthesis Report, Center for Research on Anti-Semitism, Technical University Berlin, March 2003, p. 10. Viewed online 12 October 2005 at: <http://eumc.eu.int/eumc/material/pub/FT/Draft_anti-Semitism_report-web.pdf>.
11 Phyllis Chesler (2003), p. 12.
12 Ibid., p. 3.
13 Ibid., p. 12.
14 Ibid., p. 118.
15 Ibid., p. 57.
16 *Tikkun*, May/June 2003, p. 43.
17 *The Jerusalem Report*, 8 August 2005, p. 62.
18 *Tikkun*, May/June 2003, p. 43.
19 *The International Jerusalem Post*, 7–13 April 2006.
20 *Perceptions of Anti-Semitism in the European Union: Voices from Members of the European Jewish communities*. Report, European Monitoring Centre on Racism and Xenophobia, p. 13. Viewed online 12 October 2005 at: <http://www.europarl.europa.eu/ studies/ eumc_report/eumc_interviews_en.pdf>.
21 Ibid., p. 12
22 Ibid., p. 33
23 See Ryhnold's chapter in this volume.
24 Nathan Schransky, speech to the Europe against anti-Semitism for a union of diversity seminar, Brussels, 19 February 2004.
25 Email correspondence with Jean-Yves Camus.
26 *Perceptions of Anti-Semitism in the European Union: Voices from Members of the European Jewish communities*. Report, European Monitoring Centre on Racism and Xenophobia, p. 37.
27 Ibid., p.12
28 <http://www.jafi.org.il/forum> and <http://www.jewish-issues.com/aliyah_news.html>, accessed 20 September 2005.
29 *Jewish Chronicle*, 22 September 2006.
30 *The Australian*, 20 February 2006, p.16.
31 *The Jewish Week*, 16 January 2004.
32 *Perceptions of Anti-Semitism in the European Union: Voices from Members of the European Jewish communities*. Report, European Monitoring Centre on Racism and Xenophobia, p. 14. Viewed online 12 October 2005 at: <http://www.europarl.europa.eu/studies /eumc_report/eumc_interviews_en.pdf>.
33 *Manifestations of anti-Semitism in the European Union* (Berlin: Technical University Berlin, March 2003), p. 8.
34 Gabriel Schonfeld, The Return of Anti-Semitism (San Francisco: Encounter Books, 2004), p. 155.
35 "We have a debt to Israel", *Ha'aretz*, 16 August 2006.
36 Abraham H. Foxman, *Never Again? The Threat of the New Anti-Semitism* (San Francisco: Harper, 2003), pp. 65–66.
37 Abraham H. Foxman (2003), p. 67.
38 *Los Angeles Times*, 8 May 2002, p. B13.
39 *International Jerusalem Post*, 20 October 2004, p. 23.

40 Danny Ben-Moshe, *Jewish Community Attitudes Towards and Engagement with Israel: An Intergenerational Study, Melbourne, Australia* (Draft Report to United Israel Appeal (Victoria), Melbourne, 2005).
41 Ibid.
42 Ibid.
43 Ruth Eglash, "Unrest Spurs Venezuelan Jews' Interest in Aliya", *Jerusalem Post*, 18 May 2006.
44 Address by Deputy Prime Minister and Minister of Foreign Affairs Silvan Shalom to the European Jewish Congress, 2 February 2004.
45 Yossi Shain and Barry Bristman (2002), p. 69.
46 Ibid., p. 83
47 *Perceptions of Anti-Semitism in the European Union: Voices from Members of the European Jewish communities*. Report, European Monitoring Centre on Racism and Xenophobia, p. 25. Viewed online 12 October 2005 at: <http://www.europarl.europa.eu/studies/eumc_report/eumc_interviews_en.pdf>.
48 *The New Statesman*, 28 June 2004, p. 31.
49 "Europe's Leaders Confront Antisemitism", viewed online 19 March 2004 at: <www.ncjs.org> .
50 Brian Klug, "The collective Jew: Israel and the new anti-Semitism", *Patterns of Prejudice*, 37, 2 (2003), p. 133.
51 Ibid., p. 133.
52 Ibid., p. 134.
53 Ibid., p. 136.
54 Ibid., p. 135.
55 Ibid., p. 130.
56 *The Weekend Australian*, 6–7 December 2003, pp. 22–23.
57 Nathan Schransky, speech to the Europe against anti-Semitism for a union of diversity seminar, Brussels, 19 February 2004.
58 Larry Luxner, "Venezuelan Jews Flee to Florida", *Baltimore Jewish Times*, 2 October 2005.
59 Gabriel Sheffer *Diaspora Politics: At Home Abroad* (Cambridge: Cambridge University Press, 2003), pp. 11–12.

ISRAEL COMMENTATOR

The Jewish Addiction

Neil Lazarus

The chapter presented by Professor Ben-Moshe provides an interesting example of the inability of Jewry to recognize their addiction with anti-Semitism. It lacks qualified proof that there is a *new* anti-Semitism. Moreover the chapter's title poses Zionism as the *question* rather than Jewish identity and fails to comment on the most poignant issue that it raises itself — that of how to ensure that a generation of Jews does not grow up with an identity defined by those who hate them. The article fails to recognize that a new relationship between Israel and the Diasporas is urgently needed; a relationship not defined by an exaggerated threat of anti-Semitism, but one that enables Zionism to solve the new question of Jewish identity.

Anti-Semitism and the Jewish Addiction

The need for anti-Semitism is a Jewish addiction. As with most addictive substances it enables the consumer to function temporarily with a heightened capability. Yet with all addictions there is an irrational dependency despite the threat to long-term health. Indeed, the old idiom that where there are no Jews, the anti-Semite will invent them can be reversed — to where there is no anti-Semitism, Jews will invent it.

In order to ascertain the influence of anti-Semitism on the Diaspora's relationship with Israel it is necessary to distinguish between different Jewish communities and their different experiences. This is not a question of Israel and the Diaspora — but rather the relationship between Israel and the Diasporas. The problems of American Jewry are different to those in Croatia or France.

The addiction to anti-Semitism is perhaps most predominant in American Jewry. Whilst many American Jews *perceive* a threat of anti-Semitism — the number of Jews who actually encounter anti-Semitism are minimal.

> American Jews are commemorating 350 years of life on the country's shores, recalling the first arrivals to New Amsterdam from Recife, Brazil. As a result, there is a lot of stocktaking about the American Jewish experience.
>
> At the Anti-Defamation League, we are among those engaged in this activity. Our latest public opinion poll on the attitudes of Americans toward Jews in America — a survey of 1,600 Americans conducted by the Marttila Communications Group from March 18–25 — provides an opportunity to do just that.
>
> Clearly, America is different. The Jewish experience in the US, it can be argued, is different from every other Diaspora community. The level of integration and the comfort of American Jews in US society is unmatched.
>
> This duality of America being a hospitable place for Jews, but also one where anti-Semitism can resonate, surfaced once again in our 2005 survey. The most important finding of the poll — that 14 percent of Americans had anti-Semitic attitudes — was confirmation that anti-Semitism has dramatically declined since our initial survey in 1964.[1]

The Jewish community of America is not suffering from anti-Semitism but continues to *perceive* it as a problem. Ironically, the year 2005 was marked by a *decline* of anti-Semitism in the United States. It is difficult to argue that there is a threat to the American Jewish community from anti-Semitism. There has not been a substantial rise of anti-Semitism in America, new or otherwise. Indeed, according to the ADL, levels of anti-Semitism in 2001 were approximately the same as in 1998, and even at the alleged new *peak* of anti-Semitism activity in 2004, there were more recorded anti-Semitic incidents in the USA in 1990, 1993 and 1995.

Little scientific research has been conducted regarding which types of Jews, religious or non affiliated, perceive the threat of anti-Semitism to a greater extent. Indeed it would be fair to speculate that for many secular Jews, the practice of Israel advocacy provides a means of Jewish identification. Advocating for Israel provides an attractive alternative to praying at synagogue. Others, if not many, see Israel as a security check against an exaggerated threat of anti-Semitism.

The strongest affiliation to Israel can be found in religious American Jews and not the unaffiliated. In an American Jewish Identity Survey of 2001,[2] 58 percent of religious Jews defined themselves as very attached to Israel, compared to 15 percent of secular Jews. Moreover, 47 percent of religious Jews had visited Israel, whereas 74 percent of secular Jews had not. It would appear that religious affiliation and not anti-Semitism, perceived or otherwise, is the strongest influence on the identification of American Jews with Israel.

Indeed 2005, which saw a drop in anti-Semitism in America, saw a significant rise in American *aliyah* — the highest in 22 years.[3]

It was not because of anti-Semitism that American Jewry emigrated to Israel — but rather that the implementation of a substantial financial incentive and the creation of a new *aliyah* organization (Nefesh B'Nefesh) three years earlier enabled a religious identification with Israel to be fulfilled.

Indeed since its launch in 2002, Nefesh B'Nefesh has aided the immigration of some 7,000 Americans to Israel, around double the number before the organization existed. Anti-Semitism has not influenced American Jewry's decision regarding *aliyah* — monetary comfort has.

> These immigrants to Israel (olim) are unique in that they are being sponsored by Nefesh B'Nefesh. Nefesh B'Nefesh, a Florida-based group, is offering one-time grants of $5,000–$25,000 and help with job placement to North Americans who will immigrate to Israel.[4]

Whilst many official Jewish organizations such as the Anti Defamation League and the Simon Weisenthal Center continue to feed the anti-Semitism addiction, American Jewry continues to lose its sense of Jewish identity. An increased perception of anti-Semitism does not prevent an increased assimilation rate of American Jews. So whilst "thirty percent of Americans said Jews were responsible for the death of Jesus",[5]

> more than one third of the Jews in the United States are not married to Jewish spouses, according to a new study commissioned by the Jewish American Committee, Israel's leading newspaper *Yedioth Ahronoth* reported Monday.
>
> Furthermore, 1.5 million people in the U.S. today have one Jewish parent and one non-Jewish parent, the study shows.
>
> The report found three levels of converted Jews:
>
> Active Jews: 30 percent of converts do so out of choice and are more devoted to Judaism than most Jews by birth are.
>
> Assimilated Jews: 40 percent of converts did so because their spouses asked them to and they are not involved in setting the religious standards in the home.
>
> Ambivalent Jews: 30 percent of converts have doubts about their conversion and feel guilty about the beliefs and practices left behind; their children exhibit ambivalence and view themselves as "half-Jewish".[6]

American Jewry, whilst exaggerating the problem of anti-Semitism, does not consider the threat serious enough to neither make *aliyah* nor slow its rate of assimilation. Both it would seem, are more influenced by a perception of comfort and wealth.

Anti-Semitism, Israel and Jewish Identity in Europe

The experience of European Jewry provides a useful opportunity to contrast the influence of anti-Semitism on Jewish identity with their American counterparts. But we need to be wary of simplification. In the same way that we should be wary of the term Diaspora Jewry rather than Diasporas, we also need to differentiate between the experiences of different European communities.

In May 2005 the ADL commissioned a report entitled *Attitudes Towards Jews in Twelve European Countries*. Their conclusions provided interesting reading.

To the question "Are Jews more loyal to Israel than this country?" the percentage of respondents answering "Probably true" was highest in Italy with 55 percent, second highest in Poland with 52 percent and third highest in Spain with 51 percent. France was in last place with 29 percent.

When asked whether Jews have too much power in the business world the percentage of respondents answering positively was as follows: first place was Hungary with 55 percent, second place was Spain with 45 percent and third place was Poland with 43 percent. France was only seventh place with 25 percent.

To the question "Do Jews have too much power in international financial markets?" the percentage of respondents answering positively was as follows: first place was Hungary with 55 percent, second place was Spain with 54 percent and third place was Poland with 43 percent. France was in eighth place with 24 percent.

When asked "Do Jews talk too much about what happened to them in the Holocaust?" the percentage of respondents answering positively ranked as follows: first place was Poland with 52 percent, second place was Germany and Switzerland, both with 48 percent, and third place was Italy with 49 percent. France was seventh with 34 percent.

To the question "Are Jews responsible for the death of Christ?" the percentage of respondents answering positively was as follows: first place was Poland with 39 percent, in second place were Hungary, Spain and the UK with 20 percent, and third place was France with 13 percent.

When asked "Is your opinion of Jews influenced by actions taken by the State of Israel?" the percentage of respondents answering positively was as follows: first place was Switzerland with 41 percent, second place was Spain with 37 percent and third place was Austria with 36 percent. France was last with 15 percent. [7]

The relatively low percentage of anti-Semitic attitudes in France is surprising, as 2005 marked the highest French *aliyah* rate in thirty-four years.[8] Even in Europe, where a new wave of anti-Semitism has arisen, there seems to be little relation between anti-Semitism, Jewish identity and Israel. As in the USA, Israel is attracting French Orthodox Jews enticed by financial benefits:

> Those involved with French aliya said the boost in numbers had as much to do with the appeal of funding and services AMI provides immigrants and Israel's new programme of "community absorption," where immigrants settle together in neighborhood clusters around the country, as with the push given by anti-Semitism.
>
> "The main reason is an ideological reason, a Zionist reason," said Arieh Azoulay, chairman of the Jewish Agency's aliyah and absorption committee, pointing to intermarriage rates over 50% which threaten the next generation's ability to retain its Jewish identity.

> "The wave of anti-Semitism [only] enhances the Zionism of Jews in France," he said.
> "We know that the potential is enormous" when it comes to French aliya, said AMI director Avi Zana. "We decided in this last year to create AMI because we know a lot of people have decided to make aliya but are waiting for somebody to help them take this very important step."
> Families on the flights, arriving from Paris and Marseille, will get an average of $6,000, while the 70 students on board will be receiving scholarships for study in Israel.
> One third of the immigrants — 70% of the families — will be participating in "community absorption" programmes in Jerusalem, Netanya, Ashdod, Beit Shemesh, Eilat and Netanya.
> Most of the immigrants arriving, according those helping with preparations, are either Orthodox or traditional in their observance.[9]

Despite the higher levels of anti-Semitism in Europe in the last half a century, the biggest threat to Jewry, and the biggest challenge to Jewish identity, is not anti-Semitism but assimilation.

Summary

With all addictions, the more of the substance you consume, the less effect it has. Regular coffee drinkers need to drink more coffee to feel its influence.

One cigarette a day is seldom enough for the nicotine-dependent smoker.

The cry of anti-Semitism is wearing thin — even the rebranded, ready to go, even nastier "new" anti-Semitism is having little appeal to a new generation of Jews who do not remember the Holocaust.

> A December 2002 study by the Jewish Agency's Institute for Jewish People Policy Planning found that the number of Jews in France fell from 535,000 in 1980 to some 500,000 in just two decades, a loss of over 6 percent . . . It is therefore hardly surprising that in a lengthy article appearing in the 2002 edition of the American *Jewish Year Book*, Della Pergola estimated that, "French Jewry will experience a slow but steady decline from 520,000 in 2000, to 480,000 in 2020, to 380,000 in 2050, and 300,000 in 2080." Meanwhile, across the Channel, he wrote, "The Jewish population in the United Kingdom will decline to 240,000 in 2020, 180,000 in 2050, and 140,000 in 2080."
> In effect, this means that within just 75 years or so, French and English Jewry will only be half their current size.
> In smaller Jewish communities in Europe, the retrenchment rates have been even more pronounced.[10]

The effect of anti-Semitism on the identity of world Jewry is minimal — even the so-called new anti-Semitism. Political events in Israel are having a marginal influence on the majority of Jews in the Diasporas. As one student said to me in a recent seminar: "Neil, you just don't get it . . . apathy is 'in'."

The challenge we face is not to continue to define our identity through the supposed negative attitudes towards Jews of others — but to define it in a way that will appeal to a new generation. We need to ask the hard questions about the future of Jewry in the Diasporas. The threat is not to be found in repainting the tired picture of the swastika — but will be realized when Diaspora Jewry looks in the mirror.

In recent years, attempts to place Israel as a positive element of Jewish identity have been encouraged — and Israel is presented more than just as a place of possible refuge.

Programmes such as *birthright israel* (see p. 35 *et seq.*) and MASA (see p. 39 *et seq.*) which encourage young Jews to visit Israel have been very successful in their aim at rekindling a Jewish identity. This is a positive step forward. Indeed, Israel may well hold the key to strengthening the identity of those Jews who see neither *aliyah* or religion as attractive. Yes, the image of Israel must be positive and not simply portrayed as a place of refuge.

When Jewry in the Diasporas see Zionism as an answer and not as a question, then the first step in revitalizing a truly authentic identity will have been taken. Without it, we will be forced within 50 years to rename the Diaspora Museum in Tel Aviv, The Museum of the Diaspora. I will be the first to suggest its relocation to Jerusalem — across the road to Yad Vashem (Israel's Museum of the Holocaust).

Notes

1 Abraham H. Foxman, "After 350 Years, Still A Lot To Do", *Ha'aretz*, 22 April 2005.
2 American Jewish Identity Survey, Jewish Virtual Library, viewed online 18 October 2006 at: <http://www.jewishvirtuallibrary.org/jsource/US-Israel/ajis.html>.
3 Keren Hayesod, "Aliya 2005: Record Immigration from the West", *Solidarity Update No. 320*, Press Release from Communications and Marketing Division, Jewish Agency For Israel, 17 January 2006.
4 Lisa Katz, "The Americans are coming", *About.com*, viewed online 18 October 2006 at: <http://judaism.about.com/library/1_culture/bl_aliyah_nefesh3.htm>.
5 Abraham H. Foxman (2005).
6 Ynet, 16.4.2207.
7 Anti Defamation League (2005) *Attitudes Towards Jews in Twelve European Countries*, Anti Defamation League, viewed online 18 October 2006 at: <http://www.adl.org/anti_semitism/european_attitudes_may_2005.pdf>.
8 Keren Hayesod (2005).
9 Hilary Leila Krieger, "French aliya headed toward record numbers", *The Jerusalem Post*, 24 July 2005.
10 Michael Freund, "The Real Threat to Europe's Jews", *The Jerusalem Post*, 7 March 2004 reproduced by *aish.com*, viewed online 18 October 2006 at: <http://www.aish.com/jewishissues/jewishsociety/The_Real_Threat_to_Europes_Jews.asp>.

DIASPORA COMMENTATOR

Anti-Semitism and Israel in Jewish Identity

Jean-Yves Camus

As Danny Ben-Moshe points out, the Holocaust and the subsequent creation of the State of Israel placed the Jewish state at the core of Jewish identity in the Diaspora. This is not to say that Israel had been absent from the heart and mind of Jews since the destruction of the Second Temple and the dispersion, but the word "Israel" in the daily prayers evoked the Holy Land and the future gathering of the Jewish people there after the coming of the Messiah. What was new after 1948 was that Israel existed as a *State*. Herzl's legacy remains ambiguous to this day: anti-Semitism is still central to the development of Zionism, but Zionism is first and foremost about the fundamental right of the Jews to be recognized as a people entitled to live in their own country, on the land of their forefathers. Thus, even if anti-Semitism were non-existent, Zionism would still be an option because it is an answer to what is seen by both religious and secular Jews as an anomaly; being discriminated against as a distinct people and not being allowed to live as such.

There are three options for the Diaspora: distancing themselves from Israel; moving closer to the Jewish state; and the "Bundist" approach. Even before the emergence of the "new anti-Semitism" with the Second Intifada, however, the overwhelming majority of the Jews had made their choice. I shall write here with particular reference to the case of French Jewry, which is the largest in Western Europe. In France, as elsewhere, the Jewish population was almost entirely non-Zionist before 1948. After 1948, Zionists were still a minority and they certainly still are, if one defines being a Zionist as making *aliyah*. However, the openly anti-Zionist factions almost completely disappeared after the Six Day War for two reasons. First, in France, as everywhere in the world, the Israeli victory and the return of Jerusalem to Jewish sovereignty was interpreted as a sign of G-d within the religious segment of the community, which means that the Zionist–Religious faction progressively won over the Orthodox non-Zionist one. Second, in the 1960s and the 1970s, the Jews *en masse* left the French Communist Party and the Leftist movements, moving to more moderate positions on the issue of Israel–Palestine — to such extent that today, the bi-national, one-State position has very few supporters. There is also a very important factor that I think Ben-Moshe underestimates in his essay: in France, and to a lesser extent in Belgium, Italy, Spain and Switzerland, the *Sephardi* element coming from North Africa and the rest of the Arab world is stronger than in the 1950s, holding a very different perception of Europe to that of the native *Ashkenazi* Jews. They tend to see their presence on European soil as a transient situation, of which Israel is the logical conclusion. They are also more observant and more receptive to the Zionist–Religious ideology which means, in the case of France, that a significant number of them are staunchly pro-Zionist, while at the same time quite disillusioned with the Israeli establishment, and especially the political Right for having made concessions such as the Gaza pull-back in 2005/6.

The fact that since 2000 many Jews have indeed less trust in the broader public, as a result of rising anti-Semitism, is often interpreted as proof that the end of the Diaspora is close. I do not think so. First of all, even though French *aliyah* is on the rise, it is still a tiny minority and the *yeridah*[1] rate is high (about one-third). Furthermore, the Diaspora has managed to get through this difficult situation by finding new allies on the political spectrum, so that it is not as isolated as some may think, and can even take a new strength. It is not the entire Left globally that has failed: the British, French and German Social-Democratic parties have a balanced approach to the Middle East issue. The anti-Semitic Right is on the decline, and in Italy the former fascist party *Alleanza Nazionale* has even become a supporter of Israel. Even the foreign policy of France has been slowly but markedly changing since 2002. So most Jews in this country think of Israel as a possible refuge, *while at the same time* asking for a more efficiently organized, close-knit community which would act as a political lobby; something that was unbelievable in France some 20 years ago, given the traditional reluctance of French Jews to consider themselves an ethnic minority.

It is clear that, as a result of the present situation, the community, at least in France, has become more parochial, and this in itself has had unexpected results. For example, a growing number of those who do not plan to emigrate are learning Hebrew. Communal life is thriving and religious observance is on the rise. Jews are certainly more suspicious of their non-Jewish environment, but never have there been so many children with Hebrew surnames (something totally alien to the French assimilationist tradition) and so many people wearing *kippot*,[2] and even the full religious garb in public places. One spectacular result is that, although most of the Jewish schools in France are strictly Orthodox, Israel is an important part of their curriculum. The New anti-Semitism has definitely not transformed every French and European Jew into a Zionist, but it has certainly slowed down assimilation and made many Jews return to some form of identification with the Jewish people. In this context, the Jewish community has adopted an attitude which is a mix between two approaches: identification with Israel and working towards a more secure place within the European countries. The Jews of Europe are closer now to Israel than they have ever been, but they still believe in their future as a part of their respective host countries. They are asking the State and the non-Jewish population for support and recognition, which ultimately means that they are not yet ready to end the experience of the Diaspora.

Notes

1 *Yeridah*: As opposite to *aliyah*, means the fact that one leaves Israel for the Diaspora.

2 *Kippot*: Skullcaps; a sign of religious observance that, when worn outside of the synagogue, is specific to Orthodox Jews.

2

Jewish Continuity and Israel Visits

David Mittelberg

The relationship between Jewish continuity and Israel visits can no longer be understood without an appreciation of the nature of contemporary globalized Western society, the nature of modern identity and the differential bases of attachment, longing and belonging of the individual to the collective. The collective may include some or all of the following: the State, the Nation, an ethnic group or perhaps a transnational People. Moreover, international travel or in this case the Israel visit, may be better viewed in its special binding role between homelands and their diasporas.

I have been working for over 30 years on Israel–Diaspora relations and the role of the Israel experience in that relationship. Primarily I have used the historical paradigm born of the particular experience of the Jewish people: The unique case of the Jewish Diaspora *vis-à-vis* the homeland of Israel, rather than looking at the Jewish Diaspora as a part of a broader typology of diasporas.

The Israel–Diaspora Jewish discourse does take place within one language, but it is a contested language, not consensus-based, dominated by the *migration paradigm*. I mean by this that Jewish peoplehood is literally exhausted by the question of whether Diaspora Jews do or do not migrate actually or metaphorically to Israel. This prescriptive metaphor has come to imply that an authentic experience of the Diaspora migrant in Israel could be achieved only by *immersion* into the host culture, then distancing from the culture of origin, and ultimately the abandonment of the culture of origin for the new chosen alternative culture of the country of destination, namely Israel.

Today, a new context and debate is emerging that reflects a radical and rapid globalization of the phenomena of diaspora itself and consequently the growth of diaspora tourism, its analysis and its celebration. Indeed if the meta process is the globalized proliferation of the diaspora condition the responses are often local or rather multi-local.

Globalization and Ethnicity

Giddens (1991) points to a mode of social organization that separates time and space without the "situatedness of place". Put another way, this refers to the integration of people in "lived time" — not only in their presence but often, typically, in their absence (Featherstone 1995). More specifically, Featherstone views globalization as:

> producing a unified and integrated common culture . . . (where) . . . (we find the most striking examples of the effects of time–space compression, as new means of communication effectively make possible simultaneous transactions which sustain 'deterritorialized cultures'. (Featherstone 1995, pp. 114–115)

If the genesis and persistence of ethnicity has been traditionally understood as a residual outcome of migrant national ancestry and religious affiliation, the *dissipation of ethnicity* was then anticipated as a function of both generation-time and modernizing secularization. In contrast to this thesis of linear attrition, globalization presents an unanticipated contemporary macro genetic force which generates the invention or reinvention of ethnicity as a response to those very same global forces of cultural homogenization, social meaning, deconstruction and the atomization of social relationships (Mittelberg 1999).

In this world, identity is privatized — an outcome of personal choice. Indeed, the preservation of this personal choice has itself become the metavalue of postmodern society. That is to say, in the emerging postmodern North America, what matters most is the fact that you can choose which ethnicity to assume as well as the timing, intensity and salience at any given time throughout the life cycle.

Hence, the contemporary world becomes one in which the ethnic is not disappearing, rather one where postmoderns typically live through personal multiple identities in a pluralized world (Mittelberg 1999). With this backdrop it now becomes necessary to engage in a reappraisal of the homeland–diaspora dichotomy outside the old migration-based paradigmatic teleology. What is a Diaspora and what is Diaspora tourism?

Diaspora and Diaspora Tourism

The process of rapid globalization and localization of the last thirty years, together with mass movements of labour and other migration, have fundamentally transformed the nature of diaspora–homeland categories and thought, while multiplying the number of peoples who in 2005 live simultaneously in a homeland and a global diaspora. Gabriel Sheffer (1999, p. 400) has made a short list which includes:

> Turks in the United States, Germany and Sweden . . . Moroccans in France, Spain and Germany . . . South Koreans in the US, Canada, and various countries in the Middle East; Filipinos in the US, Japan, and various Asian and Middle East countries . . . the 25 million Russians in the former Soviet republics.

How should these different diasporas be understood? One scholar has generated a nine-fold generic typology of diaspora (see Coles and Timothy 2003, pp. 4–5). These include both dislocation and relocation, the maintenance of collective memory or myth including an ongoing relationship to the homeland and the possibility of return. In addition, diaspora members share an alienating relationship with the host society as well as a solidarity relationship with co-ethnics in parallel geographic sites, what Clifford calls "multi-local diaspora cultures" (Clifford 1997, p. 246). Here I will primarily utilize the definition of cultural diaspora, which attempts to elucidate the issues of collective identity of homeland and nation recognizing, following Mitchell (1997), that diaspora identities are:

> multifaceted and composed of complexly interwoven strands of ethnicity, religion and ancestry. Diaspora communities have specific geographies and histories, they have multiple loyalties, they move between regions, do not occupy a single cultural space and, perhaps most importantly, operate exterior to state boundaries and their cultural effects. (Cited by Coles and Timothy 2003, p. 7)

What then is diaspora tourism? Clearly there is a great deal of conceptual overlap and symbiosis between diaspora and tourism.

Coles and Timothy (2003) offer six distinctive patterns of travel and tourism that are derived from three characteristics of ***Diaspora***. They are: (1) *the duality of home and host country;* (2) *the real and imagined collective memory of the group;* (3) *the contrasting and distinctive nature of diasporic identities "abroad"* (Coles and Timothy 2003, p. 13). The six patterns of diaspora tourism which are not as distinctive analytically from each other as the authors suggest, include the following: first, diasporic tourist seeking roots in homeland; second, genealogical or family tourism; third, homeland tourists visiting the diaspora spaces; fourth, diaspora destinations as tourist sites for mainstream non-diaspora tourists; fifth, homeland and diaspora members travelling to transit spaces such as concentration camps in Poland; sixth, travel by diasporans to vacation spaces in the host state.

Where does this leave the Jewish people, whose supposedly unique historical condition has been appropriated by analysts as only one case among many? It seems that it locates the reconstruction of Jewish peoplehood in a very mobile and better integrated world on the one hand, but subject to a stressful process of postmodernization, privatization of religion and community on the other, combined with acutely heightened possibilities and probabilities of personal cultural choice for the moderns.

I now move on to the question of precisely how this Jewish peoplehood is to be articulated. Contemporary Jewish Israel–Diaspora discourse continues to be dominated by the language of migration as either a moral imperative (contemporary Zionism) or as a heritage that may now be *passe* and irrelevant for existential questions of Diaspora Jewish life. By maintaining, albeit antithetically, *the same migration paradigm both in Israel and in the Diaspora*, both sides continue to share (though in a weakened mode in the last five years) a rejection of the other, as a part of everyday life. The result is a minimal interconnection and interdependence between the vast majority of Israeli and Diaspora Jews on the foundation of the worlds they actually live in. Instead, they are engaged with each other, if at all, either in the imagery of ancient historical and ethical language of the synagogues or in the rarified sociopolitical debates and reportage of CNN and the *New York Times*. The first has important though limited relevance by virtue of religion, whether as an essential or only a symbolic part of Diaspora Jewish lives. The second draws relevance from affirmation or alienation from

Israel as a basis of Diaspora public collective identity as Diaspora Jews, for thus the non-Jewish world defines them in good times as well as in bad. What is still required is a paradigmatic redefinition of the structure of Jewish peoplehood; one that encompasses the everyday worlds in which Jews in Israel and its diasporas actually live. I will return to this question below. It is now necessary to consider the role of visits to Israel by Jewish Diasporans within the broader context of Jewish peoplehood.

The Visit to Israel

The data on the Israel visit is growing very fast, dominated by the overriding concern of how that visit contributes to the Jewishness of those who make that journey. Previous research has demonstrated the Jewish impact of Israel educational trips on participants (see, for example, Mittelberg 1988, 1992, 1994; Horowitz 1993; Israel and Mittelberg 1998; Chazan 1997; Saxe et al. 2002, 2004). In an extensive survey of this literature, Chazan (1997) has prepared an updated and comprehensive analysis of over 100 items of recently reported research investigating the impact of the Israel experience on identity formation among youth. The research supports the conclusion that youth visits to Israel have positive outcomes for measures of Jewish identity in adulthood, both as part of a cluster of other experiences and also with an independent causal weight. As Chazan (1997) makes clear, important questions still remain to be answered, involving the weight of ideological content on programme outcomes, and the role and definition of pedagogical excellence. In addition, we know very little about the degree to which the measured impact on adult behaviour is a function of the Israel visit itself, or post-visit environment and programming, or combinations of these. Much additional work is called for, particularly in regard to the role of the post-trip environment in sustaining long-term attitudinal change.

The Visit to Israel: A North American Jewish Population Survey (NJPS) Decennial Comparison

Based on analysis of the North American Jewish Population Survey 2000–1 data (NJPS), provided by Len Saxe and colleagues (Saxe et al. 2004b) from the Brandeis Center for Modern Jewish Studies,[1] it is possible to make some cautious comparisons between data I reported a decade ago (Mittelberg 1999) and data based on NJPS 2000–1. These comparisons allow us to determine changes in patterns and the strength of the connection to Israel between North American Jews who have visited Israel and Jews who have not. I will limit myself to only a few dimensions of comparison, leaving a more detailed analysis for a later essay. It needs to be mentioned, however, that such a comparison is fraught with many methodological issues that have been the subject of intense public and scholarly debate. Notwithstanding these issues, I do conclude, as do all the disputants, that important analyzes can be made and certainly broad patterns can be confidently observed.

1. Who visits Israel? Saxe (2003) distinguishes between two sectors in the NJPS 2001 data. The first includes the total population, including both self-identified Jews and those who are of Jewish background (together totaling 5.2 million Jews), out of

whom only 36 percent have ever visited Israel. The second sector comprises only the self-identified Jews (4.3 million Jews), out of whom 42 percent have ever visited Israel. In 1999, I reported that out of the total 5.5 million population of core Jews only 26 percent had ever visited Israel, while out of those who identified as Jews by religion this number rose to 31 percent (Mittelberg 1999, p. 144). On the face of it, a significant increase in the number of North American Jews visiting Israel at least once. But who are these Jews and what is the source of this increase?

In 1999, I reported that out of all core Jews representing a population of 5.5 million, 60 percent of Orthodox Jews have visited Israel, 39 percent of Conservative Jews, 23 percent of Reform Jews, and 21 percent of Other Core Jews (Mittelberg 1999, p. 68). In 2001, Saxe reports that 75 percent of Orthodox Jews have visited Israel, 54 percent of Conservative Jews, 35 percent of Reform Jews and 34 percent of Secular/Just Jewish. This again seems a remarkable increase but it must be stressed that the population that Saxe's data is based on, as the authors explicitly point out, refers to a population of 4.3 million Jews today in North America and NOT the 5.2 million that the sponsors of the survey, the United Jewish Communities (UJC), regard as the total population of American Jews. The Saxe data analyzes the more connected Jews, presumably on the grounds *inter alia* that this data is more reliable than the broader data set. In addition, respondents of Jewish background only, in NJPS 2001, were not asked many important questions related to Israel, thus complete comparisons cannot be made between the two sets of data. Despite all this, what remains interesting to me is how similar the *relative* patterns have remained over the ten-year period, indicating that the data and findings are more robust than both sets of disputants may have felt.

Thus while there may remain some quite significant dispute about the *size* of American Jewry and therefore the size of the increase in the rate of visiting Israel, the overall relative percent gap in the frequency of visits between the denominations has remained the same.

2. Age Here I believe the most important pattern-breaking finding is revealed. While the 1990 and 2000 studies both report in different ways that the rate for first time visitors to Israel is higher amongst the older sections of the public, in 2001 Saxe reports an increase in 18–29 aged respondents visiting Israel, namely 38 percent. In 1999, I had reported that only 22 percent of core Jews aged 18–35 had ever visited Israel (Mittelberg 1999, p. 147).

3. Income Both the 1990 survey and the 2000–1 surveys show that there does not seem to be a great difference in the number of visitors to Israel from the lower and moderate-income groups. The 2001 survey showed that those who earned less than $15,000 were the least likely to visit Israel (29 percent), compared with those who earned $75–100,000 (41 percent), $100–150,000 (40 percent), and more than $150,000 (56 percent). All middle income earners seemed to visit Israel at the same rate. Providing similar findings, the 1990 survey said that both low and moderate-income persons visited Israel at a rate of 14 percent. The highest earning group, those making over $80,000, visited Israel more. I concluded that, "this pattern shows people with a high income visit Israel more frequently. This implies that a subsidy for a first-time, young adult, single visitor could have a leverage effect on the rate of visiting Israel" (Mittelberg 1999, p. 67).

Emotional Attachment to Israel and a Visit to Israel (NJPS 2000–1)

This data is presented here as a comparative base line for the programme analyzes that will follow below. Based on the NJPS data, Saxe and colleagues report that 30 percent of 18–29 year old self-identified Jews responded that they were emotionally attached to Israel, 26 percent of 30–39 year olds, 30 percent of 40–49 year olds, 29 percent of 50–59 year olds, 35 percent of 60–69 years olds, 41 percent of 70–79 year olds and 34 percent of 80+ year olds. The general pattern seems to be that people over 60 maintain a deeper emotional connection to Israel than those in the younger groups. However, 18–29 year olds maintain a deeper connection than 30–39 year olds and 50–59 year olds, and they maintain the same connection to Israel as 40–49 year olds. At the same time, Jews *who have been to Israel* maintain a far deeper connection to Israel than those who have never visited Israel. Fifty-two percent of Jews who have visited Israel feel emotionally attached to Israel compared with the 16 percent of Jews who have never visited Israel. From this data it can be inferred that visiting Israel does serve to strengthen the connection a Jew develops to the Jewish state.

In another recent study by Mayer, Kosmin and Keysar (2002), attachment to Israel is strongly correlated with religiosity, both on measures of actually visiting Israel (where we find that 47 percent of religious Jews report visiting Israel compared to 23 percent of secular Jews), as well as in regard to the degree of attachment to Israel. Here the authors report that 58 percent of religious Jews see themselves as *very* attached to Israel compared to only 15 percent of secular Jews. The authors are perturbed and perplexed by the disconnect between secular Jews in the Diaspora and secular Jews in Israel, calling for more research on the trend. But really is it any wonder when one considers that the primary paradigm of the discourse is first, in religious terms itself, and second, dictates a one way migration imperative? Interestingly enough, Mayer et al. also report that both religious and secular Jews report an increase in travel to Israel compared to the findings of the 1990 NJPS of a decade earlier. On the other hand, previous research indicates that the visit to Israel enhances attachment to Israel and the Jewish people both for the religious *and* the secular Jew (Mittelberg 1999). Is there then a connection to be made between the apparently inexorable attrition of attachment of American Jews to Israel (especially younger American Jews) and the increasing opportunity of travel to Israel of younger American Jews? It is to this question I now turn.

The Short-Term *birthright israel* Israel Experience Programme

The *birthright israel* programme was launched in the winter of 1999–2000, when nearly 5,000 young college students from Diaspora Jewish communities responded to an unprecedented invitation to visit Israel as a gift of the Jewish community. This marked the start of a massive educational experiment, funded by a partnership that included the government of Israel, the Jewish Agency for Israel and Jewish Federations, as well as a consortium of private philanthropists. Later on, during the summer of 2002, the programme was expanded to include Former Soviet Union (FSU) Jews.

Since the launch of *birthright israel* at end of 1999, nearly 50,000 young adults aged 18–26 from North America have visited Israel on a free educational trip for ten days. An additional 22,000 from 26 Diaspora countries have participated. Research by the evaluators of the programme, Saxe et al. (2002, 2004), as well as independent research by this author, demonstrates that the programme elicits a consistent set of normative and attitudinal changes in participants, as will be seen below. However, the larger question that remains is, to what degree do these changes persist over time back in the countries of origin? While it may be still premature (given the short number of years that this programme has been in existence) to draw final conclusions, this question has nevertheless been examined in both sets of data analyzed here, with the trend further corroborated by reference to research on longer term programmes (referred to briefly below).

This question has been analyzed at two separate levels of resolution and by two independent analyzes. Saxe et al. (2004), show that changes do persist over time and that they are statistically significant both longitudinally (over a three-year time period) per participant, as well as when compared with non-participants in the programme. The non participants, being interested registrants who actually never participated for one reason or another. Our own research (Mittelberg and Lev Ari: forthcoming) was also based on a longitudinal design of pre and post questions administered at both ends of the short visit, however the degree of analysis of actual programme detail was of a higher resolution than that of the Brandeis study, primarily since the unit of analysis was actual complete busloads of participants, their staff and actual programme itinerary.

The *birthright israel* visit to Israel was designed to be an educational experience, not just a tour, in order to connect college-age Diaspora Jewish youth with their heritage and to strengthen their Jewish identity. These ten-day trips have been run in winter and summer cohorts, timed to coincide with university inter sessions.

> Birthright['s] only eligibility requirements were that applicants consider themselves to be Jewish, fall between the ages of 18 and 26 and not have participated previously in a similar 'peer educational program' in Israel. Birthright (*Taglit* in Hebrew) is an umbrella organization that authorizes and coordinate[s] the efforts of approximately 30 university-based, community-based, religious, for-profit, and secular not-for-profit trip providers. (Kelner 2004, p. 4)

The empirical data for the article quoted below was collected from the participants of one such provider. Underlying the itinerary designed for each trip was a carefully planned set of experiences whose goal was to influence participants both intellectually and emotionally (Saxe et al. 2000). Thus *birthright israel*'s short-term goal was to provide participants with " . . . a stimulating encounter with Israel — and by extension with their own identity" (Post 1999).

Shaul Kelner, a member of the official Brandeis *birthright israel* evaluation team, sums up succinctly the core structure and educational strategy of the programmes as experienced by over 5,000 participants. This structure and its educational rationale were mandated to all providers, including of course the participants of the provider under review here.

> The experience itself was a fast-paced bus-trek across Israel. Each group of approximately 40 people had its own itinerary, tour bus, driver, American or former Soviet Union staff, responsible for group building and an Israeli facilitator, charged with presenting a narrative about the sites. Itineraries — relatively standardized — included visits to Jewish holy sites, tours of ancient and modern historical areas, nature hikes, meeting with Israeli youth, social events, and guest lecturers on a variety of topics regarding Israel and Judaism. (Kelner 2004, p. 4)
>
> Birthright arranged its presentation of Israel in a way that encouraged tourists to project Jewish and Zionist meanings onto the sites. All trips address the following themes: (1) The nature of contemporary Israeli Society, (2) meetings with young Israelis, (3) Jewish values, (4) Zionism then and now, (5) an overview of Jewish history, and (6) the Holocaust and Jewish life. In order to ensure a personal implication in the collective Jewish narrative for the participants the final theme of 'what it all means for us' is implemented. (Kelner 2004, p. 7)

Elsewhere Kelner articulates the theoretical underpinnings of this educational strategy (Kelner: forthcoming, p. 3), whereby "group tourism is a potent medium that can be manipulated to enable the illusion of a singular core self and thereby effect profound changes in the self concept of the individuals"; *birthright israel* engaged in a purposeful project designed to achieve precisely that.

Data Analyses

The comparison that follows is between Oren birthright data with the national *birthright israel* longitudinal impact study conducted by the Center for Modern Jewish Studies at Brandeis University (Saxe et al. 2004). The data of the latter is based on the Winter 2003–4 cohort for which 15,0000 young adults applied in Fall of 2003. Seven thousand of these actually took part in the inter session break of December 2003–January 2004. The data is based on 7,660 respondents to a pre-trip survey and 6,097 respondents to a post-trip survey; actual participants comprised 72 percent of the first group and 45 percent of the second group, the remainder being non-participants (Saxe 2004, p. 67). The data of the former is drawn from the same period.

In their important study Saxe and colleagues (2004, p. 6) demonstrate the impact of the experience in Israel on participants. In their analysis they describe two kinds of persisting effects.

1. *Conversion* effects; the degree that a participant is changed by the programme trip, for example, on a measure such as a feeling of connection to Israel. Indeed they report a strengthening of connection to Israel, to the Jewish people and to Jewish history.
2. *Preserving* effects; which refer to the absence of erosion of pre trip positive attitudes towards Israel and the Jewish people (*ibid.*, p. 7).

The strongest effect reported is the connection to Israel followed by connection with Jewish peoplehood and Jewish history (Saxe 2004, p. 42). Perhaps not surprisingly, given the short duration of the programme, no impact was reported on measures of religion or religious practice, nor, must it be added, were these goals of the programme.

In addition to pre and post at both ends of the programme, Saxe et al. (2004) studied the **long-term** impact of the trip, two years after the conclusion of the programme (see *ibid.*, Appendix A, pp. 59–66 for methodological details of the study). For these purposes and in addition to the above analysis, they studied a sample of participants from the year 2002 cohort (N = 281), which they compared to a group of non-participants from the very same cohort (N = 268), making a total survey population of 549 students. With respect to the impact of the programme on the participants' feeling of connection with Israel, while both groups began at a common benchmark base of 44/47 percent of a high degree of connectedness to Israel, programme participants increased their score on this measure to 75 percent at the end of the programme and maintained this higher rate at 62 percent even after two years (Saxe et al. 2004, p. 20–22). At the very same time, the non-participants hardly increased their measure of connectedness over the same period. Similarly the analysis was repeated with a random sample from the year 2001 cohort (N=501), with follow up being after three years. Here, too, the same pattern was observed, namely, that while the pre trip benchmark was a 25 percent/20 percent pre trip score of feeling of connection to Israel, at the end of the programme participants' score had increased to 58 percent, while after three years their score was maintained at 49 percent, compared to a score of only 27 percent for the non-participants (Saxe et al. 2004, pp. 19, 60).

The above rich and comprehensive data refer to a series of national samples of both participants and non-participants, while in our own study of *birthright* groups, the overall sample studied is smaller in number. However, in our own study, it should be noted that the samples are based on unit analyses of complete buses of *birthright* participants studied by pre and post questionnaires (without, however, any opportunity to study non-participants). In this data similar patterns can be reported. What can we learn from the Oren *birthright israel* data, which reports the responses of *birthright israel* participants from North America as well as the former Soviet Union?

A: Post-Trip changes in Jewish Identity, Diaspora Identity and Attitudes towards Israel among North American (NA) and Former Soviet Union (FSU) birthright israel *Short-Term Participants*

As can be seen from table 2.1, following the trip, in response to the question: "Is it important to you to belong to the Jewish community?" a positive significant change was reported by participants, both from North America and the Former Soviet Union. Regarding the question: "Does being Jewish play an important part of your life?" the respondents indicated a similar slightly higher sense of identity at the conclusion of the programme (although the change itself was not statistically significant among the FSU respondents). In response to the question: "Is Israeli culture important to you?" participants in both groups reported a positive (and significant) change. Regarding the question: "To what extent do you see Israel as a source of pride and self-respect for Diaspora Jewry?" there is almost no change found, though the pre- and post-scores on this measure remained high in both groups. In both of these measures of identity, the scores were already high at the beginning of the programme and were preserved high at the conclusion of the programme. However, the most dramatic change amongst participants from both groups is to the degree of *emotional attachment to Israel*, which was not very high at the beginning of the programme and was strengthened during the trip. This outcome, together with the higher importance now attached to belonging to their Jewish community, all contribute to a heightened sense of Jewish peoplehood. These impacts are better reflected in the participants' own words:

> "The trip was a once in a lifetime journey, both spiritual and mental."
> "This trip gave me the insight into my heritage that would have otherwise been unavailable to me."
> "I somehow truly feel connected to other Jews in a way previously unknown to me."
> "The Israeli soldier experience was the best part of the programme and a huge influence in my and the others on my bus's want, to come back to Israel to study or to live."
> "I feel a closer connection to Israel and have a greater understanding of the issues facing the state."
> "The trip was an experience that somewhat has changed my life. Because of this trip, I feel more connected to the Jewish culture, religion, and heritage. I feel that I want to be more involved in the Jewish community when I get back to [the] USA."
> "The trip has inspired me to make aliyah and I know that it has inspired some of my friends on the trip as well . . . it is really important to expose all kinds of Jews to Israel." (Lev-Ari and Mittelberg 2005)

By way of comparison, in both groups of North American and FSU participants, *no change*, either positive or negative, was recorded on the measure of Diaspora *Citizenship* Identity (namely, the importance of their attachment to their country of origin) as an outcome of the visit to Israel.

B. Long-Term Israel Experience Programmes

Almost two decades ago (1986), I had the privilege to be associated with the launching of two long-term programmes in one year (*Oren* and *Otzma*), each a forerunner of the entirely new MASA initiative launched in 2005. This new initiative of the government of Israel and the Jewish Agency for Israel was aimed at radically increasing (by subsidizing) the participants in long-term (semester to one year) programmes in Israel in order to quadruple the number up to 20,000 by the year 2008. These two programmes (*Oren* and *Otzma*) have been extensively researched and findings published. They are briefly referred to here both as examples and predictors of the likely outcomes of this new but belated initiative of global Jewish leadership, allowing us to explore its long-term implications (Mittelberg 1988; Mittelberg and Lev-Ari 1995; Mittelberg 1999; Mittelberg et al. 2003).

Similarly to the *birthright* data just reported, respondents in both programmes reported a sustained heightened importance of being Jewish in their personal lives, as well as continuing to see Israel as a national cultural and religious centre of the Jewish people. Unlike the *birthright* participants however, these alumni experienced a weakening of their American identity compared to their scores at the outset of their longer term programme.

Summing up, the centrality and salience of the Jewish and Israeli ethnic components of self-identity were seen to be strengthened in increased measures over time; withstanding attrition over the follow up period back home in North America. However, this Jewish peoplehood identification was correlated with a slight decline in the weight of the American component of their identity. All in all, one can say that the visit to Israel changed the *relative* weight of different components of the ethnic identity of young American Jews on their return home to America. As has been shown elsewhere (Mittelberg 1988; Mittelberg and Lev Ari 1995), these impacts are neither automatic nor guaranteed. The primary factors of the Israel experience that contribute to this ethnic impact include: close social interaction with the host, the sense by the participants that they contributed to the host society, and finally, high satisfaction with the educational and social programme that was provided for them.

The visit to Israel for American Jews is made possible by the globalization of travel and tourism, allowing integration of American Jews with Israelis within time, without sharing a permanent place of residence. This process results in the relativization of American identification as part of global Jewish identity, within which belonging to a wider *imagined community* is incorporated.

Ultimately, the burden of integration of the different worlds of experience into a pluralized American Jewish identity remains incumbent on the participant-alumni, as he or she renegotiates their identity in the pluralized world of the community on their return home.

Jewish Continuity and Israel Visits

It is often asked to what extent Jewish continuity is possible in the Diaspora today. The honest answer is that we don't really know but we can perhaps determine the lines of analysis. We can ask to what degree is the Jewish culture of most Diaspora Jews filled with content that determines behaviour (often characterized as "ethnic"), or whether this content is reduced to the symbolic, lacking behavioural consequences. To what degree is this culture — however rich — made plausible to the individuals who share it by virtue of a community structure that reinforces its reality status and maintains processes of socialization (both formal and informal) from generation to generation? We can further ask what proportion of Diaspora Jewish children grow up in ethnically homogeneous households that serve as the source of the historical memory and culture that is being transmitted to them. By the same token, we need to know what sort of ethnic outcome arises from dual-identity households where the adults choose to be ambiguous about their multiple ethnic heritages. In these cases today, it is unclear what the children of such households will adopt as their nominal or symbolic ethnicity, if any, and what will be its subsequent strength.

Finally, we can ask about the role of Israel in this emerging ethnic culture of choice. Israel is the one place in the modern world where Jewish values are nominally those of the dominant culture of society. This situation is in contrast to the minority status of Jewish ethnicity in the Diaspora. Israel, therefore, has the potential to be a focus (partial or otherwise) of Jewish identification for all Diaspora Jews, or to act as a locus of Jewish experience — whether physical or virtual — to be lived through.

Diaspora Jewish youth today share a set of common background experiences, which can be termed *agents of re-ethnification*. These include formal Jewish education, the celebration of rites of passage such as the bar/bat mitzvah, participation in informal Jewish youth groups, educational trips to Israel at all ages, and Jewish studies courses at universities (Mittelberg 1999).

The *visit to Israel* is a potentially important agent of Jewish ethnicity, precisely because it stands at the interface between the private and the public, the religious and the secular, and the particular and universalistic aspects of Jewishness. In Israel, the visitor experiences a manifestation of Jewish sovereignty which is nonreplicable beyond Israel's borders. Israel contributes affect to Diaspora symbolic ethnicity. Israel supports Diaspora Jewish identity by acting as the object of organizational efforts in the areas of philanthropy and politics. Ultimately, the effect of the Israel experience is to influence North American Jewish teens and young adults toward Jewish marriage, volunteer social involvement, and communal responsibility. Its normative and behavioural consequences may then contribute to the *re-ethnification of Diaspora Jews.*

Israel represents a partner for enriching Diaspora Jewish consciousness, for Israel is itself at present involved with its own process of defining Jewish continuity in ways different but no less significant than those of Diaspora Jewry. Although Israel and Diaspora Jewry have different challenges with regard to Jewish continuity, they need to explore a common and shared solution. This involves a programme of reciprocal personal, cultural, and economic interchange between Jews in Israel and the Diaspora. Modern Jewish identity is incomplete without the contribution of both communities. Israelis should seek greater integration of the forms of Jewishness represented in the Diaspora. Diaspora Jewry could develop a better understanding of the historical role and opportunity inherent in the Jewish sovereign state — something that no minority Jewish culture could ever generate. Modern Jewish ethnicity will develop in its fullest form from all that the Jewish people can collectively offer.

However, the *Israel connection* can be relevant to Diaspora Jews only if the latter are *existentially relevant to Israeli Jews*; currently they are hardly at all. To this end, Diaspora-based Jewish institutions will be compelled to work with *grass-roots Israeli institutions* in order to build together a new common culture that is relevant to Jewish people everywhere. It is perhaps somewhat ironic that today we find that the issues of (a) what makes up being Jewish in Israel, and (b) how that Jewishness determines or affects all the other aspects of Israeli public and private life, stand at the centre of Israel's own quest for identity. This issue challenges, indeeds threatens, in its divisiveness, the very sense of peoplehood without which Israel's existence is unthinkable or even justifiable. A significant part of the Jewish identity crisis in Israel resides in the absence of a sense of belonging, both to the Jewish people and to one's local community. Any serious grappling among Israelis with the issue of *their own* Jewish identity and culture must include a *continuous dialogue with Jewish peers from the Diaspora.* Through this dialogue, Jews in both communities must interrelate so that we may understand and deal with the complexity of Jewish identity — an identity that embodies cultural, national, and religious components.

Thus the Jewish communities in the Diaspora today could assume a *new* historic role of *partner* with Israel, to ensure the Jewish future of Israel in the Diaspora and the Diaspora in Israel — the Jewish future of the Jewish people. Diaspora Jewry together with Israeli Jewry would pursue this goal by engaging intentionally, purposefully, and programmatically in *Jewish People Building* through lateral Israel–Diaspora Jewish programmming: that is, social engagement and interaction between different Jews from different communities who mean something personally to each other and who live out existential commonalities in partially shared communities, even if only for segments of their daily lives, or at important stages in their biographies. Some successful programme examples have already included (1) Israel–Diaspora Twin Community Leadership Development, (2) Israel–Diaspora Family Life Cycle

Celebration and (3) Israel Experience Peer Encounters. Today it is painfully clear that the image of Israel cannot serve the Diaspora as a surrogate for a community that is absent. The challenge to and responsibility of Diaspora Jewish leadership is to reconstitute the role of Israel in community life by *transforming the image of Israel to an experience of Israel.* They must move the Israel–Diaspora relationship from the *transcendent but ephemeral to the contractual but central.*

Finally, Diaspora Jewish leaders must transform the individual experience of Israel to a community relationship with its own bilateral institutional basis. The next steps beyond the Jewish Agency's Partnership 2000, which is essentially programmatic, is the establishment of concommittant structures, *Regional Israel–Diaspora Federations* which would maintain — along the whole spectrum of twinned local community functions — the intrinsic Israel–Diaspora relationship.

A contract binds two sides. The implication here is for nothing less than the reconstitution of the basis of Jewish peoplehood. At the base of such a contract lies the view that Jewish continuity in Boston and Haifa, for example, is not only dependent on what goes on *within* each community, but also on what goes on *between* each community. While each community can in principle go its own way, the Jewishness of neither will be strengthened by it.

This is the Israel connection to Diaspora Jewish continuity; it is as well, somewhat paradoxically, the Diasporan connection to Israeli Jewish continuity. *Jewish peoplehood requires the input of both ends of the assymmetrical though symbiotic relationship* in order to be sustained.

Travel to Israel: Migration of Another Kind

Fifty years after the establishment of the State of Israel, but especially following the Six Day War, travel to Israel has been transformed from a demand of external migration to a case of internal migration — internal, that is, to the Jewish people, with temporary travel of a round trip nature.

As such, the visit to Israel that is now understood as an educational programme in Israel (not the migration to Israel) represents a broad consensus between the Jewish elites of Israel and Diaspora society. Witness especially the *birthright israel* program and the entirely new MASA initiative launched at the time of writing, between the Government of Israel and the Jewish Agency for Israel, with the aim of radically increasing (subsidizing) the participants in long-term (semester to one year) programs in Israel in order to quadruple the number up to 20,00 by the year 2008.

In all of these efforts, the consensus of both lay and professional leadership — and one which is supported by research — is that an educational experience in Israel has a transformative impact on the Jewishness of the traveller (even though there is much debate regarding the power, weight and sustainability of the educational experience in Israel).

From the perspective of the sociology of tourism, the Israel experience of those who travel there, can be understood as a particular case of diaspora cultural tourism, in all its six forms cited above, often more akin to a pilgrimage than to recreational tourism.

The Jewish Diaspora now can be understood as a particular case of contemporary peoples that live *in a multi local environment with an embedded homeland and lateral dias-*

poras. That is to say, modern Jews may well simultaneously live in and feel a belonging to a number of places, all of which are part of their spiritual home. They may belong to a given Diaspora community as well as to one in Israel sustaining the social fabric that joins both communities. Israel–Diaspora relations therefore may be best viewed within the context of a particular case of a transnational peoplehood which, in the Jewish case, predated the rise of the nation state in the midst of which was born the Zionist movement and the Jewish state.

International travel from the Diaspora to Israel then can be seen as a particular form of cultural tourism which has the effect on the traveler of building a level of attachment to a physical society outside the locale in which he or she resides permanently, as well as generating an attachment to the imagined people to which *both* the traveler and the hosts purportedly belong.

Summary

The current Israel–Diaspora discourse maintained almost exclusively by the elites of both Israeli Jewish society and Jewish Diaspora institutions has been antagonistically dominated by the *one way migration paradigm*, as a categorical imperative demanded by the State from its distant and dissident fellow (Western) Jews. As categorically as it was demanded, so, too, was it denied; certainly at the personal level of Diaspora leadership and the Jewish masses. Failure to fulfill this goal invited both sides to participate in a choreography of mutual rejection, and not to an opportunity to rethink the paradigm itself. This missed opportunity is especially poignant in view of the fact that significant sections of both Israeli and Diaspora Jews do indeed maintain long-term family, business and career relations with Jews in their opposite community. Globalization brings a growing number of Israeli Jewish young adults into the labour and social markets of Diaspora community and institutions. The reverse is also true, both as part of the "push" programmes of educational travel to Israel and the pull of the Diaspora for exploration and growth for Israeli youth in search of higher education and/or post army growth and experience.

Alongside this paradigm of discourse has also blossomed the default philanthropic paradigm, the Diaspora-sponsored trade-off for the absence of migration just referred to. This philanthropic support (as important as it undoubtedly is, both for the donors and the recipients) was and remains often captive to the images most likely to serve the interest of capital mobilization rather than the generation of Israel–Diaspora reciprocity and interdependence. Relationships were often, if not always, marked by an emphasis on vivid images of the needs of the recipients, and the weaknesses of Israeli society, thus defining Israel as a place to support but not to join..

While the importance of the educational visit and its impact are recognized, it begs the question with which we began. The overarching question that has yet to be answered is: what sort of Jewish continuity do we seek and hope for? What continuity will the visit to Israel sustain, and what kind of people will modern Jews sustain?

Towards Global Jewish Peoplehood

- Can we see Jewish peoplehood as a de-territorialized culture in the existential sense? Can Jewish peoplehood be not limited to only one territory?

- Can we discuss this possibility without being accused of denying the centrality of Israel in Jewish history and contemporary Jewish peoplehood?
- Can we discuss being Jewish without having to see the Diaspora as a liminal event; liminal to primordial Jewishness which can only be found in Israel?
- Are we obliged by the recognition of multilateral Jewish peoplehood to deny the messianic vision and the Zionist programme of the ingathering of the Jewish people in its own land?
- Can there be perhaps an affirmation of the role of Israel in the structure of global Jewish peoplehood, as well as Israel being an agent for, and dimension of, personal Diaspora Jewish identity?
- Can Israeli Jews include Diaspora Jewish life worlds into its collective vision without making the demands of immediate physical residence in the land?
- Finally, can we leave the issue of personal permanent migration to the forces of biography, marriage and money markets, and concentrate on the global platform on which Jewish identity and social structure needs to be firmly placed in the twenty first century?

Diaspora tourism which is exemplified in the Jewish case by *birthright israel* and now MASA, points to the universal blurring of boundaries between home and host country and to the need to *redefine both the real as well as the imagined collective memory of contemporary Jews*. It furthermore invites us to take into account, openly and explicitly, the ways in which different Diaspora identities contrast with each other, as well as with the Jewish identity of Israelis in their homeland.

None of the issues raised by these questions can be dissolved into religious ideology — whether pluralist or fundamentalist ideology — nor can they be reduced to and exhausted by the exclusive political demand of migration to Israel. Rather, the debate needs to be structured on a more inclusive and broader paradigm of late modern Jewish peoplehood. Indeed, this discourse must be expanded to include the contemporary local community structures and the diverse cultural paradigms of the global Jewish community, in order to forge anew the binding affinities, common language and shared destiny that makes belonging to a people concretely relevant for its members.

If the discourse is restricted to the *synagogue-driven* religious paradigm in the name of the American ethos, or to the *state-driven* migration paradigm in the name of the Israeli ethos, the opportunities offered by a more inclusive global transnational paradigm of peoplehood may be overlooked or eliminated.

Whatever the future holds for the Jewish people, it seems clear that not all the cards are held today in only one community. Moreover, interdependence and reciprocity between the different communities is a *sine qua non* for the continuity of the Jewish people. Finally, educational travel between Israel and its diasporas, in *greater numbers and at earlier ages* is likely to contribute to these very consequences and thus to the continuity of the Jewish peoplehood to which modern Jews widely aspire.

Table 2.1 Pre-Trip and Post-Trip changes in Jewish Identity, Diaspora Identity and Attitudes towards Israel among North American (NA) and Former Soviet Union (FSU) *birthright israel* Short Term Participants

NA: N=326; FSU N=155

Key: 1 to 5 scale; 1 = low degree, 5 = high degree

Identity and attitudes	*Pre-Trip*	*Post-Trip*	*t-value*	*Significance (2-tailed)*
I Diaspora Jewish Identity				
(a) Importance of belonging to the Jewish community				
NA participants	3.67	3.89	-5.20	0.000
FSU participants	3.53	3.72	-2.78	0.006
(b) Being Jewish plays an important part in my life				
NA participants	3.98	4.14	-4.38	0.000
FSU participants	3.78	3.89	-1.57	0.116
II Homeland Component of Diaspora Jewish Identity				
(a) Israeli culture is important to you				
NA participants	3.64	3.78	-2.85	0.005
FSU participants	3.68	3.83	-2.19	0.030
(b) Israel as a source of pride for Diaspora Jewry				
NA participants	4.04	4.04	0.06	NS
FSU participants	4.25	4.29	-0.57	NS
(c) Emotionally attached to Israel				
NA participants	3.41	3.92	-3.93	0.000
FSU participants	3.45	3.94	-6.98	0.000
III Citizenship Component of Diaspora Jewish Identity				
Being American/FSU plays an important part in my life				
NA participants	3.62	3.59	0.70	NS
FSU participants	2.72	2.78	-0.48	NS

Note

1 I wish to record my indebtedness to Prof. Len Saxe and Dr. Bruce Phillips at CMJS Brandeis, for their important methodological assistance with regard to utilization of NJPS 2001 data.

References

Braziel, J.E. and Mannur, A. (eds), *Theorizing Diaspora. A Reader* (Malden, MA: Blackwell Publishing, 2003).

Chazan, Bary *Does the Teen Israel Experience Make a Difference*? (New York, NY: Israel Experience Inc., 1997).

Clifford, J., *Routes Travel and Translation in the Late Twentieth Century* (Cambridge, MA: Harvard University Press, 1997).

Cohen, R., *Global Diasporas* (London: Routledge, 1997).

Coles, T. and Timothy, D. J. (eds), *Tourism, Diasporas and Space* (London: Routledge, 2004).

Featherstone, M., *Undoing Culture: Globalization, Postmodernism and Identity* (London: Sage Publications, 1995).

Giddens, A., *Modernity and Self-Identity: Self and Society in the Late Modern Age* (Stanford, CA: Stanford University Press, 1991), p. 16.

Hollingshead, K., "Tourism and the restless peoples: A dialectical inspection of Bhabba's halfway populations", *Tourism, Culture and Communication*, 1, 1 (1998): 49–77.

Israel, S. and Mittelberg, D., *The Israel Visit — Not Just for Teens: The Characteristics and Impact of College-age Travel to Israel* (Waltham, MA: The Maurice and Marilyn Cohen Center for Modern Jewish Studies, Brandeis University, 1998).

Kelner, S., Saxe , L., Kadushin, C., Canar, R., Lindholm, M., Ossman, H., Perloff, J., Phillips, B., Teres, R., Wolf, M. and Woocher, M., *Making Meaning: Participants' Experience of Birthright Israel* (Waltham, MA: The Maurice and Marilyn Cohen Center for Modern Jewish Studies, Brandeis University, 2000).

Kelner, S., *Somebody Else's Business: The Deliberate Attempt to Influence Individual Belonging through Israel Experience Programs.* Paper presented at Conference on Dynamic Belonging: Shifting Jewish Identities and Collective Involvements in Comparative Perspective, at the Institute for Advanced Studies, Hebrew University of Jerusalem, Israel on 20 June 2004.

Kelner, S., "The Stone the Builders Scorned: Constructing Jewish Belonging Through Mass Tourism." In Cohen S.M., Goldberg, H. and Kopelowitz, E. (eds), *Dynamic Belonging: Shifting Jewish Identities and Collective Involvements in Comparative Perspective* (forthcoming).

Mayer, E., Kosmin, B. and Keysar, A., *American Jewish Identity Survey 2001* (New York, NY: CUNY Graduate Center, 2002).

Lev-Ari, L. and Mittelberg, D., "Four Years of Oren-IGT Hillel's *birthright israel* Trip: Summary of Research Reports (2002–2005)". Internal Research Report, Oranim, Academic College of Education, Tivon, Israel, 2005.

Mittelberg, D., *Strangers in Paradise: The Israeli Kibbutz Experience* (New Brunswick (USA) & Oxford (UK): Transaction Books, 1988).

Mittelberg, D., "The Impact of Jewish Education and the 'Israel Experience' on the Jewish Identity of American Jewish Youth", *Studies in Contemporary Jewry*, Vol. 8 (1992).

Mittelberg, D., *The Israel Visit and Jewish Identification*, The Institute on American Jewish–Israeli Relations, Issues Series No. 4 (New York, NY: American Jewish Committee, 1994).

Mittelberg, D. and Lev-Ari L., "Jewish Identity, Jewish Education and Experience of the Kibbutz in Israel," *Journal of Moral Education*, 24, 3 (1995).

Mittelberg, D., *The Israel Connection and American Jews* (Westport, Connecticut & London: Praeger, 1999).

Mittelberg, D., Lev-Ari, L. and Mansfeld, Y., "Globalization and the Role of Educational Travel to Israel in the Ethnification of American Jews", *Tourism Recreation Research*, Special Issue on Volunteer Tourism, 28, 3 (2003).

Post, M., "Don't Bash Birthright", *The Jerusalem Post*, 20 December 1999, p. 54.

Saxe, L., Kadushin, C., Pakes, J., Kelner, S., Sternberg, L., Horowitz, B., Sales, A. and Brodsky, A., *Birthright Israel Launch Evaluation: Preliminary Findings* (Waltham, MA: The Maurice and Marilyn Cohen Center for Modern Jewish Studies, Brandeis University, 2000).

Saxe, L., *American Jews and Israel: Insights from NJPS* (Waltham, MA: The Maurice and Marilyn Cohen Center for Modern Jewish Studies, Brandeis University, 2003).

Saxe, L. and Kadushin, C., *Ten Days to Launch a Life-long Connection to Israel: The Impact of* birthright israel. Paper presented at the Fifth Annual Herzliya Conference at the Maurice and Marilyn Cohen Center for Modern Jewish Studies, Brandeis University, Waltham, MA on 15 December 2004.

Saxe, L., Kadushin, C., Hecht, S., Rosen, M.I., Phillips, B. and Kelner, S., *Evaluating* birthright israel; *Long-term Impact and Recent Findings*. Research Report on *birthright israel*, November 2004, The Maurice and Marilyn Cohen Center for Modern Jewish Studies, Brandeis University, Waltham, MA, 2004.

ISRAEL COMMENTATOR

Israel Experience and Jewish Peoplehood

Alan D. Hoffmann

In his essay, Dr. David Mittelberg posits that the global nature of today's modern world has changed the discourse regarding the "Homeland–Diaspora dichotomy". He states that, as Israel and Diaspora maintain antiquated paradigms for viewing the other, there is little connection between these groups on the everyday level. Ultimately, he asks the question: what kind of Jewish continuity will Israel visits sustain, and in what directions are the Jewish people heading? Though Mittelberg presents some data reflecting the importance of Israel visits, I will argue that modernity has not only had an impact on the nature of Israel educational trips for Diaspora Jewry, but has also created a new necessity for these transformative experiences for Diaspora Jewish youth.

The issues facing the Jewish people today are unprecedented. Barely three generations ago, Jews throughout the world — most of whom were new immigrants, whether in the United States, Europe, South America, the Soviet Union or Australia — struggled for basic economic and sometimes physical security. These external threats, certainly in the first half of the twentieth century, but even later as well, prevented the Jewish community from truly confronting modernity and its impact on Jewish life. Today, although Jews throughout the world have achieved the basic economic and physical security they once lacked, an entirely new set of threats has emerged.

In under a century, the modern Jewish community has managed to realize many of its grandparents' dreams. In the wake of these incredible successes, however, new threats to the survival of the Jewish people have emerged. For the first time in history, Jews have the opportunity to *choose* to be Jewish. Whereas in the past, Jews were still identified and labeled as Jews by the outside society, even if they chose not to affiliate with Judaism in any way, Jews today can "opt out" of Jewish affiliation and identification completely. Being Jewish today is completely voluntary, and, as nearly every demographic study undertaken in the last decade has shown, many young Jews are choosing not to affiliate.

Thus, modernity, with all of its advantages, has created a problem that threatens the future of the Jewish people. Young Jews today need motivation to *be* Jewish; no longer does society force Jewishness on them, and no longer is having Jewish parents enough to ensure that children will remain committed Jews. We know that the old model of Jewish communities, centred around synagogues, is not enough to attract the next generation. The concept of Jewish peoplehood, which encompasses all aspects of the culture — including history, homeland, religion and spirituality — offers a fresh and exciting entry point for many young people. In the face of this crisis and these obstacles, Israel has a unique role to play in securing the Jewish future through strengthening Jewish peoplehood.

The Role of Israel

Since the founding of the State, Jewish communities around the world have cast Israel as the victim, primarily for fund-raising purposes. Although Israel still faces many challenges to its identity and Jewish nature, the vibrant, dynamic, and growing Israel of 2005 now has the potential to provide much-needed help to world Jewry. The connection to Israel is of utilitarian value in addressing the challenges of Jewish life around the world. At the same time, inculcating young Jews with a strong connection to Israel has intrinsic value as well.

From 1948, unmediated engagement with Israel has had the power to motivate and inspire Jews. It is in Israel that Diaspora Jewry can sense for the first time this notion of Jewish peoplehood and what it means to be part of the broader narrative of Jewish history. Exposure to the remarkable diversity of Israel, the rich tapestry of Israeli society, the modern Hebrew language, and the use of Jewish time has a profound effect and provides an answer to the all-important question of "why be Jewish?". Israel offers multiple gateways to Jewish peoplehood and, as such, is the single most powerful resource we have in ensuring the Jewish future. The experience of Jewish sovereignty, especially for prolonged periods of time, has a dramatic effect on many indicators of Jewish identity, behaviour and belief.

The transformative power of an Israel experience affects young and old alike and provides a unique anchor for the concept of Jewish peoplehood. Extensive research has shown that spending time in Israel can have a strong impact on people. Jewish education has to consider this transformative potential on all possible levels. Short-term programmes, including *birthright israel* and summer seminars for high-school students, can have a tremendous impact on young people, at precisely the key identity formation stages of their lives. Indeed, the Jewish community must strive to send no less than 50 percent of Jewish young people to Israel for short periods of time. Yet this is not enough. Long stays in Israel have been proven to definitively strengthen Jewish identity and generate a long-term connection to Jewish peoplehood.

According to a study that compared alumni of Young Judaea's Year Course with those who applied to the programme but ultimately did not attend, a year in Israel has a transformative effect. Of those who participated in the programme, 91 percent went on to marry Jews, in contrast to the control group where only 48 percent did so. Synagogue membership is 79 percent among alumni and only 43 percent among those who did not come to Israel. Over 70 percent of Young Judaea Year Course graduates have been back to visit Israel more than two times, compared to 20 percent of the other group. Those who spent a year in Israel were also far more likely to send their children to Jewish day school, volunteer in a Jewish framework and to contribute to Federation campaigns (Steven M. Cohen and Alan Ganapol (1998) *Building Jewish*

Identity: A Study of Young Judaea Alumni <http://www.youngjudaea.org/html/alum_study.html>).

It is, in fact, these statistics, combined with the growing concern for the Jewish future, that led to an historic policy shift by the Government of Israel. For the first time, the Prime Minister of Israel has decided to invest in the future of the Jewish people through a joint initiative with the Jewish Agency's Department for Jewish Zionist Education. This programme will ultimately bring one in every five young Jews to Israel on semester or year-long programmes. MASA: The Gateway to Long-Term Programs was launched this year and serves as a platform for all semester and year-long programmes for Diaspora Jewry.

Not only will MASA ultimately bring 20,000 people between the ages of 18–30 to Israel annually and help countless individuals embark on their Jewish journeys, but it will help shift the cultural norm among Diaspora Jewry. Spending time in Israel will become as commonplace as synagogue membership once was. After completing high school, thousands of Jewish youths, from all denominations and backgrounds, will participate in a MASA programme. Israel will become a core part of Jewish identity for a significant percentage of the Jewish world, uniting diverse Jewish communities around the world and inspiring young people to explore and own their rich heritage.

The major challenge facing the Jewish people today is the openness of modernity and the newly voluntary nature of Judaism. By placing the engagement with Israel at the centre of Jewish education, both as a source of resources and as a locus of intrinsic and unique value, Israel has the potential to provide much-needed inspiration and motivation for young people to commit themselves to seeking Jewish meaning. Israel education, however, is just one piece of the broader struggle to deal with issues that modernity has imposed on the Jewish community. As Mittelberg argued, the issues he raised can only be addressed by structuring a debate on a broad, modern paradigm of Jewish peoplehood. Peoplehood is a unifying concept that can encompass all aspects of Judaism, and Israel education is the ideal gateway to Jewish peoplehood.

DIASPORA COMMENTATOR

Jewish Continuity and Israel Visits: The Latin American Experience

Gabriel Trajtenberg

David Mittelberg's essay accurately describes new focuses on the Israel–Diaspora relationship. His essay provides an excellent analysis on the impact of different experiences as regards duration as well as the knowledge about Jewish identity of its participants.

I would like to review the ideological aspects of the underlying discourse in this exchange called Israel–Diaspora.

The Israel Perception About the Command

How Israel is perceived varies from country to country in the Diaspora. Commonly, the approach tends to be generalized as from the American Jewish experience. This experience, prevalent due to its heavy demographic weight, differs greatly from others such as the Jewish and Zionist experience in southern Latin America. My personal experience has taught me that, within a globalised context, the South American Jew thinks, lives and feels Israel differently from his northern brothers.

Predominant Jewish and Zionist education in southern Latin American Jewish communities has generated an extraordinary bridge with Israel. This educational approach tends to place Israel in the subconscious of children and young people as the final destination of the Jewish people. Regardless of personal, family or working aspects that may postpone or call off the decision to migrate to Israel, Israel is our home; our final destination.

It is important to keep alive this paradigm mentioned by David Mittelberg as the "*migration paradigm*". It is essentially the living spirit of the Zionist movement; the expression of the final destination, the historical understanding and the sense of Jewish people.

Each voyage to Israel should be considered as a remembrance of the revolutionary miracle of the Zionist experience and of the creation of the modern Hebrew State. As the famous phrase from the sixties says: *When something extraordinary turns into something ordinary, we're witnessing a revolution.* Israel is the Jewish people living a revolution. The core goal of Jewish Zionist education is simple: *to keep Israel's extraordinary nature alive.*

For a Latin American Jew, being a tourist in Israel is a mixture of six patterns described by Coles and Timothy (2003). Though there have been no studies into direct family bonds between Jewish tourists from our continent and Israel, it might be stated that the rate of visits of Latin American Jews to Israel is high. Educational Jewish tourism from Latin America to Israel during the seventies, eighties and nineties was dominated by short-term programmes averaging one to two months long over January and February. These educational experiences, headed by the Jewish Agency for Israel, were the final destination for young activists. The core programme was composed of three experiences of Israeli life. The first one was the educational programme itself, that is, the *Tapuz* plan (living in a *kibbutz*), Jewish studies, etc. During these programmes, the ideological transmission was so strong that the trip's transcendence was indelibly stamped. The second essential element was the encounter or re-encounter with the Israeli family bond. This usually took place during Sabbath when the young could experience Israeli life through the eyes of an uncle, brother, cousin, etc. Finally, participants spent some extra days experiencing Israel — its streets, smells, transportation and pubs — on their own, without any *madrich* (youth leader). This last component was fully subjective because the young activist could put into practice the legacy of their Zionist education by means of the intensive use of Hebrew.

The Effects of Globalization on the Latin American Tradition of Visits to Israel

The new millennium brought new changes and reactions in the Jewish world, especially for the American Jewish community. The data collected by the National Jewish Population Survey (NJPS) in the mid-1990s on young American Jewish identity led to the *birthright israel* programme being enthusiastically created. *Birthright israel* is an historical milestone that builds a new bridge between the North American Jewish community and Israel. In my opinion, *birthright israel* has been a wise and successful answer to the growing challenge of assimilation within the North American Jewish community.

The emergence of *birthright israel* coincides with a particular juncture in Jewish communities from the southern region of Latin America, especially in Argentina, and within a background of economic recession in Brazil, Uruguay and Argentina. From the mid nineties, the mystique and structure of mid-range programmes began losing strength and the number of participants decreased. In conjunction with this reality, the economic depression made it difficult for families to finance their children's trips, generating a gap between 1999 and 2001. Within this context, the programme spread to the Latin American regional market and strongly called, thanks to its generosity, to hundreds of young people imbued with the historical mysticism of traveling to Israel.

From 2005, MASA long-term programmes have gained rapid popularity among young people. In my opinion, MASA provides the optimum experience that any Latin American young Jew can have of Israel.

Globalization, in terms of educational tourist programmes to Israel, has both benefited and harmed Latin American Jewish communities. On the one hand, we have benefited from having amongst us members of the community who have experienced *birthright israel* programmes (short-term) and MASA (long-term). On the other hand, there is now decreased attendance in mid-range programmes (one to two months), which were once part of the tradition and spirit of the region. Mid-range programmes should be a complementary element to function as a link between the programmes mentioned above. They should be promoted as a gradual bridge to define longer-term programmes in Israel.

About Hebrew

If English is the language of globalization, then Hebrew is the language of the Jewish tribe and its Israeli State.

Educational tourist programmes to Israel should be the final closure of the long process of Jewish Zionist education, with Hebrew being the main access gate to Jewish culture and Israeli life. Hebrew is the link that gets us connected to the real Israel; to its music, television and everyday life. The deeper our knowledge of this language is, the stronger the link between the young from Israel and from the Diaspora should be.

To support Hebrew is to support Israel and Jewish people's nature among the global concord of nations. If English is the language of globalization, then Hebrew is the language of the Jewish tribe and its Israeli State.

3

Israel in Orthodox Identity: The American Experience

Chaim I. Waxman

When the connections of American Jews to Israel are examined denominationally, it is evident that denomination plays a very important role with respect to emotional attachments to Israel. For example, table 3.1, which is based on data from the 2001 National Jewish Population Survey (NJPS), shows the distribution of responses to the question, "How emotionally attached are you to Israel?"

Table 3.1 Level of Emotional Attachment to Israel, by Denomination,

	Orthodox	*Conservative*	*Reconstructionist*	*Reform*
Very	72.1	45.1	27.4	22.5
Somewhat	22.7	37.3	50.8	45.1
Not very	2.1	15.1	11.1	22.8
Not at all	3.1	2.4	10.7	9.7
Total	100.0	100.0	100.0	100.0

Source: NJPS, 2001.

The data indicate rather dramatically that Orthodox Jews have much stronger emotional ties to Israel than do Conservatives who, in turn, have much stronger ties than Reconstructionists who, in turn, have stronger ties than the Reform Jews.

The denominational significance also manifests itself in terms of having visited Israel. As indicated in table 3.2, Orthodox Jews are much more likely to have visited Israel than are their Conservative, Reconstructionist, and Reform fellow Jews, and the denominational pattern seen with respect to emotional attachment repeats here.

Author's note: Although my focus is on American Orthodoxy, it is reasonable to assume that the patterns are essentially similar among Orthodox Jews in other Western diaspora communities.

Finally, among those who have visited Israel, there is a similar pattern of denominational variation with respect to the number of times the respondent visited. Twenty-five percent of the Orthodox respondents who visited Israel, did so more than five times, and that far exceeds the percentages of the other denominations who visited Israel more than five times. The only deviation from the denominational pattern previously noted is in the Reform Jews having a higher percentage than the Reconstructionists of those who visited more than five times.

Table 3.2 Ever Been to Israel, by Denomination

	Orthodox	*Conservative*	*Reconstructionist*	*Reform*
Yes	81.4	61.2	34.6	37.8
No	18.6	38.8	65.4	62.2
Total	100.0	100.0	100.0	100.0

Source: NJPS, 2001.

Table 3.3 Number of Times Have Been to Israel, by Denomination

	Orthodox	*Conservative*	*Reconstructionist*	*Reform*
1 time	27.5	52.3	51.8	71.2
2–4 times	38.7	29.7	38.2	19.4
5–9 times	14.1	8.0	–	4.8
10 or more times	15.1	5.2	–	4.0
Resided in Israel	4.7	4.8	10.0	.5
Total	100.0	100.0	100.0	100.0

Source: NJPS, 2001.

With respect to *aliyah*, Goldscheider (1974: 381–82) found that patterns among the American *olim* "of over-concentration and selectivity among religious and Orthodox Jews relative to the American Jewish population" also manifested themselves in their patterns of synagogue attendance and ritual observance. Specifically, among the *olim* (immigrants to Israel), the rate of synagogue attendance and observance of such rituals as fasting on *Yom Kippur* and dietary regulations was disproportionately high when compared to the overall rates for the Jewish population of the United States.

Data from Israel's Central Bureau of Statistics likewise indicated the disproportionate religiosity of American *olim* and the increasing proportion of the religiously observant among them. Of the 1978–80 North American *olim*, a majority, 54 percent, identified themselves as "religious," 21 percent as "traditional," 11 percent as "not very religious," and only 14 percent as "not religious at all" (Central Bureau of Statistics 1986: 14–15; Della Pergola 1987: 126).

Since those studies, there are strong indicators of a significant increase in the percentage of Orthodox Jews among American *olim*, despite the fact that their percentage in the American Jewish population has but increased moderately at best. For example, it has been reported (Barkai 1987) that "of the [approximately] 1,900 [*olim*] who arrived from the United States [in 1986] more than 1,200 are Orthodox Jews and the remainder defined themselves as somewhat religiously observant, etc." This report is consistent with estimates, in 1976, of the assistant director of the Aliyah Department of the World Zionist Organization–American Section, and discussions with others connected with that department at that time, that about 60 percent of current American *olim* are Orthodox. More recent estimates, including those of the major American *aliyah* organization, Nefesh B'Nefesh, suggest that about 80 percent of contemporary American *olim* are Orthodox (Bayme and Liebman 1999; Wenig 2003).

In his study of American *olim*, Avruch (1981) suggested a social–psychological basis for the *aliyah* of the American Orthodox. He found that they tend to be people who, "in America, by investing heavily or increasingly in their Jewishness, effected a primordialization of their social identities." In other words, these are individuals who defined themselves primarily in terms of their Jewishness. Their Jewishness took precedence over other aspects of their identities, and their *aliyah* was an attempt to live their lives as Jews within the family of Jews. Orthodox Jews were over-represented among the American *olim*, Avruch suggests, because they are more likely to have been those for whom, in America, Jewishness took precedence over other aspects of their identities.

My analysis of American Orthodox Judaism provided an explanation which is both ideological–cultural and social–psychological. It suggested that the two major approaches adopted by Orthodoxy in its confrontation with modernity have been those of compartmentalization and expansionism (Waxman 1989). In the former, a sharp boundary is drawn between the world of the sacred and the world of the secular, and those adopting this approach seek to live their lives as much as possible within the world of the sacred. When necessity requires that they leave that world and enter the world of the secular, they are shielded from its impact by their consciousness of that world as secular and, hence, of no real value. In expansionism, on the other hand, there is no clear boundary between the worlds of the sacred and the secular, and the two are not kept totally apart. On the contrary, the expansionist attempts to bring sanctity to the secular, to make the secular sacred. This approach, which has among its ideological fathers Rabbi A. I. Kook, is that of those who are Modern Orthodox in principle, that is, those who view integrating sacred learning with secular knowledge, *Torah Umadd'a*, as an inherent value, a "*lekhathilah*," rather than as a necessary evil, a "*bede'avad*" (Lamm 1990). Those who adhere to expansionism seek wholeness in their lives and, thus, perhaps are more likely to go on *aliyah* as part of their quest for leading more whole, complete Jewish lives. It was also suggested that this might also explain the disproportionate number of Americans among the settlers in Judea and Samaria (Waxman 1989). They seek "wholeness" religio-culturally and geographically, and geographical wholeness is comprised of what they define as the entirety of "*Eretz Israel*" according to the maximalist position.

Although ideology is central, structural factors can, of course, slow down or speed up the rate of *aliyah* among the Orthodox. Interestingly, economic factors have been suggested as both impediments and as promoters of *aliyah* from the American Orthodox. Thus, Isaac Berman (1983–84) argues that even though ideology is an important variable influencing *aliyah,* so is reality; that is, economic conditions. All other things being equal, he maintains, the *aliyah* rate goes up when the economic conditions in Israel are good, and the rate declines when the conditions decline. However, when one examines the figures on American *aliyah,* it appears that there is much more involved than economic conditions in Israel. The patterns of ups and downs do not seem to be explainable in terms of the patterns of the Israeli economy. For example, the figures on American *aliyah* for the years 2001–2004 indicate a consistent rise despite the fact that during those years the Israeli economy was in a rather poor state.

On the other hand, economic factors might, in part, explain the *aliyah* figures during those years if it were assumed that the vast majority of those *olim* were Orthodox. Carmel Chiswick (1994) offers a somewhat unique economic basis for the *aliyah* of the Orthodox. She attributes at least part of their higher rate of *aliyah* to the fact that:

> the greater the emphasis placed on traditional observance, the greater the conflict between rhythms of Jewish and secular life and hence [the] greater the lifestyle cost of being Jewish. Within the American Jewish community, the more observant the family the greater the lifestyle costs of being Jewish and hence the greater the "savings" achieved by moving to Israel. Thus the rate of return to aliyah would be higher among more religiously observant Americans, and immigration to Israel would have been stimulated by a revival of Jewish observance among Jews with high-level secular occupations in the United States. (Chiswick 1994)

In my study of Jewish baby boomers, based on the 1990 National Jewish Population Survey, the data indicated that Orthodox Jewish baby boomers had lower family annual incomes than did Conservative and Reform families, and that the "cost of Jewish living" was higher for Orthodox than for others:

> there is a gap of more than $10,000 between the mean family incomes of Orthodox and Conservative, and a similar gap between the mean family incomes of Conservative and Reform baby boomers. Almost two-thirds of the Orthodox baby boomers reported combined annual family incomes of less [than] $45,000, whereas only half of the Conservatives and 42.5 percent of the Reform did . . . Since Orthodox have more children than Conservative and Reform do, this means that the economic constraints are even greater than these data indicate. The lower income of the Orthodox, combined with their larger families, means they have considerably less disposable income than others. In addition, their ideological commitments compel them to join synagogues at a higher rate than others, . . . and to send their children to private day schools, as well as to contribute to a variety of other Jewish communal institutions. There is, thus, ample evidence that the Orthodox are disproportionally affected by what has been called, "the high cost of Jewish living". (Waxman 2001)

The lower income of the Orthodox continued to be evident in the 2001 NJPS. For example, of those identifying as Orthodox, 80 percent had incomes of less than $100,000, as compared to 77 percent of those who identified as Conservative and 7 percent of those who identified as Reform Jews. Five percent of those who identified as Conservative had incomes of $300,000 or more, as compared to 3 percent for the Reform Jews and only 1 percent for the Orthodox. Those figures assume that the family sizes are the same but, in fact, we know that they are not and that the Orthodox have larger families. In other words, the significantly higher cost of Jewish living for the Orthodox persists.

If it is assumed, therefore, that the declining economic conditions in the United States during 2001–2004 had even greater consequences for the Orthodox, because their "lifestyle cost of being Jewish" in America resulted in their having even less "disposable cash" than other American Jews, they would have had a greater incentive to go on *aliyah*, even if the Israeli economy was faring poorly because their religious-lifestyle cost would be much lower in Israel.

Indeed, the major organization promoting American *aliyah*, Nefesh B'Nefesh, and the American branch of the Israel Aliya Center are now directing their messages to Orthodox families with small children, the most likely candidates for *aliyah*, and emphasizing the economic incentive of *aliyah* (Heilman 2005). There has been some debate about the wisdom of this approach but it does reflect the reality of the immediate economic concerns of young American Orthodox families.

Aliyah aside, the denominational significance of Israel also manifests itself in another aspect of Jewish culture in the United States on which there are some data, namely knowledge of Hebrew. The same denominational patterns found with respect to ties to Israel are present here.

Table 3.4 Ability to Read Hebrew, by Denomination

	Orthodox	*Conservative*	*Reconstructionist*	*Reform*
Not at all	4.6	23.9	33.1	44.3
Can sound out words slowly	15.0	41.6	38.4	38.6
Can read words fluently	80.4	34.5	28.5	17.1
Total	100.0	100.0	100.0	100.0

Source: NJPS, 2001.

As table 3.4 indicates, the Orthodox are much more fluent in Hebrew than are their non-Orthodox fellow-Jews. The Conservatives are more fluent than the Reconstructionists, while the Reform Jews are the least fluent. Although there are no empirical data on it, there is reason to suspect that American Orthodox Jews read Israeli newspapers, including *Ha'aretz*, *Ma'ariv* and *Yediot*, and are familiar with a broader range of Israeli society and culture than are their Conservative, Reconstructionist and Reform colleagues. (This does not refer to Israeli–Americans, that is, Israelis who live in the US.)

The argument is frequently heard that the reason that the Orthodox have stronger connections with Israel is because of the Orthodox domination of establishment Judaism in Israel. Non-Orthodox, it is alleged, are less connected because they feel less comfortable in Israel, and they feel less comfortable there because of the Orthodox discrimination against them. However, the NJPS data do not appear to support this contention. Indeed, the denomination variation manifests itself in a wide range of issues relating to both religious and communal identification, such as feelings of a common destiny with Jews elsewhere, and whether they attend an adult Jewish education class or any other kind of adult Jewish learning (Waxman in DellaPergola and Even (eds) 2001; Waxman 2004).

Israel is central specifically to those for whom being Jewish is central. As I have argued elsewhere, Jewishness is a role which one experiences when playing that role and the more frequently one plays the role, the stronger the sense of being Jewish. All evidence indicates that there is a stronger sense of Jewish identity among Orthodox Jews. Apparently, this is because Jewishness plays a more central role in their lives. Because of their religious requirements, there are countless more moments in the everyday life of Orthodox Jews when they consciously "play the role" of Jew. For the majority of American Jews, however, Jewishness and Jewish identity are limited to infrequent intervals, their identity is in general rather abstract, and, thus, Israel does not really play any central role in their lives.

The bonds of Orthodox Jews to Israel are religio-ethnic. In addition to many of the prayers in the services and almost all of the holidays, which are rooted in and directed toward Israel, there have been, when feasible, empirical connections between Jews in the Diaspora and Israel which manifest the value of Israel as the highest religio-ethnic plane. One example is that of *Torat Eretz Israel* (studying Torah in Zion, the Holy Land). A well-known biblical verse states, "For out of Zion shall go forth the Torah, and the word of God from Jerusalem" (Isaiah 2: 3). As a result, there is in Jewish tradition a special value in Israel. Ancient Jerusalem was the first community to implement the notion of public Jewish education, based on that very verse (Bava Batra 21a) and, thus, the notion of *Torah miZion*, Torah in and from *Eretz Israel*, also had special status in the tradition. During much of the two thousand years since the destruction of Jerusalem and the Second Temple, the small Jewish communities in *Eretz Israel* sent out emissaries to Diaspora Jewish communities, and one of the major requirements of those emissaries was that they be able to bring Torah to the diaspora communities (Abraham Ya'ari, *Sheluhe Eretz Israel.* Jerusalem: Mossad Harav Kook, 1951). It is, therefore, not surprising that, even when the Eastern European *yeshivot* (institutes for the higher learning of Talmud) were the most prominent, there were American Jewish young men who went to learn in *yeshivot* in the Holy Land, *Eretz Israel.* Jonathan Sarna relates that Behr Manischewitz, the founder of the well-known B. Manischewitz *matzah* (unleavened bread) company, had very close ties with Jerusalem and, at the onset of the twentieth century, sent two of his sons, Max and Hirsch to study there. The first, Hirsch started learning there in 1901, at the age of ten, and remained there for thirteen years, during which time he studied at the yeshivot Etz Chaim (1901–1907), Torat Chaim (1908–1910), and Meah Shearim (1910–1914). Max, who was two years older, went when he was older and he also studied for the rabbinate at Yeshivat Etz Chaim (Sarna 2005).

R. Avraham Hezroni, who lives in Jerusalem and was at the *yeshiva* in Hebron in 1929, stated, in an interview with the author on 13 January 2005, that there were approximately two dozen American students there that year. Several of them were killed in the infamous massacre, among them, William Berman and Benjamin Horowitz, who had previously studied for about a half-dozen years at the Yeshiva Rabbenu Yitzchak Elchanan (later, Yeshiva University), and Aaron David Epstein, the son of Rabbi Ephraim Epstein of Chicago and the nephew of Rabbi Moshe Mordecai Epstein, Rosh Yeshivah of the yeshiva in Hebron (Gottesman 1930).

Instances such as these continued and, after the destruction of European Jewry and its *yeshivot*, and the establishment of the State of Israel, the numbers of American Jewish young men who studied at Israeli *yeshivot* increased. Until the second half of the 1950s, however, all such activity was unorganized, on an individual basis, and was on a very small scale.

Today, it is almost a norm for both male and female Orthodox high school graduates to spend a year or more of study in Israel, primarily in a *yeshiva* or seminary. In his pioneering study of the phenomenon, Shalom Berger found that, by the middle of the 1990s, up to ninety percent of the graduates of Modern Orthodox high schools were in such a programme (Berger 1997). Although those figures may not be representative of all American Orthodox high school graduates, Jay Goldmintz (1991) indicates that "there are graduates who report that their parents are forcing them to go to Israel for the year against their will and there are high schools who use the number of their graduates who go to Israel as part of their publicity campaign[s] drive for prospective students. There can be no doubt that the post-high school yeshiva experience has become a mass movement within the Orthodox community." Berger's analysis suggests the Israeli experience probably intensified their ties with the country and its Jews.

Because of the deep and extensive ties of Orthodox Jews in the United States, it is not easy to indicate the impact of the Year in Israel programme specifically on the American Orthodox community. American Orthodox Jews are intertwined with Israel in a myriad of ways and, as a result, Israel has impact upon that community in many ways. Israel has affected the religious habits of American Orthodox Jews — many kosher food products available in the US are produced in Israel; most American Jews who purchase *etrogim* (citrons which are part of the rituals of the holiday of Succot, the festival of booths) buy Israeli *etrogim*; many Orthodox Jews buy religious books from Israel, adopt Israeli religious music as their own and, as has been indicated, travel to Israel frequently. For many, Israel is probably the only country outside the United States which they have visited.

One area in which it appears more likely that it was the Year in Israel programme, in particular, that influenced American Orthodox patterns is in a number of synagogue-related customs. For example, until the 1960s, it was rare to find an Orthodox synagogue in which the Friday evening service, *Kabalat Shabat*, was begun with the singing of *Yedid Nefesh*. That was an Israeli custom which has now been incorporated into American Orthodox culture. Likewise, until the 1960s, the custom in most Ashkenazi synagogues was that the two chapters of Psalms said after *Kabalat Shabbat*, Psalms 92 — *Mizmor shir leyom hashabat* — and Psalms 93 — *Hashem malakh* — were said together, and the Reader, *ba'al tefila*, repeated only the last verse of *Hashem malakh*. Since then, however, it is customary for the congregation to stop after *Mizmor shir* and for the Reader to repeat the last two verses of it before everyone continues with *Hashem malakh*. This, too, is the adoption into American Orthodox culture of an Israeli custom. One other to be noted here is the reciting of *Birkhat kohanim* on the Shabat of the Intermediate Days of a holiday, *Shabat chol hamo'ed*. For whatever reason, the custom in Ashkenazi synagogues until, approximately, the 1960s, was not to recite it on *Shabat chol hamo'ed*. Since then, it is increasingly the custom to recite *Birkhat kohanim* on a *Shabat chol hamo'ed*, as is the custom in Israel. In all of these cases, the changes were typically introduced by young men who returned from learning in an Israeli yeshiva where they had seen the Israeli custom both in the yeshiva and in *shuls* there. And just as these influences were subtle and, individually, almost unnoticeable, so has American Orthodox culture been influenced by Israeli culture in many other ways. Indeed, American Orthodoxy and Israel are so intertwined that one can visualize a "Orthodox global village" with Israel as its centre.[1]

Whatever the distinctions between the "Ultra-Orthodox," or *Haredim*, and "Modern Orthodox," deep connections to Israel characterize both. Whether or not the State of Israel is "the first flowering of redemption," Israel is of great religious significance for both Haredim and the Modern Orthodox, as *Eretz Israel*, the Holy Land, as well as the home of the largest or second largest Jewish community and certainly the home of the largest number of Orthodox Jews. Contrary to popular mythology, the Haredim are overwhelmingly not anti-Zionist and certainly not anti-Israel. On the contrary, as the 2001 National Jewish Population Survey (NJPS) reconfirms, Orthodox Jews in the United States, including the "Ultra-Orthodox" or "Hasidic" or "Haredi," have much stronger ties with Israel than do other American Jews. Surveys from several decades have consistently showed that the extent of Orthodox Jews' attachments to Israel — however measured — greatly exceed those among other denominations, and that differences between Orthodox and non-Orthodox are sharpest with respect to the most demanding measures of Israel involvement, be it receptivity to *aliyah* rather than pro-Israel feelings, or having closer ties with individual Israelis, or fluency in Hebrew rather than just a rudimentary knowledge of Israel's language (Waxman 1992). This, again, is true of Haredim as well as modern Orthodox. Indeed, as for the Haredim, perhaps the only newspapers that they read, at least in public, are *Hamodia* and *Yated Ne-eman*. In Monsey, New York, there are today private homes with newspaper boxes out front specifically for the delivered *Hamodia*, an English-language edition of the Israeli newspaper of Agudat Israel. *Yated Ne-eman* is similarly the English-language edition of the newspaper of the more Lithuanian-oriented Haredim of the Degel Hatorah party. Both of these newspapers, as well as most of the domestic weeklies which cater to the Orthodox community, such as the *Jewish Press*, focus on Israeli news and events, and they cater to and foster deep and perhaps penultimate ties between American Orthodoxy and Israel.

These patterns, although quite a contrast from the stereotypical image of haredim as anti-Zionist and isolationist, are not all that surprising, especially for those in Western societies. Even in Israel, research indicates a growing "Israelization" of haredim, politically, linguistically, and in many other cultural patterns (Caplan and Sivan 2003).

Until mid-2005, the emotional ties to Israel of American Orthodox Jews expressed themselves in a variety of ways. The Orthodox openly rejoiced and/or cried with Israel, and they had no questions or hesitation in expressing their deepest concerns for Israel's welfare. They were ever-ready to recite *Tehilim*, Psalms, and other prayers, as well as to undertake fasts for the variety of dangers facing Israel. Isolated deviant cases aside, their concerns were not exclusively for their fellow Orthodox Jews in Israel but for Israel in its entirety.

The summer of 2005 marked a major turning point for American Orthodoxy with respect to its relationship with Zionism and Israel, especially the government of Israel. After Israel's disengagement from the Gaza Strip/Gush Katif, in the summer of 2005, American Orthodoxy, following their counterparts in Israel, became increasingly critical of the Israeli government and of secular Zionism as whole. Facing the impending disengagement, the official positions of the major organizations of centrist and modern American Orthodoxy — the Orthodox Union and the Rabbinical Council of America — issued calls which urged restraint, civility, and sensitivity but were not in the least critical of the Israeli government.[2] It is likely that these public positions did not reflect the personal positions of their members; the members were almost assuredly much more critical of the disengagement.

After the violent dismantling of Amona in early 2006, even the organizations have become more overtly critical of the Israeli government. The Orthodox Union wrote a strong letter to Acting Prime Minister Ehud Olmert:

> to express our deep dismay regarding the violent scene that was broadcast around the world from Amona last week. We cringed as we viewed the images of members of the elite Yassam unit, tasked with carrying out the rule of law, enter a house and proceed to mercilessly beat fellow citizens who were merely sitting on the floor exercising their right to civil disobedience. We never thought we would see such a dark day in the State of Israel where Israeli citizens are trampled by the horses of their own police force.

The letter continued with more harsh criticism of the police, with only part of one sentence directed at the actions of the protesters: "While we reject the actions of the those protesters who resorted to violent tactics such as throwing stones, bricks, glass and paint at soldiers . . . " The contrast between the positions of the Orthodox Union *vis-à-vis* the disengagement from Gush Katif and that of the dismantling of Amona appears to be reflective of a broad shift in the attitudes of American Orthodoxy toward both the Israeli government and the broader, non-Orthodox, Zionist movement.

Following patterns within Israeli society, though not as overtly, there appears to be a growing rift between the Orthodox and the non-Orthodox, with the Orthodox manifesting a deepening alienation from non-religious Zionism. It is much too early to predict how this will develop. It is already clear to many in the leadership of the American Religious Zionist community that the alienation and rift will, at least, pose a formidable challenge to the Modern Orthodox educational system in its ability to inculcate an appreciation of and loyalty to Religious Zionist values as well as to Modern Orthodoxy, in general.

Notes

1 Some years ago, Prof. Menachem Friedman, of Bar-Ilan University's Sociology Department, suggested to me that the connections between the Orthodox in the United States and Israel could appropriately be analyzed within the context of such concepts as the "*haredi* global village" and "Modern Orthodox global village." The notion I suggest here is built on Friedman's suggestion but extends it beyond the confines of a particular Orthodox sub-community.

2 For a critique, as well as a rationale of the official position, see the debate between Emanuel Feldman and Yosef Blau 2005.

References

Avruch, K., *American Immigrants in Israel: Social Identities and Change* (Chicago: University of Chicago Press, 1981), p. 117.

Barkai: A Journal of Rabbinic Thought and Research, 1987, 4: 408 [in Hebrew].

Bayme, S. and Liebman, C., "Forward" in Yair and Sheleg, *The North American Impact on Israel Orthodoxy* (New York and Ramat Gan: Institute on American Jewish–Israel Relations, American Jewish Committee, and the Argov Center of Bar-Ilan University, 1999).

Berger, S. Z., "A Year of Study in an Israeli Yeshiva Program: Before and After." Ph.D. dissertation, Azrieli Graduate Institute for Jewish Education and Administration, Yeshiva University, 1997.

Berman, I., "Immigration to Israel: Ideology vs. Reality", *Forum* 50 (1983–84): 25–30.

Caplan, K. and Sivan, E. (eds), *Israeli Haredim: Integration without Assimilation?* [in Hebrew] (Tel Aviv: Van Leer Jerusalem Institute/Hakibbutz Hame-uhad Publishing House, 2003).

Central Bureau of Statistics, State of Israel, *Survey of Absorption of Immigrants: Immigrants of the Seventies — The First Three Years in Israel*, Special Series No. 771 (Jerusalem: Central Bureau of Statistics, 1986).

Chiswick, C.U., "Impact of the Six-Day War on American Jewry: An Economic Perspective." Paper presented at the conference on The Impact of the Six-Day War, The Hebrew University, Institute of Contemporary Jewry, Jerusalem, Israel, 1994.

DellaPergola, S., "Demographic Trends of Latin American Jewry." In *The Jewish Presence in Latin America*, Elkin J. L. & Merkx G. W. (eds) (Boston, MA: Allen & Unwin, 1987), pp. 85–133.

Feldman, E. and Blau, Y., *Jewish Action* 66, 2 (Winter 5766/2005): 38–42.

Goldscheider, C., "American Aliyah: Sociological and Demographic Perspective." in *The Jews in American Society*, M. Sklare (ed.), (New York: Behrman House, 1974), pp. 335–384.

Gottesman, L., *The Martyrs of Hebron* [New York: 1930] and now online at: <http://www.hebron.org.il/pics/tarpat/martyrs.htm#Aharon%20David%20Epstein>.

Heilman, U., "Shh! Don't Tell Them it's Aliya." *Jerusalem Post*, 21 July 2005, p. 5.

Lamm, N., *Torah Umadda: The Encounter of Religious Learning and Worldly Knowledge in the Jewish Tradition* (Northvale, NJ: Jason Aronson, 1990).

National Jewish Population Survey (NJPS) 1990.

National Jewish Population Survey (NJPS) 2001.

Sarna, J.D., "The Americanization of Matzah: Manischewitz and the Rabbis of the Holy Land," [pamphlet] (New York: Graduate School of Jewish Studies, Touro College, 2005), p. 12.

Waxman, C. I., *American Aliya: Portrait of an Innovative Migration Movement* (Detroit, MI: Wayne State University Press, 1989), pp. 119–38; 167–68.

Waxman, C. I., "All In the Family: American Jewish Attachments to Israel." In Medding, P.Y. (ed.), *A New Jewry? America Since the Second World War* (Studies in Contemporary Jewry, Vol. 8) (New York: Oxford University Press, 1992), p. 136.

Waxman, C. I., "Congregation, Community, and Continuity: Denominational Affiliation as an Indicator of Jewish Identity," in DellaPergola, S. & Even, J. (eds), *Studies in Jewish Demography, 1997* (Jerusalem: Institute of Contemporary Jewry, Hebrew University, 2001), pp. 281–293.

Waxman, C. I., *Jewish Baby Boomers: A Communal Perspective* (Albany: State University of New York Press, 2001), p. 35.

Waxman, C. I., "The Enduring Significance of Denomination" [in Hebrew], *Gesher: Journal of Jewish Affairs* 50, 150 (Winter 2004): 24–31.

Wenig, G., "Making Dreams of Israel Come True." *Jewish Journal of Greater Los Angeles*, 15 August 2003.

Ya'ari, A., *Sheluhe Eretz Israel* (Jerusalem: Mossad Harav Kook, 1951).

ISRAEL COMMENTATOR

Modern and Haredi Orthodox American Jews and Their Attitude to the State of Israel

Eliezer Don-Yehiya

Chaim I. Waxman has written an interesting and stimulating essay on the attitudes of Orthodox American Jews to Israel. There is still a need to differentiate between the positions of various sections in American orthodoxy on this issue. (To a large extent, this also applies to Orthodox Jews in other Western countries, especially Britain.)

The main division in American orthodoxy is between the so-called "Modern Orthodox" and the "Ultra-Orthodox," best known as "Haredim". Waxman is right in claiming that, contrary to common wisdom, American Haredim care about Israel's security and well-being and take much interest in Israel's affairs. Many Haredim visit Israel quite often and tend to send their sons to study in Israeli Yeshivot (Torah academies). Nevertheless, there is a marked difference between the source and nature of Haredim identification with Israel and the way that Modern Orthodox Jews identify with the Jewish state. While most contemporary Haredim support Israel and reject any attempt to endanger its security and international standing, they are doing this mainly for pragmatic reasons.

Israel is home to millions of Jews and to the greatest Haredi community in the world. It is also the greatest centre of Torah study. Many, if not most, Haredim have relatives or friends in Israel. It is only natural then that most of the Diaspora Haredim would care for Israel and its Jewish inhabitants. However, unlike most Modern Orthodox Jews, the Haredim do not perceive the contemporary Jewish state as the "beginning of redemption", and they do not attach to it a religious significance. As a matter of fact, the Haredim identify not with the State of Israel but rather with the Land of Israel and its Jewish residents. The Land of Israel is for them (as it is, indeed, for every orthodox Jew) the Holy and chosen Land, but the holiness of the Land is not applied to the State and certainly not to its government and other institutions. A case in point is the Lubavicher Rabbi, R. Menachem Mendel Schneeorson, who never used the term "The State of Israel", but spoke only of "The Land of Israel" or "The Holy Land". The reason for this was that for him (and for other Haredim), a secular state cannot bear the holy name of "Israel", even if most of its residents are Jews. It should also be noted that when Haredim, especially their spiritual leaders, use the term "Israel" they are often referring not to the State, but rather to the people of Israel.

This phenomenon is related to the fact that Israel does not play a significant role in the symbol system of Haredim. To this day even "moderate Haredim" reject Zionism, which they perceive as a dangerous ideology that strives to replace the traditional Judaism of Torah and religious commandments with a modern secular nationalism based on language, territory and state. Many Haredim are therefore anxious to avoid any action that could be interpreted as lending a sacred or ideological significance to that creature of Zionism, the State of Israel.

In this respect (as well as in other aspects of Haredi attitude to Israel), Israeli and Diaspora Haredim have much in common, but there are also certain marked differences between the two. On the one hand, the place does make a difference. Haredim living in Israel are much more involved in Israeli society and concerned about it than their brethren in America and other western countries. On the other hand, Haredi rejection of Israel's symbol system is more firm and widespread in Israel than in the Diaspora.

Thus, almost all Israeli Haredim do not celebrate Israel's Independence Day and do not recite the prayer for the welfare of the State of Israel. They are also not willing to wave the Israeli flag, nor to recite Israel's national anthem, Hatikva. Many American and other Diaspora Haredim share this attitude. However, a considerable percentage of American Haredim do take some part in Independence Day celebrations and recite the prayer for the State of Israel.

The difference in this regard between Israeli and American Haredim has to do with the fact that Haredi society in Western countries is more diversified and pluralistic than its counterpart in Israel. Admittedly, Israeli Haredi society is also divided into various groups, but they all have in common distinct attitudes and ways of life that set them apart from the rest of Israeli society, including Israeli religious Zionists (who are similar but not identical to American Modern Orthodox Jews). Thus, most Israeli Haredim engage in Torah study as their main preoccupation, reject modern Western culture and avoid secular studies, especially in academia. By contrast, most American Haredim are working for their living and do not segregate themselves from Western culture. Many American Haredim pursue secular studies at universities, even while they are studying in the Yeshiva.

These and other practices of Diaspora synagogues attest to the diversity and pluralism of Western Haredi communities, which is reflected in their attitudes to Israel, as well as in other aspects of their life. The various aspects of Haredi diversity in the Diaspora are interrelated. Thus, in many Diaspora synagogues Haredim and Modern Orthodox Jews pray together, which is one of the reasons that even the Haredi members of these synagogues celebrate Independence Day and recite the prayer for the State of Israel. What all this means is that the borders between the two main streams of American orthodoxy are not as clear-cut as they are in Israel, and this is also reflected in the attitudes of Orthodox American Jews towards Israel.

There are still marked differences between the ways that the various groups in American orthodoxy relate to Israel. Thus, in contrast to most Modern Orthodox Jews, even the more "liberal" or moderate American Haredim do not attach any messianic or religious significance to the State of Israel. This is manifested in the fact that even those Haredi synagogues in America who do recite the prayer for the State are anxious to omit the verse "the beginning of redemption" from this prayer. There are also Haredi Diaspora synagogues that have authored their own version of the prayer, which is significantly different from the "official" prayer authored by the Israeli Chief Rabbinate. Thus, in a Haredi synagogue in London they recite a prayer for the "inhabitants of the Land of Israel."

The above characterization of American and other Diaspora Haredim does not apply to the case of Diaspora Hasidim who are very similar to Israel's Hasidim in their ways of life and their attitude toward Israel. Waxman argues that "American orthodoxy and Israel are so intertwined that one can visualize a 'Orthodox global village' with Israel as its centre". This argument is certainly valid with regard to the Hasidim, but, as I have tried to demonstrate, it cannot be applied to other variants of Jewish orthodoxy and especially not to the non-Hasidic Haredim.

DIASPORA COMMENTATOR

Israel in Orthodox Identity

Françoise Ouzan

Chaim I. Waxman's analysis is subtle and complete. Focusing on the place of Israel in American Orthodoxy, he provides us with its various facets. His main analysis is interestingly both socio-psychological and ideological-cultural. Two concepts are used to articulate the two major approaches adopted by Orthodoxy: "compartmentalization" and "expansionism".

The former expresses a radical way of confronting modernity as well as an ability to draw a boundary between the world of the sacred and that of the secular, thus creating a shield "when necessity requires that [the Orthodox] leave that world [of the sacred] to enter the world of the secular". Waxman justifies this attitude of compartmentalization by adding that the nature of the shield lies in the consciousness that the secular world is of "no real value".

When comparing to the French context, we may say that such a compartmentalization, which has been achieved for years by Orthodox and Ultra-Orthodox Jews, is made more difficult in times of crisis, such as the one Jews are undergoing in France today. Indeed, showing one's Jewish identity in some public places may create extra tensions. Because of anti-Semitic attacks, a separation between the secular and the religious world is enforced upon Jews. Ultra-Orthodox Jews in France wear a beard and a hat, signs of Jewishness that are more negatively perceived today than they used to be. Some Ultra-Orthodox French Jews, whose religious life is much more difficult in France than in America, are led to think of *aliyah*.

In contrast to Orthodox and Ultra-Orthodox Jews, Modern Orthodox Jews do not make such a sharp separation between the secular and the religious world. Yet, they also suffer from the fact that visible signs of their Jewish identity may endanger their lives in certain areas. Indeed, Chief Rabbi Joseph Sitruck recently made a public announcement to advise French Jews not to wear a *kippa* in public. Although denominations are not the same in France as in America, the most observant amongst the Modern Orthodox are led to consider making *aliyah* in order to be able to do the *mitzvot* freely. If they cannot emigrate to Israel, the double identity they have in France may lead to a form of schizophrenia. Indeed, a number of Ultra-Orthodox and Modern Orthodox French Jews are convinced that they will not succeed in finding a job in Israel because of age discrimination.

For Chaim Waxman it is rather "expansionism" and not "compartmentalization" that leads to *aliyah*. The former concept is thus defined: as opposed to compartmentalization, *there is no clear boundary between the world of the sacred and the world of the secular*. Therefore, the "expansionist" aims at making the "secular sacred" in his search to lead a more complete Jewish life. That approach, which consists in integrating sacred learning with secular knowledge, is that of Modern Orthodoxy in America and that of most French *olim* who are either Orthodox or "traditional" in their observance ("*Traditionalistes*"). In fact, among the Jews from France who live in Israel, Rav Kook's ideas (mentioned by Waxman in relation to Modern Orthodox American Jewry) are central. They are voiced through the writings of the French Orthodox Rabbi Léon Ashkénazi.

Of course, Jewishness does not prevail over the numerous other identities for all Jews. When it does, it is likely to prompt *aliyah*. In France, the attachment of Orthodox or "Traditionalist" Jews to the State of Israel being strong, Jewishness can come into conflict with the diasporic society when the image of the State of Israel is debased in the public sphere.

However, as Chaim Waxman underlines it, ideology is the prime incentive for the *aliyah* of the Orthodox in the United States, even if structural factors have an impact on the rate of *aliyah*. This is also true of France. Zionism is meant to be the main reason for emigration to the Jewish state, according to Arieh Azoulay, chairman of the Agency's *aliyah* and absorption committee, mentioning intermarriage rates of over 50 percent and anti-Semitism that only "enhances" Zionism (*The Jerusalem Post*, 24 July 2005). There is also a highly significant relationship between religious outlook and attachment to Israel. Among French Orthodox Jews, too, the greater lifestyle cost of Jewishness in France compared to that in Israel is not the prime motive of *aliyah*, although it may be taken into account and act as a "trigger".

As in the United States, the average number of visits to Israel by the Orthodox is higher than for secular Jews. Data from the survey conducted in 2002 on the Jews of France (*Les Juifs de France, valeurs et identité*) by Erik H. Cohen and Maurice Ifergan for the *Fonds Social Juif Unifie* (*FSJU*) indicate that the traditionalist religious-based attachment to Israel extends to considerations about *aliyah*. French Orthodox Jewry is estimated at about 5 percent of all Jews, which appears to be a small figure. These are Jews who obey the strict rules of Orthodoxy. However, among those who consider themselves "Traditionalistes", there are Jews who also observe Shabbat, keep kosher and resemble some of those falling under the American heading of "Modern Orthodox". Statistics reveal that the majority of Jews (51 percent) consider themselves "traditionalists", as this label does not refer to a religious denomination or affiliation, but to levels of observance that are in conformity with Jewish tradition without obeying the strict rules of orthodoxy. Others call themselves "Libéraux" ("liberals") (15 percent) and the remainder consider themselves non-observant (29 percent). In 2002, 6 percent of all French Jews planned to make *aliyah* (3 percent in 1988), and 58 percent were against the idea. However, 81 percent would consider themselves satisfied if their children settled in Israel.

According to the organizations facilitating *aliyah* (The Jewish Agency, and The AMI Fund, a new private venture), most of the immigrants who arrived in Israel in 2005 were either Orthodox or "Traditional" in their observance. Furthermore, there is a link between the *aliyah* of the "Traditionalistes" and their involvement in Jewish structures of education or affiliation to youth movements such as "Eclaireurs

Israélites" or Bnei Akiva in which the centrality of Israel is noteworthy.

In summation, although the main patterns are essentially the same among Orthodox Jews in Western Diaspora communities, it is impossible to compare denominations that overlap or do not refer to the same social context. In that respect, place does matter when considering Israel within religious identity. The United States is one of the two biggest centres of Judaism and a country where religiosity is high, whereas France is a secular state with a Christian tradition and a centralistic political culture. As a consequence, being an Orthodox Jew in France is more complex. By identifying strongly with Israel after the Six Day War, Orthodox Jews expressed their wish to identify as part of a pluralistic Jewish community in France. They did not merely voice the centrality of Israel in their identity or their desire to make *aliyah.*

Among the key variables influencing attachment to the Hebrew state, religious outlook and group identity are indeed the chief explanatory variables for individuals' levels of attachment to Israel and *aliyah.* It is important to note that these characteristics are acquired and thus are open to influence (*The Attachment of British Jews to Israel*, Jewish Policy Research Report, 1997).

References

Hilary Leila Krieger, "French Aliya Headed Toward Record Numbers", *The Jerusalem Post*, 24 July 2005.

Cohen, E. H. and Ifergan, M., *Les Juifs de France, valeurs et identité* (Unpublished survey, Fonds Social Juif Unifie [FSJU], 2002).

Barry Kosmin, Antony Lerman and Jacqueline Goldberg, *The Attachment of British Jews to Israel*, JPR report (London: Institute for Jewish Policy Research, 1997).

4

Conservative Judaism, Zionism and Israel: Commitments and Ambivalences

Daniel Gordis

In contemporary Jewish life, there is not a single mainstream movement that expresses anything other than wholehearted support for a Jewish, democratic State of Israel. While all the movements, from left to right, do sometimes differ with Israel about specific policies, all are careful to word their critique as a disagreement about policy, rather than an indication of a lack of support for Israel herself. Today, these profound commitments to Israel and her security seem commonplace; virtually unworthy of mention.

But such widespread support for the notion of a Jewish state was not always so automatic. Indeed, both Orthodoxy and Reform had stages of being opposed to the creation of a Jewish state, each for their own reasons. Orthodoxy, now perhaps the most ardently Zionist movement,[1] has long had elements with profound misgivings (see chapter by Chaim I. Waxman). As Professor Michael Rosenak notes, when speaking about the radical religious right-wing Neturei Karta and Satmar Hassidic sects:

> Zionism is the most pernicious movement in Jewish history, for it has flouted the oath imposed upon Israel not to . . . attempt to conquer *Eretz Yisrael*, and not to rebel against gentile domination. In rebelling against the nations, Zionists have, in fact, rebelled against God and are thereby delaying the true redemption.[2]

Even more mainstream Orthodox movements have struggled with some of the complexities raised by Zionism, such as the work it requires in the public sector on Shabbat, or the uneasy alliance with radical secularists that it forces upon a much more traditional community.

Similarly, significant segments of the early Reform Movement, due largely to the movement's principled universalism, also initially opposed the idea of a Jewish state. Professor Rosenak notes this dimension of Reform history as well, and asserts that classical Reform adopted a "theology of negation". "Indeed," he writes as he describes the Reform position, in the worldview of much of classical Reform ideology, "the dispersion of Israel was providential, making possible a realization of the biblical prophecy that Israel be 'a light unto the nations.' Zionism is thus a regressive conception, and the State of Israel seeks to narrow Jewish identity by creating a secular version of what was but an early stage in Israelite religion."[3]

Conservative Judaism, however, never manifested such objections to the formation of a Jewish state.[4] The Movement was never so universalistic as to deny the legitimacy of Jewish particularism and the specific needs of the Jewish people in the wake of the demise of European Jewry, and at the same time, was never so divorced from secular Jews or so committed to a theological stance which demanded that the building of Jewish state be relegated to a messianic era, that it could not support the efforts of the Zionist movement from the outset.

Thus, Naomi Cohen notes that "it has long been commonplace in scholarly accounts to note the special bond between Conservative Judaism and Zionism",[5] and cites Samuel Halperin's claim that "the American Zionist movement derived its most unanimously enthusiastic and dedicated supporters from the ranks of Conservative Judaism".[6] Much more recently, Ismar Schorsch, Chancellor of the Jewish Theological Seminary of America, the academic centre of Conservative Judaism — at least in the United States and possibly worldwide — listed a commitment to modern Israel as chief among the seven prime commitments of contemporary Conservative Judaism (the "sacred cluster"), writing:[7]

> The centrality of modern Israel heads our list of core values. For Conservative Jews, as for their ancestors, Israel is not only the birthplace of the Jewish people, but also its final destiny. Sacred texts, historical experience and liturgical memory have conspired to make it for them, in the words of Ezekiel, "the most desirable of all lands (20:6)." Its welfare is never out of mind. Conservative Jews are the backbone of Federation leadership in North America and the major source of its annual campaign. They visit Israel, send their children over a summer or for a year and support financially every one of its worthy institutions. Israeli accomplishments on the battlefield and in the laboratory, in literature and politics, fill them with pride. Their life is a dialectic between homeland and exile. No matter how prosperous or assimilated, they betray an existential angst about anti-Semitism that denies them a complete sense of at-homeness anywhere in the Diaspora.

Conservative Liturgy and the State of Israel

This commitment to Israel and to Zionism may be seen in numerous ways in the Conservative Movement, its liturgy chief among them. And as it is to the movement's liturgical publications that the laypeople are most commonly exposed, our examination of the way in which Israel is manifest in the identity of Conservative Judaism begins there. The Movement's first major liturgical publication was the *Festival Prayer Book*, published by the United Synagogue of America in 1927, some twenty years before the State would be created, and even before the Holocaust. As Israel did not yet exist, the furtive prayers for Zion as they had long existed in the liturgy seemed sufficient, it would seem. Even though the prayer book was published a decade after the 1917 Balfour Declaration, the issue of Jewish statehood as a pressing political or spiritual concern does not appear in this edition.

However, by the time the Movement's next major liturgical publication appeared, matters had changed. The *Sabbath and Festival Prayer Book*,[8] published in 1946, appeared shortly after the horrors of the Holocaust had subsided, and just two years before the declaration of Israel's independence. In 1946, the Jewish battles with the British in Palestine were well under way, and the specter of Jewish sovereignty was on the minds of many. One might have expected, therefore, a liturgy openly engaged with these issues.

Interestingly, although the *Sabbath and Festival Prayer Book* contains a long and articulate foreword describing the commitments and principles which underlay the creation of this new prayer book, this foreword does not mention the Holocaust at all, and its discussion of the emerging Jewish state is also rather minimal. The foreword does state that "a prayer book is not a museum piece. It must express our own aspiration, and not merely those of our ancestors".[9] And yet, the only mention of Zionism in the foreword is found in a discussion of the *Musaf* service, where, it is noted, "Also implied in the prayer is the recognition that sacrifice is essential for the fulfillment of all human ideals. Then, too, we cherish the hope that Palestine will again become significant not only for Israel but for the spiritual life of mankind as a whole."[10] Beyond this, however, Zionism is not mentioned. *Ha-Tikvah*, the anthem first of Zionism and then of the Jewish state, is included in a group of hymns at the conclusion of the prayer book, but without a note as to what it signifies, or that it is the Anthem of the Jewish state.[11] Even as late as the 1973 printing of the prayer book, this had not changed.

Interestingly, though, in a liturgy that appeared a decade earlier, we do find engagement with the State of Israel as a religious issue. The Rabbinical Assembly's *Weekday Prayer Book*, which appeared in 1961,[12] embraced the State wholeheartedly. In this publication, the Movement added a prayer for Israel Independence Day in the *Al Ha-Nissim* section, a section which heretofore had been reserved for the miracles of Hanukkah and Purim. The English translation, a relatively literal rendering of the Hebrew, reads:

> We thank You for the miraculous deliverance, for the heroism, and for the triumphs in battle of our ancestors in other days and in our time.
>
> In the days when Your children were returning to their borders . . . the gates to the land of our ancestors were closed before those who were fleeing the sword. When enemies from within the land . . . sought to annihilate Your people, You, in Your great mercy, stood by them in time of trouble. . . . You gave them the courage to meet their foes, to open the gates to those seeking refuge, and to free the land of its armed invaders. You delivered the many into the hands of the few, the guilty into the hands of the innocent. You have wrought great victories and miraculous deliverance for Your people to this day, revealing Your glory and Your holiness to all the world.

While today, revisionist history might lead some to quibble with the ease with which the authors speak of "free[ing] the land of its armed invader[s]", the inclusion of Israel Independence Day in a cluster alongside Hanukkah and Purim makes an undeniable statement that the creation of the State of Israel is accorded much significance. The inclusion of Torah and Haftarah (prophetic) readings for Yom Ha-Atzma'ut in the same prayer book only strengthens this perspective. It is worthy of note, however, that the use of the *Al Ha-Nissim* structure makes the case for Israel as a dramatic *historical* event for the Jewish people. This is not necessarily a theological claim. Theological grapplings with the State of Israel, such as those found in the works of Orthodox thinkers (for instance, Rabbi Joseph B. Soloveitchik[13]) are not found as readily among those of Conservative thinkers.

Why the 1961 weekday prayer book would make this change, but the *Sabbath and Festival Prayer Book* is more reticent in addressing issues of Israel and Zionism (even in the printing of 1973, particularly in light of the fact that this printing appeared in the aftermath of the euphoria of 1967) is difficult to explain.[14]

The significance of Israel to the Conservative Movement's worldview is further attested to in the *Siddur Sim Shalom*, the Movement's all-inclusive prayer book, published first in 1985. There, a version of the Prayer for the State of Israel as adopted by the Chief Rabbinate of Israel is included, and reads:[15]

> Our Father in Heaven, Rock and Redeemer of Israel, bless the State of Israel, the first manifestation of the approach of our redemption. Shield it with Your loving kindness, envelop it in Your peace, and bestow Your light and truth upon its leaders, ministers, and advisors, and grace them with Your good counsel. Strengthen the hands of those who defend our holy land, grant them deliverance, and adorn them in a mantle of victory. Ordain peace in the land and grant its inhabitants eternal happiness.

At first blush, a serious engagement with Israel seems to be emerging with this edition.

Conservative Jews and Zionist Discourse: Complicating the Picture

As we have seen, Conservative liturgy has consistently recognized the importance of the State of Israel, and has made significant changes to reflect that altered condition of the Jews in light of Israel's creation, while, at the same time, avoiding a declaration of the centrality of Israel in the lives of contemporary Jews. But beyond liturgical formulations, what about the members of the Movement themselves? How much has the view reflected in these texts seeped into their own consciences and identities?

The truth is that the picture is complex. Conservative Jews rank high on surveys in terms of support for Israel, and thus, one might expect American[16] Conservative Judaism to produce significant *aliyah* (immigration to Israel). However, though no precise numbers are available, it is clear that the vast majority of American *olim* are products of American Orthodoxy, which comprises barely 10 percent of the affiliated Jewish community, while Conservative Jews, who comprise approximately 26 percent of the affiliated community, produce few immigrants to Israel.[17] Why is that?

As we will now see in a variety of additional texts, there is another side to the Conservative Movement's engagement with Israel; a side somewhat more ambivalent, or put otherwise, a side less inclined to negate the "at-home-ness" which American Jews often feel in America. This phenomenon is evident even in the Prayer for the State of Israel, which we cited above. For just as interesting as the fact that the prayer is included in the *Siddur Sim Shalom*, is the issue of exactly which sections of the prayer were omitted by the Conservative Movement.

The first section of the prayer, which *is* included, is identical to the standard formulation. What is significant is what *Sim Shalom* chose *not* to include. That is the section that reads:

> And remember all our brethren of the House of Israel, in all the lands of their dispersion, and lead them quickly to Zion Your city and to Jerusalem, the abode of Your glory, as it is written in the Torah of Your servant Moses: "Even if your outcasts are at the ends of the world, from there the Lord your God will gather you, from there He will fetch you. And the Lord your God will bring you to the land that your fathers possessed, and you shall possess it; and He will make you more prosperous and more numerous than your fathers.
>
> Unite our hearts together to revere and venerate Your name and to observe all the precepts of Your Torah, and send us quickly the Messiah son of David, Your righteous anointed, to redeem those who await Your deliverance.

The deletion of the latter paragraph may reflect a general Conservative discomfort with messianic imagery in the *siddur*. But much more interesting for our purposes is the omission of the major paragraph about the Diaspora. That paragraph, which prays for the ingathering of Jews from across the world to the Land of Israel, is palatable only for those willing to live with an internal dialectic born of commitment to Israel and a sense of comfort in one's Diaspora homeland. But *Sim Shalom* seems uncomfortable with that notion of dialectic. And therefore, it simply omits this section, without even noting in the Notes section that any changes have been made to the original prayer.[18]

The literary structure of the original prayer is quite simple. It contains an opening, followed by a prayer for elements of the Jewish people who need God's help: (1) the State (2) her leaders (3) her defenders, and (4) the Diaspora. The prayer then concludes with a messianic flourish.

Siddur Sim Shalom deletes the conclusion (perhaps because of other theological considerations), and omits, as well, the Diaspora from that cluster of Jews who need God's intervention. Nothing is wrong with the Diaspora (at least in terms of its relationship to the Land of Israel), the prayer book intimates. And that, in turn, seems to mute some of the Zionist fervor of the prayer book.

This "muted" Zionist fervor, we should note, may be more prominent among Conservative Jews than, say, Orthodox Jews, precisely because Conservative Judaism is so inherently American. And American Jews, as is commonly known, seem to exhibit a more tenuous connection to Israel than do others. Thus, while a 1997 study showed that 78 percent of British Jews had visited Israel, the corresponding figure for American Jews was only 37 percent: less than half.[19] To be sure, distance and cost are a factor, but the "at-homeness" in America that Chancellor Schorsch denies does seem to exist, and would seem to account for at least part of this phenomenon.

But American–Jewish "at-homeness" in the United States explains only part of the picture. For even in British circles, the levels of commitment to Israel and the rate of visits to Israel are higher among Orthodox than they are among non-Orthodox Jews, and the further to the "left" one moves, the lower the rates and the level of commitment become.[20] The Conservative communities in places such as France and Australia, where Zionist activity is much more central to Jewish life in general than it is in the U.S., also exhibit great attachment to Israel. Those Conservative communities, however, are extremely small relative to those in the US and even in England.[21] (There is virtually no Conservative Jewish life in the former Soviet Union.)

The above-mentioned tendency to avoid the internal cognitive dissonance which might result from people committed to living in America expressing their profound enthusiasm for the State of Israel (to which they do not intend to move) is apparent in a wide array of other central texts from the Movement, beyond the prayer book at which we have already glanced. For our purposes, we will look briefly at two such examples. The first is a statement of the Movement's principles, while the second is a textbook written for Conservative teenagers. In both cases, I believe, we find commitment to Israel, along with the ambivalence which the emendation of the Prayer for the State of Israel seems to reflect.

Conservative Jews and Zionist Discourse: A Statement of Principles

Emet Ve-Emunah, the Statement of Principles of Conservative Judaism,[22] is a classic example of the Movement proclaiming commitment to Zion, while immediately thereafter mitigating that commitment with the (perhaps quite understandable) declaration that life in the Diaspora is equally legitimate. The Statement claims that:

> We rejoice in the existence of *Medinat Yisrael* (the State of Israel) in *Eretz Yisrael* (the Land of Israel) with its capital of Jerusalem, the Holy City, the City of Peace. We view this phenomenon not just in political or military terms; rather, we consider it to be a miracle, reflecting Divine Providence in human affairs. We glory in that miracle; we celebrate the rebirth of Zion. . . . Throughout the ages, we have revered, honored, cherished, prayed for, dreamed of, and sought to settle in Jerusalem and the Land of Israel.

Thus far, we have the view reflected in the liturgical sections we examined above. Almost immediately, however, the *Emet Ve-Emunah* proclaims its fealty to America, and continues:

> This zealous attachment to *Eretz Yisrael* has persisted throughout our long history as a transnational people in which we transcended borders and lived in virtually every land. Wherever we were permitted, we viewed ourselves as natives or citizens of the country of our residence and were loyal to our host nation. Our religion has been land-centered but never land-bound; it has been a portable religion so that despite our long exile (*Galut*) from our spiritual homeland, we have been able to survive creatively and spiritually even in the *tefutzot* (Diaspora).
>
> Indeed, there have been Jewish communities in the Diaspora from the days of the Prophets. The relative importance of the Land of Israel and the Diaspora fluctuated through the centuries. Whether the Diaspora was more creative than Zion or Zion was more vital than the Diaspora is of little importance. What is important is [that] Eretz Yisrael enriched world Jewry even as world Jewry enriched *Eretz Yisrael*.[23]

One can easily understand the predicament facing Conservative leaders. As the most classically American of the Movements, Conservative Judaism feels a sense of at-home-ness in the United States that makes a wholehearted Zionism difficult. For somewhere on the spectrum of Zionist ideological commitment lies a grappling with the possibility of leaving one's home for Israel. That is, quite simply, part and parcel of most Zionist ideologies. *Emet Ve-Emunah* struggles to straddle the divide, and does so elegantly. But it does so at the expense of ideological clarity, and of passion. This phenomenon appears more than once in *Emet Ve-Emunah*. Shortly after the previous citation, the following appears:[24]

> We staunchly support the Zionist ideal and take pride in the achievement of the State of Israel in the gathering of our people from the lands of our dispersion and in rebuilding a nation. The State of Israel and its well-being remain a major concern of the Conservative Movement, as of all loyal Jews. To be sure, the Conservative Movement has not always agreed with Israel's positions on domestic and foreign affairs. We have often suffered from discriminatory policies, but we remain firm and loving supporters of the State of Israel economically, politically and morally.[25]

The claim about "discriminatory policies" is not without basis. Conservative institutions have, quite clearly, not received the support that Orthodox institutions in Israel receive. However, that this becomes a major issue in a "Statement of Principles" is noteworthy. So is the fact that in a fifty-seven page booklet, Israel and Zionism occupy approximately three or four pages.

A similar phenomenon is evinced in Conservative Judaism's chief educational document, a book produced for teenagers and designed to express to them the fundamental commitments of Conservative Jewish life. In *Conservative Judaism: Our Ancestors to Our Descendants*,[26] four pages are devoted to Zionism.[27] One page is devoted to a history of those Jewish ideologies that opposed the creation of the State, and one explains the difference between political Zionism and religious Zionism.

Soon, however, it becomes clear why the author, Dorff, dedicates a substantial amount of space to this distinction. He writes in the next paragraph:

> If your motivation and hopes for Israel are solely political, then the only way to be a true Zionist is to live in Israel . . . On the other hand, if you see Israel as the religious and cultural *center* of world Jewry, then you are not denying the legitimacy of the Jewish communities of the Diaspora. On the contrary, you might even say that the existence of Jewish communities outside of Israel is necessary for the . . . well-being of Israel. . . . [T]he Jewish communities of *both* Israel and the Diaspora are legitimate and important for the future of Jews and Judaism.[28]

Again, the argument itself may be legitimate. Ahad Ha-Am might have said something very similar. However, Dorff's book for adolescents is not meant to be scholarship. It is pedagogy, and intended to assist in identity formation. And here, too, it is clear that Dorff, like his colleagues, is ambivalent about the commitments he would like his charges to develop.

Towards the end of this section, Dorff writes, "The Conservative Movement has had some problems in Israel, however, and you should be aware of them."[29] What follows is a discussion of the hegemony of the Orthodox rabbinate, the fact that Conservative rabbis are unable to perform life cycle events in Israel and the inequality in the funding of religious institutions, all of which culminates with Dorff's assertion that "This is clearly an intolerable situation, and Conservative leaders in Israel and North America may have to take strong steps to rectify it."[30]

The readers of Dorff's book will learn much more about inequities in the distribution of religious power in Israel than they will about the revival of the Hebrew language, or the cultural, literary, theatrical and even religious creativity of a people at home in its own land. It is not that Dorff denies these. But he, like *Emet Ve-Emunah*, ultimately expresses a profoundly ambivalent approach to Israel. Conservative Jews are Zionists, he tells his charges, but not so Zionist that they ought to feel uncomfortable living in the Diaspora. That is both because the Diaspora is legitimate, and because Israel is far from perfect. Indeed, it is important to note that both *Emet Ve-Emunah* and Dorff's book are not idiosyncratic. Rather, they reflect a commitment to Israel but an unwillingness to engage in serious dialogue about the implications that the existence of the State of Israel has for Conservative Jewish life; an unwillingness that is found throughout the ranks of the Movement's leadership. *Conservative Judaism Magazine*, the official publication of the Rabbinical Assembly (the professional organization of Conservative Rabbis worldwide), illustrates quite clearly a somewhat dispassionate approach to Zionism and Israel among the Movement's leaders. Although the journal published a special issue on the occasion of the 25th Yahrtzeit of Rabbi Abraham Joshua Heschel,[31] a special issue on health care,[32] and even an entire issue devoted to theology,[33] there has been no special issue on Israel. Astonishingly, the theology issue did not include a single article on the theological significance of Israel or Zionism.

There was no issue of *Conservative Judaism* dedicated to the 50th anniversary of the creation of the State of Israel. Nor was there an issue, or even a series of articles, dedicated to the signing of the Oslo Accords. Indeed, the most noteworthy article of the last few years on Conservative Judaism and Zionism is an argument for the diminution of the centrality of Israel in Conservative Jewish ideology.[34]

Those who might wish for greater Zionist passion in Conservative Judaism must acknowledge, however, that this ambivalence is not new. In the heady days of the spring of 1948, just as the Jewish state was achieving independence, students at the Seminary (the academic centre of Conservative Judaism) wished to ensure that *Ha-Tikvah* would be played at their graduation ceremony. But then-Chancellor Finkelstein refused. A student from that year later related that:[35]

> Finkelstein was ideologically close to Judah Magnus, the chancellor of Hebrew University and a pacifist. We gathered from what he told us that there were plans afoot to form a government in Palestine with Finkelstein's participation, as an alternative to Zionist leadership. Apparently, he was in touch, if not in collusion, with the Martin Buber led Brit Shalom group which opposed the establishment of a Jewish state. . . .[36] As to Hatikvah, the cause célèbre, it was both part and not part of the graduation exercises. The orchestra indeed played the anthem of the new State of Israel, but only as a musical rendition, without singling it out for special attention, with the audience remaining seated.

The Ambivalence Persists.

Yet, it persists as a genuine ambivalence. Many Conservative Jewish institutions do engage with Israel seriously. Participants in Camp Ramah each summer are exposed to Hebrew, to Israeli staff members and to a variety of programmes about Israel. Israel Independence Day is certainly celebrated in the vast majority of Conservative Schools. And the Conservative Movement's Israel programmes, such as summer programmes and the year-long *Nativ* programme, are deeply Zionist in their orientation.

Where the passion begins to subside is among adults. While Solomon Schechter schools celebrate Yom Ha-Atzma'ut with passion, the synagogues which these children's parents often attend pay less attention to this day, or to other Israel events on the calendar. By adulthood, it seems, even many committed Conservative Jews have internalized the ambivalences to which Elliot Dorff points, leading to the complexities to which we have sought to point.

Summary

Ismar Schorsch, Chancellor of the Jewish Theological Seminary, the academic centre of Conservative Judaism, set out a decade ago to articulate the fundamental commitments of Conservative Jews. In an article entitled "The Sacred Cluster," he argued, among other postulates, that for Conservative Jews, "life is a dialectic between homeland and exile. No matter how prosperous or assimilated, they betray an existential angst about anti-Semitism that denies them a complete sense of at-homeness anywhere in the Diaspora.[37]

That dialectic, though, has been difficult to sustain. Conservative Judaism is the only major American Jewish movement without an anti-Zionist past, and its liturgy has consistently engaged with the new reality of Israel. At the same time, Conservative Judaism is also, at its core, deeply American, and as such, a sense of comfort with and in America is one of its key commitments. That is why even though Chancellor Schorsch asserts (as we noted at the outset of this chapter) that American Conservative Jews cannot feel completely at home in America, the reality is not that stark. American Jews, and Conservative American Jews, *do* feel at home in America. Their support for Israel, therefore, is of necessity different from that of Jews in Europe and elsewhere, where continued Jewish thriving in the Diaspora is still seen with a tenuousness that American Jews have long since abandoned.

American Conservative Judaism *is* committed to the survival and flourishing of the State of Israel. But it is also committed to a vibrant American Jewish community. And Jacob Neusner is correct when he asserts that:

> Zionism maintains that Jews who do not live in the Jewish state are in exile. There is no escaping that simple allegation, which must call into question that facile affirmation of Zionism central to American Judaism. . . . American Jews . . . do not think that they are in exile. Their Judaism makes no concession on that point.[38]

That is the bind in which Conservative Judaism finds itself. It is the tension reflected in its texts, and the ambivalence reflected in the behaviour of its adherents. It is, as well, the challenge that awaits the attention of a new generation of Conservative leaders. And there are indications that change might well be possible. A recent study of American Conservative college students revealed that an increasing number had now visited Israel, and this during a period of perceived dangers in Israel:[39]

Percentage of Respondents Who Had Ever Visited Israel, 1995–2003

1995	*1999*	*2003*
24%	55%	60%

The implications of this increased travel to Israel, made possible largely by the Birthright Program, are significant. As the authors of the study state:[40]

> One of the most striking findings of . . . our study is the students' increased attachment to Israel. Emotional ties to that country have strengthened since 1995. While only 56% said that Israel was "very important" to them when they were age 13, presently 66% feel that Israel

is "very important." We attribute the strengthened attachment to Israel of this cohort over the years to the increase in travel to the Jewish state. While only 24% had visited Israel by the start of high school, that proportion jumped to 60% during the college years. . . . Studies of participants in the Birthright Israel program, a diverse population of young Jews 18–26 years old across the spectrum of Jewish denominations, also emphasize the receptivity of young North Americans to the message of Zionism and their enthusiasm for Israel.

A renewed and intensified Zionism in Conservative circles remains possible. It will require, in all likelihood, increased travel to Israel for young adults and more mature adults, and an all out educational effort as well. But ultimately, for such a programme to emerge with seriousness, the Movement leaders and lay membership will first have to acknowledge their deep ambivalences about Israel; ambivalences which stem from their ties to Diaspora life in general, which, in turn, lie at the very root of contemporary Conservative Jewish identity.

Notes

1 How one measures the "Zionism" of a movement is, quite obviously, not simple. However, every estimate of the percentage of American Jews who make *aliyah* places the number somewhere in the high 90s. The numbers of participants in Orthodox programmes during the Second Intifada were also much less impacted by the security situation than numbers in other non-Orthodox programmes.

2 Michael Roseank, "State of Israel," in Arthur A. Cohen and Paul Mendes-Flohr (eds), *Contemporary Jewish Religious Thought: Original Essays on Critical Concepts, Movements and Beliefs* (New York: The Free Press, 1987), p. 912.

3 Rosenak, "State of Israel," p. 912.

4 The situation at JTS, the academic fountainhead of the Movement, was actually somewhat more complex than this. For a fuller discussion, cf. Naomi W. Cohen, "Diaspora Plus Palestine, Religion Plus Nationalism: The Seminary and Zionism, 1902–1948" [hereinafter "Diaspora Plus Palestine"], in *Tradition Renewed: A History of the Jewish Theological Seminary of America* (New York: JTSA, 1997), Volume II.

5 Cohen, "Diaspora Plus Palestine", p. 115.

6 Samuel Halperin, *The Political World of American Zionism* (Detroit: Wayne State University Press, 1961), p. 101. Cited in Cohen, *ibid.*

7 Chancellor Schorsch's article originally appeared in *Conservative Judaism Magazine*, as an (unacknowledged) response to my critique of contemporary Conservative Judaism, "Positive Historical Judaism Exhausted: Reflections on a Movement's Future," in *Conservative Judaism*, Vol. XLVII, No. 1 (Fall 1994), pp. 3–18. It was later published separately as Ismar Schorsch, *The Sacred Cluster: The Core Values of Conservative Judaism* (New York: Jewish Theological Seminary, 1995), p. 4. The text quoted here is taken from the JTSA web site, at <http://www.jtsa.edu/about/cj/sacredcluster.shtml#1>.

8 Morris Silverman (ed.), *Sabbath and Festival Prayer Book: A New Translation, Supplementary Readings and Notes* (New York: The Rabbinical Assembly of America, and the United Synagogue of America, 1946).

9 *Sabbath and Festival Prayer Book*, p. vi.

10 Ibid., p. ix.

11 Ibid., p. 370.

12 Gerson Hadas and Jules Harlow (eds), *The Weekday Prayer Book* (New York: The Rabbinical Assembly, 1961, fourth printing 1966).

13 Cf., e.g., *Fate and Destiny: From Holocaust to the State of Israel* (New York: Ktav Publishing House, 2000).

14 Of course, it is clear that the prayer book was simply reprinted, and not revised. But that is not the point. The question is, in light of all that had changed in Israel, *why* was there no revision when the prayer book was reprinted?

15 Jules Harlow (ed.), *Siddur Sim Shalom: A Prayerbook for Shabbat, Festivals, and Weekdays* (New York: The Rabbinical Assembly, The United Synagogue of America, 1985), p. 417.

16 This essay is exclusively about American Conservative Judaism. The references here to Conservative Judaism make no claim to being an adequate representation of the views of European arms of the Movement. The situation in Masorti Judaism, the branch of the movement in Israel, is obviously completely different.

17 Estimates I have been given by staff members of the Jewish Agency claim that the combined percentages of Orthodox and Haredi *olim* bring the total to almost 98 percent of American *aliyah*. The number of Conservative *olim* is clearly very small, and of those Conservative Jews who do come, many are rabbis or Jewish professionals. The number of Conservative laypeople, they assert, who make *aliyah* is miniscule. This intuitive sense was corroborated in a conversation with Karni Goldschmidt, who served for three years as the New York based JAFI *shelichah* to the Conservative Movement.

18 *Siddur Sim Shalom*, p. 875.

19 Barry Kosmin, Antony Lerman and Jacqueline Goldberg "The Attachment of British Jews to Israel", JPR Report No. 5 (London: Institute for Jewish Policy Research, 1997), p. 11.

20 Ibid., pp. 16–17. The Kosmin et al. study does not specifically refer to Conservative Jews in this data, but to "Orthodox, Traditional, Progressive, Just Jewish and Secular." But the fundamental point emerges with clarity from their data.

21 Of the approximately 1500 Conservative rabbis listed in the 2003 "Rabbinical Assembly Membership Directory," for example, only two reside in Australia. Three live in France, and not a single one is to be found in the FSU.

22 *Emet Ve-Emunah, Emet Ve-emunah* — Statement of Principles of Conservative Judaism (New York: Jewish Theological Seminary, Rabbinical Assembly, United Synagogue of America, 1988) [hereinafter *Emet Ve-Emunah*], pp. 37–38.

23 Then why raise the question here? Or is the goal to deny the centrality of the Land of Israel?

24 Ibid., p. 38.

25 Note that physical presence in Israel is not mentioned as one of the ways in which the Movement is supportive of Israel.

26 Elliot N. Dorff, *Conservative Judaism: Our Ancestors to Our Descendants* (New York: United Synagogue of America, 1981).

27 The title of the section is the section called "Beliefs Held in Common Within the Conservative Movement: Zionism."

28 Ibid., pp. 201–202. Italics original.

29 Ibid., p. 202.

30 Ibid., p. 203.

31 Volume L, No. 2–3, Winter/Spring 1998.

32 Volume LI, No. 2, Summer 1999.

33 Volume LI, No 2, Winter 1999.

34 Aryeh Cohen, "Permeable Boundaries: Zionism, The Diaspora and the Conservative Movement", in *Conservative Judaism*, Vol. LIV, No. 1 (Fall 2001).

35 Rabbi Gershon Winer, z"l, who later moved to Israel and who died in 2003, sent this account in an email to Ravnet, an on-line discussion group of Conservative rabbis, on Tuesday, October 08, 2002. He introduced his remarks as follows: "In response to Rabbi Richard Rubenstein's request on Ravnet for more information on Dr. Finkelstein attitude to Zionism in 1948, I have excerpted the following from a book I am now completing. The specific episode was recorded not long after it occurred." [As Rabbi Winer disseminated this in email form, it was understandably in somewhat informal style. I have corrected a

few spellings and changed punctuations slightly. The rest remains unchanged from his original posting. I am grateful to a number of colleagues for their assistance in locating this posting, particularly Rabbi Leon Rosenblum, who was able to provide me the entire text.]

36 Cf. *The Jewish State: The Struggle for Israel's Soul* (New York: Basic Books, 2000), esp. "Ben-Gurion's Jewish State and Buber's Dissent, 1948–1961), pp. 267–283 for a fascinating account that fundamentally corroborates Weiner's assessment of Buber's stance.

37 Chancellor Schorsch's article originally appeared in *Conservative Judaism Magazine*, as an (unacknowledged) response to my critique of contemporary Conservative Judaism, "Positive Historical Judaism Exhausted: Reflections on a Movement's Future", in *Conservative Judaism*, Vol. XLVII, No. 1 (Fall, 1994), pp. 3–18. It was later published separately as Ismar Schorsch, *The Sacred Cluster: The Core Values of Conservative Judaism* (New York: Jewish Theological Seminary, 1995), p. 4. The text quoted here is taken from the JTSA web site, at <http://www.jtsa.edu/about/cj/sacredcluster.shtml#1>.

38 Jacob Neusner, *Stranger at HomeL "The Holocaust," Zionism and American Judaism* (Chicago and London: The University of Chicago Press, 1981), pp. 99–100.

39 Ariela Keysar and Barry Kosmin, *'Eight Up' — The College Years: The Jewish Engagement of Young Adults Raised in Conservative Synagogues, 1995–2003* (New York: Ratner Center for the Study of Conservative Judaism, 2004), p. 18.

40 Ibid., p. 43.

ISRAEL COMMENTATOR

Reflection on Israel and Identity in Conservative Judaism

Reuven Hammer

On the whole I believe that Dr. Gordis' analysis of the relationship of the Conservative Movement to Zionism and Israel is correct, although I disagree with some details. For example, Dr. Gordis is somewhat dismissive of the liturgical efforts of the Conservative Movement to include Israel in the prayers, citing the use of the *Al Ha-Nissim* framework as "not necessarily a theological claim". I feel that, on the contrary, the liturgical work done on *Yom Ha-Atzmaut*, and specifically the use of that prayer, is the strongest possible theological statement. The Conservative/Masorti prayer books go far beyond the Orthodox prayer books in stating that the creation of the State of Israel is to be seen as an act of religious significance on an equal par with such events as Hanukkah and Purim. I am not convinced that our liturgy avoids "a declaration of the centrality of Israel in the lives of contemporary Jews".

Conservative Zionism, however, is the embodiment of American Zionism, that is, support for the establishment and the strengthening of the Jewish state with little or no commitment to *aliyah*. There are many versions of Zionism that do not posit the negation of Jewish life outside of Israel, however it seems to me that to be authentic,

Zionism must include the option of *aliyah* as a path to personal and Jewish fulfilment. It is on this point that Conservative Zionism has been too understated.

Perhaps the most serious consideration of the place of Zionism in the Conservative Movement took place in a conference devoted entirely to that subject convened at the Jewish Theological Seminary in New York in 1988. This conference resulted in a book, *Zionism and the Conservative/Masorti Movement* (New York: Jewish Theological Seminary, 1990), which included essays by leaders of the Movement. A perusal of these essays reveals the entire gamut of thought on this subject, including criticism of the lack of commitment to *aliyah* and to the establishment of a Conservative Movement in Israel, as well as affirmation of the legitimacy of the Diaspora.

Writing in that volume I suggested that the following steps be taken:

1. Accurate translations of all the prayers that refer to the ingathering of exiles.
2. Honest teaching of the Bible's focus on *Eretz Yisrael.*
3. A liturgy for Yom Ha-Atzmaut that reflects this focus.
4. Publications stressing that the creation and sustenance of the Jewish homeland is the supreme task of the Jewish people.
5. Greater emphasis on Israel in the curriculum of our religious schools.
6. Centralization of the movement in Israel.
7. Bringing every Jewish teenager to Israel.
8. Bringing families from our congregations to visit Israel for extended periods.
9. Creating an *aliyah* fund.

To the best of my knowledge little has happened since then, with the exception of point three which can be found in the newest edition of the *siddur Sim Shalom.*

In addition, consideration must be given to the place of the Conservative/Masorti Movement within the State of Israel itself and the effect of that on the Conservative Movement in America and elsewhere. This is certainly implied in the writings of the spiritual fathers of Conservative Zionism; men such as Schechter and Friedlander, who voiced a vision of the Jewish state which was couched in religious, spiritual, cultural terms. The Zionism that they taught stressed the following ideas:

1. The aim of Zionism is to build a spiritual centre for the Jewish people.
2. Zionism's goal is to allow Judaism to flourish and to rebuild itself in a free environment.
3. The state must promote and be the embodiment of the great ideals of morality and justice that are found in the Torah and in the teachings of the prophets.
4. By doing that, the State of Israel will have an effect on all of humanity, just as Judaism in the First and Second Commonwealths had a positive effect upon the history of the world and made a contribution to the "spiritual wealth of the world".

If the Conservative/Masorti Movement is committed to such a vision, it can only realize it through its efforts within the State. It is in this area that the American Conservative Movement has failed to do much more than pay lip service to the creation of the Masorti Movement in Israel. It is for this reason that I am puzzled by Gordis' remark questioning the fact that the discriminatory policies against the Masorti Movement in Israel "becomes a major issue in a 'Statement of Principles'". On the contrary, if we are truly committed to a specific vision of Israel as the religious and spiritual centre of the Jewish people, we should be actively engaged in seeking to eliminate the present situation of religious coercion and the monopoly given to the official rabbinate. Of course such activity must be accompanied by the positive actions of building a Masorti Movement and its institutions through grass roots activities which must, of necessity, be supported financially by the American Conservative Movement.

It is a given that our Zionism must come to the fore in Israel as well as in the Diaspora. I would like to see us recognize and strengthen the uniqueness and the importance of what the Masorti Movement can offer to Israeli society. What differentiates our Israeli Movement from the Conservative Movement in other countries or from other Zionist Movements? Obviously the basic principles of Conservative Judaism apply here as well:

1. Adherence to traditional Judaism and affirmation of the validity of *halakha.*
2. Readiness to re-interpret *halakha* to meet the needs of the time.
3. Readiness to embrace the fruits of modern knowledge and scholarship, rejecting fundamentalism.

In bringing Masorti Judaism to Israel we want to teach a Judaism that is based on these principles. And these principles do express our uniqueness. Our adherence to *halakha* differentiates us from Reform Jews. Our readiness to re-interpret *halakha* differentiates us from the Orthodox Jews. Our rejection of fundamentalism differentiates us from the *haredim.* All of these principles differentiate us from the secular, since ours is a religious movement, based upon belief in God and adherence to the Torah and *mitzvot.*

The existence of such a strong Masorti Movement would have a positive influence on the Diaspora Conservative Movement, providing an example of a full Jewish life and creating a place in Israel where Conservative Jews could feel at home and with which they could identify when in Israel. It would also provide a positive attitude and framework encouraging Conservative *aliyah.*

DIASPORA COMMENTATOR

Conservative Judaism and Zionism: Different Views of Jewish Unity

David B. Starr

In his masterly synthesis of American Jewish history, Jonathan Sarna argues that both Conservative Judaism and Zionism emerged from worldviews which prized Jewish unity and peoplehood above all else. Each attempted to transcend more partisan ideologies like Reform Judaism and Orthodoxy, both of which resulted in more coherent but also more limited sorts of movements. But while Conservative Judaism and Zionism emphasized unity as paramount, philosophically and practically they differed with one another, articulating diverging definitions of unity, and of peoplehood. These differences continue to separate the two approaches.[1]

Daniel Gordis accurately describes the points of convergence and divergence between Conservative Judaism and Zionism. He notes the historic support of both Conservative leaders and laity for Zionism, especially striking in pre-1948 American Jewish life, when significant elements of Orthodoxy and Reform remained agnostic concerning, or openly hostile to, Zionism, particularly in its demand for a Jewish state.

At the same time he detects a deep fissure separating the two movements — institutionally and attitudinally. The first reality to remember calls to mind the mantra of the real estate business: location, location, location. The bare fact of American Jewish life, its location in America, carried with it lasting implications. American Jews, be they Conservative or anything else, have seen themselves as American, and as being at home in America, with all of the existential ramifications that ensued. American Jews believed in American exceptionalism: they needed no other place of refuge. The guarantees and reality of American freedoms, diversity, and religious pluralism sufficed for them. Zionism remained the strategy and destination for other Jews, who could not obtain their freedom elsewhere.

The fact that Conservatism began as a diasporic movement, in the West, meant that it viewed Zionism practically and somewhat self-servingly, asking with some degree of skepticism what Zionism could possibly do for its Jews rather than what they could do for it, particularly the imperative of *aliyah.* It is also the case that peoplehood for Diaspora Jews means something different than it does for Jews self-consciously embracing Jewish nationalism as constituting the core of their identity. Western Jews may have embraced the mythic power of peoplehood, but they mediated that in many cases through their ethnic churches, and the religious expression they gave to their identity, as one American religious group among many.

In some deep sense, Zionism privileges ethnicity as the core of Jewishness; hence its strength in eastern societies that perpetuated ethnic identity. Western societies, particularly the United States as a liberal rather than nation-state, implicitly and overtly recast ethnic identity. Jews thus became a religious group, the third element in the famed Protestant-Catholic-Jewish troika popularized in the 1950s by Will Herberg. Jewish internal arguments over defining Jewishness and Judaism, particularly the large question of the authority of Jewish tradition over their lives, remained purely voluntary given that Jewish identity here remained voluntary rather than civic. American Jews carried American passports, not as Jews but as American citizens like all others

Given these dynamics, it is hardly surprising that Zionism — defined at its radical extreme as the revolution that would negate the Diaspora — enjoyed only limited success among American Jewry. American Jewry, including Conservatism, has failed spectacularly at promoting American Jewish *aliyah.* Failure seems beside the point; American Jewry never saw itself as committed to, much less as endeavoring to, promote *aliyah.* Jewish immigration suggests a policy for dealing with the problem of worldwide Jewish refugees, not for dealing with a well integrated, secure American Jewry in need of no such refuge.

Here I want to focus not so much on practicalities as on more philosophical sorts of differences. Not surprisingly, given the centrality of history and its study, and the modern methodology of historicism in Conservative Judaism, what separates the two worldviews comes down to their strikingly different readings of history, in terms of constructing a narrative of Jewish history and in terms of their philosophy of history. A reading of several central figures in American Conservative Judaism, down to the current chancellor of the Jewish Theological Seminary, shows the subtle but powerful ideas that have differentiated the two trends in modern Jewish life.

Consider historiosophy for a moment. Though not a philosopher of history, Solomon Schechter took as his hero Nahman Krochmal, a Jewish thinker and conservative *maskil* who used Hegel's notion of historical epochs and tried to adapt them to Jewish history. Hegel argued that civilizations come into being, grow, decline, give way to the next, and so on. History at its highest level tells the story of the human consciousness of the idea of God, with Christianity standing at the apex of this historical drama. Krochmal argued that all religious cultures lived subject to this iron law, save the Jews. Only Jews, owing to their covenantal status, described an upward spiral in their history rather than a mere cycle. This enabled tradition-minded but modern scholars to embrace historicism and Jewish continuity at the same time. Schechter's notion of Catholic Israel — the mythic unity of past and present, Jews and Judaism — precluded his acceptance of the Zionist "return to history". As far as he was concerned Jews had never left history; they continuously made it.[2] Schechter, like many religious figures of his time, mistrusted the Second Aliyah socialists because of their disdain for tradition. He recognized that this reflected a revolutionary disavowal of Jewish history in the conservative sense of keeping faith with that past. Practical disagreements like battles over educational philosophy and practice merely played out these deeper struggles over worldview.

The real point of Schechter's disagreement rested on the definition of *clal yisrael.* Zionism — at least political Zionism — defined the Jewish people politically, as the new civic, territorial, and politically sovereign Jewish entity. It assumed that entity and *clal yisrael* were one. Others like Schechter thought *clal yisrael* transcended such physical and political categories. Vertically that meant historical continuity; geographically it meant the unity of Israel and Diaspora. As Schechter wrote in 1896, Jewishness rested on Torah and what he called "Tradition". Tradition consisted not just of sacred texts, but of the meanings that Jews read into and derived from those texts. This made the People and its historical experience central in Judaism. As Schechter put it:

> Since then the interpretation of Scripture or the Secondary Meaning is mainly the product of changing historical influences, it follows that the center of authority is actually removed from the Bible and placed in some *living body*, which, by reason of its being in touch with the ideal aspirations and the religious needs of the age, is best able to determine the nature of the Secondary Meaning. This living body, however, is not represented by any section of the nation, or any corporate priesthood, or Rabbihood, but by the collective conscience of Catholic Israel as embodied in the Universal Synagogue.[3]

This spiritualized vision of Israel transcended and could never be reduced to Zionism, a much more materialist view of Jewish collectivity, in Schechter's view.

That philosophical difference found expression in radically different narratives of Jewish history, beginning with Schechter but taking fuller expression in successors like Louis Finkelstein, Gerson Cohen, and Ismar Schorsch. All of these writers took exception to core elements of the so-called "Jerusalem School" centred around Hebrew University scholars who viewed their historiographical positions as of a piece with Zionism. For some this took the form of anti-rabbinism, for others anti-medievalism, or anti-*haskalah*. Each view contained its own solution to some problem of Jewish history: Zionism would create a new identity supplanting the rabbinic version; Zionism would solve the problem of apolitical, powerless medieval Jews; Zionism would cure the assimilation that enlightenment had encouraged.[4]

The great figures of the seminary, each a great scholar in their own right, forcefully challenged these sorts of schema. Cohen, much like Schechter, dismissed *shelilat ha-golah* as a distortion and narrowing of Jewish historical experience. Eschewing hegemony, he argued that the greatness of Jewish history lay in its ever-shifting power relations between various communities, with peripheries becoming centres and in the process rivaling or supplanting older centres. Thus *Eretz Yisrael* gave way to *Bavel*, which in turn gave way to *Sefarad*. The unity within Jewish history consisted not of one place but of a process of cultural creativity and continuity. This enabled him to argue, in a 1982 *tour d'horizon* of Jewish contemporary life, that Israel and American Jewry must see each other in a truly mutualist, bi-polar fashion rather than in a hierarchical structure, with Israel dominating exilic Jewry.

> My spiritual home is *Jewland* . . . The real center of our lives must be our Jewishness, a Jewishness that will generate multiple loyalties: to the land of Israel, to the people of Israel, and to the Torah of Israel . . . Israel must be understood as much greater in age and dimension than the State of Israel. The State is only one aspect of Jewish rebirth; it is not the sum and substance either of Jewish identity or of Jewish eschatology. The two categories, Israel and *galut*, embrace the whole of the Jewish people, not only for our day but of every age.[5]

Ismar Schorsch, who Gordis quotes in the context of affirming his view of the centrality of Israel and Zionism to Jewish religious identity, carries other intellectual bags as well. Like his mentor Gerson Cohen, Schorsch in his historical scholarship consistently refuted the Jerusalem school's attempt to de-legitimize the history of Diaspora Jewry. In one of his most important articles, "On the History of the Political Judgment of the Jews", Schorsch derided the popular Zionist narrative that denied Diasporic Jewry political agency, a pathological social identity that could be remedied only by a Zionist return to history and political sovereignty. He confessed, "I have been bent on challenging the notions that the condition of Jewish powerlessness ended only in 1948 or that Jewish political sagacity emerged first in 1897 not only because they are a distortion of the past, but also because they are a disservice to the present." Rather, Schorsch argued that Jews always thought and acted politically, that sovereignty was not the only yardstick by which Jewish power should be measured, that medieval Jews enjoyed plenty of social and economic power, and that modern Jews could learn much from them about politesse as well. In a further irony, Schorsch took the offensive against such Zionist conceits, arguing that both medieval Jewries and modern Israel shared an important characteristic: "Underlying the idea of a Jewish homeland was a basic preference for the segregation of the medieval ghetto." For Schorsch, only modern Diasporic Jewry truly embraced what some might consider a higher identity consisting of roots and branches, a genuine universalism and particularism, a Jewishness capable of loyalty to tradition and yet in the world at the same time.[6]

Gordis correctly notes Conservative Judaism's interest in universalism, at least in universalist enlightenment values like freedom and democracy. How could it be otherwise given its strong successes in twentieth-century America. It bears remembering that the era of greatest expansion of Conservative Judaism — the interwar years through the 1970s — were years of tremendous anxiety about democracy and freedom, given the trials of the Depression, the rise of fascism and communism, World War II and the Cold War. American Jews endeavored to see their own culture and values through the prism of American ideals. Louis Finkelstein, chancellor of the Jewish Theological Seminary in those years (1940–1972) achieved great acclaim for his interfaith efforts to view America as a country distinguished by its record of religious freedom and commitment. He viewed Zionism in much the same fashion, distancing himself from Ben-Gurion's brand of statism, rather embracing the spiritual dimension of Palestinian Jewish values as akin to cherished American principles. There, in the soil hallowed by both Judaism and Christianity, the world would receive yet another needed infusion of the advance of democracy and spirituality yoked together. Thus when he provided an introduction to a reissue of Schechter's *Seminary Addresses*, Finkelstein reminded his readers in 1959 that American Jewry was not the only Jewry in danger of assimilation. He wrote of Schechter's avowal of Zionism:

> But in the very act of his affirmation of Zionism, he warned his readers that the peril of assimilation of the whole Jewish people into a secular, self-serving society was no less than that of the assimilation of any of its adherents to the majority faiths and traditions. The people of Israel is not one more group among the many that fill the earth . . . Judaism regards its very existence as a means to a transcendent goal, an instrument to an end, the fulfillment of the Divine will among all men, according to their diverse natures, temperaments, and backgrounds.[7]

In essence, it seems clear that from the beginning key thinkers who conceived, articulated, and built Conservative Judaism spoke a language that effectively qualified their commitment to Zionism, particularly of the political variety, and particularly of the Zionism that refused to accord any lasting significance or legitimacy to Diaspora Jewish life. Each of these thinkers recognized that Zionism remained an umbrella idea, hosting under the canopy more discrete forms with which these Seminary figures remained more congenial, connected by personal and intellectual ties to the religious and cultural streams of Zionism, and to thinkers in *Eretz Yisrael* such as Ahad Ha'am, Bialik, Shai Agnon. All of these JTS figures should also be contextualized as, at best, only part-time Zionists, given their commitments to building community in Diaspora; each viewed Zionism instrumentally for what it could do for American Jewry. Each questioned and often directly challenged core Zionist assumptions about politics and culture, history and destiny. To the extent that Zionism called for a revolution in Jewish life, rejecting Diaspora, rejecting rabbinism and its notion of canonical culture, rejecting continuity in Jewish history, Conservative Jewish thinkers chose to support Zionism without ever fully embracing its core assumptions and goals. That held true in Schechter's time, and it holds true in the present.

My commentary on the relationship of Conservative Judaism, Zionism, and Israel obviously dealt mainly in the realm of ideas and intellectuals. In that sense it inferred and assumed that these deep intellectual structures apply across the Diaspora. This by no means ignores real differences that Jews in various countries feel regarding Dr. Gordis' argument of "at homeness" as central to Conservative life in the Diaspora. If anything it suggests that whatever contextual factors — such as depth of civic attachment or degree of anti-Semitism in the host society — other sorts of ideational realities truly tie together Diaspora thought.

One may ask about how these ideas translate into the lived experience of Jews. As with any leadership, the figures focused upon here both led and articulated deeper sets of assumptions regarding Zionism. The fundamental point is the definition of *clal yisrael*. Diaspora Jews have a romantic, mythic sense of that incommensurate with politics or nationalism in the narrow sense of the term. In that sense Conservative Jews in America cherish the idea of peoplehood which actually transcends the reality of the State of Israel. One could argue, as did the various thinkers here portrayed, that Israel represents a shattering or diminution or rejection of *clal yisrael*: rejecting the continuity of Jewish historical experience, replacing an entire people and its millenial culture with a mere state/land and a newer, more discontinuous notion of culture. Do American Jews process all that? Perhaps not in the rigorous sense, but in the mythic sense, *clal yisrael* and Israel remain related yet distinct. Therein lies the gap between Diaspora Jewry and the State of Israel.

Notes

1 Jonathan Sarna, *American Judaism: A History* (New Haven: Yale University Press, 2004); particularly pp. 135–206.

2 Solomon Schechter, *Studies in Judaism*, first Series (Philadephia: Jewish Publication Society, 1896); Schechter, *Seminary Addresses and Other Papers* (New York: Burning Bush Press, 1959).

3 Schechter, *Studies*, xviii.

4 David N. Myers, *Re-Inventing the Jewish Past; European Jewish Intellectuals and the Zionist Return to History* (New York: Oxford University Press, 1995).

5 Gerson D. Cohen, "From Altneuland to Altneuvolk: Toward an Agenda for Interaction between Israel and American Jewry," in *Jewish History and Jewish Destiny* (New York: Jewish Theological Seminary of America, 1997), pp. 31–56.

6 Ismar Schorsch, "On the History of the Political Judgment of the Jew," in *From Text to Context: the Turn to History in Modern Judaism* (Hanover, NH: University Press of New England, 1994), pp. 118–132.

7 Louis Finkelstein, "Introduction," to Solomon Schechter, *Seminary Addresses and Other Papers* (New York: Burning Bush Press, 1959), xiv–xv; "Judaism, Zionism, and an Enduring Peace," *New Palestine* May 1943; "Zionism and World Culture," *New Palestine* September 1944; both quoted in Arthur A. Goren, "Spiritual Zionists and Jewish Sovereignty," in *The Politics and Public Culture of American Jews* (Bloomington: Indiana University Press, 1999), pp. 145–164; see also James Gilbert, *Redeeming Culture: American Religion in an Age of Science* (Chicago: University of Chicago Press, 1997), pp. 63–94. Gilbert analyzes the lengths Finkelstein went to promote Jewish–Christian understanding of America as religious in nature, contrary to Deweyan emphases on science and secularism as the keys to American freedom and democracy, in the dark hours of the 1930s and 1940s.

5

The Place of Israel in the Identity of Reform Jews: Examining the Spectrum of Passive Identification with Israel to Active Jewish–Zionist Commitment

Michael Livni

What Does Identifying with Israel Mean?

The term "identifying with Israel" straddles the entire range from pro-Israelism as a passive element of Jewish *identity* to active Jewish–Zionist *commitment*.

Simon Herman has noted that in conscious Jewish–Zionist identity the individual identifies with and is committed to Israel as an expression of "a balance between a past, present and future orientation to the condition of the Jewish people". Significantly, the title of the chapter in Herman's book on Jewish identity relevant to our discussion here is entitled "Zionism and Pro-Israelism: A Distinction with a Difference".[1]

In today's reality there is usually a continuum between these two poles. Transforming passive pro-Israelism to active Jewish–Zionist commitment is an ongoing challenge faced by the Zionist movement worldwide.

What are the implications for Jewish–Zionist commitment in the twenty-first century? Posing this question requires a brief preliminary re-examination of the concept "Zionism" in terms of commitment, for both Diaspora and Israeli Jews. Such an examination must recognize the separate historical roots and the approaches of political and cultural Zionism respectively.

These two approaches have not necessarily been mutually exclusive, despite the tension between them as far as priorities have been concerned. In fact there always was, and still is today, a "mix" of both approaches within the different Zionist ideologies.

Political and Cultural Zionism

The driving force behind the establishment of Zionism as a national (political) movement by Theodore Herzl was the existential threat posed to *Jews* from *without* in many lands of the Diaspora. Political Zionism, a State for the Jews, was a response to the emergence of a malignant anti-Semitism as a byproduct of perceived threats to indigenous national identity by "foreign elements" in a number of emerging nation-states in nineteenth-century Europe.

Hence, the *finite* aim of political Zionism was to found a State for the Jews "like all the Nations", in order to remedy the "abnormal" situation of Jewish vulnerability — everywhere a minority, nowhere a Nation.

The finite aim of political Zionism has been achieved. Political Zionists in the Diaspora have become pro-Israel — that is, supporters of the State of Israel.

Within Israel, political Zionists have become conscientious citizens, paying taxes and doing army service as required. Both in Israel and the Diaspora, political Zionism as such has, in fact, become "post-Zionism".

The motivating force within cultural Zionism of Achad Ha-am was the threat posed to *Judaism* from *within*. That threat was the result of the direct impact of modernity (the Enlightenment) on Jewish corporate society, initiated by the Edict of Emancipation (1791) in France.

The Emancipation created a particular dynamic, which resulted in the disintegration of traditional Jewish society and the exposure of the individual Jew to the Enlightenment. Judaism became a matter of individual conscience and choice. It was now possible to limit the function of Judaism to that of a creed, with its distinguishing rituals and symbols — similar and parallel to the format of various Christian denominations, particularly those of Protestantism. This was the path chosen by classical Reform at the beginning of the nineteenth century.

The response of *cultural zionism* to the threat of cultural assimilation was the establishment of a Jewish centre in Palestine to ensure the continued *creative* existence of the Jewish people, wherever they might be. Such an ongoing aim was (is) *infinite*.

The national centre would be *the place* where a Jewish polity would contend with all the challenges of modernity — political, social and economic, as perceived through the prism of the Jewish heritage. In this way cultural Zionism would renew the role of the Jewish people as a creative force in the history of the Nations; a role that had ended with the cessation of prophecy and the destruction of the Temple.

Achad Ha'am's seminal essay, "Priest and Prophet", written in 1893, posits that the creativity reflected in the Bible stemmed from the tension between the prophetic drive for social justice and the norms of the "establishment," personified by the priests (and kings). A renewal of that creative tension could only take place in an autonomous Jewish centre in the historic Jewish homeland.[2]

There never was nor is there now a consensus regarding a cultural Zionist vision of what a Jewish state should be. However, there have been three common denominators to all the visions that have had a Zionist impact either in the past or the present.

First of all, the various cultural Zionist visions have had an ideology. Gideon Shimoni explains the concept of ideology as "a coherent, action-oriented set of ideals that provides those who subscribe to it with a comprehensive cognitive map of their position and purposes".[3]

Secondly, the vision and the ideology for its realization have had to be capable of mobilizing a minimal critical number prepared to invest their personal lives and resources in realising the ideology. This usually necessitated life in partnership with like-minded others — that is, life in a community of purpose (intentional community).[4]

Lastly, in order to ensure continuity, the ideological nucleus both within and without the intentional communities had to establish an educational system, formal and informal, both in Israel and the Diaspora.

Before the establishment of Israel, the premier cultural Zionist ideology was that of Labour Zionism: Hebrew land; Hebrew labour; Hebrew language; social justice. Its role model was the *chalutz* (pioneer) within the framework of the *kibbutz* intentional community.

During the last generation the Zionist vision of *Gush Emunim*, stemming from messianic Orthodox Zionism and catalyzed by the Six Day War, has been a striking example of cultural Zionist commitment and intentional community (the "Settlements"), regardless of one's personal opinion concerning its nature.

Zionism and Postmodernism

Both political and cultural Zionism were ideological Jewish responses to modernity. The Enlightenment legitimized free will as a valid force in human affairs. Ideology proposes plans of action to realize a vision. Herzl's famous phrase "If you will it, it is no fairy tale" reflects the modern belief that ideology embodied in free human will can shape reality.

It is a hallmark of postmodernism that it rejects ideology and has recruited the social sciences to ascertain "reality" as the benchmark for proposing policy. Eliezer Schweid contrasts the "modern" with the "post-modern" thus:

> Guidelines based on 'modern' philosophy and ideology deal with what is 'desirable'. They are determined by the subjective interests of individuals, groups, classes, political parties and Peoples. Instead of this we (now) have (the 'post-modern') objective and scientific guidelines where the weighted common interests of all are objectively determined . . . this demands a reform in the social sciences . . . it demands theory which reflects actual practice as determined by objective investigation.[5] (Translation: Michael Livni)

The post-Zionism of pro-Israelism (both in Israel and the Diaspora) is in fact an expression of postmodernism. Neither is conducive to the propagation of norms rooted in cultural Zionist ideology of what the Jewish state should be.

The contemporary priests of post-modernism in the Jewish polity are the Jewish professionals who have been trained in the postmodern approach of social science and their non-ideological moneyed supporters. They have de-legitimised the prophetic demand of "the desirable that should be" no less effectively than the Rabbis who ruled that prophecy had ceased in Israel.[6]

In the light of the foregoing general discussion, we now need to examine the place of Israel in the identity of Reform Jews on the spectrum of passive pro-Israelism to active Jewish Zionist commitment.

Reform World Jewry and Identification with Israel

Simon Herman studied the dynamics of education towards Zionism fifty years ago. "The general rule . . . is that Zionist education requires Zionist groups. *Becoming a Zionist is in fact a process of growing into a group which is Zionist*" [emphasis in the original].[7] In practice, Herman was talking about Zionist youth movements and camps that constituted a significant framework for Zionist commitment at that time.

Herman also pointed out, however, that identification and commitment within such frameworks were usually mediated by role models representing a particular cultural Zionist outlook. These could be older *madrichim* (youth leaders) or *shlichim* (educational emissaries) from Israel who embodied in their personal lives a way of life (*torat chaim*) and a Jewish–Zionist vision based on a particular value world which reflected a concept and vision of what the Jewish state should be.

Active identity and commitment to the Zionist enterprise meant identifying with a particular vision of Israel.

What do statistics tell us about the place of Israel in the identity of Reform Jews? Some 90 percent of Reform Jews live in the United States. However, it is important to relate to other Diasporas in order to ascertain if the place of Israel and/or the Jewish–Zionist commitment of Reform Jews in other lands parallels that of America.

The United States

By virtue of the National Jewish Population Survey of 2000–1 (NJPS) conducted by the United Jewish Communities, the statistically best-documented group of Reform Jews is that of the United States, the largest Jewish Diaspora.

According to the NJPS there are 5.2 million Jews in the United States. Denominational identification was surveyed among 4.3 million Jews who had "stronger Jewish connections". Of those, 35 percent "consider themselves" Reform, 26 percent of Jews consider themselves Conservative, 10 percent Orthodox, 20 percent "just Jewish" and 9 percent "other." The NJPS determined that the Jewish population in Reform households totaled 1.4 million. It is also significant that some 45 percent of those considering themselves Reform had not been raised Reform.[8] In the United States, the trend appears to be in the direction of Reform.

However, it must also be noted that the NJPS records that the actual population affiliated with Reform congregations encompasses a much smaller number: 754,000.[9]

As for the place of Israel in the identity of those considering themselves Reform Jews compared to other sectors of US Jewry, the NJPS records the following results:[10]

	Orthodox	*Conservative*	*Reform*	*"Just Jewish"*
Ever Visited Israel (%)	73	53	34	27
Emotional Attachment				
Very Attached to Israel (%)	68	39	21	24

These are surely disappointing statistics from any Zionist point of view. They are even more disappointing in light of the finding that 57 percent of all Reform Jews and 68 percent of those affiliated with Reform synagogues claim to have "a strong sense of belonging to the Jewish people".[11] This disconnect surely warrants further investigation.

Another indicator of Israel involvement is youth travel under Reform sponsorship. Before the Second Intifada, the National Federation of Temple Youth (NFTY) six-week summer tours peaked at 1400 participants. This was still a modest number but, in the wake of Oslo, it was slowly climbing.

In 2001, at the height of the Second Intifada, the Union of Reform Judaism (URJ) was the only Jewish institution to cancel Israel tours outright. This was done in spite of the protest of the Israel Movement for Progressive Judaism (IMPJ) and regardless of the fact that the Netzer countries (see below) carried on. In 2005 there were again 600 participants on these tours. One hundred high school juniors attended the semester-long Eisendrath International Exchange (EIE) programme. The only post-high school programme, the recently initiated "Carmel" programme based in Haifa, had 12 participants in 2005–6.[12]

Other Diaspora Countries

There are a number of common denominators among the Reform movements outside of the United States.

1. They exist in Jewish communities that are younger, more cohesive, and more compact than Reform Jewry in the United States. Hence the Jewish ethnic connection has remained stronger. Zionism/pro-Israelism is more normative in the Jewish community as a whole.

2. The Reform community constitutes a minority, sometimes not officially recognized, within the total Jewish community. Access to the Jewish people's national institutions, such as the World Zionist Organization (WZO) and the Jewish Agency, is of particular importance to these Reform communities.

3. In the Jewish communities of the former Commonwealth countries, the venue of a semi-autonomous Zionist youth movement as a framework for informal education was much more established than in the United States, the partial exception of Young Judaea notwithstanding. In order to prevent attrition of Reform youth to secular Zionist youth movements such as Habonim, the Reform movements of countries such as Britain, Australia and South Africa found it expedient to support the establishment of Netzer.

The lack of NJPS equivalents outside of the USA presents a major methodological problem in trying to assess the place of Israel in the identity of Reform Jews in the rest of the Diaspora. In the absence of reliable statistics, the elucidation of a specific Reform behaviour as a common denominator of all Reform Diasporas becomes a problematic quest.

Netzer as Indicator of Reform Jewish–Zionist Identity

The Reform Zionist youth movement, Netzer (Noar Zioni Reformi) was established in 1980. Initially, Netzer was established in Britain, Australia and South Africa with the informal help of the Israel office of the URJ Youth Division office in Israel. The World Union for Progressive Judaism (WUPJ) adopted it as its youth arm.

For a number of Diaspora countries, the activity of the Netzer movement is at least a partial indicator of the relationship to Israel. This is so for two reasons:

1. Statistics regarding participation in long-term Israel programmes are available from the Netzer Olami office in Jerusalem.
2. Surveying the performance of Netzer has predictive implications for potential Jewish–Zionist commitment and identification with Israel in the coming generation.

In addition, the influence of cultural globalization has had an impact on the value orientations of Jewish youth, certainly Reform Jewish youth, in the entire Western world, including Israel. Thus, an extrapolation from Netzer to Reform youth in America has become increasingly relevant. This has already been a factor in the recent (2005) formal affiliation of NFTY with Netzer Olami.[13]

It is of major significance that Netzer was established as a semi-autonomous Zionist youth movement. The empowerment of youth (in the absence of money and/or availability of professional staff) and the organic unity of work with youth through into young adulthood were and are major differences between Netzer and NFTY. The implications of this are discussed elsewhere in this chapter.

In Britain and Australia in particular twenty-five years of Netzer have shown that this was a correct strategic choice for ensuring future Jewish–Zionist leadership, professional and lay, for these smaller Reform communities.

In 2004, Netzer reported a membership of 1,400 in Britain — ages 10–25.[14] The fact that 1,400 young people are active in an avowedly Zionist youth movement and are the recognized youth arm of the movement in Britain clearly indicates a high level of integration of Israel into Reform identity.

The combined Netzer movements of Britain send cohorts of 15 to 25 high school graduates for a ten-month "Shnat" Netzer programme to Israel. If we extrapolate the lower number to the 754,000 Jews actually affiliated with the congregations of Reform Judaism in the United States, we would have a youth movement of 26,000 with annual cohorts of some 280 high school graduates on long-term Israel programmes.

The Australian Netzer movement parallels the example of its British counterpart. There are probably between 15,000 and 20,000 Reform Jews in Australia, and Netzer counts 410 members. Annual cohorts of five to ten high school graduates participate in the ten-month Netzer "Shnat" programme.

In the last few years there has been an encouraging development of Netzer in countries of the Former Soviet Union (FSU). Netzer claims 2,000 members in the FSU. Reliable figures for affiliation with Reform congregations are unavailable.

There is a Netzer presence in other countries of the Diaspora as well — Germany, Holland, Spain, Argentina. Netzer has not yet found a way to establish itself in the small French Reform community. Netzer has not been organized in Canada because of the affiliation of the Canadian Council of Liberal Congregations with the Union for Reform Judaism (USA)

The major conclusion to be drawn from the Netzer experience is that there is not now any inherent contradiction between a pro-Israel Reform Judaism as such and a more intense Jewish–Zionist commitment promoted by a Reform Zionist youth movement.

Also significant is that the adult institutions of the Reform movement in countries in which Netzer operates have come to see Netzer, a semi-autonomous Reform Zionist youth movement, as normative for the informal education of their youth. In those countries where Netzer has already existed for 25 years (Britain, Australia), the adult movement has undertaken considerable financial responsibility for the financing of Netzer staff (including *shlichim*) and Netzer activities. Netzer graduates, lay and professional, are coming to play a significant role in this continuing support.

Hence, we must inevitably return to the question of which factors, particular to Reform Judaism in the United States, have made the place of Israel (and by extension, Jewish–Zionist commitment) in the identity of American Reform a challenge.

The Evolution of Reform Thought on, and Identification with, the Zionist Enterprise

The Reform attitude — specifically that of the Reform Rabbinate — to the Zionist enterprise has undergone a sea change over the last 120 years. This pertains to both the political and cultural parameters of Zionism.

The basis of the classic Reform rejection of Zionism lay in its rejection of Jewish peoplehood as such. The concept of Judaism as a religious community (*kultusgemeinde*) was influenced by the Protestant church model. The rationale of classic Reform was that it was the Jewish mission to propagate universal (prophetic) values by means of Jewish dispersion among the Nations.

A detailed history of the relationship between Reform Judaism and the Zionist idea is not within the scope of this essay. However, a good general exposition can be found in Michael Meyer's history of the Reform movement.[15] David Polish has given a "blow by blow" description of the stormy path of the Zionist issue in the arena of the American Reform rabbinate.[16]

In the twenty years between the two world wars the travails of European Jewry inexorably drove the Reform movement to amend its position. A new generation of Reform Rabbis from East European backgrounds catalyzed the process. The Columbus Platform, adopted in 1937, affirmed the concept of Jewish peoplehood and even partially endorsed the Zionist idea.[17]

What is of significance is that the Rabbis adopted a statement affirming both the physical need of some Jews for a "Jewish homeland" (*de facto* political Zionism) as well as a cultural Zionist concept — "a centre of Jewish culture and spiritual life".

The cultural Zionist affinities of many in the Reform Rabbinate were influenced by the ideas of classical Zionist thinkers: Achad Ha'am, A. D. Gordon, and the founder of Reconstructionism, Mordechai Kaplan.[18] However, it was the personal contact on the part of Reform Rabbis with cultural Zionism in its Labour Zionist variant in Palestine that had a major behind-the-scenes influence in the formulation of the Columbus platform.[19] In describing the *chalutzim*, the words of Maurice

Eisendrath, the future President of the Reform movement in America (1943–71), are illustrative:

> they take somewhat more seriously than we the ethical behests of the Torah, the categorical imperatives of the prophets . . . where has the much vaunted passion of Reform Judaism for social righteousness and justice been so tangibly adumbrated as in the labor colonies and cooperatives of Zion.[20]

Many Rabbis were more outspoken than Eisendrath. They formed a group of Labour Zionist sympathizers, but their operative influence would not come to fruition for another thirty years.

The Holocaust almost inevitably created a broad consensus, including within Reform Judaism, for political Zionism. The establishment of Israel marked a watershed in the attitude of the Reform movement as a whole.

It was the impact of the Six Day War that generated an unprecedented response on the part of Diaspora Jewry, including the American Reform Movement. It was not only a visceral reaction to the possibility of another catastrophe befalling the Jewish people, but also the realization that the Jews stood alone.

In the wake of the war there was a major shift on the part of American Jews — Reform included — from involvement in general causes (civil rights, anti-Vietnam protests) to the particularly Jewish causes. A leading figure in this shift was Rabbi Richard G. Hirsh who was one of the first to moot the idea of a Reform *kibbutz* and was instrumental in the transfer of the WUPJ Head Office to Jerusalem in 1973. In 1974, Hirsch persuaded the World Union for Progressive Judaism to affiliate with the World Zionist Organization — a process that was consummated in 1976.[21] The establishment of ARZA (the Association of Reform Zionists of America) in 1977 as a Reform Zionist party was the final step in the process.

In 1963, David Ben-Gurion granted the then president of the Hebrew Union College (HUC), the archeologist Nelson Glueck, a plot of land in Jerusalem. Glueck promised to bring rabbinic students to Israel for a year. The promise came to fruition in 1970. Unfortunately, the impact of this experience did not bring about the desired results, as is discussed below.

A dedicated group of Zionist Reform Rabbis under the leadership of Stephen Schafer took over the Youth Division. Ever-larger contingents — in the hundreds — of Reform Youth came on Israel summer trips.

The Labour Zionist orientation of many Reform Rabbis, already evidenced a generation earlier, resulted in two dialogues: with educators and with cultural activists of the *kibbutz* movement. These dialogues that were held in Oranim — the teachers' seminary of the *kibbutz* movement — in 1971 and 1973 helped pave the way for the proactive role of the UAHC Youth Division in undertaking the establishment of a Reform *kibbutz*.[22]

A key element in Schafer's rationale for being the *kibbutz*'s "point person" and establishing a seminar centre there was his awareness that Reform youth needed a place and young adults with whom they could identify. The first Reform *kibbutz*, Yahel, founded in 1976, was to be both a symbol as well as a practical venue for imparting Reform Zionist identity. The second Reform *kibbutz*, Lotan, was founded in 1983.

The 1975 United Nations Resolution equating Zionism with Racism galvanised the UAHC Biennial Convention being held at Dallas, which I also attended. From the podium, Rabbi Alexander Schindler, the UAHC President, declared:

> We are all of us Jews and whether we use the small z or the large Z we are all of us Zionists. The land of Israel, which is Zion, and the children of Israel who constitute the Jewish people and the God of Israel are all bound together in a triple covenant. At no time in our history have we ever stopped praying or longing or working for Zion.[23]

I was an eyewitness and joined the hundreds of delegates who snaked through the Convention Center singing "Am Yisrael Chai", energized and inspired by Schindler's speech.

There are no hard statistics available, but my impression is that the place of Israel in the identity of those Reform Jews affiliated with synagogues apparently peaked in the early 1980s.

During the last two decades of the twentieth century, the position of Israel and Reform Jewish–Zionist commitment lost ground rather than gaining in strength. Surely this is now reflected in the place of Israel in regard to the identity of American Reform Jews.

There is little documentation for this period. My analysis stems from my personal involvement, beginning with my *shlichut* to the Youth Division of the UAHC in 1975.

It is possible to adduce a host of general factors militating against the furtherance of either an ideology or an identity with Israel. Such factors would include a shift to individualism in America, symbolized by the election of Ronald Reagan. One could also note that the waning of an ideologically orientated Labour Zionist Movement and the ascent of right-wing Zionism to power all had a negative impact on the image of Israel. The 1982 Lebanon War added further question marks to identifying with Israel.

The retirement of Rabbi Stephen Schafer resulted in the gradual abandonment of long-term Israel programmes and the break up of *Garin Arava*, the *aliyah* framework for Reform youth. An emphasis on summer Israel trips continued, but the development of an embryonic Reform Zionist youth movement was aborted. *Aliyah* of NFTY graduates to Israel in general, and to the *kibbutzim* in particular, ceased almost entirely. Not only did this place the *kibbutzim* themselves in a precarious position with regard to their Reform identity, but they also found it more difficult to play an educational role in relation to NFTY youth groups.

The few long-term programmes still maintained were based near Jerusalem. Yahel and Lotan were "far away". Stephen Schafer's vision of Reform *kibbutzim* impacting on the Jewish–Zionist identity faded.

The professionals who replaced Stephen Schafer had a particular aversion to empowering college-age youth within an autonomous framework. In a personal conversation with me in 1978, the future director of the Youth Division made it clear that he would not continue with Schafer's policy of youth autonomy.

Nothing could have been more symbolic of the change in Youth Division priorities than the location of the *shaliach* office within the Youth Division complex. Under the aegis of Schafer the office was located near the entrance, not far from the director's office. When I visited in the mid-eighties, the *shlicha* had been relegated to a small and cramped back room.

In Israel itself the implosion of the *kibbutz* movement, ideologically and economically (in that order), eroded its credibility as a political partner. This was occurring at a time that also marked the gradual passing of that generation of Rabbis whose affirmation of the Zionist enterprise stemmed in part from their identification with the *chalutzim* and the accomplishments of Labour Israel.

In the last two decades of the twentieth century ARZA was unwilling and unable to deal with Reform Zionist education. The will was not there.

It is only in the last few years that the World Reform Zionist movement, ARZENU, influenced by the relative success of Netzer, has begun to be cautiously proactive. A youth task force has been established. ARZA has become the locus of the *shaliach*, rather than the Youth Division. The latter has become more Zionist-oriented in its Israel programming.

Rabbinic Training and the Identification with Israel

The premier Reform Rabbinical Seminary is the Hebrew Union College (HUC), with its home campus in Cincinnati. It has branches in Los Angeles, New York, and, since 1970, in Jerusalem. In my opinion, HUC has proved itself to be a Zionist and more particularly a Reform Zionist failure for a generation.[24] The vast majority of HUC graduates of that generation now leading most congregations have no commitment to Reform Zionism, despite having spent a year of their studies in Israel. If they did have Reform Zionist commitment, ARZA would have 200,000 members rather than 50,000. Congregational visits to Israel would triple. Each of the larger congregations would have student scholarships for Reform Zionist Year-in-Israel programmes.

The HUC Year in Jerusalem has missed many opportunities of exposing its students to non-academic Jewish–Zionist role models. If the cognitive understanding of the students' Zionist spirituality is negligible, the experiential encounter of the students with Zionist spirituality is closer to nil.

An extreme example of the HUC avoidance of experiential and cognitive encounter with Reform Zionism is its token involvement with the Reform *kibbutzim* — arguably the only examples of Reform Zionist intentional community currently in existence. Kibbutz Lotan rates a two-hour visit in the HUC curriculum. Nor do the *kibbutzim* figure in the programme of the Leo Baeck College in London.

The College has been unable to entertain the idea that part of the year in Israel should be spent in Israeli academic institutions rooted in a humanist Zionist philosophy — teachers' seminaries in particular — and in contact with educators (and students) who embody that philosophy, quite compatible with Reform Judaism. This would ameliorate the current situation where students are in an American Reform "ghetto". Such contact would be mutually beneficial both for the Israelis and the Rabbinic students.

The net result: most Reform Rabbis are not even partial Reform Zionist role models. The lukewarm attitude to Israel among many Rabbis is a serious impediment to strengthening the role of Israel within the identity of Reform Jews, particularly in the United States.

What Can Be Done to Improve Prospects for Reform Zionist Identity?

All the foregoing leads to clusters of working assumptions for those who seek to reinforce the role of Israel in the identity of Reform Jews.

Strengthening the place of Israel in the identity of Reform Jews is dependent on creating foci of Reform Jewish–Zionist commitment where youth and young adults can identify with people (role models), places, and communities that project a Reform cultural-Zionist vision, even if only in part. It is mainly youth and young adults who are accessible to value change as they go through the process of their personal identity formation. The process of identification must be affective *and* cognitive. Today, those loci of Reform Zionist commitment that exist, particularly the Reform *kibbutzim*, are under-utilized.

Groups realizing a Reform Zionist commitment would have a "ripple effect" (family, friends, local Jewish and even general media), thereby upgrading the place of Israel in the identity of a larger number of Reform Jews. As mentioned above, by virtue of Netzer, educational processes incorporating nuclei of Reform Zionist acculturation already exist, in part, in a number of Diaspora countries. However, by virtue of its numbers, the Reform community of North America constitutes the major challenge.

Promoting Educational Reform Zionist Process

It is *the* function of the Reform Zionist movement in the Diaspora to be proactive, directly and indirectly, in promoting an educational succession, affective and cognitive, of Reform Zionist education. A good conceptual point of departure would be to focus on the gap shown in the NJPS between the 68 percent of Reform Jews actually affiliated with congregations who have a strong sense of belonging to the Jewish people, and actual emotional identification with Israel — 21 percent of Reform Jews in general and 28 percent of those congregationally affiliated.[25]

The summer camps of the Reform movement are ideal transient intentional communities with great potential for the start of the process. Deliberate placement of Reform Zionist role models — graduates of Reform Zionist programmes in Israel — should be empowered to have some input into the camp programmes, both experiential and cognitive.

For those among the college-age youth who choose to be active there has to be a semi-autonomous framework. Professional leadership inevitably encroaches on the "living space" of young adults and saps their motivation. Optimally, informal education at this stage should be provided by role models who themselves live in Reform Zionist intentional communities (*shlichim*). This is not always possible. The *shlichim* will work in tandem with the top level professional. Young adults must make their own way within the framework of a given budget and within the framework of the WUPJ ideological consensus. This is what defines them as being autonomous, but not independent.

It would truly be in the spirit of Achad Ha'am's approach to cultural Zionism if local chapters of ARZA were to intensify initiatives for Zionist cultural events on various topics — evenings, which in addition to the cognitive, would also feature an experiential aspect. Would it not be suitable for Reform Zionist groups to sponsor the

Seder Tu B'Shvat (New Year of the Trees) in their congregation, as well as celebrations of Israeli Independence Day? Such initiatives in the local congregation could make a specific substantive contribution. No less important, in the context of such educational activity, is that specific congregation members appear as role models for fellow-congregants with less Jewish–Zionist commitment.

The centrepiece of such a succession of learning experiences would be a long-term, properly structured Reform Zionist Israel Experience. The potential of such an experience for those who return to the Diaspora cannot be properly utilized without a framework, at the college level, within which these returnees continue to function and express their Reform Zionist commitment. Such frameworks cannot be professionally run from above. They must be semi-autonomous in order to generate continued motivation. That is the essence of youth movement. I have discussed this in detail elsewhere.[26]

As the experience of Britain and Australia show, this redounds to the benefit of the Reform community as a whole and upgrades its qualitative relationship to Israel as a Zionist enterprise.

Reform Zionist Intentional Community

A major challenge facing Reform Zionism is the question of Reform Zionist intentional community in Israel — Reform Zionist *kehilla kedusha*. Currently, the term "intentional community" is used by the communal movement internationally.[27] The degree of cooperation in intentional communities varies, as does their orientation to outreach (mission, *shlichut*). The common denominator of all intentional communities is that they are composed of a group of people who have chosen to live together with a common purpose, working cooperatively to create a lifestyle that reflects their shared core values.

There can also be a spectrum of substance. For example, a Reform Zionist intentional community may choose to emphasize educational outreach. This is the path chosen by the Humanist–Zionist intentional community of Kibbutz Tamuz in Beit Shemesh.[28] Another example, Kibbutz Lotan, defines itself as a Reform Zionist *kibbutz*, maintaining a collective framework and emphasising Eco-Zionism.[29]

Let there be no misunderstanding. Within the Zionist enterprise, intentional community as an individual choice for self-realisation (*hagshama atzmit*) has always been the choice of the few. In its heyday, the *kibbutz* movement did not constitute more than 7 percent of the Jewish population. Generally it was 3 percent.[30] Its educational significance lay in the fact that tens of thousands, particularly within the youth movements, passed through it as part of a normative process of acculturation to the Labour Zionist ethos. As mentioned above, this was to be the role of Reform *kibbutzim* as envisaged by Stephen Schafer.

It is the sincere belief of most Reform Rabbis, including those truly active and committed to furthering Reform Zionism, that "the synagogue remains the foundation of Jewish life . . . ".[31] This is surely a valid statement for the post-Enlightenment Diaspora, but its uncritical transposition to Israel is a tragic conceptual error. The foundation of Jewish life has been the community: the *kehilla kedusha*. After all, the renewal of holy community in modern garb was and is a central theme in the rationale of cultural Zionism.

The historian Uriel Tal has noted that: "The community is the medium for the actualization of the covenant . . . it is the particularistic community which enables man to practice universalistic ideas . . . "[32]

Indeed, the Israel Movement for Progressive Judaism must eventually confront the question of whether it remains a federation of congregations on the Diaspora model or whether it is also the basis for a Reform Zionist movement. A central feature of such a movement has to be intentional community seeking to impact on nascent Israeli society with its unique vision of what a Jewish state should be.[33]

The direction of the IMPJ will inevitably influence the degree to which it stimulates identity and passion among the younger generation in Israel, and among Reform Jews (especially youth) in the Diaspora.

(A Reform Zionist movement in Israel would engage in other activities as well. A positive existing example is the Israel Religious Action Center (IRAC). IRAC was an ARZA initiative. As well as being of service to the IMPJ it has had an impact on Israel as a whole. However this area is not within the purview of this essay.)

Ideology and Vision

Can Reform Judaism generate a Jewish–Zionist commitment that would meld Reform values, attitudes and behaviour into a unique Reform Zionist vision, realisable through intentional community?

Creating intentional communities of Reform Zionism commitment is predicated on the assumption that there is a Reform cultural Zionist vision. Any cultural Zionist vision will be based on a world outlook that expresses itself through an action-oriented ideology. Ultimately, any cultural Zionist vision remains just that if there is no ideologically oriented process that educates towards intentional communities seeking to realize that vision.

To this end, a Reform Zionist ideology with an action plan for its implementation, piece by piece, has to be formulated (including allocation of resources).

Simply put: The prophetic (modern) element inherent in the idea of "movement" must impact upon the priestly outlook of (postmodern) "organization". Or, if you will, we can juxtapose postmodernity to modernity: "Everything is foreseen, but free will is given."[34]

If Reform Zionism can contend with the challenge of a Reform Zionist educational process, the challenge of a variety of Reform Zionist intentional communities and the challenge of Reform Zionist ideology, then it is my opinion that there will be two results:

1. The place of Israel in the identity of the Reform Jew will be significantly reinforced.
2. The profile of Reform Judaism in Israel will be markedly enhanced.

The question becomes: Is there the will in Reform Judaism and its institutions to contend with the challenge posed by Israel for the identity of Reform Jews?

The very fact of positing this question reflects a modernist as distinct from a postmodernist stance.

Summary

In summary, an action programme that would generate a process of Reform Zionist commitment can notably augment the place of Israel in the identity of Reform Jews. The focus should be a cultural Zionist educational continuum for youth and young adults. Reform Zionist commitment must be expressed through intentional communities in Israel. Such communities, with even a partial expression of prophetic ideals, can be the source of inspirational feedback and pride for Reform Jews in the Diaspora. By means of identification with Reform Zionist community in Israel, the place of Israel in the identity of Reform Jews will be enhanced.

Notes

1 Simon N. Herman, *Jewish Identity: A Social Psychological Perspective* (Beverly Hills and London: Sage Publications, 1977), pp. 116–134. The direct quote is on p. 125.
2 Achad Ha'am, "Priest and Prophet (1893)" in Leon Simon (ed.), *Selected Essays of Achad Ha'am (1912)* (Philadelphia: Jewish Publication Society,1962), pp. 125–138.
3 Gideon Shimoni, *The Zionist Ideology* (Hanover, NH: University Press of New England 1995), p. 3.
4 See Uriel Tal, "Structures of Fellowship and Community in Judaism," in *Conservative Judaism*, 28, 2 (Winter 1974):3–12. Tal relates the "intentionalist character of the Torah" to the concept of *kehilla kedusha* (holy community) and identified the Kibbutz Dati as a contemporary example. The term "intentional community" is currently in general use in the communal movements throughout the world. See below — "Reform Zionist Intentional Community".
5 Eliezer Schweid, "Humanism, Globalization, Post-Modernism and the Jewish People" in *New Gordonian Essays* (Tel Aviv: Hakibbutz Hameuchad, 2005), p. 14. (Hebrew translation: Michael Livni).
6 "Since the deaths of Haggai, Zachariah, and Malachi, the Holy Spirit has ceased in Israel." See detailed note with sources on cessation of prophecy in Yosef Hayim Yerushalmi, *ZAKHOR: Jewish History and Jewish Memory* (Seattle: University of Washington Press, 1996), p. 124, Note 28. Thus, authority passed from the prophets to the Knesset Gedola (Avot 1:1) and their inheritors — the Chachamim (the Rabbis).
7 Simon N. Herman, "Education Towards Zionism" in *Forum* 5, World Zionist Organization, Jerusalem, January 1962, p. 84.
8 National Jewish Population Survey (NJPS), "Reform Jews", A UJC Presentation of 2000–1 Findings for the Union for Reform Judaism Board of Trustees, Denver, Colorado: 11 June 2004. (There are no page numbers.)
9 Ibid.
10 National Jewish Population Survey (NJPS), "Israel Connections and American Jews", Report 12, United Jewish Communities Report Series on the NJPS — 2000–1, August 2005.
11 National Jewish Population Survey (NJPS), "Reform Jews", A UJC Presentation of 2000–1 Findings for the Union for Reform Judaism Board of Trustees, Denver, Colorado, 11 June 2004. (There are no page numbers.)
12 Terry Hendon, Administrative Secretary, URJ Touth Division Office, Jerusalem. Personal Communication, 9 February 2006.
13 At the time of writing this affiliation is mainly symbolic and does not yet express itself in joint programming. In his report to ARZENU in June 2005, Maoz Haviv, General Secretary of Netzer noted that: "We are well aware . . . that in order to fill up the decision

with real content, there is quite a lot which has to be invested by both sides . . . during the coming years."

14 All figures for Netzer membership were supplied by the Netzer Olami office in Jerusalem as of January 2006. These figures include membership from age 10 up to and including the young adult sector, TAMAR (Tnuat Magshimim Reformim).

15 Michael Meyer, *Response to Modernity: A History of the Reform Movement in Judaism* (New York: Oxford University Press, 1988). See in particular Chapters 7 and 8.

16 David Polish, *Renew our Days* (Jerusalem: The Zionist Library, 1976).

17 "Judaism is the historical religious experience of the Jewish people . . . Judaism is the soul of which Israel is the body . . . In the rehabilitation of Palestine, the land hallowed by memories and hopes, we behold the promise of renewed life for many of our brethren. We affirm the obligation of all Jewry to aid in its upbuilding as a Jewish homeland by endeavoring to make it not only a haven of refuge for the oppressed but also a centre of Jewish culture and spiritual life. " (Columbus Platform, 1937, cited from David Polish (1976), pp. 199–200).

18 David Polish (1976), p. 191.

19 The late Gideon Elad has documented in detail the evolution of the relationship between the Reform movement (in particular, the Rabbinate) and Labour Zionism which eventually led to the founding of the first Reform kibbutz, Yahel. His (2000) Hebrew thesis, "*Or B'Arava?: Yahel — Du-Siach U'mesima Bein HaTnua HaKibbutzit L'Tnua HaReformit*", unfortunately remains unpublished. See also: David Polish (1976), pp. 192–198.

20 Maurice Eisendrath, *CCAR Year Book*, Vol. 47 (1937), pp. 218–19.

21 Richard G. Hirsch, *From the Hill to the Mount: A Reform Zionist Quest* (Jerusalem: Gefen and the Zionist Library, 2000), pp. 49–67.

22 Documented in detail by Elad (2000) in "*Or B'Arava?*" in note 19.

23 Cited from: Michael Langer (Livni) (ed.), *Reform Zionist Perspective* (New York: UAHC Youth Division (offset), 1977), p. 292.

24 Michael Livni, "A Reform Zionist Policy for Hebrew Union College" in *Reform Zionism: 20 Years* (Jerusalem and New York: Gefen, 1999), pp. 254–58.

25 National Jewish Population Survey (NJPS), "Reform Jews", A UJC Presentation of 2000–1 Findings for the Union for Reform Judaism Board of Trustees, Denver, Colorado, 11 June 2004. (There are no page numbers.)

26 Michael Livni, "Aspects of Zionist Jewish Education" in *Reform Zionism: Twenty Years — An Educator's Perspective* (Jerusalem and New York: Gefen, 1999). See Section Four for a general discussion on Jewish Zionist education and Section 5 for the implications with regard to the Reform movement.

27 See for example: *Eurotopia: Intentional Communities and Ecovillages in Europe*, 2005, <www.eurotopia.de>; *Communities Directory: A Guide to Intentional Communities and Cooperative Living*, Fellowship for Intentional Community, Rutledge, Missouri, 2005, <www.ic.org>.

28 Website: <www.tamuz.org.il >.

29 Kibbutz Lotan <www.kibbutzlotan.com>. In particular see:"Vision Statement.". See also: Michael Livni (2004) *Case Study: Kibbutz Lotan-Eco-Zionism and Kibbutz*, ICSA Lectures at <www.chavruta.org.il >.

30 See Michael Livni (2004) *The Kibbutz and its Future: Historical Perspective*, ICSA Lectures at <www.chavruta.org.il>.

31 Peter Knobel, *Israel in Reform Jewish Liturgy*, paper delivered to ARZA Reform Zionist Think Tank, Malibu Calif., January 2005.

32 Uriel Tal, "Structures of Fellowship and Community in Judaism" in *Conservative Judaism*, 28, 2 (Winter 1974): 3–12.

33 See Michael Livni, "More Than Worship is Needed" in *Judaism*, 31, 4 (Fall 1982), as well as "Reform Judaism and Reform Zionism in Israel" in *CCAR Journal* (Spring 1991). Both

essays can also be found in *Reform Zionist: Twenty Years — An Educator's Perspective*, Section 2.

34 Avot 3: 19.

ISRAEL AND DIASPORA COMMENTATORS

The Place of Israel and the Diaspora

Lisa Grant and Michael Marmur

Michael Livni has written a position essay reflecting his unique and important voice in the debate about Reform Zionism. He provides contextualization and explores the contemporary challenge of strengthening the place of Israel in the identity of Reform Jews. He also offers a critique of many of the institutions within the Reform Movement that are charged with this complex task. As representatives from the educational arm dedicated to the preparation of the future leadership of the Movement, the two of us have decided to co-author this response in an attempt to contribute to a unified conversation; one which bridges the Great Divide between Israel and the Diaspora. Although differences — cultural and political — separate these perspectives, lines of division do not run in a simple way between Diaspora and Israel. Rather, the relationship between Jews "here" and "there" (as the Talmud phrases the distinction) is far more nuanced and complex. We believe that it is possible to gain depth of vision by fusing the two perspectives.

Given our institutional commitment to training Reform religious leaders in both Israel and the Diaspora, we need to develop a unified vision that articulates the role of Jewish peoplehood in shaping Reform Jewish identity. And indeed, Israel is at the heart of any conversation about Jewish peoplehood.

Attempts to deepen awareness of, and commitment to, Jewish peoplehood in North America and elsewhere are taking place on many levels. In recent years the Reform Movement has dedicated itself to cultivating a stronger sense of Jewish peoplehood, through symbolic acts such as the unification of NFTY (the North American Federation of Temple Youth) with Netzer Olami (the network of Reform Zionist youth movements), the revitalization of ARZA (the Association of Reform Zionists of America), the establishment of post-high school programmes such as Carmel at the Leo Baeck Education Center and the University of Haifa, and the recent upsurge in enrollment of high school students at the Eisendrath International Exchange programme. Congregational trips to Israel and elsewhere in the Jewish world are flourishing. Indeed, in a February 2006 survey of Reform educators in North America, 80 percent of respondents noted that their congregation has recently been to Israel, or is planning to bring a group within a year.

It might be tempting to conclude that all these indicators demonstrate that the sense of affiliation to the Jewish people is higher than ever within the Reform movement, but alas this is not the case. Indeed, there is ample evidence — anecdotal and empirical — to suggest that we are currently witnessing a significant disconnect between the lay and professional leadership of the Reform movement in this regard. For example, in a recent survey of current HUC students, 78 percent reported they were either satisfied or very satisfied with how their training prepared them for connection to, and familiarity with, Israel. Yet, only 3 percent noted that this connection to, and familiarity with, Israel would contribute significantly to their professional success. Similarly, educational initiatives within the Reform movement seem to fall far short of their goals with regard to the teaching of Israel. The same 2006 survey of Reform educators cited above revealed a significant disconnect between those who espoused a goal of connecting Israel education to Reform Jewish life (41 percent) and those who set a specific curricular objective to achieve that goal (17 percent). Likewise, 48 percent of respondents noted that one of their three top educational goals was to encourage travel to Israel, yet only 17 percent listed travel as a specific curricular objective.

These findings are sadly contextualized by examining Reform Jewish attitudes and behaviours as reported in the 2000–1 National Jewish Population Study (NJPS). Here, Reform Jews report lower levels of attachment to Israel than either of the other two major denominations. Reform Jews travel to Israel less often, and send their children to Israel less often as well. Indeed, only about 38 percent of Reform Jews say they strongly agree with the statement that Jews in the US and elsewhere around the world share a common destiny, as compared to 51 percent of Conservative and 72 percent of Orthodox Jews who strongly agree with this statement.

These data are evidence of a well-documented decline in a sense of ethnic connection among Jews in North America (and elsewhere). This is particularly salient amongst younger Jews, who are emblematic of an ethos that allows for and even celebrates the personal freedom and the constructed nature of identity in a post-ethnic world. Given this contemporary reality, we understand that we cannot recover or impose a singular ideological focus on Jewish peoplehood. The idea of total immersion in one or another aspect of Jewish expression is neither possible nor desirable from our perspective. Rather, we understand our educational and theological goal to be the provision of a complex weave of materials, sources, and experiences. As in all weavings, the warp begins with a fixed foundation, which in our case is rooted in Jewish traditions, sources and values. Individuals create the wool by interweaving their own textures and colors through that foundation to create a pattern that fits with their lives.

In our view, one of the foundational strands of any Jewish tapestry must be that of Jewish peoplehood and Israel. A Jewish identity devoid of that strong sense of peoplehood is a "thin" identity that will be difficult to sustain over time. Without this essential dimension, Jewish life becomes narrow, attenuated, and will ultimately unravel. Against this backdrop, the need to articulate and effectuate a compelling vision of peoplehood education for the future leadership of our movement is so much the greater.

Let us consider two focal activities currently underway that are designed to redress the absence of a strong sense of connection to either Israel or Jewish peoplehood in Reform Jewish identity. The first is within ARZA (the Association of Reform Zionists of America), an affiliate of the Union for Reform Judaism, the central body of the Reform Movement of North America. The second is the Year in Israel programme of the Hebrew Union College, which is mandatory for rabbinical and cantorial students at all Stateside campuses, as well as for education students enrolled at the Rhea Hirsch School of Jewish Education at HUC in Los Angeles.

In fulfillment of its mission of Israel advocacy and education, ARZA has taken the lead in striving to develop a greater consciousness about Israel and Jewish peoplehood in the daily lives of Reform Jews. Over the past two years, this work has emanated from a Think Tank whose members represent a rich cross-section of academics, rabbinical students, congregational rabbis, educators, and Reform Jewish lay leaders committed to developing a sophisticated ideological and philosophical foundation for new policies and programmes focused on strengthening both a Zionist consciousness within American Reform Judaism and a liberal religious consciousness among Jews in Israel. The Think Tank's work takes place in three domains:

(1) the ongoing intellectual exploration and deliberation on the many dimensions of the central question: "Why should Israel matter to Reform Jews?";
(2) the translation of these ideas into educational products, including publications and programmatic materials for congregations and other educational settings; and
(3) ongoing advocacy for broader integration of Israel and the Jewish peoplehood into not just what it means to be a Reform Zionist, but what it means to be a Reform Jew.

The Think Tank also creates a bridge between North American and Israeli initiatives to define and strengthen Reform Zionist identity. Israeli representatives of the Israel Movement for Progressive Judaism participate in the North American Think Tank and, starting in 2006, ARZA supported the development of a parallel initiative in Israel. This Israeli counterpart has begun to generate working papers and project ideas to further its goals for fostering Reform Jewish identity, both in Israel and the Diaspora.

Over the last five years, Israel education has come to play a central role in the HUC Year in Israel programme, and today it constitutes some 25 percent of the formal curriculum. However, we recognize that further work needs to be done to help students develop a stronger personal connection to contemporary Israel. Like many programmes and curricula, the Year in Israel programme aims to meet a number of goals, and often the tension between these goals for priority and emphasis is tangible. Some of our interlocutors would be happy to see the majority of the year given over to experiential education and ideological formation, while others are primarily concerned about the programme's academic goals. For some, it is the Hebrew of the streets we should be teaching, and for others the Hebrew of the Bible and the Mishnah. We are convinced that it is possible to build a programme in which these goals can serve each other, rather than compete. At the time of writing, an unprecedentedly frank conversation is taking place within the College community, with a view to giving the Israel and Peoplehood component its due place in the programme, both in Jerusalem and in the subsequent years of the programme.

The attempt to restructure the Year in Israel Program is rooted in the goal of helping students recognize that a commitment to Israel and the Jewish people are core ingredients of Reform Jewish identity. Ultimately, we hope that at the close of their year in Israel, students will be able to comfortably and coherently articulate an answer for themselves as to "why Israel matters" — to themselves first and foremost, and to Reform Jews in general. This kind of exploration must include intellectual inquiry, but also requires experiential activities that allow for meaningful and sustained encounters with a broad mix of Israelis, as well as opportunities for personal reflection on the significance of Israel and the Jewish people to their own lives as American Jews and as future leaders of the Reform Jewish community.

To meet this goal, a number of practical steps are now being seriously contemplated.

Our first initiatives in this arena will be to strengthen the American students' connections and interactions with Reform Jews in Israel. We will do this through a variety of means that will affect the programme's content and structure. Internally, we will align the academic calendars of our Israeli and North American programmes, so that the programmes may be better integrated. We also plan to introduce a Hebrew standard for completion of the course which will require continued Hebrew studies for those who have not gone sufficiently far during their time in Jerusalem.

One under-utilized weapon in our educational arsenal is the link between our students and the communities of Israeli Progressive Judaism. Like ARZA's initiatives in collaboration, we see that the potential for developing closer personal relationships among Reform Jews in Israel and North America will benefit all concerned. To that end, we plan to initiate a more active programme of twinning between our students and Israeli students and families. This will include creating internships in Reform communities in Israel and opportunities for North American students to shadow Israeli Reform rabbis working in the field.

Both the ARZA and HUC initiatives address the future of Reform Judaism. We believe that our task to foster "thicker" Reform Jewish identity is inextricably bound up with our challenge of creating both immanent and transcendent connections to Israel and the Jewish people. This begins by enriching aspects of Reform Jewish life that people already connect to and know something about, through conversations, texts, and images about Israel, personal encounters with Israelis, and, of course, visits to Israel.

Our work must not shy away from the complex realities. The days in which hearts and minds could be won through ideological rhetoric or fervent sloganizing have passed. If we are to teach our students and ourselves to weave, we will need to find a place in the fabric for dark shades and rough textures.

Our aim is not to raise the price of Israel stock at the expense of some other component of contemporary Jewish identity. It is rather to regard a sensitivity to the lived reality of Jewish peoplehood, and in its particular manifestation, Jewish political sovereignty, as a necessary strand in a great and rich creation — a Judaism so "thick" it can provide resilience, warmth and meaning.

6

The Jewish Left, Jewish Identity, Zionism and Israel: Attitudes to the Palestinian Intifada, 2000–2005

Philip Mendes

Prior to the Holocaust, Jews were sharply divided over the question of Zionism. Many Jews strongly opposed Zionism on political or religious grounds. Some feared that support for the creation of a Jewish state in Palestine would provoke accusations of dual loyalties. Jewish socialists, including the numerically significant Bundists, opposed Zionism as a reactionary diversion from the task of fighting anti-Semitism and defending Jewish rights in the Diaspora. Many Reform and assimilated Jews defined their Jewishness in solely religious rather than ethnic terms. And most Orthodox Jews believed that the rebuilding of the Jewish homeland must await the coming of the Messiah.[1]

However, following the Holocaust and the creation of the State of Israel in 1948, organized Jewish opposition to Zionism largely vanished. The creation of Israel was seen as a form of compensation for the Holocaust and many years of Jewish persecution. Jews increasingly came to see support for Zionism and Israel as a fundamental component of their Jewish identity. This has particularly been the case in English-speaking countries such as Australia, the United Kingdom, and the USA.

For example, a 1991 survey of Melbourne Jews asked how they felt when international events put Israel in danger. Twenty-eight percent stated that their feelings would be "as strong as if danger was to self", whilst more than half (58 percent) responded that they would feel "special alarm because it is Israel". Another 12 percent indicated they would be "more concerned than if it was another country", and only 2 percent would feel "the same as if any country was in danger".[2]

A more recent study found that the centrality of Israel to Australian Jewish life and identity was reflected in, and reinforced by, the following communal structures and frameworks: the significant political influence of Zionist organizations, Zionist education in the Jewish day-school system, high participation rates in the Zionist youth movements, the pro-Israel activities of Jewish university student groups, regular coverage of Israel in the Jewish media, extensive fund-raising for Israel, a high number of visits to Israel and a disproportionate rate of aliyah, and significant political advocacy on behalf of Israel.[3]

Similarly, a survey of British Jews found that they supported Israel through fund-raising activities, political advocacy, and emigration to Israel. Eighty percent expressed a strong or moderate attachment to Israel, 77 percent had visited Israel, and 67 percent had close friends or relatives living in Israel. Overall there was a close relationship between personal and emotional attachment to Israel, and Jewish identity.[4] US studies have also confirmed the centrality of Israel to Jewish life and identity as reflected in communal structures, fund-raising, political activity, education, and religious observance.[5]

One manifestation of this pro-Israel identity has been the belief that Diaspora Jews should unite in support of Israeli policies. This unified support is seen as enhancing Israel's international standing. Conversely, Diaspora Jewish criticism of Israel is depicted as dividing the Jewish people, and giving heart to those who wish to harm the State of Israel. This attitude is dominant in English-speaking Jewish communities, and has been reflected in constant attempts to censor or silence the minority of Jews who do not support Israel.[6]

Nevertheless, a number of Jewish Left groups in all English-speaking countries do publicly dissent from Israeli policies. Some of these groups (for example, Peace Now UK and Meretz USA) are influenced by Left Zionist beliefs, some (for example, US Jewish Voice for Peace, UK Jews for Justice for Palestinians) call themselves non-Zionist, and others (for example, UK Jews Against Zionism) are openly socialist and anti-Zionist. What they all have in common is that they explicitly reject the dominant link between Jewish identity and pro-Israel views. Instead, they base their judgements of Israel on a commitment to broader universalistic concerns and ideas,[7] and demand that Jews recognize the suffering and rights of the Palestinians as well as Israel.[8]

These groups vary in the way they construct the relationship between their Jewish identity and the State of Israel. The Left Zionist groups tend to view support for Zionism and Israel as a positive component of their identity. But this solidarity with Israel is compromised by allegedly oppressive Israeli actions towards the Palestinians, which these groups reject on moral and political grounds. They see their role as that of an internal critic seeking to reshape Israeli policies in a progressive direction.[9]

The other two groups tend to see Israel as primarily a negative factor in their Jewish identity. The reality of Israel is something they would probably prefer to ignore, but the dynamics of anti-Zionist and sometimes overtly anti-Semitic politics on the Left force them to take a stand. The non-Zionist groups reject Israeli policies towards the Palestinians as contrary to the progressive values and ideas that they hold dear. Compared to Left Zionist groups, they maintain a detachment from both Zionism and internal Israeli politics, although they, too, offer support for Israeli Left and peace groups.[10]

The anti-Zionist groups actively seek to dissociate themselves and their Jewish identity from Zionism and the State of Israel. For example, some British Jews have openly renounced their right to Israeli citizenship under the "Law of Return". They suggest that Israel does not provide a haven for Jews fleeing anti-Semitism, and that in fact Israeli policies are responsible for creating anti-Semitism. These Jews reject any notion of ethnic or religious solidarity with Israeli Jews whom they regard as the oppressors. Rather, their principal sympathies lie with the victims of Israel.[11]

This chapter explores the attitudes of three Jewish Left groups to Zionism and Israel — the Australian Jewish Democratic Society (AJDS), the UK Jewish Socialist Group (JSG), and Tikkun Magazine/Community — with particular reference to the period of the second Palestinian Intifada 2000–2005. Attention is drawn to how their views of Israel differ from the Jewish mainstream, the impact on their relationship with other Jews, and also their relationship with broader Left groups.

The Australian Jewish Democratic Society (AJDS)

AJDS was formed in November 1984 as "A progressive voice among Jews" and "A Jewish voice among progressives". These dual objectives ensured that AJDS would experience an ongoing tension or conflict between its specific Jewish loyalties, and its commitment to broader Left or universalistic causes. Members came from a range of Left and civil libertarian backgrounds, including the Communist Party, the Australian Labour Party, the Jewish Labour Bund, left Zionist groups, and various brands of Trotskyist and even Maoist organizations. Most are secular or assimilated, although there is also a smattering of traditional Orthodox and liberal Reform Jews. The majority of activists are between 45 and 60 years old, with very few in the younger age group.[12]

Four specific political aims were identified by AJDS. The first was to support activities for peace, and nuclear and general disarmament. The second was to oppose racism and anti-Semitism, and promote tolerance and harmony between ethnic communities. The third was to support the legitimate aims of the Aboriginal people including land rights. The fourth was to support peace in the Middle East based on justice and national rights for both Israelis and Palestinians.

In short, AJDS supported an Israeli withdrawal from the West Bank and Gaza Strip, and mutual recognition between Israel and the Palestinians (including the PLO) leading to a two state solution. Whilst never formally linked to the Israeli peace movement, AJDS was strongly influenced by prominent peace groups such as Peace Now and the International Centre for Peace in the Middle East. Most AJDS members and supporters would probably have supported the group of dovish parties combined in the Meretz alliance which was recently renamed the Yahad Party. AJDS was never an anti-Zionist organization, but did express some ambivalence on the question of Zionism. That is, they were reluctant to accept the view held by most Jews that support for Israel was synonymous with contemporary Jewish identity and collectivity.

AJDS was strongly critical of Israeli government policies, particularly in regards to the building of settlements in the West Bank, the refusal to exchange land for peace, and the violent suppression of the first Palestinian Intifada. These criticisms provoked regular conflict with the major Jewish organizations. However, the signing of the Oslo Peace Accord in 1993 narrowed the gap between AJDS views and mainstream Jewish opinion, and led to AJDS' affiliation with the Jewish Community Council of Victoria (JCCV).[13]

The outbreak of the second Palestinian Intifada in September 2000 led to renewed friction between AJDS and mainstream Jewish opinion. These tensions reflected communal perceptions that AJDS gave greater priority to endearing itself to its allies on the Left, rather than addressing specifically Jewish concerns and sensitivities.[14] AJDS' approach has consistently been influenced by universalistic assumptions: that judgments of Israeli actions and policies should be based on a broad concern for human rights, peace and justice,[15] rather than the narrower tribal solidarity with Israel favored by most Jews.

AJDS specifically rejects the dominant Jewish belief that Jews should display solidarity with their own people, avoid internal dissent, and show a united front to others.[16] Instead, they aim to persuade Australian Jews to "take a more objective approach", "to see both sides of the situation",[17] and "to understand the Palestinians as real people with real aspirations, rather than an enemy motivated purely by an evil desire to destroy Israel".[18]

AJDS spokespersons regularly describe themselves as "strong supporters of Israel, but not uncritical supporters",[19] and reject the notion "that right and justice are purely on one side of the conflict".[20] One AJDS statement added, "just as we mourn every Jewish death, so we mourn every Palestinian death. Let us not forget that four times as many Palestinians as Jews have been killed since the Intifada began last year".[21]

AJDS actions have incorporated a number of key strategies and agendas. Firstly, they have engaged in dialogue with, and sought to identify, common ground with local Palestinian and Arab groups. For example, AJDS participated in a Jewish–Muslim Women's Group called Salaam Shalom,[22] hosted a number of Palestinian speakers including Taimor Hazou,[23] invited Palestinian asylum seeker Aladdin Sisalem to their annual dinner,[24] and prepared statements for delivery to Palestinian rallies.[25] AJDS also agreed to participate in a protest vigil against the visit of former Israeli Prime Minister Benjamin Netanyahu.[26] Although AJDS formally withdrew from the rally at the last moment in response to a major Palestinian terrorist attack in Jerusalem,[27] more than 50 AJDS members still participated in the rally, including AJDS Publicity Officer David Zyngier who spoke to the media on behalf of the organization.[28]

Secondly, AJDS have questioned mainstream Jewish and Israeli arguments regarding the failure of Camp David, and the factors contributing to the outbreak of the Intifada. For example, AJDS blamed Ariel Sharon's visit to the Temple Mount for provoking the initial Palestinian violence, and condemned ongoing violence from both the Israeli and Palestinian sides.[29] They denied that the Barak Government had made the Palestinians a "generous offer", arguing that the continuing presence of Jewish settlements would have frustrated geographic contiguity. Instead, they argued that the creation of a genuinely viable, contiguous, and independent Palestinian State was necessary for peace.[30]

Later AJDS statements placed much of the blame for the continuing violence on the policies of the Sharon Government. To be sure, AJDS unequivocally condemned Palestinian suicide bombings and acts of terror.[31] But they also suggested that the root cause of the conflict was the ongoing Israeli occupation of the West Bank and Gaza Strip, and the oppression and suffering of the Palestinian people.[32] AJDS condemned the Israeli invasion of the Palestinian West Bank cities in April 2002 as "totally out of proportion to the violence that provoked the Israeli action".[33] They also condemned the Israeli actions in the Jenin refugee camp as "morally repugnant", whilst rejecting Palestinian accusations of a massacre.[34]

AJDS also criticized Israel's construction of the security fence or wall in the

Territories, arguing that "the only way to escape the cycle of violence is to recognize the Palestinians as partners instead of seeing them as enemies".[35] AJDS endorsed the Geneva Accord, the unofficial Israeli/Palestinian peace agreement based on a two-state solution.[36] In addition, AJDS proposed in-principle support for the right of return of 1948 Palestinian refugees to their original homes. AJDS qualified this statement by adding that "our support for the right of return is not an unconditional support and any agreement on this issue would need to maintain Israel as a Jewish state".[37] A further clarification indicated that "Israel cannot settle an unlimited number of returning refugees. Compensation and re-settlement of refugees in the emerging Palestinian state will be the key to resolution of the refugee tragedy".[38]

Nevertheless, this apparent endorsement of Palestinian demands for a right of return appeared to place AJDS totally outside the mainstream Jewish and Israeli Left. Most leading Israeli peace activists including David Grossman, Amos Oz and the Peace Now group have denounced the right of return as code for the destruction of Israel.[39] A later AJDS statement denied that the organization had ever supported a Palestinian right of return.[40] The equivocal stance taken on the right of return seems to typify the challenges faced by AJDS in attempting to reconcile both its specifically Jewish and broader universalistic loyalties.

AJDS has also rejected mainstream Jewish concerns over alleged political and media bias against Israel. For example, AJDS has denied that the public broadcaster SBS is biased against Israel, and argues that, on the contrary, SBS promotes a diversity of views on the Middle East.[41] AJDS also defended a parliamentary motion by Labour MP Julia Irwin calling for an unconditional Israeli withdrawal to the pre-1967 borders — a stance which most Jews regarded as one-sided and unbalanced.[42] And AJDS opposed the Jewish campaign against the awarding of the Sydney Peace Prize to Palestinian academic, Dr Hanan Ashrawi. AJDS argued that Ashrawi was a worthy candidate for the prize, given her support for two states, and her joint activities with members of the Israeli peace movement.[43]

AJDS' criticisms of Israeli policies resulted in confrontation with mainstream Jewish groups, and some attempts were made to paint AJDS as "self-hating Jews" and traitors to the Jewish community.[44] There were also some threats of violence by right-wing Jews towards AJDS. At a Jewish Solidarity with Israel rally in September 2001, AJDS members handing out peace leaflets were harassed, vilified and physically attacked by a group of young religious activists.[45] The AJDS perspective regarding such hostility is that they have been unfairly "demonized" for expressing views shared by many within the Israeli Left and peace movement.[46]

AJDS has criticized the views of far Left anti-Zionist fundamentalist groups such as the International Socialist Organisation which regard Israel as a racist and colonialist state that has no right to exist,[47] and has also rejected the proposed academic boycott of Israel.[48] Nevertheless, AJDS has also entered into dialogue with radical groups such as the International Solidarity Movement (ISM) which do not recognize Israel's right to exist.[49]

AJDS argues that its involvement with the broader Left helps to prevent or at least minimize the presence of anti-Semitic slogans or rhetoric within the anti-war movement.[50] For example, AJDS took credit for a number of Palestinian groups joining a Jewish-organized protest against the airing of a film by Holocaust denier, David Irving.[51]

The UK Jewish Socialist Group (JSG)

JSG is a political organization which campaigns "for Jewish rights and for the rights of all oppressed minorities in building a socialist future". [52] The group was established in 1974 to counter the growing threat posed by the fascist National Front, and the increasing tendency on the Left to provide uncritical support for Arab nationalism, and to slip from anti-Zionist to overtly anti-Jewish rhetoric.[53]

JSG favor a "socialist solution to the Israel–Palestine conflict based on equality and self determination for Israeli and Palestinian Jews and Arabs". [54] Historically, the JSG's stance on Israel resembled a Left Zionist or non-Zionist position. They defended Israel's right to exist, and favored a two-state position based on negotiations between the Israeli Government and the PLO. But over time JSG shifted to a Bundist (and anti-Zionist) perspective which rejected the centrality of Israel, and critiqued the detrimental impact of Zionism on Diaspora Jewish communities. JSG argue that history has confirmed "the basic Bundist argument that you cannot turn an international people into a one-nation people in a one-nation state".[55]

JSG has also been vigorously critical of Israel's repression of the Palestinians, and identifies with radical Left and peace groups inside Israel. Such JSG positions provoked a backlash from mainstream Jewish groups, and overt instances of violence from right-wing Zionist organizations.[56]

Today, JSG members come from three principal backgrounds: ex-Zionists including former *kibbutzniks*, members of ex-Communist Party families, and people from working class backgrounds. Most members are aged 40–65 years old. JSG remains a socialist organization given that "for us it is still much more natural to be a Jew and a Socialist than to be a Jew and right wing".[57]

JSG aims to "counter myths about the shrinking, dying and assimilating Diaspora by affirming the vitality of Jewish communities across the world".[58] JSG "rejects the negative ideology of Zionism which undermines Diaspora communities by insisting on the centrality of Israel to Jewish life and by subordinating the political, economic and cultural needs of Diaspora communities to the demands of the Israeli state".[59]

Since the outbreak of the second Palestinian Intifada, JSG have campaigned against Israel's repression and brutality in the Occupied Territories. For example, JSG have participated in a number of joint activities with Palestinian groups, including weekly protests outside the Israeli Embassy,[60] organized and participated in forums with Israeli and Palestinian speakers,[61] publicized the Palestinian view of Barak's offer at Camp David,[62] and sought to highlight internal dissent within Israel, including the significant number of soldiers (known as "refuseniks") refusing to serve within the Territories.[63]

JSG have criticized Left Zionist groups such as Friends of Peace Now for allegedly sitting on the fence, and refusing to publicly air criticisms of Israel and local Jewish apologists for the Sharon Government.[64] However, JSG have formed coalitions with newer organizations such as Jews for Justice with Palestinians (mainly comprised of academics) and Just Peace UK which seek to incorporate a broader grouping of left-wing Jews. In May 2002, the three groups organized a counter-protest of about 400 people to the large 55,000 strong "Solidarity with Israel" rally organized by mainstream Jewish groups in Trafalgar Square.

According to JSG activist David Rosenberg:

> We had to put up with a lot of verbal abuse, you know where all these people come along and say you should have died in Auschwitz, but actually some people who came to the main rally came to join ours. Our protest included slogans against the Occupation, about the reality of people getting killed, so some people engaged and had a lot of discussion with us, whereas others were abusive.[65]

JSG argue that the only solution to the conflict is an end to the Israeli occupation of the Territories, the removal of all Jewish settlements, and the establishment of Palestinian self-determination and statehood with Jerusalem as the shared capital of both Israel and the Palestinian state. JSG firmly oppose Palestinian suicide bombings, but equally they defend the Palestinian right to statehood irrespective of the "violence of the oppressed Palestinian people against the Israeli state, against its occupying settlers and soldiers, or by the terrible attacks on its citizens".

JSG call on Diaspora Jews to "cross real and invisible community boundaries to act in solidarity with the Palestinian people in their struggle for self-determination".[66] JSG specifically reject claims by Israel that it "acts on behalf of Jews worldwide".[67] Their form of Jewish identity is based on universalistic values and ideals, rather than any form of narrow association with the Jewish nation state.

JSG also support the principle of a Palestinian right of return, stating:

> We recognize that refugees everywhere in the world have a right to return home and that includes the Palestinians. We also recognize that in practice, there is probably going to be a mixed solution, some people returning and some people receiving compensation. We don't believe that the future security of the Jews in Israel necessarily depends on demographics.[68]

JSG's unequivocal critique of Israeli policies has led to ongoing conflict with mainstream Jewish groups. David Rosenberg notes that the *Jewish Chronicle* is reluctant to publish JSG letters, or even to report on JSG activities.[69] At the same time, JSG has had conflict with groups on the Left which utilize anti-Jewish rhetoric in their attacks on Israel. For example, JSG have protested manifestations of anti-Semitism in the British pro-Palestinian and anti-war movements, including overt anti-Semitic abuse and the equation of Israel with Nazi Germany, whilst maintaining that a visible Jewish presence helps to reduce such incidents.[70] In addition, JSG have rejected proposals for an academic boycott of Israel on the grounds that such boycotts are discriminatory in that they punish all Israelis, regardless of their political beliefs, on ethnic and national grounds.[71]

The US *Tikkun* Magazine/Community

Tikkun magazine, a bimonthly political journal, was established by Rabbi Michael Lerner in 1986 as a voice for liberal and progressive Jews concerned to "mend, repair and transform the world". A related concern was to introduce non-denominational religious and spiritual values via a "politics of meaning" into social change movements. In recent years, *Tikkun* magazine has expanded into a broader interfaith educational outreach community concerned to promote a world of love, generosity and kindness. Tikkun supporters include atheists, agnostics, and those involved in alternative or traditional spiritual communities, but can generally be categorized as belonging to the spiritual or religious Left.[72]

Tikkun rejects unqualified Jewish support for Israeli policies. Rather, their sympathies lie with those Israeli Left and peace groups which share their progressive values and ideals. They endorse a two-state solution to the Middle East conflict based on an end to the Israeli occupation of the West Bank and Gaza Strip, the evacuation of the Jewish settlements and the return of the settlers to Israel, and the establishment of a Palestinian State alongside Israel. Tikkun urges Israel to take major (though not total) responsibility for the Palestinian refugees including the payment of reparations, but takes no official position on Palestinian demands for a right of return. However, Michael Lerner personally favors a quota system whereby Israel agrees to take back approximately 15,000 refugees per year for the next thirty years.[73]

At the same time, Tikkun calls on the Palestinians to cease terror and violence, to end the demonization of Jews and Israel, to withdraw demands for the immediate return of three million refugees, and to pursue a strategy of nonviolent civil disobedience based on the teachings of Gandhi and Martin Luther King.[74] Tikkun describes Palestinian suicide bombings as "wrong, morally abhorrent, and never justified by reference to some other acts of oppression or murder".[75]

Tikkun provides an overtly universalistic analysis of the conflict which claims to be both pro-Israel and pro-Palestine. According to Michael Lerner, "pathologies and evils have been perpetuated by peoples on both sides . . . both sides have legitimate claims, both sides have legitimate grievances against the other, and both sides have made terrible errors".[76] Lerner aims to provide a "balanced perspective" which "affirms the fundamental decency of people on both sides of this struggle".[77] Tikkun condemns the "sins of tribalism, chauvinism, and thinking our pain is more important than anyone else's pain".[78]

Tikkun also aligns their criticism of Israeli policies with specific Jewish religious and spiritual values and morality, stating "We consider ourselves the true pro-Israel voice, as opposed to those who support the current Israeli government even when its policies are self-destructive and a disgrace to the Jewish teachings of a world based on love and justice and peace."[79] Lerner argues that "the tribalism and ultra-nationalism fostered by Israel and by some of its right-wing supporters is antithetical to the teachings of Torah that demand 'love the stranger' and recognize that every human being is created in the image of God".[80]

Since the outbreak of the Second Intifada, Tikkun has consistently attacked Israeli policies, and argued for the creation of a viable Palestinian State. [81] Tikkun rejected Ehud Barak's explanation of the failure of the Camp David negotiations, arguing that no Palestinian leader could have accepted Israel's offer for fragmented and limited sovereignty. Instead, Tikkun urged the Israelis to dismantle the vast majority of settlements, end all acts of violence by settlers and soldiers against Palestinians, acknowledge their responsibility for the Palestinian refugees, and recognize Palestinian claims to Arab East Jerusalem.[82]

Following the election of the Sharon Government in early 2001, Tikkun denounced Israel's "war of brutality against a mostly unarmed and defenceless population". Reference was made to sieges of Palestinian cities, house demolitions, denial of food and medical care, and other examples of collective punishment. Tikkun claimed that these measures only generated greater support for terrorism, and urged

Israel to address legitimate Palestinian aspirations.[83] Tikkun was highly critical of the major pro-Israel lobby group, the American Israel Public Affairs Committee (AIPAC), describing them "as the pro-Ariel Sharon lobby, who pursue policies which are actually destructive to the best interests of Israel".[84] Tikkun offered strong support for the unofficial Geneva peace accord signed by Yossi Beilin and Yasser Abed Rabbo in October 2003.[85]

Tikkun's support for Palestinian national rights has provoked significant criticism from mainstream and conservative Jewish groups. As Lerner notes, there have been continual attempts to silence Jews who question Israeli policies, including loss of donations, cancellation of magazine subscriptions, and overt death threats.[86]

Tikkun has also attacked left-wing groups and individuals (including Jews) who engage in unbalanced and anti-Semitic criticisms of Israel.[87] For example, Lerner denounced the extreme anti-Zionism propagated by the leading peace coalition group, Act Now To Stop War and End Violence (ANSWER). As a result of this criticism, Lerner was allegedly excluded from speaking at a major anti-war demonstration in San Francisco.[88] Tikkun also denounced the proposed academic boycott of Israel, referring to the "moral blindness and stupidity" involved in boycotting those academics who oppose current Israeli policies.[89] More recently, Tikkun called on members participating in a protest rally against George Bush and the Republican Party Convention to actively confront those who "carry anti-Semitic signs and bring a message of hate".[90]

SUMMARY

All three Jewish Left groups discussed — the Australian Jewish Democratic Society, the Jewish Socialist Group and Tikkun — reject the dominant link between contemporary Jewish identity and pro-Israel views. In contrast to most Diaspora Jews, they do not automatically offer solidarity to the State of Israel and its population. Instead, they define their Jewish identity in more universalistic terms, and judge Israeli actions and policies according to broader political and moral criteria. Their apparently divided loyalties have led to considerable conflict with mainstream Jewish groups.

JSG takes the most radical position in that they explicitly reject the dominant Zionist assumptions on the centrality of Israel in Jewish life. Utilizing Bundist ideology, they argue that Jews remain an international people, and that the needs and concerns of Diaspora communities are just as valid and important as those of Israel. They reject any suggestion that Jews should close ranks behind Israeli policies, and provide a vigorous critique of Israel's treatment of the Palestinians. Nevertheless, they defend in principle the right of Israeli Jews to national self-determination, and are critical of left-wing groups which blur anti-Zionism and anti-Semitism in their defence of Palestinian nationalism.

AJDS also reject any expectation that they should subordinate universalistic rights to specific Jewish concerns and agendas. Utilizing a broad left-wing ideology, they offer a critical and relatively non-partisan analysis of Israeli policies and actions. Whilst describing themselves as supporters of Israel and eschewing any overt criticism of Zionism, they appear in practice to blame Israel for the breakdown of the peace process, and to make far greater political demands on Israel than on the Palestinians.

However, they still defend Israel's right to exist, and reject far Left proposals for a one-state or bi-national solution.

Tikkun is arguably closer to the Jewish mainstream than the other two groups in that they don't overtly reject pro-Israel or Zionist assumptions. Nevertheless, they also adopt a universalistic or middle-path perspective based on reconciling the Israelis and Palestinians, rather than narrowly defending the Israeli perspective. Utilizing broad secular humanist and specifically Jewish religious values, they unequivocally reject the Israeli occupation of the Territories, and what they describe as the ongoing oppression of the Palestinian people. They also condemn Palestinian terror and violence, and critique left-wing groups which articulate unbalanced criticism of Israel.

Whilst all three groups are critical of Israel they still recognize to a greater or lesser degree the important role that Israel plays in Jewish life. This is reflected in the significant time and energy that they devote to the Israeli–Palestinian conflict relative to other prominent national and international issues such as the rights of refugees, the crisis in Sudan, and the war in Iraq. The middle-path views on Israel that they adopt reflect the dilemmas and challenges they face in dealing with their dual Jewish and Left constituencies.

In practice, Jewish Left groups seem to sit on the margins of both the Jewish and Left communities. Their universalistic agendas — including their critical views on Israel — reflect ideological beliefs that emanate from outside the concerns of their own ethnic community. Yet Jewish Left groups cannot divorce themselves completely from the aspirations of most Jews (which includes an overwhelming support for Israel) if they wish to participate in mainstream Jewish life.

Equally, their concern (however ambivalent) with specific Jewish affairs — including the well-being of Israel — poses problems for their acceptance on the Left, which tends to be highly critical of Israel. The price for acceptance is that they adopt (at least in part) the Left's questioning of explicit Jewish national and especially Zionist identity. This means that they can never join the majority of Jews in an unequivocal endorsement of Israel.

As for their impact on Israeli policies and agendas, it appears to be minimal or non-existent. Some Israeli Left groups have at times sought their support, and have actively encouraged their intervention into internal Israeli debates. But Israeli Governments have overwhelmingly ignored their views, contending that only Israeli citizens should be able to participate in Israeli political decisions.

Acknowledgements

I am grateful to David Rosenberg of the Jewish Socialist Group for the interview we conducted in London, and to Steve Brook of the Australian Jewish Democratic Society for his brief response to written questions and his comments on an earlier draft. Thanks also to Rabbi Michael Lerner of *Tikkun* for his comments on an earlier draft.

Notes

1 W.D. Rubinstein, "Zionism and the Jewish People, 1918–1960", *The Jewish Journal of Sociology* 43, 1–2 (2001): 5–36.

2 John Goldlust, *The Jews of Melbourne: A Community Profile* (Melbourne: Jewish Welfare Society, 1993), p. 155.

3 Danny Ben-Moshe, "Pro-Israelism as a Factor in Australian Jewish Political Attitudes and Behaviour" in Geoffrey Levey and Philip Mendes (eds), *Jews and Australian Politics* (Brighton & Portland: Sussex Academic Press, 2004), pp. 128–132.

4 Stephen Miller, Marlena Schmool and Antony Lerman, *Social and political attitudes of British Jews: some key findings of the JPR survey* (London: Institute for Jewish Policy Research, 1996), pp. 7–8.

5 Benjamin Ginsberg, "Identity and Politics: Dilemmas of Jewish Leadership in America" in Sandy Maisel (ed.), *Jews in American Politics* (Oxford: Rowman & Littlefield, 2001), pp. 21–23.

6 For a discussion of the merits and limitations of this argument, see Marla Brettschneider, *Cornerstones of Peace: Jewish Identity Politics and Democratic Theory* (New Brunswick, Rutgers University Press, 1996). See also Peter Medding, "Jewish Politics in Comparative Perspective", in Geoffrey Levey and Philip Mendes (eds), *Jews and Australian Politics* (Brighton: Sussex Academic Press, 2004), p. 233.

7 Philip Mendes, "Censorship or Pluralism: some personal reflections concerning the Australian Jewish debate on Israel", *Generation*, 6, 3 (April 1997): 64–69.

8 Tony Kushner and Alisa Solomon, "Wrestling with Zion: An Introduction" in Tony Kushner and Alisa Solomon (eds), *Wrestling with Zion: Progressive Jewish–American Responses to the Israeli–Palestinian conflict* (New York: Grove Press, 2003), pp. 1–9; Judith Butler, "No, It's Not Anti-Semitic", in Henri Picciotto and Mitchell Plitnick (eds), *Reframing Anti-Semitism: Alternative Jewish Perspectives* (Oakland: Jewish Voice for Peace, 2004), p. 23.

9 See, for example, Susannah Heschel, "Should Jews relinquish the right of return? No" in *Wrestling with Zion*, pp. 294–95.

10 See Ellen Lippmann, "Doing Activism, Working for Peace: A Roundtable Discussion" in *Wrestling with Zion*, pp. 351–52.

11 Melanie Kaye/Kantrowitz, "Returning the Law of Return" in *Wrestling with Zion*, pp. 284–86. See also Alisa Solomon, "Intifada Diptych", ibid., pp. 301–313; Steven Feuerstein, "Doing Activism, Working for Peace: A Roundtable Discussion", ibid., p. 351, and Joel Kovel, ibid., p. 354.

12 Email from AJDS Executive member Steve Brook, 12 July 2004.

13 Philip Mendes, "Australian Jewish Dissent on Israel: a history of the Australian Jewish Democratic Society (Part 1)", *Australian Jewish Historical Society Journal* 15, 1 (1999): 117–138; Philip Mendes, "Australian Jewish Dissent on Israel: a history of the Australian Jewish Democratic Society (Part 2)", *Australian Jewish Historical Society Journal* 15(3): 459–474.

14 Philip Mendes, "Think the Jewish left is politically bankrupt? Think again", *Australian Jewish News*, 20 December 2002.

15 *AJDS Newsletter*, August 2003, p. 2. See also Harold Zwier, *Address to Australian Fabian Society "Paths to Peace in the Middle East Forum"*, 28 July 2004.

16 AJDS statement to Palestine Solidarity Rally, 12 November 2000.

17 *AJDS Newsletter*, December 2001, pp. 11 & 14. For similar sentiments, see *AJDS Newsletter*, December 2002, pp. 10–11.

18 Harold Zwier, Address to AJDS Annual General Meeting, 3 February 2002.

19 AJDS statement to Palestine Solidarity Rally, 12 November 2000. This speech was never delivered due to a last-minute change of mind from both AJDS and the rally organizers. See Brandon Cohen, "Jewish Democrats withdraw from Palestinian rally", *Australian Jewish News*, 1 December 2000.

20 AJDS Statement to Palestinian Rally, 7 April 2001.

21 *AJDS Newsletter*, December 2001, p. 2.

22 *AJDS Newsletter*, August 2002, p. 2.

23 *AJDS Newsletter*, April 2001; Mark Briskin, "Sharon compared to Kalejs", *Australian Jewish News*, 2 March 2001.
24 David Langsam, "Sights on peace", *Australian Jewish News*, 25 June 2004.
25 Chantal Abitbol and Mark Briskin, "Jews join Palestinian rallies", *Australian Jewish News*, 13 April 2001.
26 Mark Briskin, "Bibi protests likely at Chabad House", *Australian Jewish News*, 10 August 2001.
27 Harold Zwier, "AJDS protest", *Australian Jewish News*, 31 August 2001.
28 *AJDS Newsletter*, September 2001, p. 7; Larissa Dubecki and Chloe Saltau, "St Kilda, for a day, is a M-E hotspot", *The Age*, 13 August 2001; James Crafti, "Protest and counter-protest greet Netanyahu", *Green Left Weekly*, 22 August 2001; Mark Briskin, "Tense demonstrations outside 770", *Australian Jewish News*, 17 August 2001.
29 *AJDS Newsletter*, November 2000, p. 2; December 2000, p. 11; Harold Zwier, "Sharon's provocation is unforgivable", *The Age*, 5 October 2000; Harold Zwier, "Extremists take charge in Israel", *The Australian*, 6 October 2000.
30 *AJDS Newsletter*, February 2001, p. 2; March 2001, p. 4; April 2001, p. 5; Harold Zwier, "The real issues", *Australian Jewish News*, 16 February 2001.
31 *AJDS Newsletter*, September–October 2003, p. 1.
32 Renate Kamener and Steve Brook, "Slur campaign on AJDS", *Australian Jewish News*, 4 June 2004.
33 *AJDS Newsletter*, April 2002, p. 11. See also p. 8; Renata Kamener et al., "Palestine's pain", *The Australian*, 13 April 2002.
34 *AJDS Newsletter*, May 2002, p. 6.
35 *AJDS Newsletter*, August 2003, p. 1; February 2004, p. 1. See also Harold Zwier, "Israelis and Palestinians on a road to hopelessness", *The Age*, 2 September 2003.
36 *AJDS Newsletter*, December 2003, pp. 1–6; January 2004, pp. 3–6. For the details of the Geneva Accord, see Yossi Beilin, *The Path To Geneva* (New York: RDV Books, 2004).
37 AJDS statement to Palestinian Rally, 7 April 2001, and AJDS statement to Palm Sunday Peace Rally, May 2001. See also Alana Rosenbaum, "Jewish protestors campaign for Palestinians", *Australian Jewish News*, 13 April 2001.
38 David Zyngier, "Remembering when we'd rather forget", *Australian Jewish News*, 13 April 2001.
39 Amos Oz, "Israel's Doves Must Reconsider", *The Age*, 11 January 2001; David Grossman, *Death as a Way of Life* (London: Bloomsbury, 2003), pp. 99–104.
40 Renate Kamener and Steve Brook, "AJDS Proposal", *Australian Jewish News*, 9 July 2004.
41 *AJDS Newsletter*, November 2002, p. 10.
42 *AJDS Newsletter*, December 2002, p. 2. See also Matt Price, "MPs fire barbs in Israeli troop row", *The Australian*, 12 November 2002.
43 *AJDS Newsletter*, September-October 2003, p. 5; November 2003, p. 3; Anon, "Jewish group rejects campaign against Hanan Ashrawi", *Green Left Weekly*, 29 October 2003. For a detailed discussion of this controversy, see Geoffrey Levey and Philip Mendes, "The Hanan Ashrawi Affair: Australian Jewish Politics on Display" in Geoffrey Levey and Philip Mendes (eds.), *Jews and Australian Politics* (Brighton & Portland: Sussex Academic Press, 2004), pp. 215–230.
44 Peter Kohn, "Pro-Peace or pro-Palestinian?", *Australian Jewish News*, 20 June 2003.
45 *AJDS Newsletter*, October 2001, p. 7; Renate Kamener, "Joining the protest", *Australian Jewish News*, 28 September 2001; Harold Zwier, "Suitable solidarity", *Australian Jewish News*, 12 October 2001.
46 Email from Steve Brook, 12 July 2004.
47 *AJDS Newsletter*, August 2001, p. 3.
48 *AJDS* Newsletter, June 2002, p. 1. For a critique of the academic boycott proposal, see

Philip Mendes, "Much Ado About Nothing? The Academic Boycott of Israel Down Under", *Midstream* 50, 2 (2004), pp. 9–13.

49 *AJDS Newsletter*, May 2003, p. 3; April 2004, p. 3; May 2004, p. 2; Andra Jackson, "Palestinian arrives with non-violence message for all", *The Age*, 15 March 2004.

50 *AJDS Newsletter*, May 2003, p. 2.

51 *AJDS Newsletter*, July 2003, p. 3; *Green Left Weekly*, 23 July 2003.

52 Jewish Socialist Group, *Join the Jewish Socialists' Group* (London: JSG, 2005).

53 Anon, "Our History" (London: Jewish Socialist Group, 2004), <www.jewishsocialist.org.uk/history1.html>; Charlie Pottins, "Looking Back", *Jewish Socialist*, 44, Spring (2001), pp. 30–31.

54 Jewish Socialist Group, *Join the Jewish Socialists' Group.*

55 Interview with David Rosenberg in London, 22 May 2004.

56 David Rosenberg, "It's our community too", *Jewish Socialist*, 41, Spring (2000), pp. 3 & 25; Anon, "Our History".

57 Interview with David Rosenberg.

58 *Jewish Socialist*, 42, Summer/Autumn (2000), p. 35.

59 Jewish Socialist Group, *Join the Jewish Socialists' Group.*

60 *Jewish Socialist*, 43, Winter (2000–2001), p. 3; 44, Spring (2001), p. 4.

61 *Jewish Socialist*, 45, Autumn–Winter (2001), p. 3.

62 *Jewish Socialist*, 48, Summer (2003), p. 8.

63 *Jewish Socialist*, 47, Winter (2002–2003), p. 2.

64 *Jewish Socialist*, 44, Spring (2001), p. 3.

65 Interview with David Rosenberg.

66 *Jewish Socialist*, 46, Spring (2002), p. 2.

67 Jewish Socialist Group, "JSG statement on Israel and Palestine" (London: Jewish Socialist Group, 2000), <www.jewishsocialist.org.uk/statement.html>.

68 Interview with David Rosenberg.

69 Ibid.

70 *Jewish Socialist*, 46, Spring (2002), p. 17; 47, Winter (2002–2003), pp. 5–7; 48, Summer (2003), pp. 30–31; David Rosenberg, "Tam Dalyell's mistake", *The Guardian*, 19 May 2003.

71 *Jewish Socialist*, 47, Winter (2002–2003), pp. 10–14; Interview with David Rosenberg.

72 *Tikkun*, 16, 5 (September–October 2001), pp. 9–19; 19, 5 (September–October 2004), p. 82.

73 Michael Lerner, *Healing Israel/Palestine* (San Francisco: Tikkun Books, 2003), pp. 166–167.

74 Michael Lerner, *Healing Israel/*Palestine, pp. 129–138; *Tikkun*, 17, 3 (May–June 2002), p. 10; 17, 4 (July–August 2002), pp. 7–12; 18, 5 (September–October 2003), p. 11.

75 *Tikkun*, 18, 1 (January–February 2003), p. 12.

76 Michael Lerner, *Healing Israel/*Palestine, p. xvii.

77 Ibid., pp. xiii & xviii.

78 *Tikkun*, 20, 5 (September–October 2005), *High Holiday Supplement.*

79 *Tkkun*, 17, 2 (March–April 2002), p. 10.

80 Email from Rabbi Michael Lerner to author, 8 September 2004.

81 *Tikkun*, 15, 5 (September–October 2000), pp. 6–7;

82 *Tikkun*, 15, 6 (November–December 2000), pp. 7–10; 16, 1 (January–February 2001), pp. 10 & 27; 16, 2 (March–April 2001), p. 5; 16, 5 (September–October 2001), pp. 7–8; 17, 2 (March–April 2002), p. 9; 18, 3 (May–June 2003), p. 12.

83 *Tikkun*, 16, 3 (May–June 2001), pp. 9–10. See also *Tikkun*, 16, 4 (May–June 2001), pp. 11–12; 16, 6 (November–December 2001), pp. 6–7; 19, 4 (July–August 2004), pp. 9–10.

84 *Tikkun*, 18, 3 (May–June 2003), p. 11.

85 *Tikkun*, 18, 6 (November–December 2003), p. 11; 19, 1 (January–February 2004), pp. 8–12 & 33–56; 19, 4 (JulyAugust 2004), pp. 12 & 40–41.
86 Michael Lerner, *Healing Israel/Palestine*, p. xvii; *Tikkun*, 16, 1 (January–February 2001), p. 10; 16, 4 (July–August 2001), p. 10.
87 Michael Lerner, *The Socialism of Fools: Anti-Semitism on the Left* (Oakland: Tikkun Books, 1992), pp. 87–107.
88 *Tikkun*, 18, 2 (March–April 2003), pp. 30–31; 18, 3 (May–June 2003), p. 39. For a left-wing critique of Lerner, see Philip Green, "Anti-Semitism, Israel and the Left" in Tony Kushner and Alisa Solomon (eds), *Wrestling with Zion: Progressive Jewish-American responses to the Israeli–Palestinian conflict* (New York: Grove Press, 2003), pp. 243–248.
89 *Tikkun*, 17, 5 (September–October 2002, p. 11). See also *Tikkun*, 19, 4 (July–August 2004), pp. 56–60 & 65.
90 "Demonstrate for Peace — today", *Tikkun Mail*, 29 August 2004.

ISRAEL COMMENTATOR

The Jewish Left, Jewish Identity, Zionism and Israel: Attitudes to the Palestinian Intifada, 2000–2005

Avi Katzman

Dr. Mendes' essay highlights the common tendency of Jewish Diaspora communities to shy away from critical positions regarding Israeli government policy. Such criticism from individuals or groups within the community is perceived to stem from external, unrelated considerations and to express an absence of Jewish solidarity. The results of the 17th Knesset elections on 28 March 2006 highlight the problematic nature of such an approach.

In this election the Israeli public generally, and the Jewish–Zionist public specifically, expressed agreement with the central criticisms voiced by leftist circles against the state's policy *vis-à-vis* the Israeli–Arab conflict. The majority within Zionist Israel now rejects the rightist platform that Israeli governments have supported ever since the Six Day War, and accepts an Israeli withdrawal from Palestinian areas and the establishment there of a Palestinian state. Does this mean that most of Jewish–Zionist Israel acted out of ulterior motives, and a lack of Jewish solidarity?

The election results, which the Likud leader and former Prime Minister, Binyamin Netanyahu, declared to be a plebiscite, show that the Jewish–Zionist community in Israel reached the conclusion that its previous governments had followed a flawed and wrong policy when they invested vast sums into establishing and defending settlements in the occupied territories, opposing the idea of two states for two peoples. The great majority of that community in Israel today maintains that withdrawal from Palestinian areas and evacuating settlements there is good for Israel, whose security is embodied neither in territorial expansion nor in preventing Palestinian independence.

Hence, past criticism of Israeli government policies did not necessarily arise out of ulterior motives or lack of Jewish solidarity. It may well have come from a sober, farsighted and responsible vision of "what is good for Israel", as interpreted in the state of Israel today, and from an understanding that Jewish solidarity is not summed up in answering "Amen" to the errors of Israeli governments. The constant struggle of the Zionist left in Israel and the Jewish left in the Diaspora has certainly made a substantial contribution to the historical departure taken by Israel today. By contrast, too many Jewish communal leaders' prolonged silence when they could have raised their voices, and their efforts to suppress criticism, do not necessarily testify to the love of Israel in their hearts, nor to an understanding of their public duty.

The centrality of the State of Israel in Jewish life raises difficult and problematic issues of identity, along with feelings that may range from pride to shame and from obligation to guilt. Moreover, Israel's centrality is pertinent not only in Jewish life; Christians and Moslems everywhere also look to Israel as a religious and moral source; it is laden with symbolism that is very rich spiritually, politically and mythically. World media and public opinion are obsessed with Israel as a major theme. Israel draws the attention of conspiracy theorists and biblical scholars, esoteric cults and political analysts, as the locus of action, real or imagined. Too many expectations, too many anxieties, are associated with it. And all of that seems to implicate the Jewish people at large, sometimes with life-threatening results. Diaspora Jews are almost forced to either stand up for Israel or disavow it, to identify themselves totally with it or alienate themselves just as strongly from it; not much space is left there for neutral attitudes. It is very hard to disown parts of Israel and support its key aims at the same time; to mourn the victims of terror attacks while also feeling solidarity with the women of "Machsom Watch". As complex as Israeli reality is, it yet calls for simplistic, black or white, political sensibilities. Nonetheless, efforts to suppress criticism and ambivalent attitudes towards Israel in the name of a "united front" are more worrisome than any criticism. Only totalitarian movements, organizations and regimes fear criticism and try to suppress it brutally. Criticism is essential if an open society is to thrive.

Ancient Jewish sources do not favor suppressing disagreements and avoiding criticism. From the biblical "Thou shalt indeed rebuke thy neighbor" to the Talmudic "[Both] these and these are the living word of God", Jewish dialogue is traditionally not harmonious and does not see uniformity as a value. Sharp disagreements have marked Jewish culture through the generations, while consensus has been a rarity. Few are the cases of a policy that enjoyed consensus amongst the Jewish people. Only once in modern times has there been an instance of a broad, nationally and politically significant consensus: the tremendous enthusiasm that, for a short, disastrous period, united Jewish communities worldwide behind the false messiah Shabbetai Zvi, who was to lead them to the land of Israel.

Today there is a very broad consensus as to Israel's centrality in Jewish life. But make no mistake: Israeli government policy at any given time does not necessarily represent "the spirit of the Jewish people", nor the good nor the will of the Israeli public. Nor is the Israeli government, any more than any other government, immune from error or stupidity or evil. The Israeli government, like every other, has to face criticism from the Right, Left and Center. Dr. Mendes' essay identifies support for the Israeli government with a pro-Israel attitude and is therefore both mistaken and misleading. But even this book itself reflects a bias: it deals with the "Left" movements

— right-wing Jewish movements, and anti-Zionist right-wing movements among them, are not considered an issue meriting discussion.

Israel is a democratic Jewish state. As the state of the Jewish people it is under obligation to cultivate relations with the Diaspora. This means mutuality and participation in a continuous Jewish dialogue, with possibilities of both consultation and criticism: otherwise the dialogue is devoid of meaning. As a democratic state Israel must be open to sharp and even divisive criticism, defending with all her might both the right to speak out and the right to listen. The existence of democracy depends on respect for the rights to criticize, protest, condemn and demonstrate. There is no democracy without freedom of expression, an independent and critical press, freedom to investigate and a fighting opposition. Israeli society has always had the advantage of sharp-witted intellectuals such as the late Yeshayahu Leibowitz, the late Israel Eldad, Amos Oz and Menahem Brinker on the Left, Yosef ben Shlomo and Arieh Stav on the Right, and many others whose criticism stimulates public discourse. Historians such as Benny Morris and Tom Segev, journalists such as Gideon Levy and Amira Hass, attorneys such as Avigdor Feldman and Michael Sfard, commentators such as Moshe Negbi and Haim Baram and organizations such as *Betselem* and the Civil Liberties Union allow the Israeli public to see the darker side of its existence here, and to assume responsibility for Israel's acts. These individuals and groups, seeking to preserve Israel's human face, expose the harsh facts, showing us our errors and our transgressions.

The right — or the duty — of decent Israelis to criticize what their country is doing does not cease once they leave its boundaries. What is true for Israelis is true for those to whom Israel is dear. Israel is the state of the Jewish people, a state whose policies on numerous issues affect Jewish lives in the Diaspora, and, as such it invites a multi-dimensional dialogue; open, vital and critical, in the ancient tradition that "All Israel is responsible for one another". Mutual responsibility is the foundation of Jewish existence and its spiritual essence, and the criticism within this situation is a historical commonplace of Jewish culture throughout its history.

Since antiquity, the Jewish world has known numerous radical movements. From Étienne de la Boétie and Michel de Montaigne through to Heinrich Heine and Moses Hess, Karl Marx and Leon Trotsky, Rosa Luxemburg, Gustav Landauer and Emma Goldman, to Betty Friedan and Noam Chomsky, many Jews have been radical thinkers, revolutionaries, and human rights activists, leading the struggle to change social, political and economic realities. Not a few of them did it with Messianic zeal and anti-Semitic overtones and undertones. For some, "the revolution" was a convenient way to deal with the issue of having been born Jewish, which haunted them to the last of their days. There are Otto Weiningers of sorts, people who express their Jewish identity in negative terms. But such phenomena appear to exist in most human groups; there being nothing specifically "Jewish" about it.

It is very easy to dismiss Jewish critics of Israel as "self-hating Jews", to "understand" how they became captivated by the spell of prevalent anti-Semitic views disguised as anti-Zionism. Those true lovers of Zion, who are not to be deterred from their caring critique by superficial labeling, deserve much more admiration than current Jewish public opinion would afford them.

DIASPORA COMMENTATOR

Reflections on the Place of Israel in the Identity of Non-Zionists

Jonathan Freedland

It seems an arcane field of study, the Diaspora Jewish non- or anti-Zionist Left. No matter where you find them — Britain, Australia or the US — such Jewish leftists will complain that they are an endangered species, few in number, huddled together on the margins. Some look back to a golden age — such as the era of mass Jewish trade union activity in the East End of London in the 1920s and 1930s — but most have known only a life spent in meetings of a few dozen, firmly outside the mainstream.

Nevertheless, they deserve attention for at least two reasons. First, the non- or anti-Zionist Jewish Left — our subject here — often punches above its weight, achieving greater impact than its numbers alone would suggest. Some of that impact, as the preceding essay by Philip Mendes makes clear, is negative: the Jewish leftists he discusses have a knack for stirring arguments and bust-ups in their respective communities that ensure their ideas receive constant and full-throated discussion. That is certainly true in my own country, Britain, where even a single letter in the *Jewish Chronicle* from a Jewish anti-Zionist will bring at least a dozen in response, each angrier than the one before.

But there is a second reason to examine the Jewish non- and anti-Zionist Left. For this body of people, in their dilemmas, in the often tortured balancing act they perform between their ethnic community and their political fraternity, between their families and their comrades, as it were, reflects an awkward truth about the wider Jewish Diaspora itself.

But first a couple of other observations. Mendes notes that Tikkun is "closer to the Jewish mainstream" than the other two groups he cites; namely the Australian Jewish Democratic Society and Britain's Jewish Socialist Group. I would have guessed as much. For the centre of gravity in US politics is so much further to the Right than it is elsewhere, that even a leftist grouping such as Tikkun could not function unless it tacitly accepted, in Mendes's words, "pro-Israel or Zionist assumptions". I suspect these assumptions are necessary in order for Tikkun to stay credible, not only within the Jewish community, but within *American political discourse itself.* It is not only US Jewry that takes certain Zionist principles as read, but mainstream US politics. This is in sharp contrast with Britain, for example, where the prevailing consensus outside the Jewish community is, at the very least, suspicious of Zionism.

A useful contrast here is between the different support groups for Peace Now in the two countries. Americans for Peace Now (APN) declare on every statement they make that "APN is a Jewish, Zionist organization dedicated to enhancing Israel's security through peace . . . ". Americans for Peace Now clearly feels it has to reassure Washington opinion that it seeks the best for Israel, indeed that it is Zionist. Press releases for Peace Now UK feature no such tag-line, its activists surely aware that such a declaration could, in the milieu of contemporary Britain, cause as many problems as it might solve.

This is just one tiny illustration of what is now a chasm separating the US from the rest of the world: while the starting point of US discourse on the Middle East is sympathy for Israel, close to the opposite is true for the rest of the world. That complicates life for Jewish critics of Israel. In America they are out of tune with their fellow Jews, but also with much of the wider national conversation. In Britain and beyond, such critics find themselves in step with their fellow citizen — but resented by a Jewish community that feels itself beleaguered and under siege.

A second observation: In each one of the contexts Mendes examines and, I would argue, the rest of the Jewish world, the old Left discussion of Zionism has all but vanished. Now the Bundist complaint that Zionism would distract from the greater task of fighting anti-Semitism, or the socialist claim that Jews' place was in the wider international proletariat, as national identities gave way to workers' solidarity — those arguments now sound quaint, as if historical curios. They are no longer heard. The JSG in Britain valiantly makes the Bundist case that diaspora is a virtue, rather than a plight, but, organizationally at least, it does so with the faintest voice. Today the argument against Zionism is not the debate it was — an internal Jewish discussion about which strategy offered the best hope for the Jews — but rather centres on the Israeli reality, the state's behaviour and, centrally, its treatment of the Palestinians.

This shift has had an effect on the relationship of Jewish anti-Zionists with the rest of the Jewish community. Once they might have been seen as part of the Jewish family, offering their own vision of what was best for the Jews — with even their antagonists accepting that their driving motive was the welfare of the Jewish people. Today, because Jewish anti-Zionists tend to frame their case in terms of the Palestinians, they are all too easily dismissed as being somehow *outside* the Jewish fellowship — as if their motive is not to advance Jewish well-being, but the interests of the Jews' "enemies". In Britain, the group Jews for Justice for Palestinians has antagonised many Jews simply by its choice of name — which seems to seek justice for one side of the conflict, but not for both. (Their cause is furthered still less by the fact that many of these activists have little or no involvement with Jewish life except in their work against Israel and Zionism: that, too, makes mainstream Jews less willing to hear their case.)

Still, these groups hold up a useful mirror to their wider Jewish communities, even to those who loathe them. For they suffer an extreme form of what is a Diaspora condition. They are constantly struggling with a dual identity. The AJDS slogan captures this dualism perfectly. "A progressive voice among Jews, a Jewish voice among progressives." What this can translate into in practice is a life spent on a narrow strip of political terrain where one is opposed, if not despised, by both sides — the mainstream Jewish community and the wider Left. Mendes records the contortions of the AJDS on the issue of the Palestinian right to return: the group supported the right to return enough to be ostracised by the Australian Jewish establishment, but doubtless with sufficient reservations to antagonise the Australian Left.

There will be a thousand other examples like that. In Britain, Jewish leftists who went on the anti-war march protesting military action against Iraq in September 2002 were criticised by their fellow Jews for lending legitimacy to some of the anti-Israel thrust of the demonstration. Meanwhile, they were locked in a bitter argument with the march organizers about some of the placards on display (including those that equated a star of David with a swastika).

In this, the fate of the Jewish leftist is merely an extreme form of the fate of the Diaspora Jew. They are torn between their community and their universal ideals, the same way their fellow Jews are torn between their community and their citizenship, between, say, their Jewishness and their Britishness. They might feel as if they don't fully belong in either place — neither the Jewish community nor the wider left. And in that they could not be more Jewish.

7

The Changing Identity of American Jews, Israel and the Peace Process

Ofira Seliktar

The ever-changing relationship between Israel and American Jews over the last decade or so has been especially challenging. For the most part, since the establishment of the state of Israel it has been customary to argue that support for Israel lay at the core of American Jewry identity. In fact, there was even hope that Israel would serve as an instrument for maintaining the increasingly weak identity of a secularized and assimilated minority who had been reduced to what one critic described as "a residual 'Jewishness' increasingly hard to specify, a blurred complex of habits, beliefs, and feeling".[1]

Experimenting with Israel's Role in American Jewish Identity: From a Symbol of Unity to an Agent of Polarization

Making Israel the focal point of Jewish identity was a logical choice for a community in search for a new self-identity. For starters, the "melting pot" assimilationist ethos in American life was giving way to a new sense of ethnic pride to which the Jews could bring their tribalism. More importantly, Israel became the lynchpin in the evolving "civil religion" of American Jewry; so much so that for a large segment the Jewish state replaced the synagogue and the Torah as the symbol of Judaism. The Jerusalem Programme adopted by the World Zionist Organization affirmed the centrality of Israel in Jewish life, followed by the restructuring of Jewish education around Hebrew and group trips to Israel — known as missions — for the young and adults alike.

In order to help this "sacred unity", the notion of a Zionist as a Jew who immigrates to Israel was redefined as "one for whom Israel plays a central role in personal life and identity." Relieved of the arduous task of making *aliyah* or pursuing other life changing commitments, such a "light burden" formula became attractive to a variety of Jews, including, as one observer noted, marginally attached Jews and even "Jewish atheists".[2] The Judaism-as-Israelism formula was also easily translatable into communal action on behalf of Israel. Participation in, and support for, the two major Israeli advocacy organizations, American Israel Public Affairs Committee (AIPAC) and the Conference of the Presidents of Major Jewish Organization, increased dramatically. In addition, a host of other organizations launched their own pro-Israel lobbying and support ventures, and contributions to various Israeli causes soared. At its peak, in the late sixties and early seventies, this feverish preoccupation with Israel was described by a leading expert as "Israel worship" or "Israelotry".[3]

As long as Israel was seen as a victim of Arab military aggression and Palestinian terrorism, there was little difficulty in maintaining the "sacred unity" and the mobilization model of Jewish identity built around it. However, after the right-wing government of Menachem Begin took power in 1977, some strains between the more liberal members of the community and Israel developed. The right-wing, national religious coalition that Begin had put together offended the liberal–secular sensibilities of the majority of the community. The Likud's vision of Greater Israel and the concomitant treatment of the Palestinians created more unease, despite the fact that the Likud agreed to give up the Sinai territory in its Camp David deal with Egypt in 1979. The 1982 Lebanon war and the massacre in Sabra and Shatila further eroded the consensus over Israel and diminished its symbolic importance in the identity formation of American Jewry. In retrospect, the 1982 war, which many in the community considered to be an offensive war, turned Israel from a focus of shared identity into an agent of polarization.

To understand this process it is imperative to note that by the second part of the 1980s, a new round of searching for a viable Jewish identity had begun. Early hopes that an Israeli-centred identity would keep Jews in the fold was fast fading. Even before the demographic picture of the community was fully revealed in the 1990 National Jewish Population Survey (NJPS) there was a sense that the high rate of intermarriage and equally high rates of disaffiliation had been shrinking the community (to some 5.5 million from a high of more than six million after World War II). The NJPS and the annual American Jewish Committee (AJC) surveys revealed that in terms of Jewish identity, the community had split into two groups. The larger secularized–liberal segment had embraced a universalist-prophetic definition of Judaism, first articulated by the Reform movement in the nineteenth century. In this group, commitment to social justice and progressive causes such as civil rights, abortion and gay rights was the essence of Judaism, with Israel, as the embodiment of the ethnic–tribal element, taking a back seat. The smaller contingent was composed of Orthodox Jews and right-wing secularists, with Israel being a central component to the identity of both groups.[4] As noted by one observer, these hard-core Zionists had become the backbone of the communal effort on behalf of Israel.[5]

In order to understand this development, it should be mentioned that the transformation of Israel from the Ashkenazi-dominated, egalitarian, and social justice oriented society under the Labour party to an amalgam of Orthodox, national religious and right-leaning Sephardi traditionalists in the Likud era did not sit well with the progressive sensibilities of secularized American Jewry. Even without the issue of Palestinian territories, the Orthodox push to erode what little separation there existed between state and synagogue in Israeli society provoked a harsh backlash from the Reform and Conservative branches of the community. Conversely, the changing political culture of Israel was welcomed by American Orthodoxy (historically uneasy with the liberalism of the community), as well as the hard-core nationalists who shared the vision of Greater Israel.[6]

The 1993 Oslo agreement made the split in the Jewish community official. Prime Minister Yitzhak Rabin's handshake with Yasser Arafat during the 13 September White House ceremony elicited diametrically opposed reactions among American Jews. To the liberal universalists the accord was highly welcome news. As one commentator put it, after a year of tension between Israel and the United States, "there was an audible sigh of relief from American Jewish liberals. Once again, they could support Israel as good Jews, committed liberals, and loyal Americans." The community "could embrace the Jewish state without compromising either its liberalism or its patriotism".[7] Hidden deeper in this collective sense of relief was the hope that, following the peace with the Palestinians, Israel would transform itself into a Western-style liberal democracy, featuring a full separation between state and religion. Not accidentally, many of the leading advocates of Oslo, including Yossi Beilin, the then Deputy Foreign Minister, cherished the belief that a "normalized" Israel would become less Jewish and more democratic.

However, to the hard-core Zionists — the Orthodox community and right-wing Jews — the peace treaty amounted to what some dubbed the "handshake earthquake." From the perspective of the Orthodox, Oslo was not just an affront to the sanctity of *Eretz Yisrael*, but also a personal threat to the Orthodox settlers — often kin or former congregants — in the West Bank and Gaza. For Jewish nationalists such as Morton Klein, the president of the Zionist Organization of America, and Norman Podhoretz, the editor of *Commentary*, the peace treaty amounted to an appeasement of Palestinian terrorism. They and others repeatedly warned that the newly established Palestinian Authority (PA) would pose a serious security threat to Israel.

Abandoning any pretence of unity, both segments began to develop separate advocacy and lobbying organizations. The liberal supporters of the Oslo accord worked through America for Peace Now (APN), Israel Policy Forum (IPF) and other groups friendly to the Labour government of Israel. They tried to assure Congress that American Jewry was behind the accord and defended the efforts of the administration to help the fledgling Palestinian Authority (PA), including promises of financial aid. In a battle for public opinion, IPF commissioned a number of polls showing widespread support for Oslo among the community.

Working on the other side of the fence, a host of Orthodox groups, such as the ZOA, Americans for Safe Israel (AFSI), and the Jewish Institute for National Security Affairs (JINSA) launched a major public opinion campaign against Oslo. On 10 October 1993 the opponents of the Palestinian–Israeli accord organized the American Leadership Conference for a Safe Israel where they warned that Israel was prostrating itself before a "an armed thug", and predicted that the "thirteenth of September is a date that will live in infamy". Hard-core Zionists also criticized, often in harsh language, Prime Minister Rabin and Shimon Peres, his foreign minister and chief architect of the peace accord. With the community so strongly divided, AIPAC and the President's Conference, which was tasked with representing the national Jewish consensus, struggled to keep the increasingly shrill discourse civil. Reflecting these tensions, Abraham Foxman from the Jewish Anti-Defamation League was forced by the Conference to apologize for badmouthing ZOA's Klein. The Conference, which under its organizational guidelines was in charge of moderating communal discourse, reluctantly censured some Orthodox spokespeople for attacking Colette Avital, the Labour-appointed Israel council general in New York and an ardent supporter of the peace process.[8]

Since the success of the peace process hinged on financial help for the fledgling Palestinian entity, much was riding on the willingness of Congress to allocate the resources that the Clinton administration had promised. The Oslo protocol, known as the Declaration of Principles (DOP), stipulated a $2 billion fund to restore the Palestinian economy, of which a quarter was to come from the United States. To prevent AIPAC from lobbying for the Palestinian aid, the right wingers made their objections known at the Conference, which worked to coordinate the overall Jewish response. Working directly against the wishes of the Labour governments, the ZOA, the Orthodox Union and other right-wing groups prevailed upon Senate to pass the Specter-Shelby amendment, which required the State Department to certify the PA's compliance with the DOP. Senator Arlen Specter (a Republican from Pennsylvania) became the co-chair of the ZOA-conceived congressional Peace Accord Monitoring (PAM) group. Helping the Jewish right wing were a variety of Christian fundamentalist groups, including the influential Christian Israel Public Action Campaign (CIPAC).

To counter the nationalist-Orthodox campaign, the APN, IPF and other leftist and liberal Jewish groups rushed to establish their own lobbying network in Congress. The proliferation of Jewish voices did not please AIPAC, which charged that ZOA's actions threatened its role as the community's official lobby for Israel, as well as threatening the communal "agenda for Israel". AIPAC asked the President's Conference to take official action against ZOA, but Klein refused to attend the special meeting or abide by the official lobbying guidelines subsequently issued by the Conference. The ZOA–Conference clash was the last straw that broke the community's consensual back; it institutionalized the existence of separate lobbying networks above and beyond AIPAC and the Conference, which Labour and Likud subsequently used against each other.

When the right-wing Likud government of Benjamin Netanyahu took power on 29 May 1996, it tried to slow the peace process in response to the Palestinian infringement of the DOP. Netanyahu policies aroused the ire of the Left-liberal segment of the community, which used its own channels to mobilize American public opinion and sympathetic Congress members against the new Israeli government.

The process reversed itself again after Ehud Barak won a significant victory in the 17 May 1999 election. Barak's unexpectedly large margin delighted the Jewish American peace camp, which had worked hard to elect him. APN declared that Israel rejected the right-wing coalition of "messianic settlers, religious zealots and political extremists" and the American Jewish Congress (AJC) noted that Barak's government was widely representative and very stable.[9] For the Jewish liberals, this substantial popular mandate was also a sign that the Israelis were ready at last to transform themselves into American-style liberals. Predictably, hard-core Zionists were unimpressed by Barak's mandate to conclude the peace process and even more sceptical of the willingness of the PA to do so. ZOA and AFSI, among others, mounted a campaign to publicize the numerous violations of the DOP by Yasser Arafat. To forestall what they considered a rash decision, the right wing, in collusion with Christian fundamentalists, turned again to Congress. Both ZOA and National Unity Coalition — Voices

United for Israel, a Christian lobbying umbrella group, pressured congressmen to vote against a new aid bill for the Palestinians, describing it as a flagrant misuse of taxpayers' money. The cross lobbying in Congress triggered complaints that the community's standing on the Hill was being undermined. Jonathan Tobin (1999), the editor of a Jewish newspaper, wrote that "most members of Congress worry about being caught between the Jewish peace-process skeptics and the Jewish peace-process cheerleaders".[10]

The bitter schism over the peace process came to a head during the Camp David II negotiations in July 2000. Despite the news blackout at Camp David, it soon became clear that the Barak government was prepared to offer far-reaching concessions in return for the final settlement of the conflict, including the division of Jerusalem. The scope of the proposed settlement elicited predictable responses among the community. The Left hailed Barak's resolve to reach an agreement with the Palestinians and described the occasion as an historic event. Leonard Fein (2000), a long time peace activist, argued that massive territorial concessions were justified because they would bring an end to the bloody struggle between the two people. However, the nationalist–Orthodox groups made it clear that they would challenge the expected Camp David II agreement. What is more, this time around they attracted support from what was considered the mainstream of the community, uneasy about some rumored concessions. ZOA scored a coup when, on 23 June, it published an open letter to Barak signed by thirty American Jewish leaders, including two past chairmen of the Conference, top officials of AIPAC, ADL, the State of Israel Bonds, and others. The letter embarrassed AIPAC, whose chairman of the executive committee was a signatory. Even though he was forced to resign, AIPAC's 463 member executive committee remained deeply divided over the peace proposals. The executive director of the President's Conference, Malcolm Hoenlein, had joined the fray by declaring his opposition to the division of Jerusalem. The indivisibility of Jerusalem, on which there was a relatively wide consensus, became the new red line in defining the Jewish identity of the community.

Hoenlein's position, backed by the then chairman of the Conference, the right-leaning Ronald Lauder, was especially troubling to the Barak government who counted on the help of American Jewry to push for the large aid package to settle the conflict. A Labour cabinet member was hastily dispatched to "sell" the peace agreement to individual communities, but Likud responded by sending its own emissaries to work with the ZOA and other Camp David II opponents. Among them was Nathan Sharansky, the popular former Soviet dissident, turned right-wing Israeli politician. He and others were expected to help the hard-core Zionists and their fundamentalist allies to lobby Congress against the Barak government.

The refusal of Arafat to accept what was regarded as an exceptionally generous offer and the onset of the Al-Aqsa intifada put a sudden stop to the growing rift among American Jews. The unprecedented savagery of the Palestinians' suicide bombings brought the community together in ways not seen since the Six Day War. However, any hope that this new found cohesion would revitalize the Israeli-centred Jewish identity was dashed by the deep changes in American Jewish identity at the turn of the twenty-first century.

Changing Jewish Demographics and "Niche" Identities: Whose Formula Counts?

As noted, the results of the 1990 NJPS survey promoted a chorus of calls to find viable ways to assure Jewish continuity in the United States. An army of sociologists, social psychologists and other experts generated stacks of reports and recommendations, leading one observer to wryly note that "Jewish continuity has become the biggest growth industry in the Jewish community".[11] The much-awaited 1994 report of the North American Commission on Jewish Identity and Continuity recommended more Jewish education but there was no consensus on whether the liberal-universalist or ethnic-tribalist perspective should dominate. In fact, national conservatives argued that a liberal agenda would dilute the core Jewish identity to the point of total assimilation. One of them warned against experimenting with "ferocious secular liberalism" and another stated that "many American Jews confuse the Democratic Party Platform with the Laws of Moses".[12]

Given the fierce disagreements over the peace process, the role envisaged for Israel in the Jewish continuity drive was (not surprisingly) modest. A study entitled *What Will Bind Us Now? A Report on the Institutional Ties between Israel and American Jewry*[13] detailed the declining relations between Israel and the American Diaspora. Steven Bayme , a leading expert on the subject, allowed that there had been "too much confidence placed in the Israeli experience at the expense of the Jewish continuity agenda".[14] About half of the panelists in a 1996 *Commentary* symposium on Jewish identity either did not mention Israel or mentioned it in a casual way. One observer provocatively titled his article on the subject "American Zionism in Extremis".[15]

Ironically, Israel's fiftieth anniversary provided another opportunity to take stock of the changing attitudes of the community toward the Jewish state. Even a cursory look at the numerous articles and round tables devoted to the topic revealed that what underlay the official celebratory mood was what one commenter described as an "impatient, if not downright surly tone".[16] A *Moment* magazine symposium entitled "Is Israel still Important to American Jews?" agreed that Israel had become more marginal in the Jewish identity of members of the community.[17] A special issue of the *Jewish Spectator* found that the "gap widens between American Jews and Israel"; in a veiled allusion to the Middle East conflict, the magazine noted that the old "heroic image" was gone and that new realities were "not palatable".[18] The *American Jewish Year Book*, the highly respected publication of the AJC, openly focused on the "disenchantment of U.S. Jews with Israel".[19] The well-known commentator Hillel Halkin summed up the tenor of the debate by noting that some twenty-five years after Israel was proclaimed as the "civic religion of American Jews . . . the faith is losing its congregation".[20]

The annual AJC surveys of attitudes of American Jews in the late 1990s bore out these views; only about a third of the respondents claiming a close emotional attachment to Israel, with the rest either "somewhat attached" or not attached.[21] A large 1998 National Survey of American Jews commissioned by the Jewish Community Centers (JCC) showed that 9 percent of the sample felt very much attached to Israel and 18 percent felt somewhat attached. Just 20 percent thought it essential for good Jews to support Israel and 18 percent thought it was important to visit. Indeed, when questioned about actual behaviour, only 21 percent had ever visited Israel. Steven Cohen the author of the study and a leading expert on American Jewish attitudes, pointed out the "limited extent to which Israel figures in the private lives of American Jews".[22] Interestingly, these findings illustrate that the communal organizations whose focus is on Israel are essentially out of touch with their constituencies. Similar conclusions were reached by a survey that the *Los Angeles Times* published in April 1998 to coincide with Israel's Independence Day. Controlled for age and degree of orthodoxy, the analysis attested to the growing difference that Israel held for the universalists and the tribalists. The older cohorts and the Orthodox dominated the group that reported high emotional attachment to Israel; the same respondents also made up the "frequent visitors" category. Liberal-secularists and younger individuals dominated those who reported little or no attachment to the Jewish state.[23]

These findings should come as no surprise to those who have followed the subtle but powerful change in the Reform movement — the flagship of the universalistic Jewish identity. Swept by the triumph of the Six Day War and worried by the democratic hemorrhage, the Reform Jews became converts to the ethnic peoplehood notion of Jewish identity with Israel at its core. The failure of Israel to bolster Jewish identity and the highly divisive peace process resurrected the original Reform reservations about too close an identification between Judaism and ethnic nationalism. Rabbi Eric Yoffie, the leader of the Reform movement, declared in 1996 that the "age of ethnicity is over". Although stopping short of calling Israel a "false God", as some of the left-wing critics had done, Yoffie urged to fill the vacuum left by "Israel worship" with a "serious reflection on God and on mitzvah and the meaning of life".[24] Not surprisingly, Yoffie and other liberals took a dim view of the Israeli right-wing policies toward the Palestinians and their hard-core Zionist supporters in America. Indeed, relations between the two segments of the community reached such a nadir in the late 1990s that a book *Jews vs. Jew. The Struggle for the Soul of American Judaism*[25] became a best-seller in the community.

Although the Intifada restored a measure of unity to the US Diaspora, the underlying causes of the polarizing effects of the peace process have not vanished. Regrouping after the initial shock at the unparalleled brutality of the Palestinian terrorism, the Reform movement adopted an agenda that called for a "new" understanding between Israelis and the Palestinians. Even more controversial was Yoffie's decision to cancel the Reform youth programme in Israel, followed by an ugly dispute with the Israeli government over the participation of American athletes in the 2001 Maccabee Games in Tel Aviv. Critics accused Yoffie of trying to postpone the Games, thus handing a victory to terrorists. Even without official prodding, American Jews (with the exception of the Orthodox and Jewish nationalists) virtually stopped visiting Israel during the Intifada, leading the Israelis to express bitterness over the skin-deep commitment of their "American family".[26]

While talk about the "family feud" was grabbing all the headlines, little attention was paid to a host of new proposals to bolster Jewish identity, collectively known as the Renaissance Imperative. Coming some five years after the 1995 Jewish Identity report, the new round of initiatives was a response to the continuous communal anxiety about demographic decline. As the long awaited and controversial 2001 National Jewish Population Survey (NJPS) would reveal, the total number of "core

Jews" had shrunk to some 5.5 million. The number of intermarriages was estimated at 48 percent, reflecting a low communal commitment to voluntary endogamy. The Jewish fertility rate of 1.8 had fared even less well. An eye-catching 52 percent of Jewish women between the ages of 30–34 have had no children, compared to 27 percent of all American women.[27]

The 2000–2004 annual surveys of the American Jewish Committee illustrate some of the attitudinal factors behind this decline. The sample included some 7 percent Orthodox, 31 percent Conservatives, 2 percent Reconstructionists, 29 percent Reform and 30 percent who described themselves as "just Jews." Most interesting is the relatively high tolerance for intermarriage; 56 percent of the respondents stated that intermarriage is inevitable in an open society and 50 percent argued that preventing it would be "racist." Only 39 percent said that intermarriage would "pain them," a figure born out of personal experience; whereas the parent generation in the survey reported that only 15 percent of their spouses are not Jewish, a staggering 64 percent of their children have non-Jewish spouses.

With Jewish identity too weak to prevent low birth rate, exogamy and other forms of disaffiliation, the Renaissance package of initiatives was geared toward Jewish education and synagogue transformation. Bearing names like Synagogue Transformation and Renewal (STAR), Experiment in Congregational Education (ECE) and Partnership for Excellence in Jewish Education (PEJE), the programmes were designed to make synagogue attendance and Jewish education more attractive to the secularized and tenuously committed Jews. Not surprisingly, the place of Israel in this new round of identity building was minimal, a fact that was also confirmed in the AJC surveys of popular attitudes. The centrality of Israel in the respondents' Jewish identity has almost disappeared since the heydays of "Israelotry." Despite verbal affirmation of "closeness" to Israel, only 3 percent of the sample stated that Israel should be considered the most important part of Jewish identity. As for actual behaviour, some 60 percent had never visited Israel, 20 percent reported going once and 17 percent had travelled more than once; with the Orthodox and other hard-core Zionists doing most of the traveling. That liberalism had replaced Israel as the dominant element in Jewish identity was clearly attested by the self-definition of the sample: some 74 percent described themselves as either very liberal, liberal or somewhat liberal, with 26 percent claiming a conservative identity. Sixty-two percent wanted abortion to be legal under any circumstance and 49 percent advocated legal marriage for gays.

While the secularized segment of the Diaspora pinned high hopes on melding liberalism and "universalized Judaism" into a new winning formula for bolstering Jewish identity, the Orthodox and nationalist Zionists denounced the Renaissance programmes as folly. They pointed out that it was universalist and inclusive thinking that was responsible for much of the intermarriage and disaffiliation in the first place. Using the same surveys, they argued that it was their formula of Judaism — anchored in orthodoxy and centred on Israel — that had bolstered their relative numbers among core Jews. Ironically, two major Jewish philanthropists, Charles Bronfman and Michael Steinhardt, concurred with this view by proposing to fund free trips to Israel for marginally affiliated Jewish youth. The programme, known as *birthright israel*, was launched in 1998 amid general skepticism in the community. Some prominent experts wondered whether a westernized, "MacDonaldized" Israel, in their words, would be powerful enough to impart a sense of lasting Jewish identity to the young visitors.[28] A comprehensive study in 2004 found that *birthright israel*, which was attended by some 70,000 young people, imparts a stronger sense of Jewishness and communal involvement.[29]

However, even these results may not be strong enough to overcome the reluctance of the secularized–liberal segment of the American Diaspora to accept an identity in which a strong commitment to nationalism merges with a strong commitment to Judaism. As some observers have noted, ethnic expressions of Judaism waned by the end of the twentieth century because the majority of the community had internalized the American-Protestant trend of individual connection to God as opposed to a communal connection. In addition, the restarting of the peace process in 2005 has reopened the bitter communal debates, highlighting again the divide between universalists and tribalists over the peace process.

Israel, the Peace Process and the Future of American Jewish Identity

The Al-Aqsa Intifada has sent shock waves through the American Jewish community. The violence vindicated ZOA's Morton Klein, Daniel Pipes, the head of the Middle East Forum, and other hard-core Zionists who had presciently warned that the Oslo Accord-mandated Palestinian Authority under Yasser Arafat would evolve into a terrorist state. The September 11 attack on the United States generalized the spectre of Arab terrorism, silencing even some of the more vocal of the left-wing critics of Israel. Eric Yoffie apologized for thinking that Arafat could be a peace partner, and the historically dovish American Jewish Congress switched to a more hard line position. In a sign of the times, the middle of the road AJC published a report *Intifada II: The Arab Campaign to Destroy Israel*, which repeated the charges made years ago by the ZOA.[30]

However, the newly found consensus did not survive the decline in terrorist attacks brought about by an Israeli policy of targeted killings of known terrorists and the construction of the separation fence. By the middle of 2003 there were renewed signs of division among the community, especially with regard to the "road map" proposed by the Bush administration as part of its effort to end the Intifada. Hard-core Zionists, working with Christian fundamentalists, denounced the new plan. More to the centre, AIPAC organized a letter signed by a majority in Congress asking the administration to proceed with caution. However, on 24 April, 14 major philanthropists and former chairs of the Conference sent a letter asking Bush to apply pressure on Israel. The flurry of counter-lobbying was discussed but not resolved by an emergency meeting of the Conference, with some participants describing the philanthropists' letter as a "slap in the face of AIPAC". The billionaire Edgar Bronfman, the head of the World Jewish Congress, created even more commotion when he lobbied President Bush to stop Israel's separation fence.[31]

Further to the left, an effort to pressure Washington to lean on Israel was also afoot. Led by Michael Lerner, the head of the so-called "Tikkun community" (named after *Tikkun* magazine, see chapter by Mendes) organized a mass-lobbying event on Capitol Hill in June 2003, in which dozens of leftist Jewish activists, including Rabbis for Human Rights, participated. The conference and teach-ins attracted some 200 legislators and 50 senators, including the anti-Israeli lawmakers Maxine Waters, Darell Issa and Dennis Kucinich.[32] Needless to say, the event was denounced by hard-core Zionists who argued that the presence of Waters, Kucinich and other vocal critics of Israel was a badge of shame on the Tikkun community.

The unexpected decision of Ariel Sharon, the hard-line Likud leader, to unilaterally withdraw from the Gaza Strip created additional tension. Many of the mainstream Jewish organizations such as the Anti Defamation League and the Reform movement pressured the Conference of Major Jewish Organizations to issue a statement in support of Sharon. However, the ZOA and Orthodox groups hotly objected during an emergency meeting of the Conference. According to an insider's account, the fierce debate deteriorated to a "critical point, threatening the unity of the . . . organizations" and forcing the chairman to adjourn the session without reaching a decision.[33]

More division between the two segments of the community surfaced during the 2004 election. The decades long realignment in American body politics that culminated in the re-election of President George W. Bush had its roots in the alliance between economic conservatives and evangelical Christians. During the same time, the Democrats had seen their historical majority shrink to an uneasy coalition between the shriveled trade union movement, African Americans, mainline churches, liberal Jews, homosexuals, and other progressive elites.

This historical realignment had reconfigured the parties' attitude toward the Middle East conflict. Reflecting the strong pro-Israeli stand of the evangelicals, the Republicans led by Bush, a self-proclaimed born again Christian, supported the Likud government and denounced Yasser Arafat. As noted, Christian fundamentalists organized a strong lobbying network on Capitol Hill to push for right-wing Israeli policies. During the Al-Aqsa Intifada, which destroyed the Israeli tourism industry, fundamentalists organized large solidarity tours. In one of the largest displays of such solidarity, Pat Robertson led a group of 4000 of his American followers, who joined some 16,000 Christians from other countries in celebrating the Feast of Tabernacles in Jerusalem in October of 2004.[34]

While the Republicans have travelled the extra mile to embrace Israel, the Democratic Party has seen a slow but steady erosion of its historical advocacy of the Jewish state. Indeed, by the early 2000s, the changes in the demographic base of the party have chilled relations between Israel and the Democrats. First, the highly assertive Democratic Black Caucus adopted a pro-Palestinian position as part of its embrace of Third Worldism. Individual African-American legislators like the outspoken Maxine Waters and Cynthia McKinney have verged on anti-Semitism when descrying Israeli occupation of Palestine and the "Jewish power" in American foreign policy. Hostility toward the Jewish state has also emanated from the relatively small but influential McGovernite–New Left wing of the party, which had propelled Howard Dean, the virtually unknown governor of Vermont, to the front ranks of the party's candidates for the 2004 presidential nomination.

Deeper in the bowels of the Democratic party, New Left activists associated with the anti-globalization movement have been heavily involved in anti-war and anti-Israeli activities.[35] The former vice president Al Gore raised the profile of one such group, MoveOn, when he addressed its meeting in 2004. Among others, this radical Democratic group promoted the anti-Iraq war movie *Fahrenheit 911* by Michel

Moore, whose anti-Israeli rhetoric triggered a rebuke from some Jewish groups. Theresa Heinz Kerry, wife of the Democratic presidential nominee John Kerry, has been one of the donors to the Tide Foundations, which promotes a number of anti-globalization, anti-Israel groups.[36] The mainline Protestant churches have embraced divestment in companies doing business with Israel, a strategy that was effectively used against the apartheid regime in South Africa. Jewish commentators have complained about these structural challenges in the party. Indeed, one of them went so far as to accuse the new Democrats of "echoes" of anti-Semitism.[37]

Not surprisingly, Israelis took a keen interest in the electoral fortunes of President Bush. Some polls showed that up to 90 percent of Israelis favored his reelection in 2004 against some 10 percent who would have liked to see his challenger, Senator John Kerry, win. While Bush was seen as the best pro-Israeli president in American history, Kerry was perceived as lukewarm toward Israeli security concerns at best and biased toward the Palestinians at worst. Given the Israeli enthusiasm for Bush, many observers expected the American Jewish community to change its historical voting record that heavily favors Democratic candidates. However, on Election Day, only 24 percent of the Jewish community cast its vote for Bush, with the rest going to his Democratic challenger John Kerry. A subsequent analysis revealed that the Orthodox gave Bush 68 percent of their vote, as opposed to 23 percent of the Conservatives and 15 percent of the Reforms. This pattern of electoral choice is the clearest indication yet that the real double loyalty conundrum for American Jews is not the choice between their allegiance to Israel and the United States, but rather the one between Israel and their liberal agenda. With the pro-Bush stand reflecting the tribal-nationalist identity of the Israelis, the growing universalist focus of the Diaspora identity is bound to aggravate this dilemma.

Mutual recriminations over the election results have served to accentuate bitter divisions over Israel and the place it should play in the loyalty of American Jews. The Orthodox and nationalists blamed their liberal co-religionists for abandoning Israel at the altar of liberal issues. Edward I. Koch, a former Democratic mayor of New York and a major booster of President Bush, went so far as to accuse the Jewish community of betraying the interests of Israelis for the sake of its liberal agenda. He pointed out that Jews adored F.D.R. even after it became known that he did nothing to rescue Jews from the Holocaust.[38] One hard-core Zionist complained that Jews had spurned Christian fundamentalists with a proven pro-Israeli record such as Tom Delay, the majority leader in the House and added that for the Jewish Left in America, "the war against the Christian Right should take precedence over the Arab war against Israel".[39] Louis Rene Beres, the rightist activist and professor of international law, argued that for many American Jews the people of Israel "are a minor and dispassionate concern" and urged closer ties with Christian advocates of the Jewish state. For good measure he added that the "Jewish establishment was largely silent during the Holocaust".[40]

Responding with equal vehemence, liberal leaders charged that courting Evangelical amounts to "'selling out'" the values of the American Jewish community". Others asserted that the Christian Right is using Israel as a Trojan horse to undermine Jewish civic-secular vigilance. The Jewish Women Watching group planned to distribute condoms during the 2004 Jewish Communities Assembly as part of its "Strange Bedfellows" campaign to protest contacts between Jews and Christian evangelicals. Even without such high dramatics, the November meeting of the Jewish

Communities Assembly showcased the bitter split over the role of Israel in American Jewish identity.[41]

Looming even larger on the stormy communal horizon has been the new round of negotiations between Israel and the Mahmud Abbas, who replaced Arafat as the new head of the Palestinian Authority in January 2005. Hard-core Zionists — aided by Christian fundamentalists — expressed profound misgivings over American willingness to give the Palestinians yet another chance. As indicated, the ZOA and the Orthodox groups have objected to Israel's withdrawal from Gaza; they have also announced a new drive to mobilize Congress in order to enforce strict accountability on PA.[42] Ironically, the leftists and liberals in the community warmed considerably to their long-time nemesis Sharon, switching their attacks to Netanyahu, who bolted from the government over the disengagement.

With more steps toward unilateral disengagement looming on the horizon, the specter of yet another communal quarrel does not bode well for an increased role of Israel in shaping the Jewish identity of liberal Jews. According to Steven Cohen, only about 20 percent of the community has formed a strong attachment to Israel. Forty percent are described as "well disposed toward Israel" but "uninformed" and "fuzzy" about the meaning of Israel in their lives. The other 40 percent are unconnected with Israel and, for that matter, Judaism).[43] Given the liberal leanings of many in the middle 40 percent and the polarizing effect of the peace process, even more distancing can be expected. Some commentators noted that, even by the raucous standards of Jewish communal discourse, the peace debate in which both sides have sought to de-legitimize and marginalize each other was "disreputable".[44] Added to the complexity of the Arab–Israeli conflict, such tensions might have turned off a lot of the younger liberal universalists. Reflecting his experience in the Reform movement, one leader stated that "many Jews have already checked out, saying "a plague on both your houses" . . . it is "all too complicated for me".[45]

Probably more confounding is the fact that attitudes toward the Middle East conflict are underlain by the profoundly different visions of Israel that are held dear by the liberal universalists and hard-core Zionists. The former want to use the peace process to create a small, democratic Israel where enlightened citizenship and religious pluralism predominate. The latter seek a solution to the conflict that would guarantee the continuation of the Jewish character of the state and fulfill the vision of Greater Land of Israel. With the tensions over the competing visions of Israel virtually irreconcilable, Israel's attractiveness as a symbol of identity and unity — particularly among the younger generation of secularized US Jewry — is set to virtually vanish.

Notes

1 I. Howe, *Margin of hope: An intellectual biography* (San Diego: Harcourt Brace, Janovich, 1982), p. 258.

2 C. S. Liebman, *The ambivalent American Jew: Politics, religion, and family in American Jewish life* (Philadelphia: The Jewish Publication Society of America, 1983), p. 101.

3 D. J. Elazar, *Community and polity: The organizational dynamics of American Jewry* (Philadelphia: The Jewish Publication Society of America, 1976), p. 83.

4 O. Seliktar, *Divided we stand. American Jews, Israel and the peace process* (Westport, Conn: Praeger, 2002a), pp. 145–149

5 D. Ben Moshe, "The impact of the Al-Aqsa intifada on Israel–Diaspora relations," *Israel Studies Forum* 19, 3 (2004): pp. 28–57.
6 O. Seliktar, "Separating the synagogue from the state: American Jews and the struggle for religious pluralism in Israel", *Israel Studies Forum*, 18 (2002b): pp. 57–87.
7 J. S. Auerbach, "Are we One? Menachem Begin and the long shadow of 1977" in Gall (ed.) *Envisioning Israel. The changing ideas and images of North American Jews* (Jerusalem: The Magness Press, 1996), p. 349; Auerbach, J. S., "Are we One? American Jews and Israel", *Midstream* 44, 1 (1998), pp. 20–24.
8 Seliktar 2002a, pp. 134–135.
9 Seliktar 2002a, p. 182.
10 J. S. Tobin, "Can we still ask, is it good for the Jews", *Jewish Exponent*, 14 October 1999.
11 J. J. Goldberg, "U.S. Jewry pins its future on education", *Jerusalem Post*, 6 October 1994.
12 Seliktar 2002a, p. 145.
13 S. Norich, *What will bind us now? A report on the institutional ties between Israel and American Jewry* (New York: Yivo. 1995).
14 S. Bayme, "Israel Diaspora redefining their relations", *Jewish Exponent*, 8 July 1994.
15 "What do American Jews believe: A symposium", *Commentary*, August 1996.
16 J. Wertheimer, "The disaffection of American Jews", *Commentary*, May 1998: pp. 44–49.
17 "Is Israel still important to American Jews?" *Moment*, 22–27 August 1998.
18 C. Dettelbach, "Moving apart: The gap widens between American Jews and Israel", *Jewish Spectator*, Spring (1998): pp. 40–42.
19 J. Sarna, and Jonathan J. Golden, *The twentieth century through American Jewish Eyes; A history of the American Jewish Yearbook, 1899–1999* (New York: American Jewish Year Book, 2000), pp. 3–102.
20 H. Halkin, "Ahad Ha'am, Herzel, and the end of Diaspora Zionism" in Michael Brown and Bernard Lightman (eds) *Creating the Jewish Future* (Walnut Creek, CA: AltaMira Press, 1999), p. 102.
21 Seliktar 2002a, pp. 173–174.
22 S. M. Cohen, *Diaspora–Israel contact: Rethinking the partnership* (New York: World Communal of Jewish Communal Services, 1998).
23 *Los Angeles Times*, April 1998.
24 Quoted in Seliktar 2002a, pp. 175–176.
25 S. G. Freedman, *Jew vs. Jew. The Struggle for the Soul of American Judaism* (New York: Simon and Shuster, 2000).
26 Ben-Moshe, 2004.
27 E. Mayer, "Secularization among America's Jews. Insights from the Jewish identity survey", *Humanistic Judaism* 31, 1 (2003–4): pp. 4–32.
28 S. C. Heilman, "Separated but not divorced", *Society* 36, 4 (1999): pp. 8–14; Halkin, 1999.
29 "Research finds that Birthright Israel Program helps Build Jewish identity", *Brandeis News*, 3 January 2005.
30 Seliktar 2002a, p. 204.
31 Tobin, "Redefining 'pro-Israel'", *Jewish Exponent*, 8 May 2003; Pomerance, R., "U.S. Jewish groups disagree on direction of Bush 'road map'", *Jewish Telegraphic Agency*, 9 May 2003.
32 "Tikkun Conference: Huge success in D.C.", *Tikkun Magazine*, May/June 2003.
33 S. Shamir, "U.S. Jewish leaders split over public support for pullout", *Ha'aretz*, 17 October 2004.
34 *Ha'aretz*, 3 October 2004.
35 D. Horowitz, "The McGovern syndrome," *FrontPage Magazine.com*, 27 December 2004.
36 B. Johnson, "Teresa Heinz Kerry: Bag lady for the radical left", *FrontPage Magazine.* com. 13 February 2004.

37 R. Medoff, "President Lindbergh? Anti-Semitism then and now", *Jewish Exponent*, 7 October 2004.
38 E. I. Koch, "Jews must reward Bush for standing on Israel", *Jewish World Review*, 27 August 2003.
39 Tobin 2003.
40 L. R. Beres, "Outliving the road map. What we can do personally to help save Israel", *The Jewish Press*, 12 September 2003.
41 N. Guttman, "At the GA, the fault line divides as expected", *Ha'aretz*, 16 November 2004.
42 J. Besser, "Palestinian aid fights ahead?" *The Jewish Week*, 10 February 2005.
43 Steven Cohen 1998.
44 Tobin 2003.
45 Pomerance 2003.

ISRAEL COMMENTATOR

Power Paradoxes and Jewish Identity

Avi Beker

The Israeli attitude toward the phenomenon of American Jewish power is full of paradoxes. Israelis are first and foremost surprised by how American Jews — who are in constant demographic decline — are still regarded as an overwhelming force in American politics. American Jewish power is something that challenges the traditional attitude of Zionism: that of negating the exile Jews (*Shlilat Hagalut*) and projecting contempt onto the Diaspora old style Court-Jews' diplomacy. This prevailing attitude has not prevented representatives of the Israeli government from using that Jewish political clout in Washington whenever they have regarded it as necessary, nor prevented searches for financial help for political campaigns on the right or on the left.

Israelis also wonder at what seems to be a split personality of the American Jewish community. While Jews in Israel and America regard President George W. Bush as the closest friend Israel ever had in the White House they fail to understand how most of the Jewish vote continued to go to his democratic rival. While they see how American Jews care so much about the security of Israel, they fail to understand how 70 percent of American Jews can oppose the US involvement in Iraq, an opposition rate which early in 2006 was about 10 percent higher than among the general public.

While Ofira Seliktar provides a good snapshot of the prevailing attitudes of American Jews to the peace process she is less convincing in dealing with the paradoxes of American Jewish power and its implications for US–Israel relations. There is no revelation in the fact that the State of Israel serves as a major component of Jewish identity for many Jews in the Diaspora. But it is far less evident that Jews in the Diaspora define and relate their Jewish identity according to the peace policies of a particular government in Israel. It is also true that there are differences of opinion among Jews in the Diaspora regarding the policies of Israel toward the Palestinians and the territories. But it is wrong to argue that the political debate in Israel on peace is "an agent of polarization" for American Jews, and that it has a damaging affects on their community life and Jewish identity. It is a fact that many American Jews share the so-called "light burden" definition of Zionism, and many don't even intend to make *aliyah* to Israel, but this attitude is not new and it goes back far before the establishment of the State of Israel.

While there are many American Jews who disagree with Israel's peace policies, they are far more sensitive than many Israelis to the anti-Semitic attacks which often come under the guise of criticism of those policies. This discrepancy in sensitivity between the Jews in America and Israel was evident in the reaction to a widely controversial study on "The Israel Lobby and U.S. Foreign Policy" which was published in March 2006 under the auspices of Harvard University. The writers, John Mearsheimer and Stephen Walt, two important Professors, claimed that US policy is engineered through a Zionist "stranglehold on Congress". Some Israelis from the Left welcomed the study as a reflection of the loss of patience in America with the power tactics of the pro-Israel lobby.[1] Unlike them, even leaders of the American Friends of Peace Now — a group that has often been critical of both Israel policies and the pro-Israel lobb — criticized the study for glossing over the opposition of US administration to Israeli policies, and for its selective use of evidence and failure to understand Israel's war for survival.[2] In sharp contrast to the low-key reports in Israel, American Jews and other supporters of Israel, including liberal people, didn't hide their outrage and called the study anti-Semitic. Within days the Harvard and Kennedy School logos were stripped from the title page of the study.[3]

The perceived growing trend toward Israeli right-wing policies by American Jews is due to the fact, as shown by Seliktar, that in the changing demographics of the Jewish community the percentage of Orthodox Jews is growing; both in absolute numbers, and in terms of more active participation in Jewish and general political life. The Orthodox (who are only 10 percent of the Jewish community) overwhelmingly voted for Bush and the Republicans, not only because of their positions on the Arab–Israeli conflict but also, as they claim, due to their sense of identification with the Republicans' social and religious values. This trend was reflected in an extreme fashion in the mock elections conducted by the Jewish Agency in North American campuses (and also in a few other locations around the world) on the day of the elections in Israel. These mock elections gave gave the right-wing parties led by the Likkud an absolute majority in the Knesset, gave more power to the right-wing National Unity Party and even gave several Knesset seats to the outlawed Khanna party.[4]

Among the Orthodox in America (including many of the Ultra Orthodox, except for a tiny minority of self declared anti-Zionists), support and activism for Israel comes as part of their Jewish identity. However, unlike many of the liberal and less religious Jews, their Jewish identity is not exclusively dependent on Israeli politics. As practicing and observant Jews, Israel was never their "civil religion", and even frustration with the policies of a particular government will not deeply affect their attachment to Israel. The less religious and usually the less affiliated Jews may find it more difficult to develop the alternatives for their "civil religion" — an identity based on Israel. But as shown before, the schism between left and right among American Jews is not so deep as it is in Israel. Both camps in America are very sensitive to the spillovers of anti-Semitism into the discussions about Israel and both camps strongly reject charges of "double loyalty" for their activism on behalf of Israel.

The so-called "light burden" formula of Zionism to which Seliktar refers has stood at the centre of American Zionism from the very beginning. Judge Louis Brandeis, the first Jew to be appointed to the US Supreme Court (in 1916), developed the ideological rationale for Zionism in the Diaspora. He did not see any conflict between living in America, yet being an active Zionist:

> Let us Americans . . . lead earnestly, courageously, and joyously in the struggle for the liberation of the Jewish People! American Jews have not only the right but the duty to act. My approach to Zionism was through Americanism . . . Gradually, it became clear to me that to be good Americans we must be better Jews, and to be better Jews we must become Zionists. Jewish life cannot be preserved and developed, assimilation cannot be averted, unless there be established in the fatherland a center from which the Jewish spirit may radiate and give to the Jews scattered throughout the world that inspiration which springs from memories of a great past and the hope of a great future.[5]

Among the pro-Israel activists there are Orthodox and non-Orthodox Jews who can be termed as "light Zionists" because they don't intend to fulfill the basic obligation of *aliyah.* However, the Orthodox differ in the sense that they have provided the major bulk of *aliyah* from north America for many years and, as a result, they have a very extensive network of family ties in Israel (and many among the settlers). They are also the most frequent visitors to Israel and many of their children have spent one year or more of studies in Israel. There are similar trends of Israel identity and *aliyah* among Jews in the Diaspora outside North America, though there are, per capita, more Jewish visitors to Israel from countries in Europe. Similarly, within the Jewish community, there is a stronger Israeli orientation to Jewish and Zionist education in countries such as Australia, South Africa, or Mexico. The growing trend of *aliyah* from France is also based on the more traditional and religiously oriented North-African Jews.

Both sides, Israeli and American Jews, will need to adjust their perceptions about each other in order to get closer to the changing realities of the peace process. The pro-active supporters of Israel in the US will have to reflect on the deep changes in Israeli society (the political "big bang") which brought about the disengagement from Gaza and received an overwhelming support in the election results of March 2006. Israelis, on their part, must recognize the vitality of the American Jewish community and overcome the biased attitudes and prejudices of old ideological Zionism. In the eyes of the world, the Jewish Diaspora — and particularly American Jews — are seen as a critical mass of the Jewish people. The famous historian Paul Johnson, a loyal supporter of Israel and a noted philo-Semite, makes an unusual statement which would not necessarily be approved of by convicted Zionists: "The expansion and consolidation of United States Jewry in the late 19th and 20th centuries was as important in Jewish history as the creation of Israel itself; in some ways more important." Zionism, he says, "gave the Diaspora a sovereign instrument to defend the destiny of the Jews but the power of US Jewry provided the Jews with a legitimate and important part in shaping the policies of the greatest state on earth".[6]

Notes

1 See a typical attitude by Daniel Levy in "So pro-Israel that it Hurts", *Ha'aretz*, 25 March 2006. Daniel Levy was a former assistant to Yossi Beilin, and participated in the Oslo talks and in drafting the Geneva Initiative (a joint Israeli–Palestinian agreement) in 2004.
2 Comments by Lewis Roth from Americans for Peace Now, in James D. Besser "Harvard Report Blames 'The Lobby' For War", *Jewish Week*, 24 March 2006.
3 Richard L. Cravatts, "Anti-Semitic Paranoia at Harvard", *Boston Herald*, 3 April 2006. Elliot A. Cohen, "Yes, It's Anti-Semitic" *Washington Post*, 5 April 2006. And a former Catholic Priest James Carroll, "The Thread of Anti-Semitism", *International Herald Tribune*, 4 April 2006.
4 *Ha'aretz* 29 March 2006.
5 Edward Bernard Glick, *The Triangular Connection: America, Israel and American Jews* (London: George Allen & Unwin, 1982), pp. 45–46.
6 Paul Johnson, *A History of the Jews* (New York: Harper and Row, 1987), p. 566.

DIASPORA COMMENTATOR

Israeli Politics in the Diaspora and Jewish Identity

Scott Lasensky

Writing in the journal *Foreign Affairs* in 1978, long-time Zionist leader Nahum Goldmann wrote that "among the many new states created during the last 50 years, Israel is the only one that has its origins not in reality but in an ideal, not in a factual situation but in the hope and faith of a people".[1] In this sense, the place of Israel in the identity of Diaspora Jews differs from traditional ethno-nationalist communities, like Greeks, Armenians or Palestinians. It was from the heart of the Diaspora that the homeland itself was established, or "re-born" as Zionists would prefer to say. Moreover, the Diaspora has had to struggle to reconcile the idealized Israel with the realities of state-building in an unstable and hostile region.

Political divides within the Diaspora over Israel's future, which go back as far as the origins of the Zionist movement, permeate this process. This is as much a reflection of internal cleavages as it is a mirror of Israel's own political divides, which are increasingly being exported to the Diaspora. For example, as the Oslo process roiled Israeli politics in the 1990s, this same turmoil was exported to the Diaspora and had a major impact on the American Jewish community. Although left/right divisions over Israel and the peace process expand and contract as prospects for peace and threat levels rise and fall, the centrality of Israel as an affirmative source of identity remains unmistakable.

Israel itself is wrestling with its own identity as part of World Jewry, a process that has accelerated as prospects fade for a permanent peace with Palestinians. To complicate matters even further, both processes of identity formation are influenced strongly by political and social trends in the United States. Not only is Washington Israel's principal benefactor and guarantor in the international realm, but the US is also home to the vast majority of the Diaspora. Both the Diaspora and Israel enjoy unprecedented power. "Israel carries a lot of 'hard' power and the Jewish community in the US has a lot of 'soft' power", said the Jewish People Policy Planning Institute (JPPPI) in its first annual report. "Never before has the Jewish people had so much power."[2]

As power accumulates, the "Israel–Diaspora" paradigm itself has become less relevant. Not only do cross-cutting cleavages (Ultra-Orthodox, Mizrahi, etc.) increasingly straddle the traditional Israel–Diaspora divide, but population shifts are also blurring the picture. Consider Israel's own expatriate Jewish community, which numbers in the hundreds of thousands and is becoming increasingly permanent and US-based. A quick look at the largest centres of American Jewry (New York, Los Angeles and Miami) finds a growing community of Israeli expatriates. This growing expatriate group within the ethno-nationalist whole will become more significant as time passes, and their relationship with the "homeland" will differ markedly from the traditional American Jewish perspective.

In her essay on "The Changing Identity of American Jews, Israel and the Peace Process" Ofira Seliktar has done a masterful job explaining the constantly evolving place of Israel in American Jewish life. She presents a nuanced narrative of the intra-communal debates over the proper place of Israel, and how these debates have been influenced by the Arab–Israeli peace process. Her detailed, well-researched study presents a process of identity formation that is anything but static. It is a process that has been deeply influenced in recent years by developments in Israeli foreign policy and global politics. But her analysis of left/right debates over Israel could be strengthened on a number of conceptual and methodological scores. In addition, some of her conclusions are overstated.

Is Israel an agent of "polarization" within the American Jewish community? Although Seliktar provides a detailed, engaging narrative about debates over Israel, her argument that Israel has become a polarizing force is exaggerated. Perhaps because her study focuses on the Oslo years, when internal divides ran the deepest, or perhaps because her study lacks hard data, her conclusion that Israel is more divisive than unifying is open to debate. In fact, the opposite could be argued. In the post-9/11 years, identification with Israel and group solidarity appears to have increased.

Since 2001, the fragmentation of the Oslo years has receded. As is common among Diasporic communities, when threat perceptions increase, group identity hardens. Oslo's violent demise, the 9/11 attacks and the surge of anti-Semitism in Europe have all served as convergent factors. There is no doubt that right/left divides over Israel are real and meaningful, but to claim that Israel has become an agent of polarization — without presenting causal evidence — goes a bit too far. Staunch Diaspora support for "unilateral disengagement," in contrast with the divisiveness of the Oslo years, may indeed point toward a new era of consolidated attitudes (rather than the "specter of yet another communal quarrel" that Seliktar predicts.) The return of solidarity reminds us that political support for Israel remains a defining characteristic of Jewish identity in the Diaspora. Zionism, which originally rejected exile and Diaspora, has ironically become a well-spring of identity for Diaspora Jews.

Next, Seliktar's analysis relies too heavily on a rigid, traditional Israel–Diaspora paradigm, and neglects the systemic, or transnational perspective. Left/right debates within American Jewry do not occur in a vacuum. They are part and parcel of a larger system of "Jewish foreign policy," in which World Jewry maintains external relations with the international system. Jewish foreign policy is not Israeli foreign policy, nor is it an aggregation of American Jewish political power and interests. Jewish foreign policy is not controlled by the Israeli Prime Minister, nor is it led by the myriad of Jewish communal organizations in the US or elsewhere.

Jewish foreign policy, like other systems of foreign policy, has its own distinctive set of core interests, power endowments, and actors. As with other ethno-nationalist communities, the system is de-centralized and ad hoc. For a full appreciation of the changing role of Israel within American Jewry and the impact of the peace process, both the "systems" or transnational approach, and the Israeli–Diaspora framework are necessary.

Third, there is the basic question of impact on Arab–Israeli relations: are American Jews peacemakers or peace-wreckers? What is the net impact of the Diaspora on the Arab–Israeli peace process? This question is left unanswered by Seliktar.

The conventional wisdom is that Diasporas are more conservative and more strident than their co-nationalists back in the homeland. Therefore, Diasporic communities are often assumed to represent obstacles to conflict resolution, rather than serving as instruments of peacemaking. Take the Cuban American community as an example; for many years it has pushed a hard line *vis-à-vis* Castro.

But on closer inspection, a more differentiated picture emerges. Not only does the Jewish Diaspora intervene at different stages of the conflict cycle, but its net impact has been both positive and negative. Policymakers have worked in concert with the Diaspora, but they have also been taken by surprise by obstacles put up by the Diaspora.

This was the case, as described by Seliktar, with the small but influential group of obstructionists within the American Jewish community who lobbied against the Oslo process — and created complications for American and Israeli peacemakers.[3] But, at the end of the day, the Clinton Administration was undeterred by the obstructionists at home.

Diasporas can also withdraw their support — or even oppose — co-nationalists in the homeland, in favor of working for peace in tandem with host-state governments. American Jews played a role in initiating the US–PLO dialogue in the late 1980s, against the expressed desires of the Israeli government at the time, but with the full support of US Secretary of State George Shultz and the Reagan Administration.[4]

The discussion of electoral politics raises another shortcoming of Seliktar's analysis; a lack of historical grounding. For example, the Democrats were far more divided on Israel a generation ago, when Jimmy Carter was president, than they are in the age of George Bush and John Kerry. Moreover, hard data on fund-raising, Israel travel, and domestic political action could provide further insights into the evolving relationship between American Jews, Israel and the peace process. This data is readily available, and when combined with Seliktar's qualitative analysis a fuller picture would emerge.

Setting aside these methodological and conceptual critiques, Seliktar's study does stand on its own. It makes a substantial contribution to the study of relations between

American Jews and Israel. In particular, her detailed, nuanced portrait of the ideological cross-currents among the leadership provides a window into the dynamic, evolving process of identity formation.

Notes

1 Nahum Goldmann, "Zionist Ideology and the Reality of Israel", *Foreign Affairs* (Fall 1978).
2 Sergio DellaPergola and Amos Gilboa, *Between Thriving and Decline: The Jewish People 2004, Annual Assessment No. 1*, Executive Report (Jerusalem: The Jewish People Policy Planning Institute, 2004).
3 Sidney Blumenthal, "The Western Front", *The New Yorker*, 5 June 1995, pp. 36–42; Scott Lasensky, "Paying For Peace: The Oslo Process and the Limits of American Foreign Aid", *Middle East Journal* 58, 2 (Spring 2004).
4 To be fair, this initiative came from individuals, or "lone rangers," and was not endorsed by the communal leadership in New York and Washington. See William Quandt, *Peace Process* (Washington, DC: Brookings Institution, 2001).

8

Israel's Foreign and Defence Policy and Diaspora Jewish Identity

Jonathan Rynhold

Go to a synagogue, a Jewish youth group meeting, or indeed any place where Diaspora Jews are gathered, and one will almost certainly find some discussion of Israel's foreign and defence policy. The very extensive coverage of the Arab–Israeli conflict/peace process by the international media means that Israeli policy is the most prominent public expression of collective Jewish action. Consequently, it is very difficult for Diaspora Jews to ignore Israeli actions, and even assimilated Jews have felt implicated by Israeli policies.[1]

Israeli policies affect Diaspora identity in two main ways. First, they raise the issue of political loyalty. Diaspora Jews have a civic-national identity. As citizens of their respective states they owe those states loyalty. The existence of Israel as a specifically Jewish state presents a potential alternative locus of loyalty. Indeed, prior to the Holocaust many Jews in the West opposed Zionism, as they feared that the charge of 'dual loyalty' would undermine their civic rights in the Diaspora. While Diaspora Jewry has been overwhelmingly supportive of Israel, it remains concerned by the issue of 'dual loyalty' even in established democratic countries. Consequently, Diaspora Jews have generally stressed their fundamental political loyalty to the states in which they live, while simultaneously seeking to promote good relations between Israel and their respective states. The 'dual loyalty' issue comes to the fore particularly when Diaspora Jews try to influence their countries' policies in a pro-Israel direction. In some countries, such as France, such lobbying is often viewed with suspicion. But even in the US, where such activities are usually viewed as legitimate, the charge of 'dual loyalty' remains potent. For example, in 2004, the issue of 'dual loyalty' was raised when the FBI investigated the pro-Israel lobby group, America Israel Public Affairs Committee (AIPAC), regarding the passing on to Israel of apparently classified information by a Defence Department official whose boss was Jewish and a supporter of Israel.[2]

The second way in which Israeli policies affect Diaspora identity relates to the specifically Jewish aspects of identity. Zionism started off as the preserve of young radicals, though after 1948, support for Israel became central to the Diaspora Jewish consensus. Most identifying Jews continue to support Israel, even if they are critical of its government's policies. Nonetheless, as the Diaspora debate over Israeli policies has grown, so this debate has increasingly served as the context for wider ideological debates over the meaning of Jewishness and Judaism.[3] For some relatively marginal Jews, such as British playwright Harold Pinter, or the Diaspora Jews involved in trying to organize an academic boycott of Israel, it seems as if being critical of Israeli policies is almost the sole expression of their Jewish identity.

From the Israeli perspective, concern regarding how its policies affect Diaspora identity have been subordinated to Israel's own ideological and political interests: that is, *aliyah*, coupled with political and financial support. Over the years, the ideology has mellowed, but state interests remain the main determinant of Israeli attitudes. As will be discussed further on, this has led to Israeli insensitivity regarding the civic and Jewish aspects of Diaspora identity.

The bulk of this chapter will chronologically analyze the way in which Israeli policies have had an impact on the two sides of Diaspora identity. Subsequently, the focus of this chapter will shift towards considering the extent to which Israel takes Diaspora identity into account when conducting its foreign and defence policy.

The Impact of Israeli Policies on the Diaspora

The Cautious Consensus, 1948–1966

For Western Jews in this period, Israel represented a poor relative in mortal danger, whom one felt incumbent to assist, particularly when set against the feelings of guilt for not having done enough to save Jews in the Holocaust. As Thomas Friedman put it, "Israel was [a] nation of *nebechs* . . . the place we sent our old clothes".[4] Behind the Iron Curtain, Jewish opinion was much more difficult to gauge, but the reception given to Golda Meir by Moscow Jews, coupled with the reports of *Nativ*, the clandestine Israeli organization charged with keeping up contacts with Soviet Jewry, suggested that they were supportive of the fledgling state, despite continual anti-Israel propaganda. In ideological terms, Israeli policy was not controversial for the Diaspora. The only exception to this was a brief hiccup over the Suez crisis, when the Left sided with the 'Third World' (that is, Egypt), while Israel was allied with the imperialist powers, Britain and France.[5]

In this period, Diaspora Jewish identification with Israel began to find practical expression in pro-Israel lobbying. Non-Zionists began to act, once they felt reasonably assured regarding the issue of dual loyalty. In France, this process was aided by the virtual alliance between Israel and France.[6] In the US, such reassurance was formally provided by Israeli Prime Minister David Ben-Gurion in a letter to the head of the American Jewish Committee, Jacob Blaustein, in which he recognized and accepted that 'American Jews have only one political attachment and that is to the USA. They owe no political allegiance to Israel'.[7] Nonetheless, lobbying remained somewhat restrained in this period, as even American Jews still remained wary of the 'dual loyalty' issue and instead focused their efforts on securing civil rights within the US.[8]

Affirmative Pride, 1967–1981

The Six Day War was a defining moment for Israel's role in Diaspora Jewish identity. Prior to the war, Diaspora Jewry was gripped by the fear of a second Holocaust. This led even assimilated non-Zionist Jews, such as the French intellectual Raymond Aron, to express their deep sense of solidarity with the Jewish state. Following its stunning victory, Israel became a major source of pride for the Diaspora; the touchstone of its Jewish identity. One hundred thousand French Jews attended a demonstration to celebrate the victory.[9] Israel attained an almost mythical, heroic status in the Diaspora. In the US, support for Israel enhanced Jews' civic sense of belonging: Americans in general were massively supportive of Israel, since it was a strong, democratic ally. The centrality of Israel in Western Jews' identity inaugurated a 'New Jewish Politics' expressed by a more aggressive style of lobbying: a style that was more focused on Israel, as the fear of the 'dual loyalty' issue faded.[10] In the US, the main ideological exponents of this approach were neo-conservatives, such as Norman Pordhoretz, editor of the influential *Commentary* magazine. In organizational terms, it was expressed by the meteoric rise of AIPAC to become both the de facto leading Jewish organization and one of the most powerful lobbying organizations in the US.

Meanwhile, behind the Iron Curtain, the authorities were concerned by their Jewish citizens' identification with Israel's exploits at a time when they had cut diplomatic relations with Israel.[11] A growing number of Soviet Jews defied the authorities and applied to immigrate to Israel. Thus, the 'refusenik' movement was born. *Aliyah* from Western countries also grew significantly, particularly among modern Orthodox Jews; though the absolute numbers remained low. Israel's victory enhanced the confidence of Jews in Western democracies, a trend symbolized by the willingness of young religious men to wear a *kippa* [traditional head covering] in public. The fact that important religious sites were captured in 1967, including the Western Wall, also made Israel more central in Ultra Orthodox identity, though this group remained highly critical of the secular state.[12]

The 1973 Yom Kippur War, while traumatic, did not change these basic orientations. Solidarity with Israel was at the core of Diaspora identity, despite the fact that Diaspora Jewry, particularly in Europe, began to be targeted by Palestinian terrorists. Even the rise of Menachem Begin's *Likud* to power in 1977, which made some Diaspora leaders nervous, did not initially change this situation, especially as Begin achieved peace with Egypt in his first term. In sum, this period represents the high watermark of Israel's place in Diaspora identity. The idealized Israel of Diaspora identity was all things to all Jews. The hawks and the religious lauded Israel's victory in 1967, while the doves and liberals lauded its willingness to surrender the Sinai in return for peace with Egypt. Most Diaspora Jews applauded both the military victories and the compromises for peace.

The Collapse of Consensus, 1982–1992

The 1982 Lebanon War was the first time the international media generally adopted an anti-Israeli approach. It was also the first war about which Israelis were themselves deeply divided. As a result, Israeli policy became a major source of ideological controversy among mainstream Diaspora Jewry in the West, for the first time. Matters came to a head following the massacre of Palestinian refugees in the Sabra and Chatilla refugee camps by Israel's Lebanese allies. Subsequently, the leading Orthodox Rabbi in the US, Rabbi Joseph Soloveitchik and a leading Reform Rabbi, Alexander Schindler, called for a commission of inquiry, initially opposed by Begin.[13] The massacre represented the beginning of the end of the idealized Israel 'that could do no wrong' in Diaspora Jewish consciousness. Nonetheless, despite the fact that the Diaspora was generally more dovish than the *Likud* government,[14] it did not lobby against the Begin government's policies.

Another serious blow to Israel's heroic image was dealt by the Pollard affair. Jonathan Pollard, a Jewish intelligence officer in the US, was convicted of spying for Israel in 1986. US Jews were extremely angry as they felt Israel had challenged their civic identity and raised the spectre of an anti-Semitic backlash on the basis of 'dual loyalty'.[15]

The outbreak of the First Intifada in December 1987 had a more sustained and a more traumatic effect than the Lebanon War. In Lebanon, the main point of controversy was the level of force; consequently, once Israel withdrew to the security zone, the controversy died down. However, with regard to the Intifada, the issue was not only Israel's use of force, but also more core ideological matters such as the settlements and Palestinian national rights. While Diaspora Jewry continued to identify with Israel, following the trend among the Israeli public, it became increasingly polarized regarding the policies pursued by Israel's *Likud*-led governments. Politically conservative Jews and Orthodox Jews tended to identify with Israel's policies either on the basis of an ideological attachment to *Eretz Yisrael* or because they viewed attacks on Israel as an expression of age-old anti-Semitism that demanded Jewish solidarity. Meanwhile, Jewish liberals felt increasingly alienated by Israeli policies in the Territories, which contradicted their core values. One symptom of this was the growing public criticism of Israel by well-known Diaspora Jews such as Woody Allen and violinist Yehudi Menuhin. The leaders of tens of Jewish organizations in the US even went so far as to place a newspaper advertisement informing *Likud* Prime Minister Shamir (on a visit to the US) that, while they continued to support Israel in general, they opposed his policies.[16]

In the Soviet Union, Israeli policy appeared to have little effect on identification with Israel. On arriving in Israel, the leading Refusenik, Natan Sharansky, initially refrained from expressing an opinion regarding Israeli policy towards the Palestinians, professing ignorance. Subsequently, he adopted a relatively hawkish stance, as did the majority of Russian immigrants to Israel. This suggests that the Lebanon War or the Intifada did not negatively affect their identity whilst they were still in the USSR.[17]

In the West, some liberal Jews formed groups such as Friends of Peace Now that adopted a more critical and dovish line than that of the Diaspora establishment. Nonetheless, the effects of polarization were largely confined to criticism. Thus, in the US, although a large number of Jews were opposed to Israel's refusal to talk to the PLO after 1988, they were still generally unprepared to pressure Israel to change its position. Similarly, in the UK, the Union of Jewish Students (UJS) formally supported a two-state solution that was opposed by the Israeli government. But, in practice, UJS continued to co-operate with the Israeli Embassy, while engaging in campaigns aimed at defending Israel and highlighting Palestinian terrorism and anti-Zionist propaganda.

In fact, it was not Israeli policy towards the Palestinians, but Israeli government insensitivity to Jewish identity that led mainstream Diaspora Jewish organizations, on occasion, to refuse to assist Israel. In 1988, the *Likud* leader, Yitzhak Shamir, agreed to change Israel's Law of Return to allow automatic immigration to Israel so that it applied only to persons defined as Jewish by Orthodox Jewish Law. While millions of Diaspora Jews are affiliated to non-Orthodox streams of Judaism, in practice this change would have affected only a handful of Diaspora Jews each year. However the non-Orthodox saw the proposed amendment in terms of a de-legitimization of their Jewish identity by Israel. Subsequently, even the normally apolitical Hadassah and the consensus-based Conference of Presidents of Major American Jewish Organizations (Presidents' Conference) in the US, refused to help Israel lobby against the US–PLO dialogue, unless Shamir retracted his agreement. In the end, Shamir retracted and the pro-Israel lobby did continue to co-operate with the Israeli government.[18]

The second occasion when US Jews held back from lobbying was regarding the issue of loan guarantees in 1991–2. Initially, AIPAC had lobbied strongly for the Israeli government position, with the support of Congress, against the position of the Bush administration that sought to link the granting of loan guarantees by the US, of $10 billion, to a settlement freeze. While settlements were not especially popular among US Jews, this did not prevent a major lobbying campaign against linkage taking place, culminating in a massive public demonstration in Washington DC. However, following that demonstration, President Bush made the loan guarantees a major issue and referred to opponents of his position as representing a 'foreign interest'. Subsequently, US Jewry refused to continue to campaign vigorously against linkage. Although Bush later apologized for his comment, the fact that he had inferred that American Jews' opposition to linkage was symptomatic of their dual loyalty was enough for some major American Jewish organizations to refuse Israeli demands to continue to lobby vigorously.[19]

The Oslo Era, 1993–2000: Distancing from Israel?

During the Oslo era, it was claimed that Israel and the Diaspora were growing more distant from each other. With the peace process well underway and Israel more secure than ever, the Diaspora felt able to put less emphasis on defending Israel and more on combating assimilation and promoting 'Jewish continuity' in the Diaspora itself.[20] This was reflected in a shift in funding, away from Israeli causes towards home causes. In the UK, it led to the closing of the pro-Israel lobby group: British Israel Public Affairs Committee (BIPAC). While the majority of Diaspora Jews supported the Oslo process, many pro-Israel activists felt lost or even somewhat used, as Israel reversed long-standing policies against negotiating with the PLO and giving up the Golan Heights, which they had spent a lifetime defending. Activists became annoyed at some of the declarations of the Labour government telling them that their help was no longer required. Meanwhile, the Orthodox became very critical of Israel's dovish policies under Labour, which they often referred to as post-Zionist or even post-Jewish.[21]

However, the advent of the Oslo process did not really distance Diaspora Jewry from Israel; it merely altered the nature of the relationship. Instead of focusing on defending Israel, the Diaspora gave Israel a central place in 'Jewish continuity', most obviously by promoting peer group visits to Israel — for example, within the *birthright israel* programme. Indeed, increasing amounts of Jewish youth in the UK were contemplating *aliyah*.[22] In addition, criticism of Israeli policies did not affect the underlying identification with Israel. After all, those most critical of Israel's dovish policies, the Orthodox, were also the group that visited Israel the most and were most likely to make *aliyah*. Overall, the Diaspora did not distance itself from Israel: rather the Diaspora adopted a new, more pluralistic form of engagement, in which it tried to influence the nature of Israeli society and politics.[23] With the demise of the mythological 'perfect' Israel, Diaspora Jews began trying to push Israel in their preferred ideological directions. As a result, the character of Israel became the main ideological battlefield of Diaspora Jewry.

The combination of ideological fracture and political activism found practical expression in the Diaspora's approach to the Oslo process itself. Instead of focusing on general support for Israeli policies, Diaspora Jews organized to lobby in favour of their particular ideological approach to the peace process. For this first time this included significant lobbying against the policy of the Israeli government. Thus, between 1993–6 the Zionist Organization of America (ZOA) and other politically conservative organizations such as JINSA (Jewish Institute for National Security) lobbied against Israeli policies in the US. Later, in 1996–9, Americans for Peace Now lobbied for US pressure to be applied on the Netanyahu government. In this context, for the first time, a majority of American Jews also backed US pressure on Israel.[24]

Yet the peak of the disjuncture between Israeli policies and Diaspora identity came when the left-wing government of Ehud Barak proposed unprecedented concessions to the Palestinians. The majority of US Jewry did not support some of Barak's concessions, especially the division of Jerusalem and Palestinian control over the Temple Mount. Subsequently, mainstream Diaspora leaders took part in a large demonstration in Jerusalem to protest against such plans.[25] Important Diaspora leaders, who usually emphasized Israel's right to decide its foreign and security policies alone, spoke of Jerusalem as being an issue on which the Jewish people worldwide should have a say, given its central importance to Jewish identity worldwide.[26] This, more than anything else, symbolized that while the Diaspora still identified strongly with Israel, it no longer expressed that identification through subservient support for Israeli government policies, but rather through active ideological engagement to affect Israeli policies, even on core issues related to the peace process.

The Collapse of the Oslo Process 2000–4, Pluralistic Solidarity

The collapse of the Oslo process, coupled with a massive wave of suicide terrorist attacks against Israelis, was greeted by Diaspora solidarity with Israel. According to a 2003 survey, three-quarters of US Jews felt close to Israel.[27] Some Jews in Europe felt that the heavy criticism of Israel's behaviour heightened their sense of Jewish identity, separating them from their fellow citizens.[28] Despite Prime Minister Sharon's negative image among large sections of the Diaspora, Israel's policies were not generally blamed by the Diaspora for the collapse of the peace process. This was due to the fact that the Diaspora generally interpreted the unprecedented concessions agreed to by Barak, as proof of Israel's good faith. In Europe, anti-Semitism rose sharply in response to Israeli policies. Despite recognizing this connection, Diaspora Jews did not generally blame Israel for the situation. In fact, the rise in anti-Semitism in Europe led to a doubling of the number of French Jews making *aliyah* (from 1000 to 2000 a year), while other European Jews referred to Israel as a potential refuge, if things got worse. Nonetheless, French Jews were very critical of Sharon for telling them to make *aliyah* because of anti-Semitism, as this statement raised, once again, the vexed issue of 'dual loyalty'.[29] In the US, solidarity with Israel was evident at the 2001 AIPAC conference which set new records for attendance and money raised for Israel.[30] European Jews also demonstrated solidarity with Israel, as big pro-Israel rallies in Washington and New York were accompanied by rallies of around 50,000 Jews in both London and Paris in 2002 and 2003. In France, well-known Jewish intellectuals such as Bernard Henri Levi defended Israel against the generally anti-Israel public, and even less-identifying French Jews were drawn to Israel's defence; as were the representatives of Progressive Judaism in the US and the UK, who had previously adopted a more critical dovish line.[31] In fact, 63 percent of US Jews thought that they should continue to support Israel, even if they disagreed with its policies.[32]

Nonetheless, such expressions of solidarity did not represent a return to the 1970s. Members of the Israeli Left began to promote an alternative narrative, which put the blame for the collapse of the Oslo process on both sides. This began to have an impact on liberals in the Diaspora, especially after Labour left Sharon's government in the autumn of 2003. Subsequently, liberal Diaspora Jews formed the *Brit Zedek* organization, which collected over 10,000 signatures of support for the Geneva draft permanent status agreement negotiated by Yossi Beilin and Yasir Abd Rabbo (this agreement was vigorously opposed by the Israeli government and Israeli centrists in general).[33] Believing that there was a realistic chance for peace, liberal Jewish support for Sharon's policies become more equivocal. At the solidarity rally for Israel held in London, a group of former members of the left-wing Habonim youth movement left the rally when Netanyahu spoke.[34] British Friends of Peace Now published a petition against Sharon's policies signed by 300 prominent Jews, while British Chief Rabbi Jonathan Sacks, whilst generally defending Israel in the media, also warned that, without an end to the occupation, Israel would lose its soul.[35] Meanwhile, in the US, even some mainstream organizations were publicly critical of Israeli policies regarding the separation barrier and settlements.[36] Overall then, the increased expressions of Diaspora solidarity with Israel demonstrated the continued identification of Diaspora Jews with Israel, but in practical terms that identification was expressed in a more pluralistic manner than simply support for Israeli policies.[37]

The Future

The trend in the Diaspora is that the older generations and the Orthodox identify most with Israel, while the younger generation of non-Orthodox Jews identify far less with Israel. The situation is particularly evident in the US, where surveys suggest that only about a third of Jewish students identify clearly with Israel. Of the children of mixed marriages (roughly 50 percent of Diaspora Jews marry non-Jews), only a tiny minority identify with Israel. According to one extensive study, aside from the 10–15 percent who are actively pro-Israel via traditional community organizations, another 35 percent of young US Jews (classed as members of the tribe and members of the tribe lite) are open to greater identification and engagement with Israel. However, the traditional institutions of organized Jewry, including AIPAC and Hillel, turn them off and they are not receptive to the traditional 'clichéd' ways of relating to Israel. Their post-modern[38] attitudes are more similar to American non-Jews their age, than they are to their parents' attitudes. They are positive regarding 'peace' and 'democracy', while being more negative regarding organized religion and 'security', including Israeli security. While their negative perception and even embarrassment at hawkish Israeli policies is not the main reason for this alienation, it is something that discourages people from becoming actively supportive of Israel.[39] In order for Israel to harness the practical support of this crucial group, its foreign and defence policy must be viewed as geared towards peace, and as expressing democratic values. In particular, the on-going Israeli occupation of the Territories deepens this group's alienation from Israel.

More generally, Israel's on-going occupation has the potential to irreparably damage support for Israel among the majority of Diaspora Jews in the medium-term. This does not mean that the Diaspora blames Israel for the situation, nor that it expects Israel to withdraw to the pre-1967 borders in the near future. However, by 2010 there are likely to be more Arabs than Jews within the area of Israel, the West Bank and Gaza combined. Were Israel to pursue a policy of ruling over a Palestinian majority without full civil rights indefinitely, this would contradict core Jewish and democratic values. Such a situation would generate the most serious ever crisis of Diaspora Jewish identification with Israel. Recognition of this threat may be leading to a significant shift in Israeli thinking *vis-à-vis* the importance of the Diaspora in Israeli foreign and defence policy.

The Israeli Perspective: Diaspora Identification as a Strategic Asset

> "We have to consider the interests of Diaspora Jewry . . . But there is one crucial distinction — not what they think their best interests are but what we regard as their interests."[40]
>
> David Ben-Gurion

Israeli leaders generally understood Ben-Gurion's dictum as meaning that the interests of world Jewry are equivalent to the interests of the State of Israel as interpreted by its government. Thus, Israel policy-makers have been concerned by the impact of their foreign and defence policy on Diaspora identity primarily when it is perceived to have important ramifications for Israeli interests. Classic Zionist ideology proposed to 'negate the Diaspora'. It denigrated any form of Diaspora Jewish identity and focused on promoting *aliyah*. After 1948, these ideological attitudes softened. Although *aliyah* remained a core objective, the State of Israel preferred to develop relations with the Jewish communities as a whole, including non-Zionists, rather than with Zionist organizations alone.[41] Ideological considerations came second to the need to maximise the financial and political support of the Diaspora, which was especially important in the early years of statehood.

While Israel was happy to reap the material benefits of Diaspora assistance, it was less keen to recognize its reliance on the Diaspora, for ideological reasons. Nor was Israel willing to give the Diaspora a say in Israeli foreign policy, as Nahum Goldman, head of the World Jewish Congress, wanted. Indeed, Israeli policy-makers retained a disdain for Diaspora lobbying — *Shtadlanut* — as symptomatic of the 'old Jew' that Zionism sought to replace. This attitude was most apparent during the 'Who is a Jew' crisis of 1988. Both Labour and *Likud* were prepared to change the Law of Return such that it would alienate non-Orthodox Diaspora Jews in order to obtain the backing of the religious parties in Israel to form a government.[42] Shamir only reversed the policy when American Jewry refused to lobby against the US dialogue with the PLO. In other words, Israel only really took Diaspora identity into account when it made political sense in terms of Israeli state interests.

In this vein, from the late 1980s onwards, the Israeli Left and Right sought to take advantage of ideological splits in the Diaspora to build up support for their preferred policies towards the peace process. The Right was more effective in this regard. Subsequently, in the 1990s the Israeli Left tried to minimize Diaspora involvement in the peace process. Beilin saw AIPAC as right wing; Rabin disliked the whole concept of *Shtadlanut* in any case, while Peres viewed Diaspora assistance in the realm of *Hasbara* (spin doctoring) as unnecessary in the era of peace.[43] While this approach alienated many in the Diaspora, it was accompanied, for the first time, by a greater concern for Diaspora Jewish identity in and of itself. Beilin, in particular, was keen to expand the cultural and social links between Israel and the Diaspora, irrespective of *aliyah* or Israel's political interests.[44]

The Diaspora has, generally speaking, only been a minor consideration in the making of Israeli foreign policy. Relations with the Diaspora have been handled primarily by the Foreign Ministry, which has very little influence over major foreign and defence policy decisions. Even within the Foreign Ministry, the Diaspora has not been a major consideration. Thus, when in 1986 Foreign Minister Shimon Peres sent a document to all Israeli embassies that defined the relative significance of various interests, the Diaspora was ranked only fourth or fifth.[45] The relative unimportance of the Diaspora in Israeli foreign policy was also apparent in 2002 when, following cutbacks in its budget, the Foreign Ministry closed a number of its consulates and embassies. In making the decisions regarding where to cut, the Diaspora did not hold a privileged position. For example, Israel closed its Sydney consulate despite a major campaign by the Jewish community to keep it open.[46]

As Prime Minister, Yitzhak Rabin sought to minimize any consideration of the Diaspora in Israeli policymaking. On coming into office in 1992, he publicly lambasted AIPAC for interfering in the US–Israeli relationship.[47] Subsequently, he did not bother to appoint an advisor for Diaspora affairs until 1995. He only relented when US Jews opposed to his policies began to cause Israel problems in the US Congress. In 1995, Rabin received a letter expressing concern at Israeli policies from a very prominent British Rabbi known as a general supporter of the peace process. Nonetheless, Rabin's initial reaction was terse: Israeli foreign policy is not the business of Diaspora Jews. (In the end, he was persuaded by Embassy officials to send a more diplomatic response.)[48]

While Rabin is an extreme example, the state-centric approach has dominated Israeli policy under every government. The fact is that the Diaspora variable has not had a significant effect on any major Israeli decision in the realm of foreign and security policy. The only significant exception to this state-centric approach relates to *aliyah*. On occasion, the desire of Israeli governments to encourage *aliyah* has affected

Israeli policies. One reason Israel initially adopted a neutral policy in the Cold War, and that it later restrained its pro-American stance up to 1967, was its desire to maintain relations with Jews behind the Iron Curtain in order to facilitate their future *aliyah*.[49] After the Soviets broke diplomatic relations with Israel in 1967, Israel worked very closely with Diaspora Jews, particularly in Britain, to maintain contacts indirectly with Soviet Jews. Israel also developed a close relationship with Ceaucescu's Romania in order to facilitate the *aliyah* of Romanian Jews, despite the dictator's close ties to the PLO, which at that stage was still openly committed to the destruction of Israel. Similarly, in the mid-1980s Israeli policy towards the civil war in Ethiopia was determined less by ideology or geo-strategic considerations than it was by the Zionist/Humanitarian aim of bringing Ethiopian Jewry to Israel.[50] However, not all Israeli leaders thought *aliyah* should take precedence over state interests. Yitzhak Rabin stands out in this regard. Thus in 1973 he opposed the Jackson–Vanit amendment, whereby Congress linked Détente with the USSR to a Soviet willingness to let Jews immigrate freely to Israel. Rabin feared it would damage Israel's close strategic relationship with the Nixon administration that opposed the amendment.[51]

Even when Israel assumes the mantle of official representative of the Jewish people, it often does so in order to further its own distinctive state interests. Thus, when Ben-Gurion accepted reparations for the Holocaust from West Germany in the name of the Jewish people, he did so, in large part, because he believed the money, as well as the political support of West Germany, would be very important to the security and development of the fledgling state.[52]

Israel has taken a consistent interest in helping Diaspora Jews combat anti-Semitism. In the 1950s, covert Israeli operations helped protect North African Jews. By the 1960s, most of these Jews had made *aliyah* and so the activity waned.[53] After 1967, Palestinian and Islamic terrorists began to target Jews in Western countries whom they perceived as party to the conflict.[54] In democratic countries, Israeli activities were much more restricted, consisting of liaison with the local authorities and the provision of training to community security services. On the other hand, Israel has maintained close relations with authoritarian regimes that took severe measures against Jewish communities or against liberal elements within those communities, for example, its relations with the military Junta in Argentina and with the Pinochet regime in Chile, in the late 1970s and early 1980s.[55] Furthermore, with the onset of Israeli–Palestinian violence again in September 2000, anti-Semitic attacks against Jews in Europe rose dramatically. There was a clear correlation between Israeli military activity and attacks on Diaspora Jews. While Israel was concerned by this phenomenon and sought to assist local communities by raising the issue with foreign governments, there is no evidence that it canceled or scaled back any military operation. Israel's assassination of a leading Hamas figure in Damascus in Autumn 2004 was carried out in the knowledge that by striking at Hamas outside of the Territories, Hamas might change its policy and retaliate by attacking Jewish or Israeli targets outside Israel.[56] Ultimately, the State of Israel acts primarily on the basis of its interests as a state, not out of concern for the Diaspora.

In fact, despite Israel–Diaspora solidarity, anti-Semitism can be a source of tension in the relationship. When Sharon told French Jews in 2004 that they should respond to anti-Semitism by making *aliyah*, he raised the spectre of 'dual loyalty' and made Diaspora Jews feel more vulnerable rather than safer. Formally, Israel recognizes that

Diaspora Jews owe loyalty only to the countries of which they are citizens. However, in practice, ideology and realpolitik combine to make Israeli policy insensitive to the civic identity of Diaspora Jews. The ideological component was apparent in Shamir's address to the Presidents' Conference in 1988 when he declared, "Jews abroad have a moral duty to support the Israeli government, never a foreign government against Israel".[57] Subsequently, members of the Shamir government attributed US Jewry's refusal to campaign on loan guarantees as emanating from a typically weak Diaspora mentality.[58] The most glaring example of this insensitivity was the Pollard Affair. Similarly, in 2004 members of the Jewish community in New Zealand were arrested for assisting Israeli *Mossad* agents. Nonetheless, despite the impression made by this case and occasional sensationalist reports in the media, the *Mossad* has generally been sensitive regarding the dual loyalty issue.[59]

With the collapse of the Oslo process and the onslaught of attacks on Israel's legitimacy at the UN Conference on Human Rights in Durban (and in Europe more generally), Israel began to attach a greater emphasis than ever before to the Diaspora. For the first time Israel created a Minister for Diaspora Affairs, who was charged, amongst other things, with 'The Global Forum Against Anti-Semitism'. In addition, Israel's National Security Council is dealing with the issue of Diaspora relations, because it views the Diaspora as one of Israel's most important strategic assets.[60] Against this background, Jewish Policy Planning, a Jewish Agency think tank, recommended consulting the Diaspora regarding Israel's foreign and defence policy, recognizing that the results of Israeli policy affect Jews worldwide. They feared that without consultation, ideological divisions and the ambivalence of younger Jews would prevent the Diaspora from actively supporting Israel in its battle to protect the legitimacy of the Jewish state. Indeed, Israeli leaders[61] want to strengthen Diaspora Jewish identity, even if it does not result in *aliyah*, in order to sustain a strategic asset, which they took for granted for many years. The most important example of the Diaspora influencing Israeli policy relates to the Sharon government's decision to unilaterally withdraw from Gaza and four settlements in the West Bank, which was announced in December 2003. According to the then Deputy Prime Minister Ehud Olmert, who was very close to Sharon, one of the reasons for adopting the measure was the belief that if Israel continued to occupy the Territories indefinitely it would lose the support of Diaspora Jewry.[62] What bothered Olmert and Sharon was less the emotional state of Diaspora Jewry and rather more the financial and political ramifications of such a situation for the State of Israel. In other words, even if the Diaspora is becoming more important, Israeli policy-makers still view it primarily through the prism of state interests.

Summary

The Diaspora is generally only a minor consideration in the formation of Israeli foreign and defence policy. When it does play a role, it is primarily because Israeli policy-makers view it as in Israel's state interest or Zionist interest in *aliyah*, rather than out of some sort of pan-Jewish altruism.

Israeli foreign and defence policy has had an impact on both the civic and the Jewish identity of Diaspora Jews. Israeli behaviour has, on occasion, left Diaspora Jews feeling their civic identity threatened by charges of 'dual loyalty'. Nonetheless, prior to the 1980s, Diaspora identification with Israel was expressed in unwavering support for Israeli policies. Since then, Diaspora support for Israeli policies cannot be taken for granted. Mirroring the trend within Israel itself, Diaspora Jewry has become increasingly divided over Israeli policy and increasingly willing to openly criticize and act against policies they oppose. Yet criticism has not translated into alienation from Israel, rather it represents a more pluralistic expression of identification. In practical terms, this situation constrains Israel's ability to effectively mobilize Diaspora support over contentious issues such as settlements. Only an Israeli policy clearly aimed at indefinite occupation of the Territories would lead to a major crisis of Diaspora identification with Israel. On the other hand, Israel can still count on wide-ranging support for its policies on consensus issues, such as Israel's Jewish identity.

From the Israeli strategic perspective, the Diaspora is more important than ever, as it has great potential to assist Israel in its struggle to protect its legitimacy as a Jewish state in Western public opinion, and in other international non-governmental arenas. However, to succeed, Israel will have to adopt a more sophisticated, pluralistic and open form of engagement with the Diaspora than has been the case in the past.

Notes

1 Bernard Wasserstein, *Vanishing Diasporas* (Cambridge, MA: Harvard University Press, 1996), pp. 91, 228–233.
2 Nathan Guttman, "FBI says Pentagon analyst gave secrets to Israel via AIPAC", *Ha'aretz*, 29 August 2004.
3 Yosef Gorney, *The State of Israel in Jewish Public Thought* (London: Macmillan, 1994).
4 Thomas Friedman, *From Beirut to Jerusalem* (New York: Fontana, 1990), p. 454.
5 Wasserstein, *Vanishing Diasporas*, p. 96.
6 Ibid.
7 Cited in George Gruen, "The Not So Silent Partnership: Emerging Trends in American Jewish–Israeli Relations", in Gregory Mahler (ed.), *Israel after Begin* (Albany: SUNY, 1989), p. 213.
8 Peter Medding, "The New Jewish Politics in the United States" in Zvi Gitelman (ed.), *The Quest for Utopia* (New York: M.E. Sharpe, 1992).
9 Wasserstein, *Vanishing Diasporas*, pp. 98–100.
10 Medding, "The New Jewish Politics in the United States".
11 Wasserstein, *Vanishing Diasporas*, pp. 190–212.
12 Menachem Friedman, "The State of Israel as a Theological Dilemma" in Baruch Kimmerling (ed.), *The Israeli Society and State; Boundaries and Frontier* (Albany: SUNY, 1985).
13 Milton Himmelfarb and David Singer, *American Jewish Yearbook 1984* (Philadelphia: Jewish Publication Society, 1983), pp. 84–90.
14 Edward Tivnan, *The Lobby* (New York: Simon & Schuster, 1987), p. 206.
15 On Israel's relations with US Jewry 1980–96 see Jonathan Rynhold, "Labour, Likud, the Special Relationship & the Peace Process" *Israel Affairs*, 3, 3 & 4 (1997).
16 Yossi Melman and Dan Raviv, *Friends in Deed: Inside the U.S.–Israel Alliance* (New York: Hyperion, 1994), pp. 432–33.
17 Ze'ev Chanin, "The Vision of Return: Reflections on the Mass Immigration to Israel from the Former Soviet Union". Paper submitted as part of the research project: *The Meaning of Catastrophe, Historical Knowledge, and Return of Exiles: the Predicaments of Palestinians and Jews*, Philadelphia, 24–27 October 2002.

18 Colin Shindler, *Swords into Ploughshares: Israelis and Jews in the Shadow of the Intifada* (London: I.B. Tauris, 1991), pp. 142–45.

19 Rynhold, "Labour, Likud, the Special Relationship & the Peace Process".

20 On this issue see Steven Rosenthal, *Irreconcilable Differences? The Waning of the American Jewish Love Affair with Israel* (Hanover, NH: University Press of New England, 2001); Stephen Cohen, "Did American Jews Really Grow More Distant from Israel 1983–93?" in Allon Gal (ed.), *Envisioning Israel* (Detroit: Wayne State University Press, 1996); Zvi Gitelman, *New Jewish Identities* (Budapest: Central European University Press, 2003); Barry Kosmin, Anthony Lerman and Jacqueline Goldberg, "The attachment of British Jews to Israel" *Jewish Policy Research Report No. 5* (1997).

21 *Jewish Press*, 15 September 1995, p. 14; 6 October 1993, p. 16; *Jerusalem Report*, 19 October 1995, p. 38; *Yediot Aharonot*, 11 September 1995, p. 1; *Jerusalem Post*, 17 November 1995, p. 11. For polls see *Mideast Mirror*, 13 September 1995; *Jewish Chronicle*, 13 September 1995, p. 8.

22 Kosmin, Lerman & Goldberg, "The attachment of British Jews to Israel" *Jewish Policy Research Report No. 5* (1997).

23 Yossi Shain, "Jewish kinship at a crossroads: Lessons for homelands and diasporas" *Political Science Quarterly* 117, 2 (Summer 2002).

24 Jonathan Rynhold, "Israeli–American Relations and the Peace Process", *Middle East Review of International Affairs (MERIA)*, 4, 2 (2000).

25 Shlomo Shamir, "Survey: 35% of U.S. Jews favor dividing capital", *Ha'aretz*, 7 March 2001.

26 Yossi Shain and Barry Bristman, "Diaspora, kinship and loyalty: the renewal of Jewish national security", *International Affairs*, 78, 1 (2002), p. 75.

27 <http://www.ajc.org/InTheMedia/PubSurveys.asp?did=1030>.

28 Author interviews in the UK and Daniel Ben Simon, "Notes from a French anti-Semitic heartland", *Ha'aretz*, 22 July 2004.

29 Author interviews in the UK; "Sharon urges French Jews to leave 'as soon as possible'," *Ha'aretz*, 19 July 2004.

30 Shain and Bristman, "Diaspora, kinship and loyalty: the renewal of Jewish national security" p. 85.

31 Daniel Ben Simon, "Notes from a French anti-Semitic heartland", *Ha'aretz*, 22 July 2004; Daniel Ben-Simon, "The price of brainwashing", *Ha'aretz*, 6 July 2004; Simon Rocker "'We back Israel' say Liberal rabbis", *Jewish Chronicle*, 15 February 2002.

32 <http://www.ajc.org/InTheMedia/PubSurveys.asp?did=1030>.

33 <http://btvshalom.org/>.

34 Author interview with participants.

35 "UK Jewry split over Peace Now petition", *Jewish Chronicle*, 5 April 2002; Jonathan Freedland, "Prophet of Hope", *The Guardian*, 27 August 2002.

36 Shlomo Shamir, "Bronfman: Jewish leaders creating rift between Israel, U.S.", *Ha'aretz*, July 2004; Shlomo Shamir, "Reform Movement rabbis set to condemn house demolitions", *Ha'aretz*, 24 June 2004; "Reform head blasts settlements", *Jerusalem Post*, 13 November 2003.

37 See for example the 2004 survey of British Jews, *Jewish Chronicle*, September 2004.

38 Steven Cohen and Arnold Eisen, *The Jew Within: Self, Family, and Community in America* (Bloomington, IN: Indiana University Press, 2000).

39 Sherry Israel, *Comprehensive Report on the 1995 CJP Demographic Study* (Boston: Combined Jewish Philanthropies, 1997); Frank Luntz, *Israel in the age of Eminem* (New York: Bronfman Philanthropies, 2003); Nathan Gutman, "Israel not high on young US

Jews' agenda", *Ha'aretz*, 1 June 2003; Author interview with Roger Bennett, Vice President, Bronfman Philanthropies; National Jewish Population Survey (NJPS) 2001; Kosmin, Lerman & Goldberg, "The attachment of British Jews to Israel".

40 Michael Brecher, *The Foreign Policy System of Israel* (Oxford: Oxford University Press, 1972), p. 232.

41 On Israeli policy towards the Diaspora see Alan Dowty, "Israeli Foreign Policy and the Jewish Question", *MERIA*, 3, 1 (1999); Dov Waxman, "The Jewish Dimension in Israeli Foreign Policy", *Israel Studies Forum*, 19, 1 (2003); Gabriel Sheffer, "The Elusive Question: Jews and Jewry in Israeli Foreign Policy", *Jerusalem Quarterly* 46 (Spring 1988).

42 David Landau, *Who is a Jew: A Case Study of American Jewish Influence on Israeli Policy* (New York: American Jewish Committee and The Argov Centre, Bar Ilan University, 1996).

43 David Horowitz (ed.), *Yitzhak Rabin: Soldier for Peace* (London: Halban, 1996), pp. 157–59.

44 Yossi Beilin, *His Brother's Keeper* (New York: Shocken, 2000). See also comments by Peres, *Jerusalem Post*, 9 April 1996, p. 7.

45 Sheffer, "The Elusive Question: Jews and Jewry in Israeli Foreign Policy", p. 105.

46 *Jerusalem Report*, 21 October 2002, p. 56.

47 Ibid.

48 Author interview with Embassy official.

49 Shain and Bristman, "Diaspora, kinship and loyalty: the renewal of Jewish national security".

50 Dan Raviv and Yossi Melman, *Every Spy A Prince* (Boston: Houghton Mifflin, 1990), pp. 225–227.

51 Horowitz, *Yitzhak Rabin: Soldier for Peace*, p. 157.

52 Lillian Feldman, *The Special Relationship Between West Germany & Israel* (Boston: Allen & Unwin, 1984).

53 Raviv and Yossi Melman, *Every Spy a Prince.*

54 Wasserstein, *Vanishing Diasporas*, pp. 228–233.

55 Sheffer "The Elusive Question: Jews and Jewry in Israeli Foreign Policy", p. 111.

56 Khaled Abu Toameh, "Hamas split over exporting terror campaign", *Jerusalem Post*, 26 September 2004.

57 Gruen, "Not So Silent Partnership: Emerging Trends in American Jewish–Israeli Relations", p. 217.

58 *Jerusalem Post*, 31 January 1992; Glen Frankel, *Beyond the Promised Land* (New York: Simon and Schuster, 1994), p. 306.

59 Dan Raviv and Yossi Melman, *Every Spy A Prince*, pp. 323; The CIA, *Israel Foreign Intelligence and Security Services: A Survey* (Washington, DC: CIA, 1979).

60 Author conversations with Israeli officials; Yossi Shain and Barry Bristman, "The Jewish Security Dilemma", *Orbis*, 46 (Winter 2002).

61 Yair Sheleg, "American Jewry high up on Sharon's agenda", *Ha'aretz*, 13 February 2001; Horowitz, *Yitzhak Rabin: Soldier for Peace*, pp. 163–64.

62 "Interview with Ehud Olmert", *Yediot Achronot*, 5 December 2003 [in Hebrew].

ISRAEL COMMENTATOR

Identity, Diaspora and Israeli Foreign Defence Policy

Amiram Barkat

In March 1992, 29 people (including seven Israelis) were killed, when a car loaded with explosives rammed the Israeli embassy in Buenos Aires, Argentina. Two years later, in July 1994, 86 people were killed in a similar attack on the headquarters of the Jewish community in that city. According to Israeli and American intelligence services, the two attacks were perpetrated by the Hezbollah with assistance from Iranian intelligence, in revenge for the killing of Hezbollah secretary general Abbas Mussawi by Israeli forces in February 1992. According to Israeli analysts, the assault on Israeli *and* Jewish targets in foreign countries created a "deterrent balance" that made Israel think twice before carrying out further actions on high-profile figures such as Mussawi.[1] Israel has never publicly admitted this claim but up until its withdrawal from South Lebanon in May 2000, Israel refrained from similar actions against the organization's leaders. Targeted killings were extremely rare, were limited to Hezbollah field commanders and, unlike Mussawi's case, Israel did not claim responsibility for such actions.[2]

Jonathan Rynhold claims in his article that "there is no evidence" that Israel cancelled or "scaled back" any military operation for fear of counter-responses that would harm Jewish communities in the Diaspora. Even if Rynhold's claim cannot be refuted, the Mussawi affair proves that reality is more complicated than the way it is often portrayed. Even without an Israeli admission, there is no doubt that the attack on the AMIA building significantly increased the awareness of Israeli decision-makers of the possible ramifications of a similar act on the security of Diaspora Jewry.

Rynhold precisely and succinctly covers the development of the Israeli attitude toward the Diaspora. I wholeheartedly concur with his main conclusion that the Diaspora is generally only a "minor consideration" in the formation of Israeli foreign and defence policy. Indeed, Diaspora Jewry's voice is barely heard in the forums of decision makers in Israel. Furthermore, unlike Rynhold's cautious optimism that, after the collapse of the Oslo process Israel began to attach "a greater emphasis than ever before" to the Diaspora, I do not see any such change on the ground. Rynhold mentions a few steps taken by the Israeli government, including the appointment of a minister for Diaspora affairs and the establishment of a forum for countering anti-Semitism. Even so, in retrospect I would not attribute any importance to these steps, beyond their immediate political context.

In May 2005, Minister of Diaspora Affairs Natan Sharansky resigned from Ariel Sharon's government in protest over the disengagement plan. Following Sharansky's resignation, this post gradually disappeared. The Diaspora affairs portfolio was transferred to Rabbi Michael Melchior of the Labour Party, but the rank of this position was lowered from that of minister to deputy minister. After the Labour party's resignation from the government, responsibility for the Diaspora affairs "file" was transferred off-handedly to the then Tourism Minister Avraham Hirschson. The fact that the Diaspora portfolio essentially ceased to exist with Sharansky and Melchior no longer in government, strongly suggests that the position was created out of short-term political necessity.

With the disappearance of the position of Minister for Diaspora Affairs, the global forum for countering anti-Semitism also evaporated, after it had managed to meet only twice. Another disturbing development took place in the same year when the Foreign Ministry decided to cancel the independent status of the Department of Diaspora Affairs and merge it with the Department of Religious Affairs.

Contrary to the clear downgrading of the government's attitude toward the Diaspora, it should be noted that a new body, The World Jewish Forum, was founded in 2005 at the initiative of Israeli President Moshe Katsav. The Israeli president, who shows keen interest in Israel–Diaspora relations, said that this initiative had been driven by his concern for what he described as a "deep crisis in the Jewish people." The Forum is supposed to form (within a year) a Master plan for countering assimilation and increasing Jewish education around the world. At preliminary meetings several initiatives to stop assimilation were discussed, such as financing Jewish private education for every Jewish child from kindergarten to adulthood. The resources are to come from Jewish philanthropists, communities and the State of Israel. It is too early to tell whether this new body will fulfill these high expectations, but the Forum already serves as an important and much required stage for meetings between Israeli politicians, faculty and government officials, and prominent Jewish personalities from the Diaspora. Again the picture becomes more complex than originally surmised.

Coming back to the first point of this commentary. I would like to claim that Rynhold is being too harsh with the Israeli leadership when he states that Israel is using the Diaspora only for her own selfish goals. "When it (the Diaspora) does play a role," Rynhold writes, "it is primarily because Israeli policy-makers view it as in Israel's state interest or Zionist interest in *aliyah*, rather than out of some sort of pan-Jewish altruism."

This argument, which actually puts Israel in the same category as other countries with a diaspora, such as Ireland or Russia, does Israel an injustice, because it disregards an important element in Israel's policy, and even identity. Essentially, I contend that the paradigm presented by Rynhold implodes when the issue of the physical security of Jewish communities is raised. The Israeli intelligence community has always viewed itself as a defender of the Jewish people. The *Bitzur* unit set up in the *Mossad* in the 1950s did not hesitate to act on foreign soil to defend Jewish communities. The unit decided to take action even in contravention of the Israeli Foreign Ministry's stance and while putting diplomatic relations at risk. Today, after the crises with Canada and New Zealand, Israel is much more cautious in its activities. Still, *Bitzur*'s activities are granted high priority: Meir Dagan, the current head of the Mossad, views the protection of Jewish communities around the world as one of the organization's four main goals.[3]

Rynhold indeed mentions some of Israel's efforts in protecting Jewish communities, but the official appeals to foreign governments or the training courses for Jewish youth are not incidental. These are manifestations of something fundamental in the Israeli doctrine. The concern for the safety of Jews in the Diaspora sometimes outweighs the clear Israeli interest in *aliyah*. The activities of Israeli bodies such as *Bitzur* often result in strengthening the sense of security felt by Diaspora Jewry, when in order to promote *aliyah* Israel should have undermined such feeling and imbued Diaspora Jewry with the understanding that only in Israel could they live in safety. Israeli efforts for the physical safety of Diaspora Jewry does not stem from "pan-Jewish altruism," but rather from the Israeli leadership's fundamental sense of responsibility for the lives of Jews — wherever they may be. This sense of responsibility was deeply rooted in the identity of most, but not all, Israeli leaders who viewed themselves, first and foremost, as members of the Jewish people. Prime Minister Ariel Sharon used to define himself first as a Jew and a member of the Jewish people. Just three days before his second stroke, from which he has not recovered, Sharon insisted on meeting young Jews from the Diaspora in his office. "Each and every one of us shares the responsibility for the future of the Jewish people," Sharon told his young guests, before adding that, "the future of the Jewish people and the future of the state of Israel depend on cooperation and the strengthening of ties between Israel and world Jewry".

Notes

1 In February 2003, for example, *Ha'aretz* military analyst Amir Oren wrote that the attacks in Argentina "silenced the IDF's excitement over the assassination operation against Mussawi" and noted that Israeli intelligence was surprised by the intensity of the Iranian response.
2 The August 1999 assassination of Abu Hassan, a senior commander in the South Lebanon sector, was attributed to Israel.
3 According to Yossi Melman, *Ha'aretz* security analyst, in his article from November 2003.

DIASPORA COMMENTATOR

Israel's Foreign and Defence Policy and Diaspora Jewish Identity

Dov Waxman

I have been asked to write this commentary from the perspective of a Diaspora Jew. But when I ponder this label and its implications, I wonder whether it really fits. To be sure, as a British Jew now living in the United States and having never been a citizen of Israel, I would customarily be regarded by Jews and non-Jews alike as a Diaspora Jew. But there is something about this external definition that does not cohere with my own sense of Jewish identity. The difficulty I have with the label "Diaspora Jew" is its implication that I live outside my homeland — the State of Israel. From its origins in describing the dispersal of Jews from Palestine following their defeat by the Romans in CE 70, the term "diaspora" today has come to refer to any group of people that have left their country of origin (voluntarily or involuntarily) and settled in a foreign country. Members of a diaspora, according to this contemporary meaning, retain individual and collective ties — sentimental and material — to their homeland. Although they may not return to their native land, and may not even wish to, they continue to regard it as their homeland. To be a member of a diaspora, then, is to live in a condition of displacement, uprootedness, and even marginality in one's country of residence. What is definitive of this diasporic existence is the notion of a distant homeland (however geographically near or far).

It is these implications of the label "Diaspora Jew" that I am uncomfortable with. In what sense is Israel my "homeland"? It is not my homeland in a practical sense — I was born and raised in England. Nor is it even my homeland in an emotional/psychological sense — I do not feel "at home" there when I visit and I do not feel that I belong there. Israel is only my homeland in a historical sense — being the place from which my distant ancestors originated. This does not mean that I do not care deeply about the country, but rather that I do not feel that it is *my* country. I suspect that I am not alone in feeling this. Many "Diaspora Jews" have a strong sense of attachment to Israel, but this emotional bond does not necessarily mean that they regard it as their homeland. And what about those Jews (especially young secular Jews) who do not identify with Israel? Are they, too, members of the Jewish Diaspora? Or do they cease to be a member of a Diaspora if they feel no personal connection to a distant homeland? By raising these questions, my aim is to problematize the very notion of Diaspora Jewish identity and the role that Israel plays in defining this identity. If the majority of Diaspora Jews today no longer feel displaced and uprooted, if they do not consider themselves to be outsiders within their countries, and have no intention of ever moving to Israel, then perhaps we need to revise the ways in which we have been accustomed to thinking about "Diaspora Jewry" and devise a new identity for Jews who are permanently settled outside of Israel.

The problem with the label "Diaspora Jew" is, in essence, the same problem that bedevils the relationship between "Diaspora Jewry" and Israel. This is the primacy that is accorded to Israel. Just as the Diaspora Jew is defined in relation to a distant homeland (Israel), the relationship between Diaspora Jewry and Israel has, in practice, involved privileging the latter, sometimes at the expense of the former. Diaspora Jewry has been a consistent and devoted supporter of Israel, albeit to varying degrees in different periods, as Dr Rynhold's chronological overview of the attitudes and activities of Diaspora Jewry toward Israel makes clear. By contrast, Israel, or, more precisely, its official representatives, have seldom reciprocated in kind. Despite their repeated declarations of concern for the welfare of Diaspora Jews, Israeli policy-makers have generally set aside this concern when formulating Israel's foreign and defence policies. All too often, they have ignored or neglected to consider the interests of Jewish communities in the Diaspora. During the years of the military junta in Argentina, for example, Israel supported its regime and purchased arms from it, despite its persecution and torture of some Argentinean Jews. The Pollard affair in the United States represents another example of Israel's disregard for the interests of a Diaspora Jewish community, and one that is even more striking considering American Jewry's importance to Israel. This does not mean that Israeli policy-makers have never taken into account the interests of Jewish communities in the Diaspora. The clearest instance in which considerations of the welfare of Diaspora Jewry affected Israeli foreign policy was in Israel's relations with the Soviet Union (USSR). Although it is difficult to gauge the extent of its impact upon Israeli policy towards the USSR, the large number of Jews residing there was definitely a major consideration for Israeli policy-makers, especially because the welfare of Soviet Jewry was highly precarious. But Israel's effort to secure the free *aliyah* of Soviet Jewry was hardly an act of altruism. It was carried out not only on ideological and humanitarian grounds, but also because of a pragmatic awareness of the need to increase Israel's Jewish population to counterbalance a high Palestinian birthrate (hence, Israel's opposition in the 1980s to allowing Soviet Jews to emigrate to the United States rather than Israel).

Like policy-makers elsewhere, Israeli policy-makers have sought to advance the interests of their state. Rhetoric aside, realpolitik, not Jewish solidarity, has consistently governed Israeli foreign and defence policy, as Dr. Rynhold correctly notes in his chapter. The preference accorded to Israel's interests by Israeli policy-makers finds its justification in their belief that the interests of Israel are ultimately identical with those of Diaspora Jewry. They believe that the welfare of Diaspora Jews is inextricably tied to the welfare of the Jewish state. Many, perhaps most, Diaspora Jews share this conviction. According to this Israel-centric view, Israel makes a vital contribution to the well-being of Diaspora Jewry by offering them a place of refuge and a source of pride. In other words, Israel provides essential protection against the twin dangers of Diaspora Jewish life: namely anti-Semitism and assimilation. This has always been the core of the Zionist case for a Jewish state. It is an argument that has proven itself on numerous occasions. Israel has undoubtedly saved persecuted Jews and provided reassurance to those fearing persecution. But for the vast majority of Diaspora Jews who today reside in liberal democracies (US, France, UK, Germany, Canada, Australia, Argentina), the danger of persecution seems increasingly remote and, as the trauma of the Holocaust recedes, far fewer fear a second Holocaust. While some may see the growth of anti-Semitism in Europe in recent years as evidence of the persistent threat to Diaspora Jewry, in reality this limited phenomenon is more a reaction of angry and alienated European-Arab youth to the renewal of Israeli–Palestinian hostilities than a resurgence of classic European anti-Semitism. Israel may not be the cause of this anti-Semitism, but it certainly aggravates it. Finally, one must surely wonder whether, say, a French Jew would be physically safer in Israel or in France. To describe Israel as a place of refuge is to ignore the obvious dangers of life there.

If Israel's value as a 'safe haven' for Diaspora Jewry is now questionable, so too is its value as a bulwark against assimilation. To be sure, Israel has undoubtedly helped sustain Jewish identity in the Diaspora, especially among secular Jews. Support for Israel has become the most important and common expression of Diaspora Jewish identity. Israel is a rallying point for Jews worldwide in an age when common religious and cultural ties have steadily diminished. But the centrality of Israel in Diaspora Jewish identity has not resolved the challenges of Jewish life in the Diaspora. Widespread identification with Israel has not prevented growing assimilation and intermarriage. Sending youths on summer trips to Israel is unlikely to secure the future of Diaspora Jewish identity, even if it strengthens their identification with Israel. In fact, rather than being the solution to assimilation, for some Jews in the Diaspora, Israel may be part of the problem. Afraid or unwilling to identify themselves as Jews because they do not want to be associated with or implicated by widely unpopular Israeli policies, such Jews (often young and often well-educated) distance themselves from organized Jewish life. For them, far from being a source of pride, Israel may in fact become a source of shame and embarrassment. Nor is Israel the great unifier of Diaspora Jews as it once was, especially in the years after the 1967 War when Israel's stunning victory gave it a mythic status for Diaspora Jewry. Israeli policies are now highly divisive in the Diaspora, just as they are in Israel. More Jews are willing to criticize Israel, something that used to be taboo, and more Jews feel they have the right and even the obligation to disagree with Israel. As such, Diaspora Jewish identity is now often expressed by arguing about Israel, rather than simply by supporting it.

My point in making these observations is not that Israel does not contribute to the well-being of Diaspora Jewry. Rather, its contribution is smaller and more problematic than is widely assumed. Does this mean that Diaspora Jews should insist that Israeli policy-makers do more for the Diaspora? Should we demand that they give our interests more consideration when formulating Israel's foreign and defence policies? Instead of increasing the demands that we make of each other — demands that are in any case unlikely to be met — a better approach might be for both sides to expect less. Israel has long benefited from the financial and political support of Diaspora Jews. But already, as Israel's economy has developed and become more dynamic, Diaspora Jewish monetary donations have greatly declined in their economic importance. Just as Israel no longer depends upon financial handouts from Diaspora Jews, so too in the future it should no longer depend upon the political lobbying of Diaspora Jews. Its diplomacy should be as dynamic as its economy. If Israel were to expect less political support from Diaspora Jews, then it would have to be more diplomatically active itself and make more efforts to defend itself in the court of international public opinion. Conversely, Diaspora Jews should not expect Israeli policy-makers whom they did not elect and who are not accountable to them to act on their behalf or in their interests. Making Israeli policy-makers more aware of the interests of Diaspora Jewish communities is one thing, but it is unrealistic to expect them to put these interests before Israel's national interests as they define them in situations when these interests conflict, as they sometimes do. Diaspora Jews, therefore, should confidently defend their own interests and secure their own future. In doing so, perhaps they could also stop describing themselves as members of a diaspora.

9

Gender and Israel in Diaspora Jewish Identity

Elana Sztokman

The notion of identity as complex, dynamic and fluid[1] has finally arrived in the thinking around Diaspora Jewish identity and Israel. Indeed, what was once a simplistic, binary, "either you're for us or against us" conception of Israel identity seems to have been replaced with more fluctuating and flexible schemas. Perhaps the best practical illustration of this is the new and revised mission statement of the Jewish Agency for Israel's (JAFI) Department for Jewish Zionist Education, which calls for "intensifying the unique and multi-dimensional significance of Israel in connecting the next generation to its heritage, people and homeland".[2] In other words, to have Israel as a powerful force in one's identity, Israel in one's Jewish identity need not be a monolithic and single-minded concept, but can rather be complex and multi-faceted.

With that, there exists at least one aspect of Israel in Diaspora Jewish identity that is insistently monolithic, and that is the aspect of gender. The "Israel" that Diaspora Jews prefer to usher into their identities remains a powerfully and singularly male construct. The "Israel" of Australian Jewish identity, as a prime example, has been, for most of its history, both literally and figuratively male. It has been both quantitatively male in that representatives of Israel in body and in word are almost exclusively men and it has been qualitatively male in that the type of Israel being promoted and depicted by these representations revolves around power struggles, aggression, the military, and binary constructs that are metaphorically male.

Historical Perspectives

The history of women's engagement in Diaspora Zionism is largely ignored and invisible.[3]

> One is hard pressed to find a basic chronology of the establishment, main activities, and demise of Zionist women's organizations . . . Yet to neglect the history of these women . . .

> diminishes the fact that several thousand Jewish women identified, to varying degrees, with Zionism.[4]

Women Zionists in the Diaspora can perhaps be categorized along a tension between two stances; one auxiliary and one critical. In both places, women sacrificed their own positions of power, and continue to be marginalized. And yet, the tension between these two poses forms an ambivalence and complexity which are slowly beginning to form a wider basis for Diaspora Israel identity.

The auxiliary or supportive stance is often characterized by the "Sisterhoods"; that is, the creation of organizations that sought to offer women positions of influence by sustaining men's organizations.[5] Such groups included Hadassah Women, Pioneer Women (later Naamat), Mizrachi Woman (later Amit) and Women's American ORT. These parallel organizations, while providing vital services in Israel, retained the women's status within their own communities as "Ladies Auxiliary". As Aviva Cantor argues, "securing a public role in the community was the women's main motivation," but for that they "needed the approval of the male 'leaders'".[6] This enabling position, while offering an avenue to women, allows for resistance neither to community patriarchy nor to the promotion of the mythology of equality within Israel. Thus, while "Zionism proclaimed its openness towards women, Zionist women had a difficult time making their voices heard once they were in the movement."[7] For this reason, women tended to work on programmes in Israel that were not "glamorous", such as day care, and left the more glamorous issues to the men.[8]

Significantly, the Zionist identity of the women in many of these organizations in the early part of the twentieth century included a pioneering romanticism. Early female Zionist identity did not challenge the legend of the *chalutza*, despite the inaccurate and obscuring mythology it promotes.[9]

> The Labor Zionist organization . . . functioned in the public sphere and its members identified with the women pioneers of Mandatory Palestine — with the altruism, purity, and purpose of their lives, and especially with their feminism . . . If they could not lead such a life, they would support it by raising funds for the day care centers, urban residences for single women, and various other cooperative endeavors of the Council of Working Women, with which Pioneer Women affiliated . . . The chalutza, in the words of one PW member in 1927, represented the 'advanced guard of our sex.'[10]

For early Diaspora female Zionists, then, full support of Israel mythology became, according to Cantor, a form of "vicarious feminism"; a way for the women to retain a status of auxiliary enablers while maintaining their own dreams of a different life. Thus perhaps support for Israel and mainstream male Zionist organizations was, in a certain way, a form of quiet resistance.

The promotion of the *chalutza* myth as an impetus for female support of male movements remains a potent force in the formation of female Diaspora Jewish identity. As one young woman, a Canadian Jew who after years of Diaspora Zionist involvement decided to move to Israel, writes:

> growing up in Habonim, I envisioned Israel as a utopia of egalitarianism, a place where feminism was almost built into the system — what with conscription for both sexes and a history boasting a female prime minister . . . It was nice to imagine a world where equality was natural, but whenever I looked more closely . . . the appearance of equality faded.[11]

For this woman, as for many other young idealistic women, the *chalutza* is a powerful image that formed the backdrop of some often difficult grapplings.

A very different stance *vis-à-vis* Zionism was taken by feminist Jewish women in the latter part of the twentieth century. It was a feminist resistance to this very mythologized *chalutza* and the Golda Meir pseudo-evidence of Israel as egalitarian society that prompted this shifting position. Although some Jewish feminists distanced themselves from the wider feminist movement in the mid-1970s following the proposal at the United Nations Decade on Women's first conference in Mexico City in 1975 that "Zionism equals racism", this position shifted at the start of the Lebanon War in 1982 when language of oppression came to the fore.[12]

Letty Cottin Pogrebin, one of the leaders of this movement that is both overtly feminist and critical of Israel, has described the struggles of this movement.[13] Pogrebin's relationship with Israel revolves around "the P words" — Palestinians and Peace — and is marked by a complex support of Israel intertwined with vocal, active resistance to Israel's treatment of the Palestinians. As opposed to Pioneer Women for whom a subtle gender resistance entailed a full embracing of the Zionist practice regardless of what it entailed, feminist peace groups see support of the Palestinians as a *sine qua non* of their gender identity.

Interestingly, however, even Pogrebin struggles with the dichotomy embedded in this construct. She describes her ambivalence following a Jewish feminist conference in which the late Palestinian activist Raymonda Tawil was a guest speaker in Jerusalem, and just days later a Fatah-led terrorist attack on a tourist bus left 37 dead:

> The next day [after the attack], as our plane took off from Ben-Gurion Airport, I felt mixed emotions: relief to be able to escape from the pressure cooker of vulnerability, and regret that I could not stay to be part of the healing process and the struggle to bring peace. I also tried to carry with me the dream that women could break down barriers that men have erected between peoples. I forced myself to focus on Raymonda Tawil's pain, her passion for justice and hunger for national dignity, rather than on her final apologia for terrorism or her outburst banishing 'the Jew' from the Middle East. I wanted to believe that her justification of violence was merely the rhetoric of revolution; that she had to defend PLO actions because she was being watched, but that if she had real power, she would never have condoned the attack on the tourist bus. She would have chosen the women's ways of resolving conflict — dialogue, negotiation, compromise.[14]

Rejecting the dichotomy of for Israel/against Israel, Pogrebin sets out a complex stance *vis-à-vis* Israel that rests on a different dichotomy, a male–female dichotomy around communication styles. She, like many other feminists (for example, Gilligan 1982,[15] Tannen 1990[16]) sees a culturally "female way" as non-violent and non-confrontational, and believes the culturally "male way" of battle and warfare to be unnecessarily dominant in Israeli politics, culture and identity. She ultimately chooses what she sees as a female/feminist stance rather than the more simplistic pro-peace one.

Yet the reality of Israel in which violence continues to dictate events, even within the female dialogue, is an indication of the continued marginalization of the female identity in Diaspora Jewish identity around Israel. That is, while the Pioneer Women subdued their own female resistance by becoming "enablers" in order to ensure the power of their own positions in the community, later feminists rejected that enabler position by challenging the very foundations of Israel's identity — but as a result found themselves almost powerless to affect events and attitudes. In other words, neither women — enablers or resisters — nor a female culture of politics and discourse hold a central or powerful place in Diaspora Jewish identity around Israel.

Nonetheless, the struggle between these two approaches — one of idealized mythologizing and one of active feminist political resistance — forms the main tension around which women Zionists form their identities. The tension between the idealized Israeli woman and the reality constitutes a source of tremendous inner conflict. "When I realized that modern Israel did not look like the Zionist dream", Friedrichs writes, "it seemed an imperative to stay involved".[17] That is, the tension between the *chalutza* and peace women forms a female Diaspora identity around Israel that, in an undeveloped form, is ambivalent, blurry, and doubting. But within this tension lay the foundations for the "imperative to stay involved", perhaps a feminist call to action.

Indeed, this tension is perhaps the most significant contribution of Jewish women to the effort to build Israel into Diaspora Jewish identity. American Jewish sociologist Sylvia Barack Fishman, for example, offers a complex feminist position in balancing the supportive/auxiliary stance and a critical/feminist stance.

> Some women have applied feminist perspectives to innovative efforts for peace in the Middle East . . . Many such feminists fault the Israeli government and society for their treatment of women, especially lesbians, Jews of Oriental extraction, and Palestinians and other Arabs. . . These feminists sometimes assert that a new kind of Jewish identity must be found whose basis is an uncompromising awareness of universal human values. Despite their protests to the contrary, such feminists seem to be primarily defined with worldwide feminism rather than with the Jewish people and their destiny . . . Honest commitment to Israel's best interests will no doubt occasionally put Jewish feminists in the position of being 'politically incorrect' and unpopular among some other feminists. . . . Jewish feminist universalists will have to think hard about their deepest loyalties.
>
> American Jewish feminism encompasses, of course, many other ideological agendas besides 'correcting' Israel's shortcomings. Some leaders delineate Jewish feminist goals that include ecological issues, world peace, and an end to hunger, along with the expansion of Jewish spiritual opportunities for women . . . This transformed Judaism would reflect the feminist principle of inclusiveness.[18]

Fishman's criticism of Jewish feminist universalists like Pogrebin is resonant of the auxiliary women and possibly ignores the genuine struggle that Pogrebin articulated above. Fishman argues that ultimately, the role of Jewish women is to support the "Jewish people and their destiny", perhaps more than supporting the struggles of oppressed minorities. However, despite her criticism of the peace women, Fishman — like Pogrebin — tries to break down the dichotomy between support of Israel and feminist critique, by setting forth a vision of Diaspora Israel identity that is built on complexity and core feminist values of inclusiveness and spirituality.

More importantly, Fishman constructs Israel not merely as a country at war but as a society under construction. That is, the feminist imperative here is not about supporting Israel, nor is it about supporting the peace movement, but rather it is about working towards social change and promoting a better society for all its members. For Fishman, then, the Israel of Diaspora Jewish identity should not be around the dichotomy of pro-Israel/anti-Israel, or around the feminist split of auxiliary/critical, but rather a more all-encompassing feminist vision of working towards social change.

Diaspora Jewish Power

Significantly, both of these female stances, that of the auxiliary women and that of the peace women, entail both resistance and powerlessness. For auxiliary women, activism towards a Zionist dream of *chalutza* perhaps entails a resistance to dominant gender forms but lacks a power to challenge Zionist myths. For peace women, resistance to male Israeli discourse is paramount, but often leaves the activists marginalized — even *vis-à-vis* other women.

This powerlessness with which women often find themselves within their Israel identities is reflected in the power structures of Diaspora Zionist organizations. In Beth Weizmann, the building owned by the State Zionist Council (SZC) of Victoria in Melbourne, Australia, that houses most of the Zionist groups in the community, the main boardroom on the first floor is lined with portraits of SZC presidents from more than a century. Of these fifteen large, framed photos, fourteen hold pictures of men over the age of fifty, all wearing suits and ties or bow ties, and posing formally. Each portrait has its own mounted caption, such as "Samuel Wynn Esq, Zionist Leader and Philanthropist". Only one of the frames contains a photo of a woman, the caption of which reads, "Zosia Mercer, 1984–1988". Ms. Mercer apparently remains the only woman to have ever served as lay leader of the SZC. Other Zionist organizations in Melbourne, such as the Jewish National Fund (JNF), have, to this day, never had a female president.

Interestingly, however, most of the Zionist organizations have women professional directors. These paid professionals are less visible and less vocal than their male lay counterparts, and are generally not invited to chair major functions, give important speeches, or write articles in the newspaper. Indeed, the gender hierarchy involved in these relationships reflects the classic male–female division of men as dealing with the "big picture" and women as dealing with the "day to day". The women directors working for male presidents constitute, in effect, a professional auxiliary.

Interestingly, both the JNF and the United Israel Appeal (UIA) have women's divisions: classic auxiliary organizations like the sisterhood that offer women positions within the organization without granting full leadership. Cantor maintains that "all the women's organizations — the auxiliaries and the independents — have collective second-class citizenship in the organized Jewish community; they are not involved in shaping communal direction or policy."[19] Moreover, male organizational heads rationalize the existence of women's divisions in that they encourage "plus giving". As Cantor explains, "this sexist term refers to the hoped-for extra amount a wife contributes to supplement her husband's donation, thereby increasing the total extracted from a couple. (The possibility that spouses might decide together what their total 'gift' will be has never permeated the machers' sexist consciousness)."[20] In other words, in terms of lay leadership and its connections with financial status, Israel identity in this Diaspora community is overwhelmingly male-dominated, both in terms of image and in terms of actual power.

The marginalization of women in the Diaspora Israel identity finds expression in other forms as well. For example, one of the primary means through which Zionist groups in Melbourne hope to promote an Israel identity among the community is by bringing out speakers from Israel to address various community groups. According to the annual reports of the SZC that were available, in the year 2001 the SZC brought out 14 speakers, three of whom were women — Member of Knesset (MK) Naomi Chazan, MK Naomi Blumenthal, and Leah Golan, Director of Western and District Aliyah Division of JAFI.[21] In 2002, there were fewer speakers but similar proportion — one out of four speakers was a woman.[22] In 2003, there were nine overseas visitors, all of whom were men.[23] The JNF has had three male speakers and one female speaker since 2003.

The UIA did not provide written records of speakers but provided an oral list of the main speakers from the past three to four years. According to UIA Executive Director Pini Shimon, the UIA has brought out eleven formal speakers, of whom two are women — both hospital administrators who discussed dealing with terror attacks. At some point the UIA had also brought out female soldiers who were recent immigrants from Ethiopia, but Shimon was not sure when, nor did he know their names.[24] In other words, the Ethiopian female soldiers were much lower on the hierarchy than the other speakers: not even worthy of names. Thus, the Israel that is presented to the community is an overwhelmingly male Israel.

Table 9.1 Percentage of Israel-related "Viewpoint" columns written by men, *Australian Jewish News*, September–December 2003[25]

Date	*Total number of* Viewpoint *columns*	*Number written by men*	*Number of Israel-related columns altogether (percentage of total)*	*Percentage of columns written by men*	*Percentage of Israel columns written by men*
5/9/03	6	6	3 (50%)	100%	*100%*
12/9/03	6	6	3 (50%)	100%	*100%*
19/9/03	6	4	1 (17%)	67%	*100%*
26/9/03	9	7	4 (44%)	78%	*100%*
3/10/03	7	7	3 (43%)	100%	*100%*
10/10/03	7	6	2 (29%)	86%	*100%*
17/10/03	6	5	3 (50%)	83%	*100%*
24/10/03	6	5	2 (33%)	83%	*100%*
31/10/03	6	6	3 (50%)	100%	*100%*
23/11/03	8	7	3 (38%)	88%	*88%*
30/11/03	6	6	3 (50%)	100%	*100%*
7/12/03	3	3	1 (33%)	100%	*100%*
14/12/03	3	2	3 (100%)	67%	*67%*
21/12/03	5	5	4 (80%)	100%	*100%*
28/12/03	3	3	1 (33%)	100%	*100%*

The Jewish media also plays an important role in promoting a male Israel identity. The *Australian Jewish News* is arguably the primary medium through which wide communal conversation takes place on a weekly basis. The "Viewpoints" section is probably one of the most important community forums, and one of the fundamental means through which the Jewish community discusses and develops its relationship to Israel. A gender analysis of the "Viewpoints" section of *Australian Jewish News* from a randomly selected period of September–December 2003 demonstrates the overwhelming extent to which male voices and male images dominate the communal relationship with Israel. Each week, anywhere from four to eight opinion columns are printed, and, almost invariably, some (if not all) are devoted to Israel. Table 9.1, on the previous page, indicates how many of the opinion columns that related to Israel were written by men. The table offers several compelling findings. One is that not a single week passes without anywhere from a fifth to an entire "Viewpoint" section being devoted to the subject of Israel. That is, the discussion of Israel and its place in the Australian community is considered a centrepiece of this forum. By contrast, during this period, there wasn't a single article on the issue of domestic violence, for example. That is to say, Israel-relating is considered of more importance to the community's Jewish identity than many other issues, such as movements for social change in the local community (or in Israel, for that matter).

Secondly, the male voice is dominant across all issues. During this time, there were rarely more than two women's columns at one time on these pages, and women were never a majority of the writers. There were many rabbis and politicians whose names appeared regularly, but only two women's names appeared with any frequency — Ruth Wajnryb and Donna Jacobs Sife — each of whom has a semi-regular column. Columns by other women were rare.

Thirdly, no matter how rare women's columns are, they are most notably absent from the discussion of Israel. During this whole period, there were only *two* columns on the subject of Israel that were written by women. In other words, while men dominate the communal conversation generally, they most exclusively dominate the dialogue about Israel.

During this period, one issue that particularly dominated these pages was the granting of the Sydney Peace Prize to Hanan Ashrawi and the subsequent communal reaction, and the communal reaction to the communal reaction. These events highlight some of the major issues around how the Jewish community relates to Israel — such as, whether Jews should interfere with local politics on behalf of Israel, whether the Jewish community has the right to criticize the Israeli government, and what the role of Zionist leadership is generally. During the two months of finger-pointing and chest-beating that filled these columns around what was called "The Ashrawi Affair", not one commentary related to gender. Indeed, the fact that Ashrawi is a woman was not even a matter for discussion, nor was a woman's voice heard, for or against. The work of Jewish women peace activists such as Letty Cotin Pogrebin who have worked with Palestinian women over the years was completely absent from the debate — and in fact, female voices from all sides were notably absent.

Lest one deduce that it is particularly the Australian Jewish community that constructs Israel as male, there is some compelling evidence from the international Jewish community that indicates similar tendencies. My students of gender studies did a gender analysis from three months (seven issues) of the *Jerusalem Report*, a highly regarded bi-monthly Jewish–Israeli periodical. My students examined the "Quote/Unquote" pages from late 2004 to early 2005 in order to discern the gender messages. This section was chosen because it reflects a set of seemingly random or haphazard editorial choices, a short list of quotes deemed interesting, relevant, or even quirky. It also reflects perceptions of who in society has "voice"; that is, who is seen as fit to be quoted. The following table is a quantitative and qualitative gender analysis from those weeks:

Table 9.2 Gender analysis of "Quote/Unquote" pages from *Jerusalem Report*, 2004–5

Date	*Number of quotes*	*Number of quotes on military and politics*	*Number of Jewish religious leaders quoted*	*Number of women quoted*	*Positions of women quoted*	*Topics of women quoted*
27/12/04	9	7	1	1	Rona Ramon, widow of the late astronaut Ilan Ramon	Recent theft of late husband's items
10/1/05	8	5	2	2	Reut Michaeli, lawyer for Reform movement in Israel Mirla Gal, director general of Absorption Ministry	Supreme Court petition regarding religious marriage in Israel Plan to teach immigrants Hebrew on cable television
24/1/05	8	5	2	0	N/a	N/a
7/2/05	9	6	1	0	N/a	N/a
21/2/05	7	1	4	0	N/a	N/a
7/3/05	8	6	1	0	N/a	N/a
21/3/05	9	6	1	1	Nada Alwan, an Iraqi sixth grader	Protesting adding Saturday to Iraqi weekend

The above analysis, like that of the *Australian Jewish News*, demonstrates that women are rarely if ever given a voice in the debate over Israel. Indeed, in this randomly selected collection (these issues were, at the time of the gender studies course, the most recent issues of the magazine), a total of four women were quoted out of 58 quotes, or less than 7 percent of the total. Moreover, while a majority of the quotes altogether are by people with official titles, only two of those women quoted are in positions of leadership. Of the other two, one is the wife of a national icon, and the other is an Iraqi child.

While military and politics clearly dominates these pages, not a single female Knesset member, Mayor, or cabinet member was quoted, nor was any female general or military leader. The closest was a quote by the female Director General of the Absorption Ministry, hardly a high-status position in Israeli life. Indeed, the husband of female Communications Minister Dalia Itzik was deemed quotable when he said, "Who would mess with Dalia? No one! Not even I would mess with her!"[26] In other words, while nothing Minister Itzik had said or done during these three months was worthy of quoting, her husband's stereotypical portrayal of her as overly tough was considered her most interesting contribution to Israeli life.

After military and political leaders, the most commonly quoted sources are religious leaders. Religious leaders were quoted twelve times, or in 21 percent of the cases, sometimes on politics and sometimes on religion. The overlap in Israel between religion and gender is particularly striking, even though religious groups are not the majority of the population. Significantly, of these twelve quotes, only one was by a woman, Reut Michaeli, the leader of the Reform movement. The Orthodox construct of religion as male is clearly adopted by the secular press, which does not see fit to quote Orthodox women, and only occasionally quotes women on religious issues at all. By contrast, however, women were the subjects of the discussion several times. Aside from Michaeli, who addressed the important issue of Israeli laws regarding pre-wedding education for brides, Rabbi Eliyahu Abergil of Beersheba was quoted as saying that "women may not wear red clothing, since it is a most daring color and reminds one of a rooster's comb".[27] While Abergil's quote was seemingly not intended to put him in a favorable light, the overwhelming absence of women's religious voices in this secular forum is nonetheless striking.

Thus, in the international construction of Israel in Diaspora Jewish identity through written media, this small sampling indicates that Israel is a male construct, represented by male voices whose preferred arenas are military and political, and perhaps, to a lesser degree, religious. Even women whose voices may potentially represent Israel from a position of strength and power, such as those of Knesset members and religious or community leaders, are almost never brought that way, but are also constructed as wives, children, and victims.

The Quality of Gender Identity

Apart from the quantitative analyses outlined above, there are also interesting qualitative aspects to these findings. Beyond the minimal appearance of female leadership and the female voice in relating to Israel, there also arises a question: what images of men and what images of women are promoted in the community? From the *Jerusalem Report* analysis, it is clear that the military–political Israel is the preferred construct. Indeed, further analyses from the local Australian community confirm this finding.

An analysis of the speakers brought over from Israel indicates a clear preference for political and military representatives. In 2003, of the nine speakers brought out by the SZC, six spoke about issues relating to terrorism, Israeli politics and the Arab–Israeli conflict. Similarly, the four SZC speakers in 2002 all spoke about issues of war. Interestingly, the one woman that year, Sara Weinreb, came as part of a delegation from *Gush Etzion* and did not speak on her own. In fact, in the SZC annual report, although her name is listed as a heading under "Public Speakers' Service" along with "Gush Etzion Delegation — Shaul Goldstein", the subtext omits her name entirely. "Mr. Goldstein's message to the large audience was clear . . . "[28] The fact that she purportedly spoke alongside him disappears in the text.

In 2001, eight of the fourteen speakers were Knesset members, four had other leadership positions in government and related institutions, one was an author, and one was an educational leader. In the UIA, of the eleven speakers whose names were recalled, five were politicians (for example, Ehud Barak, Shimon Peres, Dennis Ross), three were military commanders, and two were hospital administrators dealing with terror (the two women on the list). The unnamed Ethiopian women were brought in as examples of new immigrants.

Thus, not only do men dominate the image of Israel brought to the Jewish community, but the image is that of a predominantly political–military male Israel at war. Women who are brought out tend to be primarily representatives of Israel as victims of terror, though are sometimes also politicians. While men are seen as writers, as speakers, and as leaders of import, women are seen as victims, and new immigrants, and occasionally politicians.

As a final example, in the 28 December 2003 issue of the *Australian Jewish News*, there was a special "Newsmakers of the Year" section. Twenty-nine people were listed, of whom five were women. One was a terror victim, one was a Jewish madam, one was a young woman who was proposed to in a public communal event, one was the CEO of Jewish Care, and one was Hanan Ashrawi. Thus only *one* Jewish woman — that is, the CEO of Jewish Care — was noted for her positive contribution to the Jewish community. And *not one* Jewish woman was noted for her contributions to Israel or to Zionist identity in the community.

Summary

In short, the idea of a female Israel identity, of women working towards change, towards dialogue and the improvement of Israeli society, is virtually absent from all Diaspora communal discourse about Israel. Work done by Diaspora Jewish women for Israel, as Reinhartz and Raider (2004) and Berkowitz (1995) point out, remains invisible and irrelevant. Women's struggles for a more complex rendering of Israel continue to be heard only by women, and are not represented in the media nor in local politics. Indeed, women regularly challenge binary oppositions of "either you're for us or against us", the kind of dichotomy that permeated the entire debate over the Ashrawi affair. But women's complexities and promotions of dialogue are marginalized and ignored. Thus the Israel construct of Diaspora Jewish identity is not only wielded by men but is also about a male culture of conflict and power.

Jewish women seeking to build a Diaspora relationship with Israel are caught in a double bind: the lack of female military representatives means that women are absent from the dominant construct of Israel in Diaspora life, and at the same time this supremacy of the male military–political Israel construct means that the areas in which women are making strides, such as in dialogue groups and movements for social change, are not considered interesting or relevant constructs for the development of an Israel identity.

Change in the gendered quality of Diaspora Israel identity thus requires two-tiered movement. Women must at once struggle to permeate the existing power structures — whether in communal leadership, in the media, or as public speaker — to ensure that women's voices are heard. At the same time, women must challenge and fight the structures that promote a male Israel construct around military and political power. Women must strive to bring out other women — not only female generals, but women who are working on grassroots change and who challenge the basic discourse of Israel's relationship to the world. Women fighting for social change must also be represented. The Diaspora Jewish community must be exposed not to mythology but to a real

Israel, fighting battles for its social character, not just its land. Women leading these charges can be brought out as examples, as models of feminism and Zionism, and can be influential in helping develop a more complex Israel identity for Diaspora Jewry.

Notes

1 K. Woodward, "Concepts of Identity and Difference", in Kathryn Woodward (ed.), *Identity and Difference* (London: Sage Publications/The Open University, 1997), pp. 7–62.
2 Jewish Agency (JAFI) Mission Statement (2005) <http://www.jafi.org.il/ education/dept/mission1.html>.
3 S. Reinhartz and M.A. Raider, *American Jewish Women and the Zionist Enterprise*, (Hanover and London: Brandeis University Press/University Press of New England, 2004).
4 M. Berkowitz, "Transcending 'Tzimmes and sweetness': Recovering the history of Zionist women in central and Western Europe, 1897–1933" in Maurice Sacks (ed.), *Active Voices: Women in Jewish Culture* (Urbana and Chicago: University of Illinois Press, 1995), p. 42.
5 P.S. Nadell and R.J. Simon, "Ladies of the sisterhood: Women in the American Reform Synagogue". in Maurice Sacks (ed.), *Active Voices: Women in Jewish Culture* (Urbana and Chicago: University of Illinois Press, 1995), pp. 63–75; Berkowitz, 1995, pp. 41–62.
6 A. Cantor, *Jewish Women Jewish Men: The Legacy of Patriarchy in Jewish Life* (San Francisco: Harper San Francisco, 1995), p. 320.
7 Berkowitz, 1995, p. 41.
8 Cantor, 1995, p. 320.
9 L. Hazelton, *Israeli Women: The Reality behind the Myth* (New York: Simon and Schuster, 1977).
10 Cantor, 1995, p. 321.
11 E. Friedrichs, "I was a teenage Zionist", in Danya Ruttenberg (ed.), *Yentl's Revenge: The Next Wave of Jewish Feminism* (Seattle: Seal Press, 2001), p. 128.
12 S. Sharoni, "Motherhood and the politics of women's resistance: Israeli Women Organizing for Peace". In Alexis Jetter, Annelise Orleck and Diana Taylor (eds), *The Politics of Motherhood: Activist Voices from Left to Right* (Hanover: University of New England Press, 1997), pp. 144–160.
13 L.C. Pogrebin, *Deborah, Golda and Me: Being Female and Jewish in America* (New York: Doubleday. 1991).
14 Pogrebin, 1991, pp. 336–7.
15 C. Gilligan, *In a Different Voice: Psychological Theory and Women's Development* (Cambridge, MA: Harvard University Press, 1982); Hazelton, 1977.
16 D. Tannen, *You Just Don't Understand: Men and Women in Conversation* (New York: Ballantine Books, 1990).
17 Friedrichs, 2001, p. 129.
18 S.B. Fishman, *A Breath of Life: Feminism in the American Jewish Community* (Hanover and London: Brandeis University Press/University Press of New England, 1993), pp. 242–243.
19 Cantor, 1995, p. 325.
20 Ibid.
21 State Zionist Council of Victoria, *63rd Annual Assembly Reports* (Melbourne: State Zionist Council of Victoria, 2001).
22 State Zionist Council of Victoria, *64th Annual Assembly Reports* (Melbourne: State Zionist Council of Victoria, 2002).
23 State Zionist Council of Victoria, *65th Annual Assembly Reports* (Melbourne: State Zionist Council of Victoria, 2003).
24 Pini Shimon, personal interview, March 2005.

25 *Australian Jewish News*, September–December 2003.
26 *Jerusalem* Report, 7 March 2005, p. 44.
27 *Jerusalem Report*, 21 February 2005, p. 44.
28 State Zionist Council of Victoria, 2002, p. 17.

ISRAEL COMMENTATOR

Women in Israel and the Diaspora: Reverses and Symbiosis

Alice Shalvi

Elana Sztokman is correct in maintaining that the Diaspora ideal of Israel is a "powerfully and singularly male construct". Ironically, this is also the dominant construct in Israel itself. So long as the country remains in a state of conflict with its neighbours — a state that may to a certain extent be perceived as prolonged by a macho military inclination to impose continued colonial rule on the Palestinians — "civil" affairs, in which women could and should play an equal, rather than an auxiliary, role are shunted aside. Women, who constitute a majority of the Israeli population, have the status of a minority and are perceived as such.

It was not always thus. During the early days of statehood, Israelis and Diaspora Jews alike were captivated by the notion, first fostered during the *yishuv* period, that the Jewish women in the country had attained a degree of independence and equality unprecedented not only among Jews, but even in other countries and societies. To a large extent, this belief was founded on, and fostered by, what one may term Zionist propaganda, especially as evidenced in the Jewish National Fund (JNF) posters and other public relations material of the 1930s and on.

Three "icons" dominated this material so far as gender was concerned, creating — whether deliberately or unconsciously — the overwhelming impression that women were playing a major role in the development of the country: a role no less important and valuable than that played by the "new (male) Jew", and in similar spheres. The photograph of a young, blonde *halutza* (Zionist pioneer), in shorts and wielding a scythe or hoe, standing knee-deep in the waving corn, was replaced after the War of Independence by a virtually identical young woman, now clad in an Israel Defence Forces (IDF) uniform and wielding an Uzi sub-machinegun. In combination, these images were based on, and in turn engendered, a conviction that both in the upbuilding of the agriculture-based economy and in the defence of the country, women were equal citizens. This firm belief was bolstered by an additional image, frequently and prominently displayed, inter alia, in the media: that of Golda Meir, a strong woman, once significantly referred to by Ben-Gurion as "the only man in his cabinet". Golda successively filled a number of key government functions, ranging from ambassador to the USSR, through Minister of Labour and Foreign Minister, to that of Prime Minister. At that time, she was only the second woman in the entire world to have headed a government.

The images were not entirely hollow or misleading, since Israel was indeed well ahead of most countries in the world in its legislation regarding the status of women. Laws stipulated equal enfranchisement, equal pay for equal work and, most significantly, equal education for boys and girls (a truly revolutionary measure, since in European communities girls and women were on the whole denied *Jewish* education, while in many of the Arab countries Jewish girls, like their non-Jewish peers, were generally denied schooling of any kind). Indeed, Israeli women gloated at the fact that they enjoyed paid maternity leave and excellent, reasonably priced government-subsidized child-care facilities, most of them operated by the veteran women's organizations, *Na'amat*, the Women's International Zionist Organization (WIZO) and *Emunah*. Only gradually did they become aware that this benevolent legislation actually reinforced the notion that motherhood and home-making were still considered the sole responsibility of wives and mothers. This notion was further borne out by the laws governing military service: women served for a shorter period of time and only in non-combat roles, primarily clerical. They were released from even compulsory service if they married, and were exempted from reserve duty if they were mothers. Family allowances also encouraged large families, and the crowning touch was Ben-Gurion's decision to grant a woman who bore her tenth child a reward of one-hundred *lirot*. All of these, as well as additional, factors instilled a certain complacency in Israeli women and filled Diaspora women with a strange mixture of pride and envy.

The new feminism of the 1970s combined with the experiences of the Yom Kippur War to make Israeli women aware that their self-satisfaction was based on an illusion. Just at a time when the lengthy war brought to light their own exclusion from vital areas in the economy as well as in the military, numerous outstanding Jewish women — including Betty Friedan and Bella Abzug — were leading the Women's Liberation movement in the US. Israeli women, particularly the more educated professionals among them, became increasingly aware of the discrimination to which they were subjected, and of their gross under-representation not only in government and national decision-making, but also in the workforce and society in general. Despite excellent legislation, women earned less than men and were primarily relegated to the service professions which enjoy lesser prestige.

Growing awareness — sparked in large part by "Anglo-Saxon" immigrants familiar with developments abroad and by direct encounters with American feminist activists — led in 1984 to the establishment of the Israel Women's Network, the country's first non-partisan women's lobby. It was precisely this non-partisanship that enabled the Network to engage in feminist advocacy *vis-à-vis* both the judicial and the legislative authorities.

The majority of Diaspora women were appalled to learn that their Israeli female idol had feet of clay; for their part, Israeli feminists were inspired and encouraged by their North American "sisters", who also provided significant funding for the new organizations, many of them grassroots, that sprang up in Israel in the following twenty years. Together, Israeli and Diaspora feminists established coalitions, particularly relating to issues of Jewish law (such as *iggun* and refusal of divorce) and to the status of women in religious practice, which are not confined to Israel. (In fact, during my own two-week tour of Australia as a guest of the National Council of Jewish

Women (NCJW) and the Australian Jewish Council in 1994, I was able to inspire and encourage women of all ages to be more pro-active on these matters. As a result, NCJW took up the challenge regarding divorce, while a number of *Rosh Hodesh* (New Moon) and women's *tefillah* (prayer) groups were established.) Blu Greenberg, a leading American Jewish feminist, maintains that she and her fellow Modern Orthodox women in the US were inspired both by the general feminist movement and by the progress made in the Reform and Conservative movements, which ordained women rabbis. In turn, Israeli feminists were inspired and encouraged by the Americans. *Kolech*, the remarkably courageous organization of Israeli Modern-Orthodox women, was a direct outcome of its founders' participation in one of the early conferences held in New York by the Jewish Orthodox Feminist Alliance (JOFA), established by Greenberg.

An area of activity unique to Israel concerned opposition to the country's enlistment policy. The Supreme Court decision of 1995 in the case of *Alice Miller vs. the Israel Air Force*, which gave women the right hitherto denied them of applying for and being accepted into pilot-training, caused considerable satisfaction because it marked an end to aggressive macho monopolization of a highly-esteemed branch of the IDF. But at the same time a pacifist trend developed. Initially a response to the First Intifada and founded in 1988, the Women in Black movement not only became a worldwide phenomenon relating to family as well as military violence, but spawned other anti-war movements initiated by women. These movements include the "Four Mothers", who were generally credited with bringing about Israel's withdrawal from Lebanon, and Machsom Watch, which monitors IDF behaviour at the checkpoints that control Palestinians' movement from place to place. One may well conclude that the nonexistence of women's equality in the armed forces actually made it much easier for them to oppose Israel's military policy.

Yet it is precisely on the issue of the Israel–Palestinian conflict that Diaspora women (and not only they) are conflicted: wanting to think the best of Israel, they find it hard to accept or condone feminist opposition to Israel's continued presence in the Occupied Territories and resent the criticism of Israel's policy. In this the women are no different from the majority of Diaspora Jewry, who find it difficult to distinguish between legitimate criticism of the policy and actions of Israel's government, and anti-Zionism. They have not yet internalized the fact that the inevitable violence of warfare and conquest results in an equally inevitable increase of violence on the home front. The shattering of the old belief that Jewish men were "different", kind and gentle in the home and incapable of verbally or physically abusing their partners or children may well be seen as yet another way in which the experience of Israeli women has had an impact on Diaspora consciousness. Painfully, Israel has gone from being among the most advanced and admired countries in the world to being among the most backward, even where women's status is concerned.

The regrettable absence of women from the Jewish public arena in Australia, which Elana Sztokman describes, becomes a tragic phenomenon in Israel. It has led to an exclusion of women not only from key positions in management in general but especially from the vital arena of determining national policy regarding both defence and socio-economic issues. Israel might very well be a very different and infinitely better state than it has become, had women indeed enjoyed the equality which the old JNF posters sought to present.

DIASPORA COMMENTATOR

Gender and Inequality Within and Across Jewish Communities

Caryn Aviv

In "The Gender of Diaspora Israel Identity" Elana Sztokman raises some important questions about the relationships between Israel and global Jewish communities. She suggests that the location of Israel in Diaspora Jews' identities has changed; from a monolithic and static "you're either with us or against us" stance of unquestioned support for Israel, towards an identity in which one's relationship to Israel is more pliable and contested. This flexibility of identity implies that for Jews around the world, it has become increasingly necessary to *acquire* or somehow *obtain* or *cultivate* a Jewish identity that involves Israel — either through philanthropy, travel and tourism, political activism, or personal and family networks.[1]

I have argued elsewhere that this conscious acquisition of a cultivated relationship with Israel suggests that Jews in global communities are perhaps no longer "in diaspora", but at home where they are, whether Jews call that home Moscow, Los Angeles, Buenos Aires, Tel Aviv, or Sydney. This global approach to thinking about Jewish identities does not negate the importance (both historically and symbolically) of Israel as an important node in the network of Jewish communities, but nor does such a perspective assume that Israel occupies the only *centre* of the Jewish universe. Jews today around the world can (and often do) feel at home in more than one centre of Jewish life, and in an age of globalized communication, can (and again, often do) travel between those homes virtually, physically, economically, and culturally. A more transnational framework for understanding the circulation of Jewish ideas, capital, people, and identities would suggest that the traditional Diaspora/Israel dichotomy no longer serves to adequately describe the complex relationships between and across Jewish communities in a global world (Aviv and Shneer, 2005).

What does gender, or more specifically, gender inequality, have to do with this question of circulating Jewish identities and ideas among Jews around the world, including Jewish Israelis? Can a more global perspective about Jewish identity, in which Israel is an important (but not the only) centre of Jewish life illuminate analysis and practical strategies for addressing gender issues and gender inequality? To go one step further, is it possible or useful to generalize across Jewish communities in thinking about gender and inequality, to see where there are commonalities and/or points of departure? Do Jewish communities around the world (including in Israel) learn from one another about how gender inequities might be redressed through structural and political interventions or social movements? My hope is that these preliminary questions will challenge researchers, particularly those who look at the role and question of Israel in Diaspora Jewish communities, to consider different assumptions and approaches to the study of gender in its myriad forms among global Jews.

Gender as a Social Institution

What do we mean when we talk about a gendered perspective of Jews regarding global Jewish communities, including Israel? I argue that the theoretical and political unit of analysis needs to shift from talking solely about women's roles and status in society (whether in Israel or elsewhere) to a discussion of gender as a social institution in *all* Jewish communities. What I mean by gender as a social institution is the notion (articulated by Jewish feminist scholars for the past two decades) that gender — that is, variations of masculinity and femininity as being key to understanding and developing a modern self — is a central organizing category of identity and inequity in most communities around the world, including Jewish ones (Lorber 1995; Barack Fishman 1995). When discussing the issue of gender as a social institution that orders and governs basic aspects of social life and interaction, we must consider the reality of persistent gender inequalities between women and men in Jewish communities as the subject of interrogation and amelioration.

Some scholars of Jewish life erroneously equate the question of gender in relationship to Israeli identity or global Jewish identities *only* with the status of women; because to talk about men is to simply talk about ——— (fill in the blank — politics, society, history, economics, etc.). In other words, a fundamental problem in some, but not all, Jewish discourses and scholarship, particularly about and in relationship to Israel, is the idea that only *women* seem to have gender.[2] In only one obvious example, we know that women are often absent from historical accounts of war and military heroism in Israeli history — relegated to the roles of grieving wives and mothers or caretakers of the wounded in Israel's wars and conflicts (Weiss 2005). The historical and contemporary depiction and representation of Israel through wars, philanthropy, politics, tourism, education, and other means of building identity for global Jews has often been characterized by assumptions of shared universal values among all Jewish women and men. As Sztokman argues in this volume, the representation of reality in public discourse (in her case, within Australian Jewish communities) in fact usually only represents men's versions of reality, and ignores or minimizes the contributions and perspectives of women.

But thinking about gender as a social institution allows scholars to look beyond the experiences of women, and instead broadens the research agenda to think about masculinities and femininities in their various historical and sociological constructions. This way, we can analyze and investigate how both men and women "do" gender (West and Zimmerman 1987). Using gender as a central category of analysis can demonstrate how gendered discourses and practices inform and shape every aspect of social interaction and institution building, not just in Israel, but in Jewish communities everywhere, and not just for women, but indeed for all people.[3] If scholars of global Jewish communities shift the analytic lens to see all relationships, interactions, institutions, and narratives as inherently gendered, then we can avoid the problem of talking about gender as if it only pertains and applies to women. Taking a more macro view of gender politics and inequality in the context of Israel/global Jewish relationships will allow us to not only see how Jewish women have participated in Zionist philanthropy and organization-building, but also allows us to better understand how notions of Jewish masculinities and men change over time, and to identify areas of Jewish history and culture that have traditionally never been considered to "contain" gender because they assume men as the universal default position.[4]

Generalizing Across Communities

A second question emerges in thinking about gender, Jewish identities, and communities: is it possible or useful to generalize about gender (and gender inequalities) across Jewish communities, including Israel? Are the relationships regarding gender politics, masculinities, and femininities universal in Jewish communities or particular to their specific locations in any given era? Can we talk about all global Jewish communities as having a shared historical experience of relationships to and perspectives about gender or Israel? I think the short answer is no: Jewish communities around the world have developed highly divergent historical patterns regarding gender, based on a complex combination of internal, regional, and global politics. They are a reflection of their wider societies' and regions' assumptions and practices regarding gender. Perhaps one could compare cases of gender inequality in Jewish communities that have shared similar political ideologies and economic systems.

In the United States and Canada, to take one example, Jewish communities have been strongly influenced by secular feminism, particularly in the areas of liturgical innovation, the development of new rituals, and the changing demographics of the rabbinate (Ruttenberg 2001). Reflecting the structures of power in the secular societies in which these Jews live, the Jewish communities of the United States and Canada also lag behind in creating gender equality in key areas of Jewish communal development, such as the top tiers of Jewish organizations like the Federation system (Cohen, et al. 2004). However, it is less useful to compare gender inequalities in North America with a vastly different Jewish cultural milieu such as that of Russia, for example, where the impact of feminism as a social movement in the wider society, and thus, within Jewish communities, has been less pervasive.

Israel in this context is an interesting case, because on the one hand, it shares features of societies and cultures — namely, technological advances, economic development (although uneven and with growing gaps among different groups), and political/cultural ties to other Western democracies such as the United States, Canada, and the United Kingdom. But when thinking about gender and gender inequality, the case for comparative analysis across Jewish communities is more complicated, as Alice Shalvi ably demonstrates in this volume. Persistent myths about Israel's gender equality among women and men continue to circulate in global Jewish communities, despite ample demographic and sociological data that suggest gender equality is far from the norm in most areas of Israeli society.[5] There are notable differences between women from different ethnic groups (Fuchs 2005), as well as differences between women and men from similar ethnic backgrounds. Additionally, if we think comparatively across different Jewish communities, what is important to many liberal Jews in North America regarding gender and Jewish identity (synagogue participation, professional opportunities in Jewish communal organizations, cultural programmes) is not necessarily salient to the majority of secular Israelis who might happen to identify as Jewish, but do not emphasize Jewishness as a core component of their identity.[6]

If anything, the place of Israel in Diaspora Jewish identity *vis-à-vis* gender inequality and feminism is the *inverse* of traditional centre/periphery ways of thinking about Jewish communities. Rather than Israel acting as the symbolic centre of the Jewish universe in terms of gender politics, most scholars would probably agree that it is *North American* Jewish communities that are at the centre or vanguard of ameliorating inequalities, with Israel learning from various social movements, organizations, and innovations in social and legal policy that originate "across the pond". Many of the founding activists of Israeli feminism thirty-odd years ago were in fact immigrants from North America and Britain,[7] and Israeli feminists routinely seek out the opinions, ideas, strategies, and dollars of North American feminists to help guide and strengthen their movements and organizations.[8]

Transnational Networking

A final series of questions is in order. If we can safely argue that gender inequality characterizes most institutions and communities across the Jewish world (and I believe the scholarly record demonstrates this quite clearly), then where are some visions of how to change or improve these inequalities? What types of relationships are there between Jewish scholars and activists who work on these issues? Are the relationships unidirectional (that is, Jewish women in global communities around the world helping women in Israel in a traditional model of charity and philanthropy), or more multidimensional (that is, both Jewish women *and* men across communities, including Israel, learning from one another about various challenges, and about what works and what doesn't)? What change has been accomplished through global and local partnerships, thanks to activists and organizations around the world, and what remains to be done?

I'd like to briefly describe three case study organizations that highlight the global exchange of ideas, strategies, and people who are working on these questions. What I suggest by describing these three case studies is that a *transnational* lens is a more appropriate and explanatory way to view the flow of information, ideas, people, and political strategies for addressing gender inequality, rather than assuming that Diaspora communities view Israel as a model, or that Israel is at the centre of Diaspora communities' understanding of gender politics. By looking at what people are doing across different communities around the world, we can better see how gender inequity is embedded in social institutions across Jewish communities, and how it is currently being addressed through strategic action and social change.

One interesting organization is Project Kesher (<www.projectkesher.org>), which connects women (and a few men) in the United States, Israel, and the former Soviet Union in order to revitalize Jewish life in the FSU, encourage women's democratic leadership and empower women to lead full and meaningful Jewish lives. Project Kesher (PK) initially began in 1989 as an American project to address the needs of Jewish women in the FSU, who were hungry for Jewish knowledge, learning, books, ideas, and a sense of community after living under Communism for so many decades. Since its inception, PK has collaborated with several organizations and prominent individuals and philanthropists in global Jewish communities, has held conferences, workshops, training, and seminars for women across 165 communities in the FSU, and has expanded its mission to include working with people from all ethnic backgrounds and religious faiths. Project Kesher epitomizes the notion that there are multiple centres of Jewish community, and that both women and men need to address gender inequality if change is to happen.

The New Israel Fund (<www.nif.org>) is an international partnership between North Americans, Europeans, and Israelis, which aims to advance civil rights and social justice within Israel, and has worked since 1979 to adequately fund Israel's burgeoning non-profit social change sector. The NIF has identified women's rights and gender discrimination as a key factor in creating a more equitable and just Israeli society, and has generously funded the activities of major gender-focused non-governmental organizations that work on legislation and social policy, combating violence against women, expanding religious legal rights for Orthodox women, and providing empowerment programmes for young women, Arab Israeli women, and recent immigrants. What is interesting about NIF is that they believe that it is not only the task of women to uplift themselves. In NIF's vision, *both* women and men, as philanthropists around the world and as activists within Israel, see gender equality as a major component of creating more justice and a better society within Israel.

The third organization, Hadassah-Brandeis Institute (<www.brandeis.edu/hbi>), bridges the scholarly–activist divide, and according to the mission statement on its website, aims "to develop fresh ways of thinking about Jews and gender worldwide by producing and promoting scholarly research and artistic projects". Housed as the only academic centre of its kind within a prestigious university with strong Jewish historical origins, HBI attempts to increase knowledge production at the intersection of Gender and Women's Studies and Jewish Studies. Although based in the United States, HBI circulates ideas and research among a global group of scholars and activists, and has been a leader in publishing innovative books that uncover the gendered contributions of women and men to early Israeli history and contemporary Israeli society, among other areas.[9] HBI also produces a journal that is based in Israel (*Nashim: A Journal of Jewish Women's Studies and Gender Issues)* and regularly convenes conferences that attract a global audience of Jewish researchers, policymakers, and activists from major Jewish communities around the world, including many Israelis.

In the case of gender inequality, Israel is by no means at the centre of Diaspora Jewish communal identities. Rather, Israeli activists and scholars continue to look towards Diaspora communities for support, ideas, and strategies to build their own movements for social change and their own models for gender scholarship. The questions about what we mean when we say gender, and whether it is possible to generalize across Jewish communities about gender inequality highlights the need for more research about intersections between gender politics and Jewish identity in global Jewish communities, including among and between Israeli Jews. By shifting our scholarly approach towards a more transnational framework, not only would we better understand how gender is embedded in all our social institutions, but we might also identify strategies that work effectively to create more just and inclusive Jewish communities that welcome the contributions and perspectives of both women and men equally.

Notes

1 This phenomenon of being "at home" and the issue of constructed relationships to Israel is discussed extensively in Aviv and Shneer's *New Jews: The End of the Jewish Diaspora* (New York University Press, 2005).

2 Additionally, one could make the same argument about sexuality as well. Most scholars of Jewish communities assume heterosexuality as the default, and elide the issue of diverse sexual orientations and the existence of Jewish lesbians and gay men. This is particularly the case in Israeli scholarship, where heterosexuality and the imperative to "reproduce the nation" (Kahn 2000) takes on a more urgent and nationalist demographic tone. For recent scholarship in English that challenges the heterosexism of Israeli knowledge production, see Yosef on Israel film (2005), Frankfort-Nachmias and Shadmi (2005), Kadish in Aviv and Shneer (2002), and Walzer (2000).

3 This concept also applies to the lives of children. However, the area of gender identity and construction in Jewish children's lives is a woefully understudied area of research in contemporary Jewish studies.

4 Thinking about men as gendered has started to happen in scholarship about American Jewish life, but unevenly, and this is not the case with much scholarship on Israel. For example, there are few studies of how varied notions of masculinity shape men's experiences of basic social institutions, like the Israeli Defense Forces. To look at men as gendered could enhance our understanding of how those social institutions, such as the military, both shape and are shaped by, changing ideas about men and masculinity. A good example: Haim Watzman's recent autobiography, *Company C: An American's Life as a Citizen-Soldier in Israel* (Farrar, Straus, and Giroux, 2005) is *all* about men, masculinity, and gender ideologies, but is never articulated as such because the author does not look at the world through the lens of gender; it is simply an invisible, yet powerful force in his social world.

5 See the Israel Women's Network website for useful reports and documentation of ways in which gender inequality continues to characterize basic institutions and policies of contemporary Israel, at <www.iwn.org.il>.

6 Here again the issue of sexuality and sexual orientation is comparable. Both lesbian and gay Jews in the United States, Canada, and Israel are deeply concerned about improving their legal status, expanding civil rights, and combating homophobia. But while these issues are the main items on the mainstream political agenda of (mostly secular) Israeli lesbian, gay, bisexual and transgender (LGBT) people, American and Canadian LGBT Jews are also concerned with issues of global Jewish identity: building and strengthening LGBT synagogues, improving the climate and working conditions of LGBT Jewish professionals who work in the community, creating resources and education for non-LGBT Jewish educational settings to address and decrease homophobia, etc. For more information about how these global Jewish communities differ on such issues, see the website of Jewish Mosaic: The National Center for Sexual and Gender Diversity (<www.jewishmosaic.org>), and "Castro, Chelsea, and Tel Aviv: Queer Jews at Home", in *New Jews: The End of the Jewish Diaspora* (Aviv and Shneer, 2005).

7 See Marcia Freedman's *Exile in the Promised Land* (Ithaca: NY, Firebrand Books, 1990).

8 One way in which this exchange is realized is through *US/Israel Women to Women*, which according to its website "provides financing and support to Israeli women of all faiths and backgrounds in their struggle for social justice, wellness and economic empowerment . . . seeds innovative grassroots programmes and advocacy efforts that enable women to be the agents for social change".

9 For example, see *The Plough Woman: Records of the Pioneer Women of Palestine*, edited by Mark A. Raider and Miriam B. Raider-Roth, Susan Sered's *What Makes Women Sick:*

Maternity, Modesty, and Militarism in Israeli Society, Kaplana Misra and Melanie Rich's *Jewish Feminism in Israel: Some Contemporary Perspectives*, and Margalit Shilo's *Princess or Prisoner?: Jewish Women in Jerusalem, 1840–1914.*

References

Aviv, C. and Shneer, D., *New Jews: The End of the Jewish Diaspora* (New York: New York University Press, 2005).

Cohen, S., Bronznick, S., Goldenhar, D., Israel, S. and Kelner. S., *Creating Gender Equity and Organizational Effectiveness in the Jewish-Federation System: A Research and Action Project* (New York: Advancing Women Professionals and the Jewish Community, 2004).

Barack-Fishman, S., *A Breath of Life: Feminism in the American Jewish Community* (Waltham, MA: Brandeis University Press, 1995).

Frankfort-Nachmias, C., and Shadmi. E., *Sappho in the Holy Land: Lesbian Existence and Dilemmas in Contemporary Israeli Society* (Albany, NY: State University of New York Press, 2005).

Fuchs, E. (ed.), *Israeli Women's Studies: A Reader* (New Brunswick, NJ: Rutgers University Press, 2005).

Kadish, R., "Israeli Gays and Lesbians Encounter Zionism", in *Queer Jews*, David Shneer and Caryn Aviv (eds) (New York: Routledge Press, 2002).

Kahn, S. M., *Reproducing Jews: A Cultural Account of Assisted Conception in Israel* (Raleigh-Durham, NC: Duke University Press, 2000).

Lorber, J., *Paradoxes of Gender* (New Haven, CT: Yale University Press, 1995).

Ruttenberg, D. (ed.), *Yentl's Revenge: The Next Wave of Jewish Feminism* (Seattle, WA: Seal Press, 2001).

West, C. and Zimmerman, D., "Doing Gender", *Gender & Society*, vol. 1, June, 1987, pp. 125–151.

Walzer, L., *Between Sodom and Eden* (New York: Columbia University Press, 2000).

Weiss, M., *The Chosen Body: The Politics of the Body in Israeli Society* (Stanford: Stanford University Press, 2005).

Yosef, R., *Beyond Flesh: Queer Masculinities and Nationalism in Israeli Cinema* (New Brunswick, NJ: Rutgers University Press, 2004).

10

The Place of Israel in the Identity of Israelis in the Diaspora: An Ethnographic Exploration

Steven J. Gold

Israeli migrants in western nations earn incomes that match those of the native-born, learn English easily, frequently marry host society citizens and exhibit high rates of naturalization. Moreover, they have easy access to the established Jewish community within which they often live and work (Gold and Phillips 1996). Despite this pattern of mobility and access to the host society, Israeli emigrants seldom describe themselves as host country nationals, socialize almost exclusively with other Israelis, frequently describe their intentions to return home and often do so.

Migrants' hesitation to identify with host societies is not an unprecedented finding. However, a sizable literature suggests that lack of identification with their new home is commonly a result of their encounters with discriminatory treatment (Waters 1999; Portes and Rumbaut 2001; Piore 1979). Generally white, Israelis describe few encounters with prejudice (Herman 2000). Hence, their resistance to identification with the host society cannot be attributed to racism. The reason for Israeli emigrants' reluctance to identify with the country of settlement is that they have been socialized into Israeli culture and citizenship, a central tenet of which is that Jews — and especially Israelis — should live in Israel. Drawing on fieldwork and in-depth interviews with Israeli emigrants in several settings and with returned émigrés in Israel, this chapter describes the impact of Israel on the identities of Israelis living in the Diaspora.

Methods

Data for this essay were collected by American and Israeli researchers through in-depth interviews and participant observation fieldwork with Israeli migrants in several settings. A major source was 194 interviews (conducted in both Hebrew and English) with a socially diverse sample of Israeli migrants and others knowledgeable about their community in Los Angeles between 1991 and 1996. In addition, we interviewed 55 Israelis in London between 1998 and 2000, and 14 in Paris in 1999. Interviews with 30 returned migrants were conducted in Israel in 1996, 1997 and 2000. Finally, an additional 19 interviews were conducted with Israelis who had moved to London since 2001, in order to access the perspective of Israelis who went abroad during the time of the Al-Aqsa Intifada and information technology crash. Many respondents had lived in additional locations outside of Israel, including the US, Japan, South Africa, Italy, France and Belgium, so respondents' experience as migrants extends beyond the specific locations where interviews were conducted. Most interviews were tape recorded, translated into English (if conducted in Hebrew) and transcribed. All names of respondents in this report are pseudonyms. Additional data were obtained through census analysis and communal surveys collected in several points of settlement (Gold 2002).

Motives for Emigration

In order to understand the nature of Israelis' conflicting identities as associated with the country of origin and the host society, we begin by examining their motives for emigration. When asked why they went abroad, most Israelis offered one of three overlapping responses: economic opportunities (including education), family factors, and a need for broader horizons (Gold 1997; Rosen 1993; Sobel 1986; Herman 1988). In this, they acknowledge — at least tacitly — the economic, educational and cultural limitations of Israeli society. In addition, a fairly large number, generally women and children, came to accompany their husbands and fathers who sought economic betterment and educational opportunity (Kimhi 1990; Lipner 1987).

While most Israelis go abroad with the specific goals of education, economic and career advancement, or family unification, another group arrive as part of a "secular pilgrimage" of world travel: a common rite of passage following military service — which is compulsory for men and women alike (Ben-Ami 1992). Having arrived in the course of extended travel, some start relationships, obtain jobs and find themselves staying on.

Finally, since the start of the Al-Aqsa Intifada and information technology crash of 2000, more Israeli emigrants have been openly critical of Israel, citing the lack of economic opportunity, fear for physical safety, limited career options and political corruption as motivating their travel abroad (Gold and Hart 2005). Such is the case for Ilan, who describes the reason he and his wife moved to London in 2002:

> The Intifada did not affect us directly. Not on a day-to-day basis. But it was in the background, you know, the fear, the safety issues. But there were other factors. The government crumbled in front of our eyes. We felt Israel is becoming more and more a third world country. Then the high-tech industry collapsed and it was difficult to see how it will improve. That was very depressing. Also, as we say, the constant war corrupts us. There was growing corruption in the government, with everyone being on trial for some "irregularities", and that did affect us.

Emigration from an Israeli Perspective

With few exceptions, Jews who have migrated during the last 300 years have been *de jure* or *de facto* refugees, with few opportunities for returning to their countries of origin. By contrast, Israelis retain the real possibility of going back to Israel. Indeed, Diaspora Jews, the Jewish state and even the emigrants themselves generally agree that they should return. Consequently, this distinguishes Israelis from most other Jewish migrants throughout history and gives them the luxury of reflecting on the morality of their emigration.

Further, historically most Jews emigrating from Eastern Europe and Russia to countries of the industrialized West have become staunchly nationalistic soon after their arrival. US and UK Jews, for example, are notably patriotic and the saga of immigrant Jews' successful adaptation to the US has been elevated in theater, films and literature as the archetype for all immigrants in that nation of immigrants (Rodriguez 2001). In contrast, Israeli emigrants infrequently proclaim their devotion to host societies and instead, often discuss their desire to return home. Many make frequent trips back to the Jewish state, sometimes culminating in permanent repatriation. In the words of a community leader in Los Angeles:

> Israelis would always suffer a certain touch of nostalgia because they are missing the things that they grew up with. Psychologically, most Israelis did not come here to be Americans. They did not come here to swear to the flag; to sing the national anthem and to go to Dodgers (baseball) games. They came here to have the house and the swimming pool and the two cars and the job and the money.

Economic Characteristics

Israeli emigration is largely understood as economically motivated and Israelis in the Diaspora are quite successful. While Israeli journalists sometimes portray emigrants as employed in menial occupations, such as cab drivers or furniture movers, every study based on systematic analysis of census or survey data demonstrates that emigrants are far more educated and skilled than Israelis generally, and among the most highly educated of all arrivals in their countries of settlement (Ben-Ami 1992; Sabar 1996; Yinon Cohen 1996: 78).

During the 1970s and 1980s, and in the 1990s to a lesser degree, Israeli emigrants have been viewed by most Israelis and Diaspora Jews alike (who followed Israeli policy on emigration) as violators of Zionist ideology and a potential threat — demographically, militarily, economically and ideologically — to the survival of the Jewish state. As a consequence, they have been referred to as *yordim* — a stigmatizing Hebrew term which describes those who "descend" from the "higher" place of Israel to the Diaspora, as opposed to immigrants, the *olim* — who "ascend" from the Diaspora to Israel. However, in recent years, both Israel and many host Jewish communities have taken a more conciliatory approach towards Israeli expatriates. Local Jews provide Israelis with communal assistance, while Israel offers its overseas citizens a package of services and benefits, including outreach, assistance and financial incentives to encourage their return home (Rosen 1993). Hence the policies and actions of Israel and Diaspora Jewish communities have served to both facilitate and limit Israelis' merger into Jewish life in the host community.

Israelis are involved in chain migration. The presence of established coethnics in the host society is a valuable resource for later arrivals. It lowers the social and economic costs associated with emigration and plays a major role in organizing receiving communities. Israelis also ease their settlement in the Diaspora by residing in the Jewish neighborhoods in major cities like London, Toronto, Los Angeles, New York or Sydney (Herman and LaFontaine 1983). At the same time, their extensive connection with co-nationals and host society Jews reminds Israelis of their shared identity as well as their status as *yordim*. Consequently, Israeli emigrants' feelings about social membership are not simply a product of their personal ties to the Jewish state. Rather, they come into being in a complex context that also includes their relations with other emigrants, local Jews, and the host society.

Israeli emigrants are generally concerned with dilemmas of national and religious membership and identity, and spontaneously brought up these topics during interviews. While a broad range of perspectives were mentioned, our analysis suggests that three approaches were most common. The first focused on resolving such conflicts by returning to Israel, or emphasizing return if not actually doing so. The second involved acknowledging the benefits of life in the host society, while also maintaining Israeli cultural traditions and developing a hyphenated identity in a manner roughly equivalent to that of other ethnic groups in Diaspora communities. After Portes and Rumbaut (1996: 250) we call this process selective acculturation — learning host society ways while simultaneously maintaining strong bonds with the origin community. The third approach is transnationalism, whereby Israelis maintain involvements with both the host society and Israel while stressing a deterritorialized notion of Jewishness that deemphasizes national membership as a cornerstone of identity.

It is important to note that these outlooks are not mutually exclusive and that the same individual or émigré subgroup might shift from one to another as they reflect on their lives in the Diaspora and connections to Israel. Nevertheless, these approaches were reported with some consistency by our respondents and are also discussed within the popular and academic literature on Israeli emigration (Shokeid 1988; Sobel 1986).

Family issues (especially raising children) were significant in Israelis' thinking about how being abroad affected their identities. Respondents in each of the three categories all told us that raising children and providing them with a viable form of national, religious and group belonging was at the centre of their efforts to develop a stable basis of membership which could be passed on.

Returning to Israel

Studies of Israeli emigration conducted by Israeli researchers report that migrants — including those who have spent a decade or more in the host society — continue to "sit on their suitcases" and refer to their imminent return (Sabar 2000; Shokeid 1988; Uriely 1995). According to this body of research, migrants make such displays in order to emphasize their identity as Israelis while denying their status as *yordim* (Shokeid 1988; Mittelberg and Waters 1992; Uriely 1994).

During fieldwork, we found ample evidence of Israeli migrants' ambivalence about being outside of the Jewish state and their pervasive, if unfulfilled desire to return home. Aaron expressed this feeling during an interview conducted in 1991 at the pool of a mostly Israeli apartment complex in Southern California.

> An Israeli is torn apart the minute he is leaving Israel (to go abroad for an extended period). It's not like people from other countries who come here and settle down, hoping for a better life. An Israeli is torn apart the minute he leaves Israel and that's when he begins to wonder where it is better — here or there.
>
> I think that the reason so many Israelis are here is the illusion of materialistic comfort they can find here, period. It has nothing to do with spiritual, cultural or emotional values they are looking for. The issue is materialism. And it doesn't fulfill all the needs a human being has. A person needs culture and some ideals to believe in. We Israelis continue to keep a close contact with Israel as if we left for a short time only. We come here and organize our lives as if we are going to stay for a short period and our life here is a make-believe. The reality is that we live here and at the same time we don't live here. We are torn apart and that leaves the question for which I don't have an answer. — What will happen to us and where are we? We are in some kind of uncertainty.

Migrants' scripts about the debased nature of life abroad are taken from Israel-based condemnations of the Diaspora and emigration thereto. This perspective asserts that because emigration violates the basic tenets of Zionism, Israeli emigrants' experience is one of alienation, isolation and guilt regarding their presence outside of the Jewish state (Shokeid 1988; Linn and Barkan-Ascher 1996). Seen as deviant both by their countrymen and by host country Jews, émigrés become self-loathing and are incapable of either joining local Jewish communities or creating their own enclaves (Mittelberg and Waters 1992; Shokeid 1988; Uriely 1995).

Noting the identificational differences between Israeli emigrants and Diaspora Jews and the stigmatized nature of Israeli emigration, Israel-based social scientists have argued that Israeli emigrants' reluctance to identify with the local Jewish community in points of settlement makes Israelis unique among contemporary immigrant groups generally, and in relation to Jewish migrants, in particular (Shokeid 1988).

Yael, who was interviewed in Los Angeles in the early 1990s, described how she is fraught with ambivalence. While her heart is in Israel, she has not yet achieved the economic goals she hoped for and so is unable to reject the economic appeal of Diaspora life.

> I just have no motivation to do anything [in the US] because we always say we will go back in a few months, maybe in a year. So why would I start a business? I studied here for 18 months. And when I graduated, I was all motivated to start a business. Then, I went to Israel for two months during the summer and all the motivation stayed in Israel. Since then, we say we will go back eventually — maybe in a year, maybe in a year and a half. So I say "why would I work hard and start making clients and advertisements when I want to go back?"
>
> I know I don't want to succeed here because I am afraid if I have something going for me, then it will be hard for me to leave. And I say it's enough. It's hard for my husband to leave. So I keep myself a source to push back. If I do well here, it will be real hard for me to leave, so I just don't want to be successful.

Several respondents asserted that while they were not mistreated in host societies, at the same time, they didn't enjoy being outsiders. A former resident of Sydney explained that she felt no ownership of Australian political and cultural life. Realizing that she continued to celebrate Israeli events from afar, she decided to return home.

> In Australia, there is a real democracy, but it wasn't mine. It's important for me to be a part of it, to be involved. I hated the fact that I was not a part of it all. It was OK to begin with, but then, I missed the involvement. For me Yom Hazikaron (Israeli Memorial Day) is a special day and when Yom Ha'azmaut (Israeli Independence Day) comes, it is a very special moment for me — I am always choked with tears. I missed that when I was there. I really missed it. I felt sad in these events away from home. I simply felt sad and detached.
>
> I used to organize all these events for Israelis. That enabled us to celebrate these events together, but it was not the same as it is here. The real thing can only be here. So we lived in Australia and we lived like Israelis there in a little Israeli social circle. Had we learned to live in Australia like Australians — we could have stayed there. But that did not happen and at the end, that brought us back. Because if we live like Israelis there — we might as well live the real thing here!

According to Israeli census reports, a number of Israeli migrants do actually return; about 5,000 a year during the last half of the 1990s, reducing to about 3,000 annually since then (Alon 2003).

While Israelis who planned to stay on in the Diaspora reported positive relations with local Jews, those focusing on return felt distant from native co-religionists at both the communal level and in synagogues . Such was the case for Norit and Deborah:

> NORIT: I think that as a community they are rejecting us. I don't really know why. I met quite a few (Israeli) people who had unpleasant encounters with them. They felt rejected and excluded by them. Why? I think they don't like us. Those (Israeli) friends of mine who told me about it — they all live here much longer than me. And they said that they have felt uncomfortable when they visited the synagogue, and at social events.
>
> DEBORAH: Most of them (American Jews) go by the Reform stream and I tend to actually like it because it's more modern and it doesn't come [in]to conflict with family life as much as the other streams of Judaism do, but, I think that from a Jewish life perspective, it's really a lot like Christianity. There isn't that much difference.

Child Rearing and Return

As already noted, among my respondents, problems of child socialization and education were by far the most commonly mentioned negative aspects of life abroad. In fact, while Israeli adults without children often felt that they could tolerate life outside of Israel, having a child often made them much more aware of the costs of life in the Diaspora and made them much more serious about returning.

Return-focused parents often feared that their children would lose their Jewish and Israeli identity as a result of living in Christian societies. Accordingly, they face a twopronged dilemma as they plan for their children's education. If they do nothing, the kids will forsake their Jewish and Israeli heritage. However, if they enroll the youngsters in local Jewish institutions, they will be confronted with another, and to an Israeli — equally foreign — notion of identity: Diaspora Judaism. In order to avoid choosing either of two undesirable alternatives, some emigrants focused on returning.

Concerned with their children's socialization, émigré parents were involved in extensive discussions with co-nationals about available schools and youth programmes that could assist them in this endeavour (Shavit n.d.; Lipner 1987). Despite the numerous Jewish and secular options available in major communities of settlement such as London, Paris, New York, Los Angeles, Sydney, and Toronto, Israelis remained generally unsatisfied. Those in England and Australia described local Jewish schools as austere, authoritarian and employing out-dated teaching methods. A father of three characterized the academy that his children attended as "the worst combination between the strictness of the English culture and the rigidity of the religious Jewish education". American public schools were seen as academically inferior and likely to foster children's assimilation to a Christian, American standpoint. In the following quotation, a couple emphasizes their children's needs as they explained their reasoning for remigration to Israel.

> INVESTIGATOR: Tell me about the decision to return.
> GILDA: The considerations were around the kids entirely. We knew we would be going back to something which has less to offer us from many aspects and we knew we had to do this for the kids' sake.
> TEDDI: The kids were part of this decision-making process. Their adjustment was not easy. Actually, it was really difficult. We were absorbed with our own issues and adaptation, and therefore the kids had to deal with it all by themselves. The youngest really wanted to go back all the time.

As the following quote from a group interview of Israeli teenagers in Los Angeles suggests, Israeli children are themselves often critical of Diaspora life.

> NORIT: My dad came here nine months before us. And I knew one day we're going to come here 'cause of him. I didn't really want to come, you know. I know it was going to be a start again and I was like scared. But I'm here and I have to accept it.
> DAN: In the United States it was Yom Kippur. We went to the synagogue and it was so different because we like prayed and then we went home and people were driving by on the street and people were eating in restaurants and it was very hard. It was very different. I felt that I am not in the right place. I shouldn't be here. I told my parents and they said "You are in the United States, you are not in Israel. You should expect that."

Another problem cited by émigré parents is that migration prevents them from sharing a common language, culture and life-shaping experiences with their children, so depriving them of generational continuity. A woman living in London described this:

> By the time they went to school, they started talking in a language that is alien to me, singing songs I do not know, experiencing things which are unfamiliar to me. That was difficult for me. I know it sounds selfish, but I want my kids. I want to be part of their lives. I wanted them to have something in common with me. I wanted them to have the same identity as mine.

Gender and the Desire to Return

Gender patterns shape Israelis' emigration and their reactions to it. Most commonly, Israeli emigrant men are involved in study or work. They find these activities rewarding, as they provide ample earnings, a positive sense of self, and social contacts. Thus Israeli men often prefer to stay on. In contrast, Israeli emigrant women who have children are charged with settling the family's domestic affairs. Supported by their husbands' earnings, they often remain housebound in suburban communities, faced with the formidable task of recreating a supportive family environment in an unfamiliar cultural and linguistic setting. Consequently, women's encounters with the host society are often more difficult than those of co-national men. Michal described the difference between men's and women's migration experience:

> INVESTIGATOR: How would you compare the feelings of the Israeli men versus women who come to America?
> MICHAL: Frustration for some women. I am frustrated because I had a career in Israel and I have none here. And do you know what the cost is? The only rewards go to the man — the economic advances. Both spiritually and fulfillment-wise, it is a lot more important for the woman to be in Israel.

In the following quotation, Dahlia explains how gendered disagreements about returning to Israel threaten her marriage:

> DAHLIA: I do want to see myself as someone who lives in Israel. The problem is that Moshe (my husband) does not feel the same way. Today, I am in a situation where I have to decide if I will have to separate from Moshe.
> INTERVIEWER: Are you serious?
> DAHLIA: Yes. I did not try it yet, and I am not interested in trying it now. We never had serious discussion about that, but when we talk in a very light way, he always laughs, saying that we (wife and son) would have to go back without him. I am not insulted by that. I think he has to pass (through) the process and then he will be happy to come back. Meanwhile, I am not in a hurry. I am here because of my family. I am happy to live with my husband in a place which is good for him, and personally, I am gaining a lot from my staying here. Maybe in five years I will say "that's enough" — but I really cannot tell when.

In sum, return-focused emigrants retained an Israel-based understanding of emigration. Finding life in the Diaspora lacking, they hoped to return to Israel as a means of resolving emigration-related problems.

Selective Acculturation to the Host Society

In contrast to Israeli emigrants who felt alienated in the Diaspora and hoped to return to Israel, another group reacted to their Israeli identities by following in the social patterns of other migrant populations — Jewish and Gentile alike — that have settled in western industrial societies for the last century and a half. While acknowledging and even prizing their Israeli roots, these émigrés would readily admit ways in which the host society had advantages over the Jewish state. In so doing, they acted in conformity with the citizenship narratives of the host society.

Selective acculturation was generally a pragmatic endeavour that involved building desired community resources and establishing links with other Israeli emigrants, local Jews and the broader society. Such efforts were rewarded, as they provided Israeli emigrants with the social, cultural and economic benefits of life abroad without requiring them to abandon feelings of attachment to, and engagement with, aspects of Israeli life that they prized. Finally, Israelis involved in selective acculturation honored the country of origin by functioning as advocates for Israel — representing and defending the Jewish state's interests, mobilizing support, promoting Israeli culture and raising funds for Israeli institutions.

As a means of accounting for their presence in the Diaspora, several respondents discussed changes in Israel that had occurred while they were abroad — such as Israel's recent political, cultural and economic transformations — as altering their identification with the Jewish state and making host societies more desirable. For example, a leftist *kibbutznick* living in England described his anger at the increasing commercialization and Americanization of Israel: "When I go back, I find that the advertising on the radio and the whole scene — the McDonald's and the Toys R Us and the whole shit — it's coming in from America, and I don't like it." A London resident who visited Israel following her divorce from an Englishman felt that the country she left no longer existed:

> I am and always was very Israeli in all my being. And although during these years (in London) I felt less and less of that sense of belonging, I still felt I am an Israeli and felt very strong about my identity. However, when I returned, I felt I did not belong here anymore because things have happened here that I was not a part of. I belonged to that country that I left behind years ago. This country does not exist anymore apart from its existence in my memory.

Finally, as noted above, since the beginning of the Al-Aqsa Intifada in Fall 2000, some Israelis have become more open in expressing their criticism of the Jewish state and their desire to be away. This is expressed in the following comments received from an informant in London during late 2001:

> An (Israeli) woman called me to discuss schooling issues. When I asked her for how long they intend to stay here, she simply said: "I am not going back." We talked a bit about how she felt about it, and she admitted that it was difficult for her to say that when she was in Israel, but here, she is OK with it. She said she met so many other Israelis here so that she now feels comfortable to say that they have decided to stay here. She also said: "We have been brainwashed to think that we can only live there, and for years we didn't dare to think we can live here, although we both have a British passport" [They were here as kids and got British citizenship]. "Now my son is 16, my second one is 14 and my little one is 11. Three boys and I am not sending any of them to the army! I am not going through that! We have had enough of that country and all the troubles it has!"

Seeking Career Advancement

Israelis often go abroad in pursuit of economic and work-related goals, and many find success. As such, émigrés acknowledge that opportunities for work and rewards in the Diaspora often outstrip those available in the Jewish state. Like other groups of skilled migrants, Israelis represent a high quality labour force who often seek non-monitory rewards from work in addition to survival income. These include personal fulfillment, advanced training, and the ability to participate in cutting-edge occupational settings (leading universities, centres of technology, finance, and cultural production) associated with advanced nations and world cities.

When Israelis seek fulfilling careers in the Diaspora, they challenge early Zionism's emphasis on collective obligations over the pursuit of individualist fulfillment. Observing the insecure status of Jews as urban entrepreneurs, traders, wage labourers, bankers and scholars in nineteenth-century Europe, the founders of Zionism felt that Jews would only be free, secure and self-respecting if they abandoned these typically Jewish occupations in host societies and instead, settled in Palestine (Kotkin 1992; Zerubavel 1995; Zweig 1969). Here, it was thought, the "new Jew" would engage in a full range of work roles, with a stress on ennobling agriculture. Rather than acquiring money from Gentiles, or conforming to the individualistic achievement culture of the West, work would be determined by collective needs and devoted to building a safe and secure homeland for the Jewish people (Almog 2000).

In their study of Israeli emigrants in New York, Marcia Freedman and Josef Korzim explore the tension between nation building at home and pursuing careers abroad. The authors contend that in the Jewish state, the self-employed are stigmatized as self-serving and parasitic tax evaders. Consequently, the "suspect nature of entrepreneurship from a Zionist perspective" is a significant motive for business-minded Israelis' emigration (Freedman and Korzim 1986: 144). When Jewish Israelis contrast the way of life available to them in the Jewish state with that beyond, they are aware of the Diaspora's opportunities, and Diaspora Jews' accomplishments — financial and otherwise — in the world of work. Accordingly, those émigrés who have a strong orientation towards entrepreneurship and careers — especially those who went abroad prior to Israel's economic transformation in the 1990s — felt forced to choose between job and country (Uriely 1994; Gold 1994). As reflected in the following comments by an émigré in LA's garment industry, a fraction preferred the Diaspora:

> For the people who were in business in Israel, you don't even have to ask. We just know that they came to do business. America is a better country for business. Less regulations, taxes and controls. They want you to do some business. Israel, it's too much socialism.

Family Life and Selective Acculturation

As noted, issues pertaining to raising children loom large when Israelis think about where they would like to live. While those focusing on return dwell upon the negative aspects of Diaspora life, immigrants following a path of selective acculturation emphasize the ways in which the Diaspora rewards Israeli families. They refer to their enjoyment of material, cultural and social advantages that are difficult to obtain in Israel, including a higher standard of living, a greater degree of personal autonomy, cordial social relations in public settings, numerous cultural amenities, longer weekends, a wider range of occupational opportunities, easier access to higher education, freedom from military service, greater cultural and religious diversity, more intimacy and privacy, and a welcome release from what they describe as the "pressure cooker" atmosphere of the Middle East (Sobel 1986; Gold 2002). Exemplifying this position, respondents Irit and Tomer feel that their migration has provided their families with more time together, numerous niceties, and satisfying work. As a consequence, their moves have been beneficial for their entire households.

> INVESTIGATOR: How has being in London influenced your family life?
> IRIT: Very good. First, now that I am working from home it is really fine with the children. Avi (my husband) is coming at about six o'clock so we are all together. Then we have Saturday and the Sunday, full of activity trips and museums. It is great not to have all the family duties

and not to spend so much time on grandparents, sisters, brothers, etc.
Tomer: Family life is much, much better here. First, I never work here as late as I did in Israel. Miri (my wife) spends much more time at home. She never had so much time in Israel. She worked a full time job in Israel. Here, she has the time to do what she really enjoys — she plays in an orchestra — so she is much happier, and takes care of the kids. Our financial situation is stable. What can I say? It all affected our family life for the better.

Ironically, a considerable number of Israelis described becoming more religious in the Diaspora. Initially joining synagogues in host societies as a way retaining some forms of Jewish identity, they found these settings more family friendly, satisfying and compatible with their values than synagogues in Israel. A university professor describes his preference for the sort of Judaism followed in American academic communities:

In the US, the dominant flavor of Judaism is the Reform Judaism and we liked it a lot, because it allowed us to come as a family unit to the synagogue. We are not, you know, religious, observant Jews, but we do come on the High Holidays. For us, it was extremely important to be able to sit together. We also liked the equal role for women in the Jewish practice. For example, you can have a female rabbi and things like that. So, we liked it a lot, actually. We found that Reform Judaism in the US flavor is much more suitable for us. So, in a way, it opened our eyes. We said, "Now, there is some room to practice Judaism and not feel too silly about it."

Immigrant Organizations

Despite their appreciation of life in host societies, acculturation-oriented Israeli emigrants are not without criticisms of their new environment. However, in contrast to returned-focused Israelis who recoil form community building in the host society and seek to resolve such concerns via remigration, these emigrants expend considerable effort in developing organizations and activities to improve life in the Diaspora. Israeli immigrants in Los Angeles, New York, Chicago, London, Paris, Toronto, Sydney and other cities have developed many activities — both formal and informal, locally-based and international — in order to resolve their misgivings about being away from Israel. For example, in major points of settlement, Israelis, local Jews and consular officials organized celebrations of Israeli holidays, film festivals and cultural events, and mobilized philanthropic activities to benefit the Jewish state. Programmes were directed at the emigrant population as well as the local community.

David — a Los Angeles real estate developer and community activist — who has been successful in unifying Israeli emigrants and native-born Jews, elaborates on his approach to integration among American and Israeli Jews. He favors incorporation with local coreligionists (in the local Jewish Federation) as opposed to maintaining unrealistic expectations for return or creating an autonomous Israeli enclave. Pointing out that local Jews have similar origins and outlooks to Israelis, he encourages the many Israeli subcontractors that he employs to join local Jewish organizations.

The Israelis have to come into the Jewish community. I don't like the fact that some of them want to be independent. I'm not against them organizing, but we should become a part of the mainstream of Jewish-American life because we are not separate. Take for example my own family. I don't see that just because somebody's grandmother left the same village in Poland that my grandmother lived in 80 years ago and came to New York, and my relatives came to Israel, that I'm that different from that person.

So, since we are the same people, we should not have a separate Israeli Federation — for two reasons. The main reason to me is that most Israelis will not admit that most of them will stay here forever. Most of them will end up living here, and 90 percent of their children will end up living here.

I mean, all Israelis somewhere harbor the hope that they will go back to Israel. But the truth is that all of them are here temporarily, and then they die. And that's the reality. I've been here eighteen years, I would like to go back. I don't know if I will. You have your businesses, people have families. You know, they cannot just pick up and leave. And they have gotten used to the way of life here and that's their reality. So these two communities need each other. And I'm not saying the Israelis should assimilate into the Jewish community and become Americans because they won't. Their children probably will, but they won't.

And they can keep their uniqueness, but in total cooperation. I think that instead of having their divisive or divided Jewish community, we need to have one strong united community, because here, you're bringing new Israeli, precious Israeli blood into the Jewish Federation. The Federation will get stronger and I'm going to tell you that some of the nicest people I know work in The Federation and it will do a hell of lot of good for Israelis to meet these people and become one community. Not for Israelis to resent Americans and for Israelis see themselves as outsiders. I mean it will take time. This is not a process that will happen overnight, but it will happen.

Gender and Community Activism

Faced with isolation and the challenges of living in an alien culture, married Israeli women often find host societies lacking in the resources they need to maintain a supportive environment for their families and children. Making use of the free time provided by the substantial earnings of their husbands, these women often take a leading role in organizing many communal activities. Shavit (n.d.: 19) describes the importance of informal school-seeking networks as a central force among middle class Israelis in London. Upon (or even prior to) arrival in the UK, women contact co-nationals to obtain information about schools. Accepting their advice, Israeli families settle within specific neighborhoods and enroll their children in one of the "network approved" schools. This pattern of settlement opens the door for further involvement in the local community: "the school's role is as a 'mag-net,' a meeting point and a channel through which new members are introduced to the community and gain access to its networks" (Shavit n.d.: 19). On a broader level, an Israeli Sunday school connects Israeli children attending various schools. Social contacts established here then unite their families.

Motivated by their desire to provide children with some forms of Israeli-style upbringing, a number of émigré women — in consort with Israeli and host society Jewish organizations — developed programmes for the community's young people. In Los Angeles, two of the most popular were the AMI (Israeli Hebrew) school and Tzofim (Israeli scouts). (Similar programmes exist in Paris, New York, London, Chicago, Miami, Silicon Valley, and Toronto). The director of one such programme describes it:

What does a child that was born to an Israeli family that lives in the United States need to feel comfortable in his community? One thing is Hebrew. They must also know about the culture in which we grew — the poems and the riddles and the rhymes and the stories. We have lessons for the Holy Days and Shabbat. We celebrate the Holy Days the way we would in Israel. They have to know about the geography of Israel to know what's going on political-wise. They have to know the history and they should know about the different Jewish heroes from the Biblical time to modern history.

While women predominate in many activities, Israeli emigrants are also involved in non-gender specific community organizations, such as Hebrew-speaking, Israeli-oriented chapters of host society Jewish organizations like the Jewish Community Federation (Rosen 1993). By linking their activities to those of the local Jewish population, émigré activists both benefit from, and contribute to, the indigenous Jewish communal structure.

In recent years, settlement-focused Israeli emigrants have developed extensive ethnic enclaves and ethnic economies (often overlapping with those of local Jews). These feature shops, social activities, synagogues, child-care centres, Hebrew language media and a variety of other activities (Gold 2002). In the course of field work in Los Angeles, one research team identified some 27 Israeli organizations — ranging from synagogues, Hebrew schools and political groups to scouting programmes, sports teams, business associations and even a recreational flying club (Gold 2002). Other major centres of settlement reveal a similar array of organizations. Within these settings, Israelis are able to access resources, maintain social lives and develop collective strategies that help them address issues of survival and identification. This is suggested in the following interview excerpt from London.

INVESTIGATOR: when you look at the Israelis here, would you define them as a community?
ESTHER: Yes, I think so. The geographical concentration is important in creating a community. I know many people choose to live in Golders Green because of this. It is very convenient to have some people around who share the same manners — that you can just call and pop in and don't need an appointment two weeks ahead. It's an advantage. Why is it a community? Because they live near each other, because there is all the services around them — the Israeli food, doctors, etc. I think the social life is very much what makes it a community.

Reconsidering Identity

Many of those who lived outside of Israel for extended periods of time described how life abroad provided a new perspective on their connections to Israel. Such insights would not have been available had they remained at home. Natali found that the distance gave her a deeper appreciation of the world and Israel's place in it. In contrast, Dan describes how he became more protective of the homeland, and came to act as a "little ambassador" for the Jewish state.

INTERVIEWER: Would you recommend to other Israelis to live here?
NATALI: Yes, abroad in general, not only here. It opens your mind to new things. You learn a lot. You come out of the bubble where you think that Israel is the best place on earth and stuff like that. You become more modest — you learn about and from other cultures. We come to see that we don't know everything. We're very arrogant. When I was young, my parents did not allow me to read the New Testament. But I think it is important that we do

read and understand other cultures and religions. We become more modest — we realize that Israel is a province — and not very central (laughing). Not the center of the world.
DAN: I very quickly realized that my role in the Diaspora is as a spokesperson for Israel, even for my non-Jewish friends. So, it did affect my identity. I realized very quickly that I am like a little ambassador. I could not actually expose criticism against the Israeli regime as easily as I was doing in Israel. My (American) friends wanted to get more explanation on what's going on. So, I changed my role after a year or two and became, like, a little ambassador to Israel, as opposed to just expressing my political opinion.

In sum, Israeli emigrants involved in selective acculturation combined cultural and identificational aspects from the host societies with favored Israeli traditions, while also supporting the Jewish state from afar. In this, they mirror the adaptation patterns of other migrant populations (Jews and non-Jews alike) that have settled in the increasingly multicultural societies of the industrialized West.

Deterritorialized Identity

Some Israeli émigrés adopt a third strategy for addressing conflicts associated with identifying with Israel yet being abroad. They do this by maintaining a transnational outlook that involves extensive ties overseas, and by emphasizing an ideology that does not privilege national membership as central to their feelings of belonging. In contrast to sojourner or settler models that underscore migrants' links with a single nation state, transnationalism describes the experience of those who maintain concurrent social, economic, political and cultural links and involvements in two or more national settings.

Transnationals are described as engaging in frequent travel and even those who do not themselves cross borders with frequency are said to reside within "transnational social spaces" where their outlooks and values are influenced by information, norms and social resources brought in from other continents or deterritorialized collectives (Portes, Guarnizo and Landolt 1999; Faist 2000). Most versions of transnational theorizing see the economic, political and geographical mobility associated with border crossing as capable of granting migrants a high degree of agency and flexibility to avoid disadvantages associated with specific localities. Sarah Mahler asserts that "Through transnational processes everyday people can generate Creole identities and agencies that challenge multiple levels of structural control" (Mahler 1998: 68); while Michael Galchinsky refers to a specifically Jewish aspect: "Recent theorists have begun to understand Jews' history and theories of diaspora as crucial to postcolonialism's attempts to subvert identity politics of all kinds" (Galchinsky 1998: 186).

As suggested by the long history of Jews' cosmopolitan outlook as well as more contemporary writing on transnational identity, some Israelis assert their right to live where they wish (Cohen 1997; Patai 1971; Appadurai 1996; Bhaba 1994). While they generally expressed affection for the Jewish state, they do not emphasize living in Israel as a central goal. Rather than conforming to traditions of immigrant assimilation advanced by Israel or the host society, they downplayed nationality as a basis of identity. Some went as far as keeping multiple households and returning to Israel with children for extended periods.

French sociologist Reginé Azria intimates that emigration (in both temporary and permanent forms) is now an accepted feature of Israeli reality: "Thus, today, some Jews are simultaneously Israeli Jews and diaspora Jews without being concerned about either this or which passport they carry. They travel around the world simply because they feel like it, or because they need to for professional, academic, family or vacation purposes" (Azria 1998: 24). For example, a journalist involved with Middle Eastern affairs described his notion of national identification:

> There's a host of reasons for my leaving Israel, but even though I live in Los Angeles, obviously, I've never left. I believe that at birth every Jew should be given three passports of three different countries so that they can always have a place to run away to.

Despite national, ideological, and religious differences between Israeli and Diaspora Jews, Israelis do feel connections to other Jews and see themselves, Jewish migrants from other countries, and native-born Jews in settlement countries as members of the same ethnic and religious group. According to Israeli anthropologist Natan Uriely, they refer to "a common past, the observance of the same holidays, rituals and ceremonies, the retelling of the same myths and similar responses to common symbols" (Uriely 1995: 30; Liebman and Cohen 1990).

Jewish ethnicity is seen as a link to potential friends and allies. Consequently, it offers a flexible form of identification that allows Israelis to make connections with local Jews and to consume communal resources without repudiating their Israeli identities. Few members of the first generation renounce their connection to Israel and become flag-waving Canadian, British or American Jews. A considerable number did, however, begin to describe themselves as members of the deterritorialized ethnic or religious community of the Jewish people. In this way, they were able to reconcile their connections to two or more nationalities without appearing disloyal to either.

Moreover, by referring to their connection to Jewish peoplehood, Israeli emigrants present themselves as experts in Hebrew and Israeli culture rather than exiles from Israeli society. The extent to which Israelis are involved in providing training in Hebrew, and Israeli and Jewish culture to Diaspora communities is significant: as indicated by the fact that "teacher" was the most common occupation among Israeli emigrants in the 1990 US Census. In this way, many Israeli emigrants view the Jewish religion and Jewish ethnicity as sources of linkage to potential friends and allies.

A woman who returned from London to Tel Aviv refers to the inclusive sense of Jewish peoplehood that develops when Jews of all stripes are brought together by their shared minority status:

> We lived in Golders Green, so there were Jews and Israelis around. We always thought that it would have been nice to have in here (Israel) the same type of relationship that they managed to establish between religious and secular people. There, it's not their country. They are a minority. So they adjust and conform to the culture and all the rest. They would not throw stones at cars driving on Yom Kippur as they do here. Also, the secular there, including the Israelis, are much more respectful and tolerant and actually open-minded towards the religious people. There is no religious coercion — and so they can be more tolerant to the religious people.

Others take an explicitly ideological approach to world citizenship and question the notion of nationalism. A Moroccan-born writer who lives in Paris and works with various nationalities, claims that he "feels at home everywhere in the world".

INVESTIGATOR: Do you feel like an outsider or do you feel here at home?
I do feel at home. I feel everywhere in the world as if I am at home. I think that everyone should live where it is convenient for him. I don't think that this ground belongs to a certain French person or to France at all, as I think that Israel belongs to the people that live there now. I don't think that Israel belongs to the Jews. It belongs to the people that built it after the Holocaust. I don't think that we should be in Israel from historic reasons. We are there because we are there, but the Arabs who lived there should also have a space.

In a like manner, a cook living in London enjoys the possibility of expressing his free will through migration, and condemns those who would stigmatize him for doing so:

INVESTIGATOR: Do you recommend Israelis to live outside the country?
Yes. Everyone that has a passport should try it. Live in another place. I am not calling that yerida. All the time we have definitions. Either you are in the army, or you are a yored, or you are homosexual. Why do they bother to define people all the time?

Transnational Work

In addition to the ideological, cultural and identity-focused dimensions of Israel transnationalism that allow Israelis to develop connections and feel comfortable in multiple settings, Israel emigrants also develop, access and exchange practical resources — in social, political, economic, familial and religious realms — via border-crossing networks. A growing body of research demonstrates the considerable value of border-crossing social networks in shaping migrants' communal and economic lives as well as their relations with the country of origin (Gold 2002; Findlay 1995; Findlay and Li 1998; Nonini and Ong 1997; Levitt 2001). Nearly every Israeli emigrant that we contacted, regardless of occupation, background, gender, educational level or place of settlement, relied on co-nationals to achieve social and economic ends. Paradoxically, some Israeli emigrants appear to maintain their Jewish and Israeli-based traditions of collectivism and self-help, even as they pursue individualistic goals beyond the Jewish state (Sabar 2000; Cohen and Gold 1996).

In the economic realm, several respondents told us how they drew upon years of experience with international businesses to create transnational activities. Because Israel's economic development policies are, to a large measure, oriented towards the export of goods and agricultural products, the country trains and sends abroad a contingent of functionaries to engage in international economic transactions. Developing skills and contacts in various settings, a fraction of these eventually become independent workers and entrepreneurs in many different national settings (Shokeid 1988). Such was the case of a Los Angeles man referred to us by the Israeli embassy. After acquiring an advanced degree in agricultural science from an American university, he had worked for several years in the export of Israeli citrus to Japan. At the time we spoke to him, he was involved in a variety of import/export activities spanning the US and Asia.

Transnational entrepreneurs eloquently reflected on both the possibilities and problems involved in international business. For example, in the mid-1990s, Sol, a Los Angeles garment manufacturer, described his ambitious plan to produce clothes in Egypt, and then transport them, via quota-exempt Israel, to be sold in the US.

> See the thing is that manufacturers and importers in the United States always went to the Far East. Whenever they want to import electronics, toys or garments, they always went to the Far East. By now, many have become more aware that the Middle East has a great potential, especially in Egypt, where a lot of the basic items are subsidized by the government. They have all the knowledge, all the know-how, and the technology over there.
>
> The idea that I developed was that you'd be able to bring garments from the Middle East even cheaper than you can bring from countries like China or Hong Kong, because of the quota limitation. The idea was to take advantage of the Israeli–United States trade agreement where there is no duty involved. What I was hoping to do is to incorporate the neighboring cheap labor countries, like Egypt, Jordan. At the same time I would keep my distribution over here (in Los Angeles).
>
> By cooperating between Israel and Egypt, eventually you will be able to bring in the finished product. They will have to be cut in Israel, it will be assembled in Egypt and brought back to Israel and shipped from Israel. I have some Israeli partners here in LA. They pooled some money together. They see the potential.

While transnational Israeli entrepreneurs may not emphasize residence in the Jewish state, at the same time, their activities bring significant income and investment capital, as well as cultural and technological innovation to their country of origin, and play a vital role in its growing involvement in the global economy.

Transnational Families

Israelis were involved in transnational business activities to achieve economic ends. They also maintain transnational family ties to ease some of the troubles associated with life abroad. Like other high status migrants, Israelis deploy the transnational family commuting practices of "astronaut" parents and "parachute" children who reside on different continents in order to access an ideal combination of economic and educational opportunities, while relying on recurrent international air travel to preserve family unity (Ong 1999; Gold 2002). In the following quote, Gilda describes how she travels between London and Israel to care for family members in two countries:

> GILDA: It is complicated. We came here (London) while our first child was in the army. He was not in a dangerous function so we could come here. A year ago, our daughter who finished the secondary school went to the (Israeli) army. She lives now with her boyfriend in our Moshav (rural collective). My son is living with my mom (in Israel). He has a separate floor in her house with a private entrance. Almost every two months, I am traveling there for ten days or so to give them also the feeling that Mom is here.
>
> INVESTIGATOR: Must be very tiring.
>
> GILDA: Yes it is. It also takes a lot of my time. I am organizing things before and after in here, and also there, I take care of all their needs.

Youth programmes supported by the Israeli government and various Jewish organizations — including *Hetz Vakeshet* (summer in Israel), study abroad, and military service — also served to keep young emigrants (as well as the children of Israelis) tied to the land, culture, language, religion and people of the Jewish state.

With their close proximity to Israel, London's émigrés appear to be more often immersed in transnational family practices than co-nationals in the US, Canada or Australia. Many of our respondents in London reported visiting Israel four or more times a year, often for weeks at a time. Batya describes a level of on-going contact with Israel that would be rare in North America.

> I managed to maintain the relationships like they were before. I talk with them often, I meet them whenever I come or they visit here. I always meet with everybody when I come. I had organized two meetings of my kibbutz and my high school mates. These were very exciting. We are still very good friends. We write to each other — mainly e-mail, and we meet. Some of my friends visit my parents and sisters regularly, and it's like another family to them.
>
> I want to be together. They are an important part of my life even if I live in London. I still have relationships with the trainees I trained during my army service, and I meet with them as well. I invest a lot in these relationships in order to keep them as they were before. Some of my friends here — their relationships in Israel gradually disintegrated simply because they put very little into the maintenance of these friendships. Mine didn't. I don't forget my life in Israel.

Israelis in the UK may be more transnational in outlook than those in North America or Australia because England is less devoted to the assimilation of immigrants than is the States or Canada (Kadish 1998). As countries of immigration, the United States and Canada maintain strong national myths with regard to the inclusion of recent arrivals. Public schools, which are attended by a considerable fraction of Israeli migrant children in the States, have long played a major role in the assimilation of immigrants (Glazer and Moynihan 1963). Jewish school attendance also promotes the adoption of a US identity (Rosenthal 1989: 149). Further, Toronto's highly organized Jewish community provides Israeli emigrants with many opportunities for involvement (Cohen 1999). In contrast, Israeli migrant children in London often attend multicultural or Jewish schools that include a sizable fraction of Israeli children. This often discourages their acquisition of an English identity (Hart 2005).

Émigrés residing in various nations asserted that transnational family strategies addressed several concerns. They allowed children to develop an Israeli identity, master Hebrew, and stay close with relatives; reduced the chances of marriage to a non-Jew, and allowed kids raised abroad to share common experiences and outlooks with parents. Sol, an entrepreneur who returned from Los Angeles to Israel, hoped that his family's time abroad provided his children with the best of both worlds:

> My son Bar was born in LA and lived here for almost 16 years. Then we moved back. He is graduating high school this year and I told him that he has a choice either to go to college here or to go to the Army and he decided to go to the Army in Israel.
>
> Even though Bar and his brothers they grow up in the United States, they love Israel and follow what's happening. I think for the kids, it was a very good move.
>
> Bar was just in LA and he was able to keep in touch with his friends over here, so when he comes here, he has a lot of friends and he can see a lot of people. So in a way, I feel that my kids have a taste of both worlds and, I hope that they'll learn to live in this big village we call the world. Yeah they have a taste of both and I hope it will be for the beneficial.
>
> All of them are bilingual and they speak pretty good English and Hebrew and, when they'll grow, they'll decide what they want to do. But I felt it was my obligation to show them a little bit of Israel. I'm an Israeli and I thought this was the most important thing.

Summary

Socialized into the culture and ideology of the Jewish state, Israeli emigrants continue to identify with the Jewish state even as they seek goals and build lives abroad. This essay has identified three strategies by which Israelis do this: by focusing on return, through selective acculturation, and by adopting a deterritorialized approach to identity. While each approach offered certain benefits, none appeared to be fully satisfactory. As mentioned by a woman who raised her children in London, one's best efforts don't always yield the desired outcome:

> I would like to see to the three of them bringing up families in Israel. That's my aim and that's my purpose, because that's what I didn't get to do. But it looks like they will not. And now, I just feel, you know, it's their life. I did what I could. They're all grown now and now it's their life. It's their choice. As long as they are happy. . . . I have got to, how to say, release the reins. I have to let them fly now. Also, they are successful in what they are doing. They are successful in what they are doing and today, it's also important.

Whatever their reactions to emigration, to a very large extent, Israeli migrants' views are shaped by concerns emanating from the Jewish state rather than the host society. They were all affected by the stigmatized status Israel confers on emigrants and all devoted considerable thought and action to resolving it. In other words, Diaspora settings are infrequently evaluated according to their own merits, but rather, in terms of their being better, worse or different from Israel. In this, we see the centrality of Israel in emigrants' identities. At the same time, despite their involvement in an Israeli world view, over time the number of Israeli emigrants continues to grow, suggesting that such identity concerns are not strong enough to suppress emigration's appeal.

Finally, given the Jewish state's relatively short history, the tenure of numbers of Israeli emigrant in hostlands is short. Greater insight into the impact of Israel on the identities of Israelis in the Diaspora will be revealed if and when a sizeable second generation raised abroad comes of age.

References

Basch, L., Glick Schiller, N., and Blanc-Szanton C., *Nations Unbound: Transnational Projects, Postcolonial Predicaments, and Deterritorialized Nation States* (Basel, Switzerland: Gordon and Breach Publishers, 1994).

Ben-Ami, I., "Shlepers and Car Washers: Young Israelis in the New York Labor Market", *Migration World* 20, 1 (1992): 18–20.

Bhabha, H. (interviewed by Paul Thompson), "Between Identities", pp. 183–199 in Rina Benmayor and Andor Skotnes (eds) *Migration and Identity: International Yearbook of Oral History and Life Stories*, Volume III (Oxford: Oxford University Press, 1994).

Cohen, R., "From Ethnonational Enclave to Diasporic Community: The Mainstreaming of Israeli Jewish Migrants in Toronto", *Diaspora* 8, 2 (1999): 121–136.

Cohen, R. and Gold, G., "Israelis in Toronto: The Myth of Return and the Development of a Distinct Ethnic Community", *The Jewish Journal of Sociology*, 38, 1 (1996): 17–26.

Cohen, R., *Global Diasporas* (Seattle: University of Washington, 1997).

Cohen, S. M., "Israeli Émigrés and the New York Federation: A Case Study in Ambivalent

Policymaking for 'Jewish Communal Deviants'", *Contemporary Jewry* 7 (1986): 155–65.
Cohen, Y., "Economic Assimilation in the United States of Arab and Jewish Immigrants from Israel and the Territories", *Israel Studies* 1, 2 (1996): 75–97.
Enav, P., "Report: A half million Israelis live in United States", *The Miami Herald*, 20 July 2003
Faist, T., *The Volume and Dynamics of International Migration and Transnational Social Spaces* (Oxford: Oxford University Press, 2000).
Findlay, A. M., "Skilled Transients: The Invisible Phenomenon", pp. 515–522 in R. Cohen, (ed.), *The Cambridge Survey of World Migration* (Cambridge: Cambridge University Press, 1995).
Findlay, A. M. and Li, F. I. N., "A Migration Channels Approach to the Study of Professional Moving to and fromHong Kong", *International Migration Review* 32, 3 (1998): 682–703.
Freedman, M. and Korazim, J., "Israelis in the New York Area Labor Market", *Contemporary Jewry* 7 (1986): 141–153.
Galchinsky, M., "Scattered Seeds: A Dialogue of Diasporas", pp. 185–211 in David Biale, D., Galchinsky, M. and Heschel, S. (eds), *Insider/Outsider: American Jews and Multiculturalism* (Berkeley: University of California Press, 1998).
Glazer, N. and Moynihan, D.P., *Beyond the Melting Pot* (Cambridge, MA: The MIT Press, 1963).
Gold, S., "Patterns of Economic Cooperation among Israeli Immigrants in Los Angeles", *International Migration Review* 28, 105 (1994): 114–35.
Gold, S., "Transnationalism and Vocabularies of Motive in International Migration: The Case of Israelis in the U.S"., *Sociological Perspectives* 40, 3 (1997): 409–426.
Gold, S., *The Israeli Diaspora* (London and Seattle: Rutgers/University of Washington Press, 2002).
Gold, S. J. and Phillips, B. A., "Israelis in the United States", *American Jewish Yearbook 1996* (New York: American Jewish Committee, 1996), pp. 51–101.
Gold, S. J. and Hart, R., "Transnational Ties during a Time of Crisis: The Israeli Diaspora since Fall 2000". Paper presented to Middle Eastern Diasporas: (In)visible Minorities, New Haven, Connecticut, Yale University, 18 March 2005.
Goldscheider, C., *Israeli's Changing Society: Population, Ethnicity and Development* (Boulder: Westview Press, 1996).
Hart, R., *Altarity: Choosing Schools, Choosing Identities in London.* Dissertation submitted for the degree of Doctor of Philosophy, Dept. of Educational and Professional Studies, King's College, London, 2004).
Herman, P, 1988, "Jewish–Israeli Migration to the United States Since 1948", Paper presented at the Annual Meeting of the Association of Israel Studies, New York, 7 June 1988.
Herman, P, 2000, "The Jews of the Jews: Characteristics of Los Angeles Households of Israelis by Birth and Israelis not by Birth", Paper submitted for Division E Contemporary Jewish Society The Thirteenth World Congress of Jewish Studies, December 2000.
Herman, P. and LaFontaine, D., "In Our Footsteps: Israeli Migration to the U.S. and Los Angeles", Master of Social Work, Hebrew Union College, Los Angeles,1983)
Kadish, S., "'A Good Jew or a Good Englishman?': The Jewish Lads' Brigade and Anglo-Jewish Identity", pp. 77–93 in A. J. Kershen (ed.), *A Question of Identity* (Aldershot: Ashgate, 1998).
Kimhi, S., 1990, "Perceived Change of Self-Concept, Values, Well-Being and Intention to Return among Kibbutz People Who Migrated from Israel to America". Dissertation submitted for the degree of Doctor of Philosophy, Pacific Graduate School of Psychology, Palo Alto, CA.
Kotkin, J., *Tribes: How Race, Religion and Identity Determined Success in the New Global Economy* (New York: Random House, 1992).
Levitt, P., *The Transnational Villagers* (Berkeley: University of California Press, 2001).
Liebman, C. S. and . Cohen, S. M., *Two Worlds of Judaism: The Israeli and American Experiences.* (New Haven: Yale University Press, 1990).

Linn, R. and Barkan-Ascher, N., "Permanent Impermanence: Israeli Expatriates in Non-Event Transition", *The Jewish Journal of Sociology* 38, 1 (1996): 5–16

Lipner, N. H., 1987, "The Subjective Experience of Israeli Immigrant Women: An Interpretive Approach. Dissertation submitted for the degree of Doctor of Philosophy, George Washington University, Washington, DC.

Mahler, S. J., "Theoretical and Empirical Contributions Towards a Research Agenda for Transnationalism", pp. 64–100 in M. P. Smith and L. E. Guarnizo (eds), *Transnationalism from Below* (New Brunswick, NJ: Transaction, 1998).

Mittelberg, D. and Waters, M.C., "The Process of Ethnogenesis among Haitian and Israeli Immigrants in The United States". *Ethnic and Racial Studies* 15.3 (1992): 412–35.

Nonini, D. and Ong, A., "Introduction: Chinese Transnationalism as an Alternative Modernity" pp. 3–33 in A. Ong and D. Nonini (eds), *Ungrounded Empires: The Cultural Politics of Modern Chinese Transnationalism* (New York: Routledge Press, 1997).

Ong, A., *Flexible Citizenship: The Cultural Logics of Transnationality* (Durham, NC: Duke University Press, 1999).

Patai, R., *Tents of Jacob: The Diaspora Yesterday and Today* (Englewood Cliffs, NJ: Prentice-Hall).

Piore, M. J., *Birds of Passage* (New York: Cambridge University Press, 1979).

Portes, A., Guarnizo, L.E. and Landolt, P., "Introduction: Pitfalls and Promise of an Emergent Research Field", *Ethnic and Racial Studies* 22, 2 (1999): 217–327.

Portes, A. and Rumbaut, R. G., *Immigrant America: A Portrait* (2nd edition) (Berkeley: University of California Press, 1996).

Portes, A. and Rumbaut, R. G., *Legacies: The Story of the Immigrant Second Generation* (Berkeley: University of California Press, 2001).

Rodriguez, G., "Mexican Americans: Forging a New Vision of America's Melting Pot", *The New York Times, Week in Review*, 11 February 2001.

Rosen, S., "The Israeli Corner of the American Jewish Community", *Issue Series #3* (New York: Institute on American Jewish-Israeli Relations, The American Jewish Committee, 1993).

Rosenthal, M., 1989, "Assimilation of Israeli Immigrants". Dissertation submitted for the degree of Doctor of Philosophy, Fordham University, New York.

Rosenthal, M. and Auerbach, C., "Cultural and Social Assimilation of Israeli Immigrants in the United States", *International Migration Review* 99, 26 (1992): 982–91.

Sabar, N., *Kibbutz L. A.* (Tel Aviv: Am Oved Publishers, 1996) (Hebrew).

Sabar, N., *Kibbutznicks in the Diaspora* (Albany: SUNY Press, 2000).

Shavit, R., "The Glue That Holds Us Together: Enhancing Community Cohesion Through School Choice. A Case Study on School Choice in a Minority Group", Mimeo, School of Education, King's College, London (n.d.).

Shokeid, M., *Children of Circumstances: Israeli Immigrants in New York* (Ithaca: Cornell University Press, 1988).

Sobel, Z., *Migrants from the Promised Land* (New Brunswick, NJ: Transaction, 1986).

Statistics Canada, *Custom Tabulation from 1996 Census* (Ottawa, Ontario: Statistics Canada, 2000).

Uriely, N., "Rhetorical Ethnicity of Permanent Sojourners: The Case of Israeli Immigrants in the Chicago Area", *International Sociology* 9, 4 (1994): 431–445.

Uriely, N., "Patterns of Identification and Integration with Jewish Americans Among Israeli Immigrants in Chicago: Variations Across Status and Generation", *Contemporary Jewry* 16 (1995): 27–49.

Zerubavel, Y., *Recovered Roots: Collective Memory and the Making of Israeli National Tradition* (Chicago: University of Chicago Press, 1995).

Zweig, F., *Israel: The Sword and the Harp* (London: Heinemann, 1969).

ISRAEL COMMENTATOR

The Bondage to Israel of Israelis Living Abroad — A Non-solvable Conflict

Naama Sabar

In his essay, Steve Gold focuses his attention on the centrality of Israel in the lives of Israeli migrants living in the (USA) Diaspora. Gold claims that in contrast to the Jews who successfully integrate into the societies they were born into, Israeli emigrants remain marginalized and alienated, and often voice a wish to return-migrate to Israel, regardless of their economic or professional success.

Gold's analysis uncovers three strategies that Israelis use in order to cope with the conflict embedded in their emigration: returning to Israel, selective acculturation and transnationalism. Those who wish to return tend to lead a "temporary" life style and often do return. Those included in the second category seem to enjoy the benefits that life abroad can offer them, while maintaining their cultural perceptions and Israeli roots. Finally, those who adopt a transnational perspective maintain strong bonds both in Israel and abroad. All groups identify themselves as Israelis.

The tendency to remain so firmly connected to the homeland and to lead a somewhat undefined and indecisive life style while living abroad seems to derive from the socialization process that Israelis experience throughout life: the socialization into Israeli culture and citizenship. One of the most profound tenets of the value system that Israelis internalize through the socialization process is their strong bond with the homeland and the State of Israel (*moledet*) and the fundamental belief that Israelis should or indeed must live in Israel; indeed, that living in Israel and belonging to Israel is in fact the most profound expression of their identity. It may be argued that because of this potent process of socialization, Israeli emigrants experience an identity conflict that enables them to maintain their identities while abroad, and at the same time impedes their integration into the host society and urges them to return-migrate.

In what follows I aim to unpack this socialization process and to highlight the ways in which it has affected migrants' thinking of Israel and their patterns of integration in the host societies into which they have migrated. In the last section of this essay, I shall briefly discuss a related issue: the ways in which migration from Israel has affected the place of Israel in the collective thinking of those who are left behind.

The Origins of the Israeli Emigrants' "Homing Devices"

The historical title "*Sabra*" and the notion that Israelis are "shaped by the stature of Israel's landscapes" (*tavnit nof moladeto*) is one of the many idioms that reflect the profound role that Israel plays in its citizens' lives, and demonstrates the unique ways in which the individual and the private interlace with the collective and public in Israel's everyday life. In an attempt to deconstruct the *Sabra*'s cultural traits, and the methods that so profoundly embed the State in people's consciousness, Almog (1997) reveals a 'task force" of socialization agents and socialization mechanisms that work together to make the State and its citizens inseparable. Among these, the education system, the army and the media assume central functions.

The value of "*Ahavat haaretz*" (love of Israel) reflects the ideals of Zionism, which has had, and indeed still has, a central place in the socialization process that every citizen experiences throughout life — and more profoundly so between childhood and adolescence, as their transition to adulthood occurs and their identities develop and form. Today, many of the values that originally emerged from the Zionist ideals and thinking remain central in the educational system. These values are reflected in the national curriculum, in which a great number of topics are themed around and intertwined with ideologies and values that enhance the knowledge, the understanding, the sense of connection and the national identity of Israel's future citizens. Courses in the history of the Jewish people, the Holocaust, Jewish Studies (including Jewish traditions, festivals, and the bible) Jewish literature, old and modern Hebrew, citizenship studies, geography, nature studies, arts and songs are structured around themes that relate to Israel, and are studied intensively during the school years. More importantly perhaps, schools in Israel conduct ceremonies and events around national events and holidays, not only for school children, but often to wider audiences, in a repetitive cycle that is then augmented by the media and other socialization agents. Through this function of the educational system — initially meant to unify a nation of immigrants — young Israelis growing up in Israel internalize the centrality of Israel in their lives, develop an unparalleled sense of place and sense of belonging, and consider their Israeli identity to be the most profound aspect of their personality. Their Jewish identity is perceived by secular Israelis as being part of being Israeli, without them paying separate attention to their Jewish identity *per se*. Although the education system in Israel has experienced significant changes during the past decade, its ideological function is still one of its central missions.

Steve Gold's findings seem to reveal the potency of this process, and the ways in which it continues to influence Israelis who choose to live abroad. Gold's essay uncovers not only the power early socialization has on people's lives but also the strategies that Israeli emigrants adopt which enable them to maintain their national identities and connection to the homeland, despite their choice to defy the main value of Zionism, and settle abroad.

Gold's article offers valuable insights about the place of Israel among the emigrants and at the same time reveals the outcomes of Israeli socialization systems. Indeed my own research has shown that the education system has a primary role in socializing children into citizenship and has the power to reduce the tendency to emigrate (Sabar 2000).

The centrality of Israel in its citizens' consciousness is extremely important for the resilience of Israeli society in Israel, in the face of the continuous threats it must address. Social resilience can be defined as the ability of a society to defend itself and its people's fundamental human rights. More importantly, social resilience is associated with the ability of society to stay unified in the face of existential threats.

While Israel should encourage education that emphasizes humanistic and universal values, we should nevertheless encourage education that emphasizes the centrality of Israel and strengthens the connection between the individual and its society and State.

Those Who are Left Behind

An important factor that contributes to the torn soul of many Israelis abroad is what they leave behind. By this I mean the attitude that Israeli society holds towards those who have left, as well as the attitudes of their close relatives. One way of looking at this issue is from the perspective of the place of the family in Jewish culture, and how this affects Israeli Jews as individuals and as a society. However, this short note will not deal with this perspective.

Israeli society's attitude towards the emigrants is very mixed and has changed and evolved. In the early years of Israel's existence, when the dominant ideology was more outspokenly collective, those who left Israel — they were called *yordim* — were seen as traitors: the late prime minister Rabin condescendingly called them "misfits". However, as Israel has grown in numbers and power, and with the move towards greater individualism, the attitude to those who emigrate from the country has changed, too. The younger generation especially looks at the freedom to choose one's country of residence as a legitimate right of the individual.

Yet in spite of these developments, Israelis abroad still suffer from overt and covert pressure from their relatives: a pressure that takes its toll. If family relations were tense before leaving Israel then the distance often tends to have a positive effect on those who left, as well as on the relatives who stay in Israel. But if relations were warm and supportive, then the distance has a painful effect and adds to the mixed feelings about life abroad as experienced by the emigrants (Sabar 2000). The picture gets more complicated when one of the couple wants to be near his or her family and is less convinced about the advantages of living abroad. A partial solution to this is by frequent traveling between Israel and the other country.

Such travel, of course, has its cost: financial, but emotional, too, in so far as frequent travel makes it hard to develop and stick to routine in the new life outside Israel. The financial burden is on both the migrant family and the family back home, who also tries to visit as much as they can. However, more often the leavers pay the way for the family to come visit them, as they tend to be better off financially.

In addition, leaving the job for frequent trips to Israel is not seen positively by the work place; moreover, it may necessitate taking vacation or leave of absence, reducing the income. One result is that the leaver's family will either always have its vacation as a family visit to Israel or not have a vacation at all because trips "home" have already consumed all the savings the family can spend on vacations.

If the family is young, then family members may have to make concessions or special arrangements to replace a missing parent who has travelled to visit her or his family back home. Even with the best arrangements, young children will not enjoy the warmth and support that an extended family can give, and especially the unique relations with grandparents. And of course the latter will miss the joy of their grand-children. Since my space here is limited, I shall not even try to touch on the complicated issue of caring for old and ailing parents from afar, and how this affects both the parents back in Israel, and many of the siblings who stayed behind, who might resent being left to look after their aging parents.

Needless to say, all the above factors affect the emotional state of many of the Israelis living abroad. Pangs of conscience are a common state.

References

Almog, O., *The Sabra — A profile* (Tel Aviv: Am Oved, 1997). (In Hebrew).
Sabar, N., *Kibbutzniks in the Diaspora* (New York: SUNY Press, 2000).

Acknowledgment

The author wishes to thank Dr. Rona Hart for helping crystallize the thoughts outlined in this essay.

DIASPORA COMMENTATOR

Definig Choices: Relocation Without Immigration?

Rona Hart

In a recent interview with an Israeli couple living in London the husband said: "Israeli remains an Israeli! Nothing can change that or take that away from us!" and his wife added: "Israel is a part of me, I cannot divorce Israel, just like I can't divorce myself!"

In his essay, Steve Gold unfolds the drama that surfaces through such statements; the identity conflict and rupture that is embedded in emigration from Israel. His analyses reveal the profound and lasting impact of Israel on the identity of Israeli emigrants, the potency of Israeli identity, even when faced with pressures that are integral to the immigration and adaptation processes, the discord between emigrants' strong sense of belonging to the homeland and their choice to establish a home elsewhere, and the effects of the Israeli identity and its embedded conflict on emigrants' adaptation journey and its trajectory.

Steve Gold's main argument is that Israeli emigrants apply three strategies to cope with the conflict engendered by their emigration: by focusing on return and adopting a "temporary" state of mind and life style; through selective acculturation, that is, integrating and learning the host society's ways in some domains, while maintaining a strong sense of attachment and bonds with the homeland; and by assuming a transnational existence, whereby they maintain participation in both countries, while adopting de-territorialised identities.

My study of the Israeli emigrant community living in the UK (Hart 2004) revealed similar patterns to those explored and detailed by Steve Gold. Indeed, the identity of Israeli emigrants seems to inform their immigration and adaptation processes, engendering from the outset a trajectory which enables them to maintain these identities and their attachments to Israel, while establishing a new home abroad. In a sense, the Israeli identity and its embedded conflict reveals itself as both a factor that shapes migrants' adaptation process, limiting its impact on their lives, and at the same time, as an essence that is maintained and reinvented by their adaptation pattern.

In what follows I shall present two arguments that emerged from my recent study of the Israeli community in London, while building and expanding on Steve Gold's concepts. The first argues that the emigrant community has a crucial role in maintaining the identities of first generation emigrants, and in cultivating the adaptation strategies described by Steve Gold. The second argument centres on the adaptation patterns and identities of the second generation, arguing that they do not share their parents' firm identification with Israel nor do they tend to develop diasporic Jewish identities. In terms of their adaptation pattern, they seem to drift away both from the Israeli emigrant community and from the local Jewish community, and show a strong tendency to assimilate.

A Balancing Act

In analyzing the role of Israeli emigrant communities Steve Gold argues that Israeli emigrant communities function both as facilitators of the relocation process as well as socialization agents that enable the maintenance of emigrants' Israeli identities and their connection to the homeland. By fulfilling these roles (which may be seen as contradictory) these communities legitimize emigration from Israel, engendering chain emigration to certain destinations. Yet at the same time, these communities also seem to moderate the effects of the adaptation process on migrants' identities and on their ties with the homeland, thus creating certain conditions that encourage the patterns discussed by Steve Gold: transnational existence, focus on return, and selective acculturation.

In a comparative analysis conducted between Israelis who were embedded in the Israeli emigrant community in London and those who were detached from it (Hart 2004), significant differences were found, which point to the centrality of the emigrant community in maintaining emigrants' identities. The findings suggest that Israelis who were embedded within their emigrant communities tend to maintain a strong Israeli identity, to develop and nurture their ties and interests in Israel, to make contributions to Israel in various ways, to display a strong sense of attachment to Israel, to endeavour to cultivate a sense of Israeli identity in their children, and indeed, to display all three strategies explored by Steve Gold: that is, discuss return as a plausible option in their lives; exhibit selective acculturation, where the focal point of their social lives remains within the boundaries of the Israeli emigrant community; and lead a transnational life style with its respective outlook.

In contrast, those who were detached from the emigrant community — a majority of which have married non-Israeli partners (Jewish or non-Jewish) — displayed a much weaker sense of belonging to Israel, maintained fewer ties in Israel, visited Israel less frequently, were less involved in Israel's affairs, and contributed to Israel to a lesser extent. Some also adopted hyphenated identities, and were less inclined to cultivate their children's Israeli identities. Furthermore, discussions of possible return, transnational life styles and selective acculturation were rarely ever present among those who chose to lead their lives away from the Israeli emigrant community.

These findings suggest that the emigrant community plays a double role: on one hand, facilitating the immigration process and thereby encouraging emigration from Israel, and on the other, seeming to maintain the identity conflict embedded in emigration from Israel, and offering a path that enables "relocation without emigration", as one of the interviewees put it. My argument goes further, to suggest that the immigrant community, specifically the London community, has developed a culture that seems to embrace this balancing act as a collective norm. It is worth noting here that this culture is unmistakably middle class, in that it allows emigrants to "cash in" on their skills and resources in various domains of life, and enjoy the benefits of life abroad, while at the same time maintaining their strong bond with the homeland, and leading marginal and fairly separate cultural and social lives within the boundaries of the emigrant enclave.

Although the emigrant community seems to have developed a culture that supports emigrants' identities and attachments to Israel, it seems to assume this role only for first generation migrants, while second generation Israeli emigrants appear to develop a distinct trajectory. I shall discuss this next.

A Lost Generation?

Currently, there is no research on second generation adult emigrants from Israel relating to their patterns of work, marriage, general adaptation or communal affiliation, as most of this generation has not yet reached adulthood. The only research available at this point on the second generation is that collected through their parents' eyes. These studies however, do provide some indications of a plausible trajectory.

My own research findings indicate that second generation emigrants seem to dissociate themselves from the passionate and compelling Israeli identity that characterises their parents' national identity and sense of belonging. In time, most seem to adopt an additional national identity, thus identifying themselves as dual-nationals. Although most of the respondents who took part in my study acknowledged that their children do feel some sense of attachment to Israel, and expressed a wish that their children would maintain their Israeli identity, they also noted that the children's links with Israel were fragile, and that "raising an Israeli child abroad" for whom "Israel is just a holiday resort" is not a realistic endeavour: "it's a bit absurd to even try to raise an Israeli child in London" as one parent articulated it. As the children's Israeli identities became thin, some parents reasoned that with their children's progression along the cross-cultural adaptation course, they were gradually "becoming British". However, many parents felt that their children's new national identity — their British identity — was also frail; a finding that seems to agree with the research literature on second generation migrants (Zhou 1997; Rambaut 1994).

The research findings also suggest that while the emigrant community assumed a crucial role in maintaining the parents' identities and links with Israel, once children have reached a point where they direct their own social lives, most have had no links with Israeli peers nor with other members of the emigrant community, and the majority have established ties that spread beyond their parents' Israeli circles. The research findings thus indicate that while the emigrant community is at the centre of the parents' existence, affecting their adaptation patterns and identities, their children (second generation emigrants from Israel) tend to distance themselves both from their parents' emotive sense of identification with their homeland and from their community circles, to carve their own identities and attachments.

Both tendencies, however, seem to be in line with recent research on the adaptation patterns of second generation migrants (Portes and Zhou 1993; Portes, Fernandez-Kelly and Haller 2005). The question that remains unanswered is whether Israeli emigrants would affiliate with the Jewish community and develop a Jewish identity, or whether they would assimilate into the host society?

The preliminary findings suggest that in contrast to Steve Gold's findings on US-based Israeli emigrants, the vast majority of Israelis living in London do not become involved in the local Jewish communities in any meaningful way and this pattern seems to be replicated by the second generation, most of whom lead their lives unrelated to and uninterested in Jewish communal life. Furthermore, there are indications that second generation Israeli emigrants, most of which lead a secular life style, develop symbolic and fairly thin Jewish identities.

Indeed, similar to other second generation migrants, they appear to be in a most awkward position: they can no longer identify with their parents' national identity nor retain their ties with the emigrant community, they are unable to identify with and integrate within the local Jewish community, and nor are they able to wholly adopt their host's national identity. They are caught between these worlds and often need to respond to pressures emanating from all three.

As the second generation's transition to adulthood unfolds, the questions relating to their Israeli and Jewish identities are yet to be examined and addressed. The research shows clearly the significance of communal affiliation in supporting and cultivating these identities, however, the research also indicates that second generation adult migrants living in London may not have any community structures to turn to for support. The question that remains unanswered relates to communal outreach policy rather than research, that is: will the Israeli emigrant community generate structures that may support their children's Israeli identities, or will the Jewish community offer this generation a base and a new address?

References

Hart, R., *Altarity: Choosing Schools, Choosing Identities in London.* (Dissertation submitted for the degree of Doctor of Philosophy, Dept. of Educational and Professional Studies, King's College, London, 2004).

Portes, A. and Zhou, M., "The new second generation: segmented assimilation and its variants", *The Annals of the American Academy of Political and Social Sciences*, 530 (1993): 74–96.

Portes, A., Fernandez-Kelly, P. and Haller, W., "Segmented assimilation on the ground: the new second generation in early adulthood", *Ethic and Racial Studies*, Vol. 268, 6 (2005): 1000–1040.

Rambaut, R. G., "The crucible within: ethnic identities, self esteem and segmented assimilation among children of immigrants", *International Migration Review*, 28, 4 (1994): 748–794.

Zhou, M., "Growing up American: The challenge confronting immigrant children and children of immigrants", *Annual Review of Sociological Research*, 23 (1997): 63–95.

Part II

COUNTRIES AND REGIONS

11

Israel as a Source of Identification for Canadian Jewry

David H. Goldberg

The organized Jewish community of Canada is unique among contemporary world Jewish communities. While facing many of the same demographic challenges experienced by most other Western Jewish communities (that is, declining birth rates, and increased dependency rates resulting from a rapidly growing aging sector[1]), Canadian Jewry nevertheless has the distinction of being one of the few significant world Jewish communities (along with those of Israel, Germany and Australia) that is presently experiencing population growth. Canada's Jewish population in 2005 stood at 372,000, representing a 30 percent increase since 286,000 in 1970; demographers project Canadian Jewry's population will reach 381,000 by 2020.[2] The adverse effects of the virtually flat rate of natural growth experienced by Canadian Jewry is off-set by continued steady Jewish immigration from the former Soviet Union, Israel, South Africa, Argentina, France, North Africa and the United States.[3] After a natural period of adjustment, these various immigrant groups become important contributors to a community that has been characterized as having "an active, participating and committed membership . . . known for the quality of Jewish life".[4] Because of this continued population growth rate as well as its well-developed day school system and social service institutional infrastructure, McGill University sociologist Morton Weinfeld predicts that Canadian Jewry is "on its way to becoming the second most important Diaspora community, after the United States".[5]

This chapter argues that identification with the State of Israel always has been and will continue to be a major factor contributing to the vitality and viability of the Canadian Jewish community. The validity of this proposition is reinforced through the consideration of the following three variables: the legacy of Canadian Jewry's commitment to Zionistic principles; the multiple and diverse ways in which this commitment continues to be expressed; and the significant and enduring factors that help to explain Canadian Jewry's ongoing commitment to Israel.

"A Strong Zionist Impulse"[6]

From the outset, Canadian Jewry exhibited a strong and almost universal commitment to the principles, goals and aspirations of political Zionism. Unlike the case in the United States, where early challenges to Zionism were ideological and divisive, in Canada such challenges were largely non-existent or confined to the periphery of organized communal life. While the intra-communal debates among Jewish Canadians about Zionism were often passionate, they tended to be tactical rather than strategic; about the specific methods for accomplishing Zionist aspirations in Palestine rather than about the fundamental legitimacy of those aspirations.[7]

Canadian Jewry quickly became one of the most generous contributors per capita among Diaspora Jewish communities to Zionist pioneering projects in Palestine. The 1921 convention of the Federation of Zionist Societies of Canada adopted a resolution to raise $1 million in support for the *Keren Hayesod* (Palestine Foundation Fund). Some 300 Jewish Canadians volunteered for the Jewish Legion, the military unit formed by volunteers from Jewish communities in Western democracies to fight alongside British forces to achieve the liberation of Palestine from Turkish rule in World War One. A sizeable proportion of these Canadian Zionists chose to remain in Palestine after the end of the war or arrived during the years of the Palestine Mandate (carrying British passports) and made important contributions to the development of the pre-state *Yishuv*.[8] A disproportionate number of Canadian Jews (along with many Canadian Christian veterans of World War II moved by the Western world's indifference to the plight of Jewish suffering in the Holocaust) fought as *Mahalnikim* ("Volunteers from Abroad") in Israel's 1948–9 War of Independence.[9] Canadian Jews, again supported by a significant number of prominent Christian Zionists, advocated aggressively on behalf of Canada's support for the UN Partition Plan of November 1947 and then for recognition of the State of Israel upon its establishment in May 1948.[10] It is upon this foundation of solid identification with the goals and aspirations of Zionism that Canadian Jewry's enduring emotional and material identification with and commitment to Israel and Israeli-based causes and institutions has been built and reinforced.

Expressing the Identification

Canadian Jewry continues to score well on major indicators of identification with Israel relative to other Diaspora communities, most notably the United States.

Personal Connectedness

Eighty-seven percent of Canadian Jewry believes Israel is "important to being a Jew". An equal proportion contends that if Israel were destroyed it would be a "personal" tragedy. Seventy percent say they often talk about Israel, whereas 42 percent define themselves as Zionists and 35 percent say they have considered immigrating to Israel. Seventy-nine percent can identify the year of Israel's independence, and 72 percent the year of the Six Day War.[11] The data for Canadian Jewry's sense of personal connectedness to Israel is consistently higher than is the case for American Jewry, where surveys indicate that the decline in personal concern about Israel, especially among young American Jews, continues unabated.[12] While there are some age-related variations in terms of personal connectedness to Israel, with older Canadian Jews tending to feel a greater connection to the Jewish state than younger people,[13] the generational distinction is not nearly as pronounced as in the United States, perhaps owing to much higher rates of day-school attendance among Canadian Jewry. (See discussion below.)

Ever Visited Israel

Having visited Israel at least once in one's lifetime (or having sent one's children to visit Israel) is considered a key expression of a Diaspora Jewish community's identification with Israel. A sizeable proportion — 66 percent — of Canadian Jews have visited Israel at least once. By contrast, only 35 percent of Jews from the United States have done so.[14]

Day-School Attendance

There is believed to be a strong positive correlation between a Jewish day-school education and an individual's identification with Israel. Here again, Canadian Jewry scores markedly better than its US counterpart, with a 55 percent rate of day-school participation compared to 29 percent for American Jewry.[15]

"Israel Experience" Student Missions

Canadian Jewry has disproportionately supported the multitude of programmes designed to give Jewish youth from the Diaspora a "taste" of life in Israel. While not unaffected by regional tensions, *birthright Canada* missions were cancelled only in 2002, at the height of the Al-Aqsa Intifada. The readiness to continue to support youth missions despite the threat of terrorism speaks to a profound commitment to Israel among Canadian Jewry that was not paralleled in the United States and other Diaspora communities. Many Jewish parents, especially those from smaller communities outside of the major cosmopolitan centres of Toronto, Montreal and Vancouver, tend to view their children's participation in Israel missions as an important hedge against inter-marriage and other challenges to "Jewish continuity".[16] Moreover, it is perhaps not coincidental that one of the founders of the international *birthright* programme is a Canadian Jew from Montreal, Charles Bronfman. For, perhaps only someone with the experience of growing up as a Jew in Canada, and even more so, as a member of an "identifiable minority" in the Province of Quebec, could appreciate the importance of young people having the opportunity to broaden their identity as Jews by experiencing Israel, and to express this identity in three inter-related ways: as proud and confident citizens of their home country, as proud and confident Jews, and as members of a Diaspora Jewish community that is deeply committed to the welfare of the State of Israel.

Tourism

The same determination that moved the vast majority of Canadian Jewry to ensure the continued viability of *birthright* and other student missions despite the threat of terrorism is also reflected in very strong support for tourism to Israel generally. Overall, Canadian Jewish tourism to Israel rose by 17 percent from 2004 (42,000) to 2005 (50,800); 58,000 Canadians (mostly Jews) are expected to travel to Israel in 2006. But this only tells part of the story. As the general manager of El Al in Canada commented recently, "The Jewish community in Toronto has very strong ties to Israel. During the height of the Intifada, the Jewish organizations, especially led by United Jewish Appeal Federation of Greater Toronto, were relentless in sending trips to Israel on a monthly basis, and it remained a key issue for the people of Toronto to be in Israel at a difficult time. Now that the situation has been quieted down, the Jewish community recognized the importance of traveling to Israel and that it's a great place to visit."[17] The El Al official went on to note that the highly successful Canada–Israel Experience and other student mission programmes have created a "multiplier effect", with hundreds of Canadian Jewish families picking up on their children's enthusiasm for Israel and planning family visits.[18] The Toronto experience has been replicated in Jewish communities throughout Canada. In Montreal, Israel is planning on opening a tourism office in the hopes of better servicing not only the city's 90,000-strong Jewish community but also groups from other faith communities that have expressed an interest in visiting Israel.[19]

Aliyah

A significant number of Canadian Jews emigrated to pre-state Israel during the years of the Palestine Mandate, many using Canada's membership in the British Empire to circumvent restrictions on the numbers of Jewish immigrants imposed by the White Paper of 1939.[20] Among Diaspora communities in Western countries, Canadian Jewry has continued to be among the largest contributors of immigrants per capita to Israel. There was a 63 percent increase in *aliyah* from Canada between 2003 (229) and 2005 (374).[21] While most Canadian Jews cite the "pull" of Israel as the primary factor in contributing to their decision to emigrate, some also acknowledge the "push" of increased concern about tacit or explicit challenges to the comfort of Jewish life in Canada, including "signs of a retrenched anti-Semitism".[22] (See discussion below.)

Public Advocacy

One final major expression of Canadian Jewry's identification with Israel has been in the area of public advocacy. Even before the end of World War II, Canadian Jewry began to petition their government to support a sovereign Jewish homeland in Palestine. In the immediate post-war period, Jews remained uncertain about their status in a Canada dominated socially, economically and politically by a "vertical mosaic" comprised of English-speaking Protestant elites and their French-speaking Roman Catholic counterparts from Quebec.[23] Moreover, Canadian Jewry remained more comfortable with the process of private interventions to government by designated communal representatives — *shtadlans*[24] — rather than large public demonstrations. Nevertheless, the enormous pressures of the moment, specifically the need to help build international support toward the creation of a safe haven for the survivors of the Holocaust in an independent Jewish state, forced Canadian Jewry to put aside its inhibitions and to aggressively lobby the Canadian government to support the UN Partition Plan and to recognize Israel.[25]

After Israel's statehood was proclaimed in the 1948 War of Independence, Canadian Jewry turned its immediate attention to consolidating its contribution to Israel's welfare through direct investments in Israel and the promotion of bilateral commercial ventures involving the governments of Israel and Canada.[26] One of the major communal actors in most such initiatives was Samuel Bronfman, founder of the Montreal-based Seagram's liquor empire. Bronfman contributed the lion's share of the seed money for the multi-million dollar Canada–Israel Development Corporation (1961) and he and his cohorts were instrumental in the founding of the founding in 1961 of the Canada–Israel Chamber of Commerce to stimulate private commercial ties between the two countries.[27] Three decades later, another generation of Bronfmans was instrumental in facilitating the completion of two important bilateral commercial agreements between Ottawa and Jerusalem: the Canada–Israel Industrial Research and Development Fund in 1993, and the Canada–Israel Free Trade Agreement in 1996 (in the latter case, overcoming a vigorous political counter-campaign spearheaded by Canada's pro-Palestinian community and its supporters).[28]

Politically, primarily under the leadership of the Canada–Israel Committee (CIC), Canadian Jewry has organized "pro-Israel" and "Israel solidarity" rallies and has raised impressive sums of money in support of emergency campaigns in times of crisis and in periods of renewal in Israel. The CIC has organized study missions for Canadian parliamentarians and other senior influence-makers to Israel, and has developed numerous other projects to emphasize the "shared values" that Canadians and Israelis have in common and that are the basis upon which the strong bilateral relationship between the two democratic countries has been constructed.[29] Moreover, the CIC has encouraged the Canadian government and media to adopt positions on the Arab–Israeli conflict sensitive to Israel's perspective.[30] It weathered the "dark days" of the Al-Aqsa Intifada when, like Diaspora Jews throughout much of the Western world, Israel's supporters in Canada felt that the Jewish state was subjected to unfair criticism by their government and by influential elements of the Canadian media.[31] Since 2003 and under the rubric of a new super-agency known as the Canadian Council for Israel and Jewish Advocacy (CIJA),[32] the Canada–Israel Committee has been accorded additional resources by the leadership of the organized Jewish community. These additional resources are being devoted to the challenge of influencing the consideration and formulation of Canada's Middle East policy in an increasingly multicultural marketplace in which Canada's rapidly growing Arab and Muslim communities are now active (and often, aggressive) participants.[33]

Explaining the Identification

The final section of this chapter seeks to provide explanations for the consistently strong identification with Israel on the part of Canadian Jewry. The explanatory variables to be considered bring to the fore socio-demographic, historical and political factors that are in many ways unique to the Canadian Jewish experience.

Impact of the Holocaust

Until Israel's creation, the Holocaust was considered the single most significant event in the modern history of the Jewish people. Indeed, for many Jews, the two events — the Nazi's systematic destruction of European Jewry and Israel's establishment — are inseparable. For those Jews fortunate enough to survive the Holocaust, and for their families, Israel's survival and security tends to be of paramount importance. Canada, acting out of both a general sense of "Christian Guilt" (one it shared with all Western countries) for the failure to act on the early evidence of Nazi persecution of German Jewry, as well as a particular guilt arising from the racist actions of senior Canadian bureaucrats who summarily denied entry visas to all but a handful of European Jewish refugees,[34] opened its shores to Holocaust survivors at the end of World War II.[35] It is roughly estimated that 1 in 18 Canadian Jews is a Holocaust survivor; this translates to about 5.56 percent of the total Jewish population of Canada (or 20,700).[36] While not necessarily monolithic, the "survivor community", based largely in Toronto and Montreal, tends to be very well organized and highly committed in its devotion to Israeli-based institutions such as *Yad Vashem* (The Holocaust Martyrs' and Heroes' Remembrance Authority), and to Israel in general. Moreover, Holocaust survivors and their families have tended to take on a disproportionate leadership role in Canadian Jewry,[37] thereby increasing the likelihood that their strong identification with and commitment to Israel will remain among the community's top priorities for the foreseeable future.

Impact of Sephardic Jews

Jews originating from Arab and Muslim countries (*Sephardim*) tend to be more "traditional" in their religious practices than their counterparts who have roots in Central or Eastern Europe (*Ashkenazim*). There is a positive correlation between degree of religiosity and identification with Israel.[38] Montreal, largely because of the commonality of language and culture, is a highly desired point of immigration for Jews from Algeria, Morocco and Tunisia as well as from elsewhere in the Arab and Muslim world where French is spoken. Montreal's Sephardic, French-speaking Jewish community, while choosing to operate in a parallel fashion to its Askhenazi-dominated Anglophone counterpart on some issues, joins with it on issues affecting Israel, normally under the rubric of the Quebec–Israel Committee. Indeed, given shifting demographics, it is the Sephardim, with a slightly more assertive ideological orientation, who are increasingly dominating the agenda-setting on Israel-related matters in the Montreal Jewish community. While much of the effective balance of power in Canadian Jewry has now shifted from Montreal to Toronto,[39] the concerns and interests of Montreal's 90,000 strong Jewish community still remain an integral component of Canadian Jewry's overall identification with Israel. However, now part of that identification must be translated into French!

Israelis in Canada

As in the United States and some Western European countries, Canada has an increasingly large community of expatriate Israelis; there are believed to be at least 30,000 in the greater Metropolitan Toronto area alone. While occasionally reflecting a measure of reserve toward communal events that some elements of Canadian Jewry choose to interpret (rightly or wrongly) as "Israeli *chutzpah*", this expatriate group has established and maintained a sub-culture within the broader Jewish community that is premised solely on an identification with Israeli culture, sports, literature, food, commerce, and, of course, politics.[40] In many local communities, it is this sub-cultural group that takes (or is given) primary responsibility for organizing communal observances of Israeli public events such as *Yom Hazikaron* (Memorial Day for fallen soldiers) and *Yom Ha'atzmaut* (Independence Day). And it is frequently the local Israeli sub-culture that is looked to for communal leadership in moments of crisis in Israel, such as the Rabin assassination and in the aftermath of mass casualty terrorist bombings. The presence of this Israeli sub-culture, while not necessarily unique to Canada, helps to explain Canadian Jewry's continuing strong identification with the State of Israel.

An Anchor in Troubled Seas

Modern political Zionism was founded on the proposition that the only solution to the Christian world's age-old "Jewish Question" was the creation of an independent, sovereign Jewish state.[41] The hatred of Jews — anti-Semitism — has historically been a critical factor in explaining the identification with Israel on the part of "distressed" Jews from Central and Eastern Europe, Russia, and from Arab and Muslim lands. While less overt than in other parts of the world, anti-Semitic attitudes have nevertheless served as an important source of identification with Israel for Canadian Jewry.[42]

In the mid-1940s, strict quotas on the numbers of Jews admitted to universities, professions and country clubs[43] contributed to the decisions of a disproportionate number of young Canadian Jewish veterans of the struggle against Nazi tyranny to volunteer to fight for Israel's independence and then become permanent citizens of the Jewish state.[44]

In March 1988, Canadian Jewry was shocked when its official "voice" on Israel affairs, the Canada–Israel Committee (CIC), was accused of "dual loyalty" for challenging Foreign Affair Minister Joe Clark's critique of Israel's "iron fist" treatment of Palestinians participating in the Intifada, as well as his implication that it was Israeli "recalcitrance" that was the primary obstacle to regional peacemaking.[45] Within hours of Mr. Clark's confrontation with the CIC, major Canadian newspapers, in both official languages, published editorials that crudely challenged the "loyalty" of Canadian Jews. Canada's largest circulation daily, *The Toronto Star*, commented that, "Clark's remarks may have cost his party votes in the next federal election. But his message was a timely one. It was also a necessary reminder to members of the Jewish community in Canada that they are citizens of Canada, not Israel."[46] Such commentary was deemed unfair even by critics within the Jewish community of Israel's handling of the Intifada, for a much more fundamental principle was at stake: the right, in a democratic society, of an organized community to express itself without fear of public ridicule or sanction. The social historian Harold Troper encapsulated the despair felt by Jewish supporters of Israel in the face of this unprecedented assault on their rights as Canadian citizens in the following way:

> Canadian ethnic groups remain particularly vulnerable to the disloyalty charge. Can one imagine those lobbying against free trade being smeared as disloyal? Would the [Toronto] Star feel it necessary to remind pro-life or pro-choice groups that they are Canadian? Obviously not. Why then is it necessary for ethnic communities to be subject to this form of abuse when exercising their rights as Canadians?[47]

The so-called "dual loyalty affair" left an indelible impression on Canadian Jewry: the sense that despite their significant accomplishments in not only smashing the anti-Semitic quotas of the 1940s but in becoming fully integrated and contributing members of Canadian society, Canadian Jews were still taking a "risk" in identifying with and advocating publicly on behalf of the State of Israel.[48]

The university campus has become a "platform for Israel-bashing" in Canada.[49] Since the mid-1990s, pro-Israel students (and Jewish students expressing no particular concern about Israel) are being aggressively challenged by campus coalitions comprised of Palestinians, Arabs, Muslims and extreme left-wing groups. These coalitions target Israel not only on Middle East issues but also for its status as a close ally of the United States and symbol of Western colonialism and globalism, as well as an accused violator of human rights. A riot by Arab students and their supporters denied former Israeli prime minister Benjamin Netanyahu the ability to speak at Montreal's Concordia University in September 2002;[50] however, the threat of a similar riot did not deter the Middle East historian Daniel Pipes from exercising his right to freedom of speech at Toronto's York University in February 2003.[51] In an expression of what Canada's former Justice Minister Irwin Cotler refers to as a "new anti-Semitism . . . that rejects the right of the Jewish people to live as an equal member in the family of nations", by the systematic process of delegitimization and demonization of Israel,[52] most Canadian campuses now have annual "Israel Apartheid" weeks and the like.

On 5 April 2004, the United Talmud Torah day school in Montreal was fire-bombed. A note tacked to the school door implied that the bombing was in retaliation for Israel's targeted killing of Hamas leader Sheikh Ahmed Yassin; a suspicion seemingly confirmed by the arrest of individuals of Lebanese descent.[53] At virtually the same time as the Montreal Jewish community was coming to terms with the Talmud Torah firebombing, its counterpart in Toronto was experiencing a surge in anti-Semitic incidents, involving the demolition of gravestones, the daubing of synagogues, and the destruction of private property.[54]

In December 2004, the Supreme Court of Canada heard the appeal of Rwandan war criminal, Leon Mugesera. His Quebec-based lawyer argued that Mr. Mugesera, accused of war crimes against other Africans, was the victim of a "Jewish conspiracy". He argued that Justice Minister Irwin Cotler, a Jew, spurred on by a lobby of prominent Jews, appointed a Jewish judge, Rosalie Abella, to the country's highest court just to rule against Mugesera's appeal against deportation. In rejecting these racist remarks, the Supreme Court (minus Justice Abella, who had withdrawn from the case) reprimanded Mr. Bertrand, who claimed, in response, that he had been "crucified".[55]

On a national television programme, Mohamed Elmasry, the president of the Canadian Islamic Congress, claimed that Israel's universal compulsory military service makes all Israeli adults fair game for attack.[56] On another occasion, Elmasry called on the Canadian government to fire two senior Jewish policy advisors because their support for Israel rendered them unable to impartially advise the cabinet ministers who appointed them.[57]

The obvious question to be asked is: What might be the implications of such incidences of anti-Semitism (and anti-Israelism) for Canadian Jewry's identification with Israel? On the one hand, there is great symbolism to be drawn from the fact that the first communal reaction of Montreal Jewry to the Talmud Torah firebombing was to rise defiantly and sing *Hatikvah*, Israel's national anthem. On the other hand, is it realistic to assume that the recent rise in anti-Semitic incidents in Canada, many in the guise of the more "politically-correct" anti-Zionism, will prompt large segments of Canadian Jewry to emigrate to Israel? According to Mordechai Ben-Dat, editor-in-chief *of The Canadian Jewish News*, the objective circumstances confronting Canadian Jewry do not warrant such extreme measures: "It isn't as if this is Germany of 1939 . . . It isn't even England of 2005."[58]

Notwithstanding such rational reassurances, and despite socioeconomic status and the predictions of demographers about continued communal growth, Canadian Jewry can be expected to maintain its close identification with Israel as a hedge against an underlying uncertainty of their continuing status as full citizens of Canada.[59]

Notes

1 Charles Shahar, "The Major Demographic Challenges Facing Canadian Jewry", *The Canadian Jewish News*, 29 September 2005, pp. B. 60–65.

2 Sergio DellaPergalo, Yehezkel Dror and Shalom (Salomon) Wald, *Annual Assessment of the Situation and Dynamics of the Jewish People. Annual Assessment Number Two* (Jerusalem: The Jewish People Policy Planning Institute, July 2005). <http://www.jpppi.org.il/main_projects/project.asp?fid=390&ord=1>.

3 Quebec's Jewish communal leadership is quietly anticipating a significant jump in migration of French Jews in the aftermath of the recent upsurge of anti-Semitic incidents, including the brutal murder of Parisian Ilan Halimi. Personal interview.

4 Harold M. Waller, "The Canadian Jewish Polity", *The Canadian Jewish News*, 29 September 2005, pp. B. 18–22.

5 Morton Weinfeld, "Canadian and U.S. Jewry: Similar, Yet Different", *The Canadian Jewish News*, 29 September 2005, pp. B. 8–13.

6 Zachariah Kay, "Canada: Relations with Zionism and Israel", in Geoffrey Wigoder (ed.), *New Encyclopedia of Zionism and Israel* (Madison, NJ: Farleigh Dickinson University Press, 1994), pp. 240–242.

7 Michael Brown, "Zionism in the pre-Statehood Years: The Canadian Response", in Ruth Klein and Frank Dimant (eds), *From Immigration to Integration: The Canadian Jewish Experience* (Toronto: Malcolm Lester, 2001), pp. 121–134; Bernard Figler, "History of the Zionist ideal in Canada", in Eli Gottesman (ed.), *Canadian Jewish Reference Book and Dictionary 1963* (Ottawa: Central Rabbinical Seminary of Canada, 1963); Leon Goldman, "History of Zionism in Canada", in Arthur D. Hart (ed.), *The Jew in Canada: A Complete Record of Canadian Jewry from the Days of the French Regime to the Present Time* (Toronto and Montreal: Jewish Publications, 1926).

8 Dov (Bernard) Joseph, formerly of Montreal, arrived with the Jewish Legion in 1918 and remained in Palestine. On 5 August 1948, he was appointed Military Governor for the

besieged Jewish Quarter of Jerusalem, a position he retained until January 1949. He subsequently served in several governmental capacities with distinction. He wrote about his experiences as Military Governor in *The Faithful City: The Siege of Jerusalem, 1948* (New York: Simon and Shuster, 1960).

9 David Bercuson, *The Secret Army* (Toronto: Stein and Day, 1984); Ben Dunkelman, *Dual Allegiance: An Autobiography* (Toronto: Macmillan–New American Library, 1976).

10 Canada was a member of the United Nations Special Committee on Palestine (UNSCOP) and was among the majority group that supported partition. See David Bercuson, *Canada and the Birth of Israel. A Study in Canadian Foreign Policy* (Toronto: University of Toronto Press, 1985); Zachariah Kay, *Canada and Palestine: The Politics of Non-Commitment* (Jerusalem: Israel Universities Press, 1978).

11 Morton Weinfeld, *Like Everyone Else . . . But Different. The Paradoxical Success of Canadian Jews* (Toronto: McClelland & Stewart, 2001), p. 361.

12 Shlomo Shamir, "Poll: Most U.S. Jews oppose Iraq war, have never visited Israel", *Ha'aretz*, 21 December 2005; "Israel not focus for younger Jews", Associated Press, 9 January 2006.

13 Morton Weinfeld, *Like Everyone Else . . . But Different. The Paradoxical Success of Canadian Jews* (Toronto: McClelland & Stewart, 2001), p. 361.

14 Sergio DellaPergalo, Yehezkel Dror and Shalom (Salomon) Wald, *Annual Assessment of the Situation and Dynamics of the Jewish People. Annual Assessment Number Two* (Jerusalem The Jewish People Policy Planning Institute, July 2005). <http://www.jpppi.org.il/main_projects/project.asp?fid=390&ord=1>.

15 Ibid.

16 Author's interviews.

17 Cited in Paul Lungen, "Canadian travel to Israel continues to recover", *The Canadian Jewish News*, 9 February 2006.

18 Ibid.

19 Janice Arnold, "Israel plans on opening Montreal tourism office", *The Canadian Jewish News*, 2 February 2006.

20 Author's interviews with expatriate Canadians who entered Palestine under the Mandate.

21 Israel Aliya Center, Toronto. See, Jenny Hazan, "Canadians arrive in group aliya project", *Jerusalem Post*, 27 August 2003; Tsahar Rotem, "Young Canadians fulfil the Zionist dream in the Negev", *Ha'aretz*, 12 November 2003; Nicholas Kohler, "Canadian Jews fill jet in mass move to Israel", *National Post*, 11 July 2005.

22 Nicholas Kohler, "Canadian Jews fill jet in mass move to Israel", *National Post*, 11 July 2005.

23 John Porter, *The Vertical Mosaic: An Analysis of Social Class and Power in Canada* (Toronto: University of Toronto Press, 1965).

24 According to the late political scientist Daniel J. Elazar, North American Jewry inherited the political tradition of "aristocratic republicanism" from its forebears in central and eastern Europe, whereby contact with non-Jewish authorities was entrusted to the wealthy and well-born, who more often than not performed their functions, on behalf of the wider community, through quiet interventions "out of the public eye". See Elazar's seminal *Community and Polity: The Organizational Dynamics of American Jewry* (Philadelphia: Jewish Publication Society, 1980), p. 320. This principle is applied to the case of Canadian Jewry by Harold M. Waller in "Power in the Jewish Community", in Morton Weinfeld, William Shaffir and Irwin Cotler (eds), *The Canadian Jewish Mosaic* (Toronto: John Wiley and Sons, 1981), pp. 151–169.

25 See note 10.

26 Zachariah Kay, *The Diplomacy of Prudence: Canada and Israel, 1948–1958* (Montreal & Kingston: McGill-Queen's University Press, 1996).

27 Peter C. Newman, *The Bronfman Dynasty* (Toronto: McClelland & Stewart, 1978).

28 See, for instance, Michael Lynk and Atif Kurbursi, "The Canada–Israel free-trade deal: a step backward for peace", *The Globe and Mail*, 5 November 1996. See also the testimony of Lynk and Kurbursi before the Standing Senate Committee on Foreign Affairs, Ottawa, 4 December 1996.

29 In his opening address to the 74th annual General Assembly of the United Jewish Communities (UJC) in Toronto in November 2005, Canada's then prime minister Paul Martin said that "Israel's values are Canada's values, shared values: democracy, the rule of law and the protection of human rights."

30 See David Taras and David H. Goldberg (eds), *The Domestic Battleground: Canada and the Arab–Israeli Conflict* (Montreal & Kingston: McGill-Queen's University Press, 1989); and David H. Goldberg, *Foreign Policy and Ethnic Interest Groups: American and Canadian Jews Lobby for Israel* (New York: Greenwood Press, 1990).

31 In April 2002, CIC National Chairman Joseph Wilder expressed concern about the "self-contradictory position" articulated by Canada's new foreign minister, Bill Graham, with regard to Israel's right to defend its citizens: "While Mr. Graham affirms Israel's right to self-defence in light of the horrific toll of Palestinian terrorist attacks . . . he then faults Israel for exercising this right of self-defence by going after the sources of terrorism in the same way that Canadian and U.S. forces are seeking to defeat terrorism in Afghanistan." Canada–Israel Committee News Release, 2 April 2002.

32 Paul Lungen, "CIJA takes over: Umbrella agency sets new course", *The Canadian Jewish News*, 4 December 2003; Pat Johnson, "Friends needed: New national group aims to protect Jews and Israel", *The Western Jewish Bulletin* (Vancouver), 26 March 2004.

33 David Ouellete, "Muslim Power in Canada", *Jerusalem Post*, 17 August 2004; Michael Valpy, "Canadian Islam gets media savvy", *The Globe and Mail*, 18 February 2006. On the organized Jewish community's status in an increasingly multicultural Canadian social and political milieu, see: Irving Abella, "Multiculturalism, Jews and Forging a Canadian Identity", in Howard Adelman and John H. Simpson (eds), *Multiculturalism, Jews, and Identities in Canada* (Jerusalem: Magnes Press, 1996); Irving Abella, *Canadian Jewry: Past, Present and Future* (Toronto: Center for Jewish Studies, York University, September 1998); Morton Weinfeld, "Canadian Jews and Canadian Pluralism", in Seymour Martin Lipset (ed.), *American Pluralism and the Jewish Community* (New Brunswick, NJ: Transaction Books, 1990); Morton Weinfeld, *Like Everyone Else . . . But Different: The Paradoxical Success of Canadian Jews* (Toronto: McClelland and Stewart, 2001).

34 Irving Abella and Harold Troper, *None is Too Many: Canada and the Jews of Europe 1933–1948* (Toronto: Lester & Orpen Dennys, 1982).

35 On Canadian Jewry's reaction to the Holocaust see Frank Bialystok, *Delayed Impact: The Holocaust and the Canadian Jewish Community* (Montreal & Kingston: McGill-Queen's University Press, 2000).

36 Toronto Holocaust Centre.

37 Harold M. Waller, "Power in the Jewish Community", in Morton Weinfeld, William Shafir and Irwin Cotler (eds), *The Canadian Jewish Mosaic* (Toronto: John Wiley and Sons, 1981), pp. 151–169; Daniel J. Elazar and Harold M. Waller, *Maintaining Consensus: The Canadian Jewish Polity in the Postwar World* (Lanham, MD: University Press of America, 1990).

38 Morton Weinfeld, *Like Everyone Else . . . But Different. The Paradoxical Success of Canadian Jews* (Toronto: McClelland & Stewart, 2001), p. 361.

39 Harold M. Waller, "The Canadian Jewish Polity", *The Canadian Jewish News*, 29 September 2005.

40 Gerald Gold and Rina Cohen, "The Myth of Return and Israeli Ethnicity in Toronto", in

Howard Adelman and John H. Simpson (eds), *Multiculturalism, Jews and Identities in Canada* (Jerusalem: Magnes Press, 1996), pp. 179–191.

41 Shlomo Avineri, *The Making of Modern Zionism. The Intellectual Origins of the Jewish State* (New York: Basic Books, 1981); Arthur Hertzberg (ed.), *The Zionist Idea. A Historical Analysis and Reader* (New York: Atheneum, 1979).

42 Alan Davies (ed.), *Antisemitism in Canada: History and Interpretation* (Waterloo, Ontario: Wilfrid Laurier University Press, 1992); Manuel Prutschi, "Antisemitism in Canada", *Jewish Political Studies Review* 16: 3–4 (Fall 2004); Derek J. Penslar, Michael R. Marrus and Janice Gross Stein (eds), *Contemporary Antisemitism. Canada and the World* (Toronto: University of Toronto Press, 2005).

43 Pierre Berton, "No Jews Need Apply", *Maclean's*, 1 November 1948.

44 Robert S. Eisen, "We felt it was a Sacred Mission", in B. Goldstein and J. Shulman (eds), *Voices from the Heart: A Community Celebrates 50 Years of Israel* (Toronto: McClelland & Stewart, 1998), pp. 62–63.

45 David H. Goldberg and David Taras, "Collision Course: Joe Clark, Canada Jews, and the Palestinian Uprising", in David Taras and David H. Goldberg (eds), *The Domestic Battleground: Canada and the Arab–Israeli Conflict* (Montreal & Kingston: McGill-Queen's University Press, 1989), pp. 167–185.

46 *The Toronto Star*, 11 March 1998.

47 Harold Troper, cited in a special April 1988 issue of *Comment*, a publication of the Institute for International Affairs, B'nai Brith Canada.

48 Irving Abella, *Canadian Jewry: Past, Present and Future* (Toronto: Center for Jewish Studies, York University, September 1998).

49 Sam Ser, "Oy, Canada", *The Jerusalem Post*, 28 July 2005.

50 Sheldon Gordon, "Campus Bans Activism After Anti-Bibi Riot", *The Forward*, 20 September 2002.

51 Howard Adelman, "Pipes on Campus: Who's Intimidating Whom?" *The Canadian Jewish News*, 6 February 2003; Margaret Wente, "Welcome to York U, where tolerance is no longer tolerated", *The Globe and Mail*, 11 March 2003.

52 Sam Ser, "Oy, Canada", *The Jerusalem Post*, 28 July 2005.

53 Gary Dimmock, "Firebombing at Jewish school linked to killing of Hamas chief. Imported Mideast hatred hits Montreal school", *The Ottawa Citizen*, 6 April 2004.

54 Jason Tchir, "Cemetery 'Cowards'; Community reviles graveyard vandals", *The Toronto Sun*, 22 May 2004.

55 Marvin Kurz, "Is the glass half full or half empty for Canada's Jews?" *The Globe and Mail*, 4 October 2005.

56 *Michael Coren Live*, CTS, 19 October 2004.

57 "Islamic Congress Urges Re-Examination of Two New Liberal Appointments: Strong Pro-Israel Voices in Foreign Affairs and National Security Making Canadian Muslims 'Nervous'", Canadian Islamic Congress News Release, 15 August 2005, Volume 8, Issue 64.

58 Sam Ser, "Oy, Canada", *The Jerusalem Post*, 28 July 2005.

59 Anna Morgan, "Anxious time for Canadian Jews", *The Toronto Star*, 16 August 2005.

12

The Reflection of Israel within British Jewry

Colin Shindler

A Special Role

British Jewry has played a unique role in the often ambivalent relationship between Britain and Israel. Sometimes the community has been characterised as an emboldened advocate for Zionism during the Atlee government during the late 1940s. On other occasions, it has been seen as an interlocutor between more liberal British administrations and hard line Israeli governments. For example, the views of the Thatcher governments in the 1980s were closer to the dovish policies of the Labour opponents of the Likud governments of Menachem Begin and Yitzhak Shamir. This produced friction in British interactions with several Israeli administrations. Yet this pivotal role was not one that British Jews had actively sought.

The Zionist movement historically arose in Eastern Europe and it was here that the Jews first became a people in the modern sense of a nation. The *Haskalah* and the legacy of the French Revolution, however, affected the two halves of Europe in different ways. Eastern Europe integrated the new ideas into tradition and political discourse as a means of coping with the breakdown of Judaism and Jewishness. Various solutions — as many as 22[1] — were on offer. Territorialism was one solution and within this, Zionism as a specific sub-section. In Western Europe, the effect of the Haskalah and the French Revolution was disintegrative where assimilation, acculturation and conversion were attractions for many Jews. Although establishment Britain formally distanced itself from the new philosophies, the liberal-conservative nature of the society in the early nineteenth century gently absorbed the general view that Jews had a right to full citizenship and the vote. London was not the address for revolution and ideological violence, but instead the exemplar of gradual change through the parliamentary system. Britain was admired for its civilised pedestrian approach by the oppressed East European Jewish masses, and this attitude was shared by most shades of Zionist opinion. For example,

Jabotinsky, an inveterate critic of British policy in Palestine, told a meeting of Polish Revisionists in October 1937:

> We may have a number of grievances against England but the English government is and will be the government of a well-disposed mother. We must have patience. We shall finally achieve our aim of a Palestine on both sides of the Jordan. This will be achieved with the aid of the England who always puts obstacles in our way and always helps us.[2]

Although the idea of a Jewish return to the Holy Land had gained currency in Victorian Britain, it was the defeat of the Ottoman Turks and subsequent British governance of Palestine that parachuted British Jewry into the cauldron of Zionist politics. British Jewry was famously fragmented over the question of Zionism. There was severe opposition to the Balfour Declaration, both from Jewish grandees as well as Jewish organizations. Even within the Government, there were differences. Herbert Samuel attempted to advance the cause of Zion while his kinsman, Edwin Montagu, tried to thwart it. The Balfour Declaration became for British Jews a question of identity politics — in essence British Jew or Jewish Briton. While some fervently embraced Jewish nationalism, others defined their Jewishness by transcending it. Although the centre of Zionist activities had moved to neutral Scandinavia during wartime, the Balfour Declaration and the British invasion of Palestine meant in reality that London was the city of negotiation and deliberation. Yet it was not indigenous British Jews who led the Zionist initiative, but anglophile East European immigrants and émigrés — such as the academic and scientist, Weizmann, the writer Sokolov and the journalist Jabotinsky. Indeed, on the eve of World War One, the English Zionist Federation could claim less than 6 percent of British Jews as its members.[3] Jews had indeed settled comfortably into their English environment — Jewish nationalism was the prerogative of a peripheral minority. London provided a home where these East European Zionists could conduct their struggles with successive British administrations, which attempted to provide new interpretations of the Balfour Declaration in an attempt to backtrack on the commitments of Lloyd-George and his government. But perhaps the first success of Zionists based in London was Weizmann's reversal of the political consequences of the Shaw Commission and the Passfield White Paper through the MacDonald letter of 1931. The hapless Lord Passfield, Colonial Secretary, better known as the Fabian Sidney Webb, was highly influenced by his chief civil servant Sir John Shuckburgh[4] who wished to expunge the Balfour Declaration of any meaningful content. His wife, Beatrice Webb compared the Zionists to the white settlers in Kenya and was quite open in her dislike for Jews per se.[5] Passfield complained about the deluge of protests from Zionists in Britain over his policies and indeed was perplexed by the outburst.[6]

1948 and After

With the establishment of the State of Israel in 1948, Zionism entered its post-revolutionary phase. There had previously been a broad acceptance that the term "Zionist" defined someone who immigrated to Israel and wished to participate in the construction of a new society there. By the 1950s, Ben-Gurion extended the title of "Zionist" to Jews who wished to identify with Israel. If formerly, Zionism had been the property of the Zionists, it now embraced the entire Jewish people. Although there was undoubtedly a strong and personal identification with Israel after 1948, this allowed for the expansion of the political hinterland for the policies of successive Israeli governments. British Jews were expected to unquestioningly support views which could abruptly alter at any moment. The success of Zionism meant the subservience of the Diaspora. If Jews chose not to live in Israel and did not avail themselves of the right to vote in elections, why, it was argued, should they have a right to express contrary opinions while in self-imposed exile? No doubt many in leadership positions in the Jewish community in Britain saw themselves as participants in the historic Zionist revolution in the Ben-Gurion mould and as loyal servants in the struggle against Israel's enemies — and thereby this intellectually justified their unquestioning political stand. The first sign of fragmentation came with the election of Menachem Begin's Likud in 1977 and its increasing dominance in Israeli politics. Begin and his policies hitherto had been anathema to the leadership of British Jewry — now they were asked to embrace him as the elected leader of Israel. Indeed his first official visit to Britain as leader of the Likud in the early 1970s catalysed demonstrations by "Zionists Against Begin". The watershed in this looming crisis was undoubtedly the exceeding of the stated aims of the "Peace for Galilee" incursion of Lebanon under the political leadership of Begin and Sharon.

Up until the summer of 1982, the formal organizational leadership of British Jewry through bodies such as the Board of Deputies of British Jews or the Zionist Federation traditionally decried criticism of the policies of an Israeli government. With the invasion of Lebanon in 1982, this consensus finally broke down. At that time, Jewish intellectuals, academics and writers established the British Friends of Peace Now which attracted large numbers of younger people. This organization's views and activities questioned the traditional communal methods of utilising a crisis to raise unified political and financial support for the policies of a particular Israeli government. In this war, Israel, itself, was divided and large sections of its population disagreed with Menachem Begin's view that it was a war of no choice. This schism was reflected in Britain and in the Diaspora as a whole. The activities of leaders in the Diaspora also provoked criticism from Israeli liberals. Abba Eban — who had close ties with the British Jewish community — described the practice of Diaspora Jews of blind support for Begin's policies as "the vulgarity of the fund-raisers".[7] Young people were also found to be more discerning about who was an enemy of Israel. In contrast, the older generation argued that their views had been formulated through experience, as observers and participants in the tragedies that had overwhelmed the Jewish people in the earlier part of the twentieth century.

Ironically, following the election of Menachem Begin in 1977, philanthropists had begun to breach the consensus themselves. After each election in Israel, the State Comptroller now began to publish details of Diaspora donations of over $10,000 to specific parties, thereby clarifying who was supporting their policies. The Jewish public could now discover the real allegiance of their philanthropic leaders. Ironically, it was the right-wing opponents of the Oslo Accords and the Rabin government who punctured the argument of "no interference in the internal affairs" of Israeli politics by Diaspora Jews. The rationale of this *volte-face* in the 1990s was that the political situation was now so dire that the very future existence of the state was in question, and that the Zionist imperative to avert this catastrophe superseded any previously held convictions of not criticising Israeli government policy. The implicit conclusion was that it was not the right to criticise that was in question, but the nature, context and future implications of the criticism. Yet both the Israeli and Diaspora Right had not made this differentiation in the 1980s — and particularly during the period of the war in Lebanon.

British Jews who were close to the leadership of the British Labour Party often utilised their positions to bring about an Israeli–Arab dialogue and negotiations. Thus the discussion between Shimon Peres and King Hussein was facilitated by and took place in 1987 in the home of Lord Victor Mishcon (who had previously held high office in the Board of Deputies).[8] Lord Michael Levy, a friend of Tony Blair and fund-raiser for the British Labour Party, served as an intermediary on behalf of the British government in facilitating contacts between the Arab world and Israel. It was surely no accident that his wife and other members of his family repeatedly added their signatures to Peace Now advertisements in the Jewish Chronicle.[9] Levy's son was a prime mover in facilitating the Geneva Agreement of Yossi Beilin and Yasser Abed Rabbo.

There has been a growing acceptance of the plurality of views about Israel as the succeeding generation has taken over the reins of authority in the Jewish community — in general recognition of the increasingly complex nature of Israeli politics. The sense of subservience to an Israeli government has become less important. Thus the current President of the Board of Deputies criticised the appointment of the new Israeli Ambassador in 2004 because of his lack of experience as a diplomat. Moreover, representative Jewish organizations have become more selective in the Israeli policies which they choose to defend. For example, no Jewish organization — apart from those on the Right or who support the National Religious in Israel — now declares its allegiance to the principle of settlement in the West Bank and Gaza. A former Israeli Ambassador in London, Moshe Raviv, and the late Chief Rabbi, Lord Immanuel Jakobovits thereby shared a Peace Now platform on the eve of Ehud Barak's election in 1999 — this would have been unthinkable a decade earlier. It was perhaps also a reaction to the recognition that Diaspora affairs — with perhaps the exception of the United States — did not rank highly on the agenda of the Israel Foreign Ministry. In 1986, the then Foreign Minister, Shimon Peres, circulated a list of Israel's priorities to embassies around the world. Interest in the Diaspora ranked fifth.[10]

What Do Jews Really Think?

The trauma of division in the 1980s raised the question of whether organizational policies on Israel were truly representative of the community at large. Throughout the 1980s, the surveys of American Jewish attitudes towards Israel by Steven M. Cohen on behalf of the American Jewish Committee indicated considerable, if qualified dissent from so-called official views. It was only in the mid-1990s that Jewish organizations in Britain began to consider what "the ordinary Jew in the street" thought. Indeed, the factual results of such research often confronted the unelected and the unrepresentative in the community with a challenge to their views. Previously, research into attitudes towards Israel had featured peripherally in communal surveys in two London suburbs: Edgware in North West London in 1968 and Redbridge in East London in 1978. The report of the Institute for Jewish Policy Research (JPR) in

November 1997 on *The Attachment of British Jews to Israel* was the first scientific analysis, based on a sample of 2,194 British Jews, to be carried out and not simply based on supposition.[11]

The report confirmed that attachment to Israel was a fundamental component of Jewish identity — and the stronger the sense of Jewishness, the stronger the adherence. When asked to define themselves, only 26 percent of respondents felt "more Jewish than British". A majority — some 54 percent — felt "equally British and Jewish", while a minority of 18 percent regarded themselves as "primarily British". When asked about attachment to Israel, 43 percent responded that they had strong ties to Israel, 38 percent were moderately attached, 16 percent felt they had "no special links" and only 3 percent projected negative views. When the minority of those Jews who defined themselves as "more Jewish than British" were questioned, 73 percent professed a strong affiliation with Israel, compared to 43 percent of the general sample. It was clear that a majority of British Jews identified with Israel with varying degrees of intensity. This was emphasised by the fact that 66 percent of the general sample had visited Israel at least once during the previous ten years and 70 percent stated that they had close friends or family in Israel. The survey also indicated an age factor, with the over-50s feeling more strongly about Israel than their younger counterparts. While visiting Israel undoubtedly heightened a sense of identification, it was significant that even among those who had never been to Israel, 34 percent of older people felt a strong attachment to the state while this diminished to a mere 3 percent of younger people. Clearly, those closer to the *Shoah*, the establishment of the state and the broad twentieth-century saga of the Jews were more aware of the centrality of Israel in Jewish life. The report commented that this was evidence of a connection with Israel "based on ideology and emotion rather than experience". It concluded that the relationship between British Jews and Israel was very much age-related and in apparent decline.

British Jews as Liberals

Given that the JPR survey had been carried out in the few months before Yitzhak Rabin's murder, 69 percent agreed with the land for peace formula, with 62 percent of this group advocating the return of most of the West Bank. A similar percentage agreed with the Rabin administration's approach to the peace process, with only 9 percent opposed. The liberal attitudes of British Jews also applied to the establishment of new settlements. Only 5 percent advocated new outposts. Nearly half the respondents wanted a settlement freeze while allowing existing ones to remain, while another 32 percent desired a freeze and a gradual evacuation. The liberal outlook — admittedly elicited during the optimistic phase of the peace process — towards Israel and its political problems reflected a broader finding of other JPR surveys. These surveys showed that British Jews were far more liberal in their world outlook than their non-Jewish counterparts from the same socio-economic background.

Significantly, this liberal outlook reflected more the view of Jewish advocacy groups in Britain on behalf of the Israeli peace camp than it did the formal approach of communal organizations on behalf of an Israeli government. Significantly, the views of those who actually immigrated to Israel were more symptomatic of the post-1967 swing from a secular socialist-Zionist ethos towards a right-wing national religious direction. Moreover, the JPR survey did not ask questions about Zionism, but only about identification with Israel. It thereby did not make a differentiation between the national religious who embraced Zionism and supported the religious settlers on the West Bank and the *haredim* who opposed Zionism and were lukewarm towards the settlers. Yet the "strictly orthodox" of the JPR survey visited Israel more often than any other group and opposed the Oslo peace process and the "land for peace" formula more than any other group. No doubt *yeshiva* study — which had become a peer group vocation for many young Jews — contributed to the high number of visits.

The JPR survey, carried out in 1995, testified to the dominance of a pronounced "Israelism" as a component in the Jewish identity of British Jews. But was this the same as Zionism? While classical Zionism had ended with the establishment of the Jewish state in 1948, it was unclear what had taken its place. Ben-Gurion commented as far back as the 1960s that "the title of Zionist now embraces entirely different things among which there is no connection, and to speak of Zionism *per se* has no real meaning".[12] Yet a central facet of classical Zionism is understood as immigration to Israel and building a just society because the Diaspora represented past failure and future assimilation. The JPR survey of the mid-1990s effectively distinguished between those who were classical Zionists and those who identified with Israel as part of a broad "Israelism". When presented with the statement that "the only long-term future for Jews is in Israel", 61 percent rejected this view. Moreover, within the 18–39 age range, rejection of this view was far higher. Even amongst those who strongly identified with Israel, 46 percent disagreed with the proposition that "the only long-term future for Jews is in Israel".

Contemporary Events

In March 2000, on the eve of the breakdown of the peace process, a JPR Commission on the representation of the interests of the British Jewish Community asked opinion-makers and communal leaders vital questions about British Jewish opinion on Israeli affairs. The Commission concluded:

> There was no great appetite for British Jewish representative bodies to take political positions *vis-à-vis* Israeli government policies, from either an ideological or a geopolitical perspective. Some felt that single-issue groups should be free to do as they wished in representing their views on Israel through a variety of means; others felt that there should be no public criticism of the government of Israel — an argument which has been made repeatedly for many years in the community. However, in the event that issues of concern did arise, it was felt that the proper channel of communication should be through the Israel Embassy via a 'central body' such as the Board of Deputies, or by means of special-interest bodies and Zionist organizations, which would then communicate their concerns via corresponding channels in Israel.[13]

This approach reflected the overall conservatism of the leadership of the community in openly espousing dissenting views. It also reflected the desire of some in positions of authority to accept that there were clear differences of opinion on Israeli policies within the leadership, which should be aired, and that groups such as the British Friends of Peace Now should be allowed to express such views. A differentiation was thus made between "official" representative groups who should not speak out and "single-issue" ones who should. This was, effectively, an unofficial, unspoken division of labour. This policy appears to have continued during the current Intifada.

In 2004, the United Jewish Israel Appeal (UJIA) published a study of Jewish identity in Britain, which was, however, based on a sample of "moderately engaged Jews".[14] The report remarked that the UJIA spent £3.5 million on Jewish renewal each year in Britain and thereby needed to target its funding on real needs rather than postulated ones. Although a more narrowly defined group than the broad JPR sample of 1995, 47 percent of those questioned agreed with the proposition "I am a Zionist", 26 percent were unsure and 27 percent disagreed. Yet when it came to identifying with Israel rather than with Zionist ideology, the choice was much more decisive. Seventy-eight percent of respondents agreed with the statement "I care deeply about Israel", while 17 percent were unsure and only 5 percent disagreed. This differentiation between "Zionism" and "Israelism" even amongst "moderately engaged Jews" was striking. Significantly, 91 percent of respondents had visited Israel, and 68 percent had visited three times or more.

When questioned about the media's coverage of Israel, 75 percent felt that it was biased, but believed that the consequences were not immediately threatening. Significantly, the study remarked that non-Jewish friends and colleagues did not share such a commitment to Israel and were described as "neutral or passive" on the issue.

When asked whether they supported the Sharon government's policies, only 6 percent of respondents strongly concurred, while another 22 percent provided moderate agreement. A similar percentage disagreed, but a majority were unsure or ambivalent in their responses. Asked to identify themselves as "hawks" or "doves", 63 percent preferred not to commit themselves to either category. Yet for those who did, the doves outnumbered the hawks by almost four to one.

Regardless of their personal views, media attacks on Israel *per se* rather than on the policies of the Sharon government appear to have galvanised British Jews. In 2002, between 45–55,000 people turned out for a demonstration in central London in support of Israel. Even given the absence of the *haredim*, the aged and the infirm, those who came alone as the sole representative of entire families, those who refused to come through fear of a terrorist attack, and those Zionists who stayed away in protest against the presence of Netanyahu as the main speaker, this was an impressive fraction of Britain's 300,000 Jews.

The attachment of British Jews to Israel in 2005 thus does not appear to have waned. This attachment has been fortified by a strong educational programme in Israel for Jewish youth to counteract a declining interest in the fate of the Jewish state within British society generally. British Jews appear to have maintained their broad liberal credentials while moving away from the Left, which is perceived to be hostile to Jewish interests and Israel. For those who choose to participate in the debate on the Israel–Palestine conflict, there is a continuing identification with dovish policies.

Notes

1 Ezra Mendelsohn, *On Modern Jewish Politics* (Oxford: Oxford University Press, 1993), p. 3.

2 Vladimir Jabotinsky, *11th Hour*, 24 October 1937. (The *11th Hour* was a weekly periodical of the Revisionist Zionist movement in South Africa.)

3 Joseph Finklestone, *Zionism and British Jews*, Jewish Year Book (London: Vallentine Mitchell, 1997), p. xxii.
4 Sir John Chancellor, Memo to Lord Passfield, 17 January 1930, PRO CO 733185/3.
5 Beatrice Webb in her diary (2 September 1929) in *The Letters of Sidney and Beatrice Webb Vol. 3, Pilgrimage 1912–1947*, Norman Mackenzie (ed.) (Cambridge: Cambridge University Press, 1978), p. 315.
6 Sidney Webb, letter to Beatrice Webb (22 October 1930) in *The Letters of Sidney and Beatrice Webb Vol. 3, Pilgrimage 1912–1947*, Norman Mackenzie (ed.) (Cambridge: Cambridge University Press 1978), p. 334.
7 Colin Shindler, *Israel, Likud and the Zionist Dream: Power, Politics and Ideology from Begin to Netanyahu* (London: I.B. Tauris, 1995), p. 163.
8 Ibid., p. 212.
9 *Jewish Chronicle* 28 October 2002; 10 October 2004.
10 Colin Shindler, *Ploughshares into Swords? Israelis, Jews in the Shadow of the Intifada* (London: I.B. Tauris, 1991), p. 87.
11 Barry A. Kosmin, Anthony Lerman and Jacqueline Goldberg, *The Attachment of British Jews to Israel*, JPR Report No. 5 (London: JPR Publication, November 1997), <www.jpr.org.uk/Israel>.
12 David Ben-Gurion, *Where There is No Vision, the People Perish in Unease in Zion*, Ehud Ben-Ezer (ed.) (Jerusalem: Quadrangle, 1974), p. 71.
13 *A Community of Communities: Report of the Commission on Representation of the Interests of the British Jewish Community*, JPR Report (London: JPR Publication, March 2000), <www.jpr.org.uk>.
14 *The UJIA Study of Jewish Identity: A Survey of Jewish Parents* (London: United Jewish Israel Appeal, 2004).

13

The Place of the State of Israel in Latin American Jewish Identity

Graciela Ben Dror

Zionism and the position of the State of Israel within the context of the Diaspora identity are at the very heart of modern Jewish existence in Latin America. The Zionist movement emerged in Latin America mainly during the 1930s, and was greatly affected by the establishment of the State of Israel in 1948. Zionist identity was expressed in ideological, political, educational and social terms, with an emphasis on concrete aid and support — material, spiritual, and personal voluntary *aliyah* — to assure the existence and development of the State of Israel.

Even though a large majority of the Latin American communities originated as a result of immigration during the twentieth century, they still embody and manifest their own unique features and customs. The development of the Zionist movement within Latin America, therefore, was a result of these features.

Certainly, the Zionist movement has become a significant reference for the Jewish population in several Latin American countries since the 1920s and the 1930s. The role of that movement, which had begun with an ideological background, was increased further by the personal encouragement provided by the visits of several prominent Jewish leaders from all over the world. The visit of Natan Bistriezki — a *shaliach* (emissary) of the Jewish Agency who was sent in order to improve the organization of the Zionist youth Movements in Latin America in the mid-1930s — added a particular strength to what was labeled in Latin America's Jewish Zionist youth movements as "Zionut Magshima" (personal commitment and *aliyah*).[1] The ground of Latin American countries was fertile for the emergence and development of Zionist identity for reasons which will now be discussed.

History and Characteristics of Latin American Jewry

Despite the fact that there had been Jews and *marranos* (false Christian converts from the time of the Spanish Inquisition) in Colonial America since the discovery and conquest of the continent, these communities generally did not flourish and grow.

A new kind of Jewish community began to develop in these countries since the last decade of the nineteenth century in Argentina and during the few first decades of the twentieth century in other countries as Brazil, Uruguay, Chile, Mexico, Cuba, Venezuela. Very small Jewish communities also appeared in most of the other countries of the continent at this time, with the size of each community varying from country to country.[2]

The immigration wave toward Latin America brought first of all a wave of *Ashkenazi* Jews from Eastern Europe, who settled in most of the countries. In addition, a smaller *Sephardic* community came from various Balkan countries, North Africa, Turkey, and other places. In some places, such as Rio de Janeiro, this Sephardi community came before the arrival of the Ashkenazis.[3]

The majority of Jewish migration to Latin America came from countries in which socio-economic issues and anti-Semitism were among the most important causes of migration to the new world. When the doors of the United States were closed by the quota regime in 1924, the Jewish population from Eastern Europe began to emigrate to Argentina, Brazil, Uruguay, Mexico and Cuba.[4]

Their background as workers, skilled workers and door-to-door salesmen led them to identify themselves with social problems, so that many Jews entered socialist frameworks, parties and syndicates.

Community Structure

The *kehilah* (community) was structured as a social organization attempting to respond to problems such as work, education, setting up and running the *Chevrah Kadisha* (burial services) and other services, imitating the way in which Eastern European *kehilot* were organized. Religious service was relegated to the synagogue, and was certainly not a central issue for most of the immigrants. Everyday maintenance was the main focus, but the immigrants very quickly began to develop communitarian social welfare, health, cultural and social services. Synagogues and community buildings were a core feature of community infrastructure. Though many came from religious homes, the immigrants generally retained a traditional background without any strong orthodox practice. The communities thus developed, for the most part, with tradition strongly in mind, but rather unconcerned with orthodoxy. The everyday struggle for existence, together with the traditional background of many of the Jewish immigrants, gave them the opportunity to assimilate economically and socially in these liberal countries, which were in those days open to European immigration. The immigrants expressed their response to this open and welcoming hospitality by sending their children to the public schools, establishing Jewish Yiddish education, social and cultural frameworks alongside, within which to develop their Jewish life.[5]

Distinctive Features of Latin American Jewish Communities

Latin American Jewry is quite unique, but nonetheless maintains parallels with other Jewish societies in the Diaspora. The first distinctive feature lies in the way these communities were established. Since it was part of the Spanish Colony, Latin America was virtually closed to Jews — as was the Iberian Peninsula — until the nineteenth century. Thus Jews coming to Latin America did so illegally. They could not live openly as Jews personally, and certainly not as active, united communities, despite a few rare exceptions. In contrast to countries such as the United States, Canada, Australia and South Africa comprising mostly Protestant populations, Jews migrating to Latin America were faced with a Catholic continent *par excellence*, founded by countries in which the Inquisition had not been abolished. The legitimacy of Jewish existence in the eyes of the majority of the population, therefore, was one of the basic problems confronting Jews within this staunchly Catholic homogeneity.

Another distinguishing feature was the fact that while most occidental Jewry in the Diaspora lived in developed countries, Latin American Jews lived in non-developed regions, belonging to what is known as the "Third World" — areas of acute social and economic polarization. Most of the Jewish Latin American communities were centred in the more progressive republics: Argentina, Brazil, Uruguay in the South, and Mexico (with its great social and political differences) in the North. The Jewish community experienced high levels of social change; moving socially and economically from lower to middle and upper classes from their arrival, mainly during the twentieth century. Jews that had been poor immigrants generally came to inhabit and comprise some of the more affluent sectors of society. Thus, in a still monolithically Catholic society, the topic of dual identity and dual loyalties came up often, and still does today.

Countries of Origin

An interesting feature of Jewish people in Latin America lies in the origin of its emigration.[6] While in other Occidental countries Jews arrived predominantly from eastern and central Europe, Latin American Jewry came, as previously mentioned, from all parts of the World. Eastern European Ashkenazim constituted the majority until the Holocaust, but in Venezuela, Brazil and Buenos Aires, they were preceded by North African Jewish immigration. Many Jews from Syria — Damascus and Aleppo — settled in Argentina and in Mexico.[7]

The community life of Latin American Jews reflected, for the most part, their European Jewish background. For example, the Ashkenazi community in Buenos Aires replicated Polish Jewish society. Their standing, both economic and social, improved markedly from working to middle class over the years. In the organizational and cultural field too, a new institutional life emerged in order to preserve and strengthen Jewish affiliation. A broad Jewish education system was created and implemented, and was expanded after the Holocaust. Jewish continuity was a primary concern throughout Latin America.[8]

Zionism in Latin America

Affiliation with the Zionist movement has to be seen within this context. There was total commitment to Zionism in many Latin American Jewish communities as part of the endeavours of the Zionist movement in the aftermath of the Holocaust. After the establishment of the State of Israel, Zionist ideology and implementation was very much reinforced. As Herzl said "the conquest of the communities" became a reality amongst Latin American Jewry after the creation of the State of Israel.

Given that the Jewish immigrants that had arrived in these countries were mostly non-religious in everyday life, the identification with Zionism became the main national Jewish identity, including in places where the Bund culture and ideology had been strong before the Holocaust in several Ashkenazi communities.[9]

Anti-Semitism did not embody violent features in Latin America, despite its Catholic tradition, but rather was culturally demonstrated through verbal expression, originating in European (French and Spanish) anti-Semitic cultural tendencies.

Argentina can be seen as the country with more anti-Semitic tradition and activities than any other.[10] There was significantly less anti-Semitic tradition in Brazil and Uruguay.[11] In Argentina, violent anti-Semitism did manifest at certain times, such as in 1919 or during Eichmann's capture in the 1960s. Even in these cases, however, it was expressed mostly in the press, books and social terms, and never reached high levels of violence, as it did in Europe.[12]

The *Shoah* (Holocaust) had a real impact on Latin American Jews. During the 1930s and the 1940s, anti-Semitism was more evident than ever before, legitimised by nationalistic and fascist groups. Its presence persisted even after the Holocaust.[13]

On an ideological level, the Latin American Diaspora developed mostly on the model of the Zionist Movement, and even more so after the impact of the Holocaust. This development was implemented in several aspects of community life: including education, the political field, social interests and the psychological realm.

In terms of education, the Jewish school curriculum after the establishment of the State of Israel suffered a dramatic change — from Yiddish to Hebrew language — mainly a result of the changes toward Israel and Zionism.[14] The "Hebraist" movement tried to include Hebrew language and culture into the school curriculum and was finally triumphant after a long series of internal dilemmas and discussions. These discussions were held in Buenos Aires, a place that, due to its centrality, was able to influence other Latin American communities.[15]

Politically the Bund suffered the consequences of a shift, both in ideology and reality, after the Holocaust. They dwindled to only a very small, peripheral movement after the establishment of the State of Israel, while Zionism gradually came to encompass the mainstream of the organized community. Before the State of Israel the political sphere in Latin America Jewish society reflected that of Eastern Europe. After the establishment of the State of Israel, however, Latin America Jewry mirrored the political panorama of Israel.[16]

The political, ideological and social predominance of the Zionist Movement was particularly evident in the marginalisation of non-Zionist contingents, as with the communist Jews. They found themselves set apart and isolated, suffering a kind of Diaspora within the Diaspora, in countries such as Argentina and Uruguay, and, to a lesser extent, Brazil. Communist Jews had their own clubs and schools, and were segregated from mainstream Jewish social life.[17]

The Jewish communities from the southern part of Latin America not only accepted a Zionist identity, but moreover embraced the ideology as a national value to be implemented in their everyday life. From these countries, particularly Argentina and Uruguay, there have been various waves of *aliyah* to Israel since 1947 until today, each with different causes and intensity.[18] Until the 1970s, this *aliyah* was primarily motivated by ideological Zionist grounds. From then on, political, economic, and local reasons began to play a decisive role in the immigration of several thousands to Israel.[19]

Against this Zionist backdrop the question arises as to the meaning of this belief system to these communities. The ideological debate surrounding the significance of Zionism had widespread impact on the Zionist movement in Latin America after the establishment of the State of Israel.[20]

The discussions of the Zionist movement worldwide brought into general awareness the fact that there were numerous differing views concerning Zionism and its implications for and in the Western hemisphere. One of the more prevalent stances spoke of the centrality of the Israeli State, advocating total personal commitment to Israel, *aliyah* and the Hebrew language. Another mainstream view took into account the (occidental) Diaspora; seeking solutions for issues, such as Jewish education, or lack thereof, awareness of assimilation, and proper preparation and training for educators, so as to be able to ensure Jewish continuity. This concept described the necessity of strengthening and deepening Jewish (community) life and presence in the Occidental diasporas — cognizant of the fact that *aliyah* would not be a massive movement in these countries — as a vital precondition to Zionist activity and personal *aliyah*.[21]

In Latin America, these two distinct standpoints focused on three major topics:

1 The significance of the centrality of the State of Israel.
2 The place of personal *aliyah* and "*Chalutziut*" (pioneering) within Zionist ideology.
3 The future of Jewish life in Western countries and the fight against assimilation.

The historiography of Argentinean Zionism shows that on the one hand the main argument given in the public arena for the establishment of the State of Israel was that of a historical compensation for Jews after centuries of suffering in the Diaspora. On the other hand, the Jewish press noted that the identification *en masse* of Argentinean Jews with the State of Israel could potentially give rise to the dilemma of double loyalty: to Argentina and Israel at the same time. After all, in a society of both cultural and religious homogeneity, such double loyalty could be seen as a problem by the local non-Jewish society. By the second half of the twentieth century, Latin American Jewry comprised of first, second, and third generation immigrants trying to integrate both socially and economically, while also attempting to maintain and express loyalty toward the countries that had welcomed them in difficult times during the 1920s and 1930s.[22] In spite of the dilemmas and rhetorical differences, the centrality of the State of Israel in the public voice of Zionism was generally accepted in Jewish everyday life and reverberated through the Jewish press and leadership — most notably in Argentina[23] and Uruguay.[24]

There were differing viewpoints with regard to personal *aliyah* ("*hagshama*") and the emphasis put on the *Chalutziut* (pioneering) movement. For the Zionist Youth movements (*Hashomer Hatzair, Habonim Dror, Betar, B'nei Akiva, Hanoar Hatzioni*)[25] there was only one possible meaning of Zionism, which often caused real verbal confrontation with the local Zionist leadership. While the representatives of youth movements on the whole very actively stressed their personal commitment to *aliyah* in the Ben-Gurion *hagshama* (personal fulfillment) mould, the Zionist leadership was more flexible in its definitions.[26]

These different approaches were publicly depicted in the Jewish Spanish press in Argentina, and several newspapers and weeklies argued for the view of Zionism in terms of active *aliyah* and *Chalutziut*. The press also asserted, however, that the process did not necessarily have to override the idea of integration into Argentinean society and the fight against assimilation through the establishment and preservation of Jewish education, society and cultural life. This was the point of view expressed by the major newspaper, *Mundo Israelita*, in Buenos Aires.[27] Other newspapers and weeklies, like *Davar*, defended the Diaspora ideal as being a vision of Israel as simply the spiritual home of world Jewry, as opposed to an actual settling place for all the Jewish people. *La Luz*, a Sephardic weekly, stressed the importance of maximum solidarity with the State of Israel — placing particular emphasis on the need for economic aid, the necessity of resisting assimilation, and the reinforcement of community life in the Diaspora.[28]

The public discussion concerning the meaning of Zionism has been a constant subject of discussion in the Spanish Jewish press since 1949. This discussion has reflected the various approaches to the topic — as personal commitment to *aliyah*, or mainly solidarity with the State of Israel — and their meaning in terms of personal identity and aid to Israel. This issue was central to some of the Latin American Zionist movements in the southern countries up until the Six Day War.[29] Until that time, the primacy of personal *aliyah* was a steadfast ideal within Jewish youth movements, in contrast to the Latin American Zionist movements and Jewish press, who advocated the need for social integration so as to avoid double loyalty accusations.[30]

Summing Up

The contribution of the Latin American Diaspora to both Zionism and the State of Israel has ultimately also resulted in a contribution to itself. From the beginning of its establishment the State of Israel offered these communities a sense of purpose, an objective to defend, and a certain directed sense of Jewish *national* identity as an alternative to a purely religious one, thereby facilitating a global vision and structure for a common future for the Jewish people.

The State of Israel stood as a primary centre for (Latin American) Jewry, despite neglecting to take into consideration the vulnerability of these communities within the arenas of national everyday politics. The case of Adolph Eichman's kidnapping from Argentina in 1960 clearly demonstrates that any local problems befalling the Jewish communities as a result of the abduction were not taken into account by its masterminds.[31]

Being a relatively young Diaspora, Latin American Jewry flourished to become a real organized community over the course of the twentieth century. Even if the Ashkenazi communities developed to mirror their Eastern European predecessors, their predominant character was neither religious-minded, nor orthodoxly observant, but rather, more centred around traditional and secular Judaism. These attributes left a broad space for the development of Zionist national ideology and practice, thus gradually transforming Jewish society from a pluralist community — traditional, Bundist, Zionist and Communist before the Holocaust — to a much more collectively Zionist one after the establishment of the State of Israel.

In that respect, Zionist ideology and the State of Israel undoubtedly contributed to and broadened the scope of Jewish identity, both among youth and adults. It offered the possibility of a national secular identity with Zionism and the State of Israel, granting an entirely new meaning to Judaism and Jewish community life in Latin America.[32]

In this way the Zionist Movement and the establishment of the State of Israel has had a great impact on local Jews. After the Holocaust they saw themselves as the vehicle for the continuity of Jewish life after the Holocaust in Europe.

In any case, the future of Jewish life in their own new countries has been a constant preoccupation within these communities. Furthermore, despite identifying themselves as Zionist, the Latin American Diaspora has placed great importance and emphasis on local Jewish education, and the struggle against assimilation in order to, above all, carry on the existence of Jewish social and cultural life.

The emphasis that has been put on the teaching and dissemination of Hebrew in Jewish schools in Latin America — and more specifically in Argentina and Uruguay — has been the result of two factors: (1) A deep identification with the Zionist solution to the "Jewish question", meaning the young State of Israel that had materialized from a dream into reality. (2) A reinforcement of this tendency by the impact that the Holocaust has had on Latin American societies.

The "Jewish question" in Jewish Zionist circles signified the reality of a tragic situation born out of the Jewish people having lived in the Diaspora for decades, and the creation of the State of Israel being the only real solution. Other alternatives of Jewish life given in modern times (such as Communism and Bundism) became less appealing in the light of the impact of Israel's establishment. Zionism and personal *aliyah* were seen as the answer to Jewish weakness. The Hebrew language therefore became an essential resource, not only to prepare young people for personal *aliyah*, but also as a new avenue and medium of communication between the centre of the Jewish people – the young State of Israel, and the periphery, the Diaspora.

As previously mentioned, the Holocaust had a very strong impact on the Latin-American Jewish population, as most of the Ashkenazi population lost their families under the Nazi regime in Europe. These Jews, who were both personally and emotionally involved in the Jewish tragedy in Europe, saw the State of Israel — and the corollary Hebrew language — as a hope and a new way of identification. The shift from teaching Yiddish to teaching Hebrew was a process that was generally accepted as a natural way of adapting to the new situation of the Jewish mainstream under the impact of the Holocaust and the establishment of the State of Israel.

Notes

1 Silvia Schenkolewski-Kroll, *The Zionist Movement and the Zionist Parties in Argentina, 1935–1948* (in Hebrew) (Jerusalem: Magnes Press, 1996), pp. 75–120, 121–48, 187–220, 233–95; Rosa Perla Raicher, "Uruguayan Jewry, Jewish National Identity and Assimilation Tendencies in its Historical Development — from the first decade of the 20th Century up to the fifties". Dissertation submitted for the degree of Doctor of Philosophy, The Hebrew University of Jerusalem, 1998 (in Hebrew), pp. 238–244.

2 Leonardo Senkman, "Argentina's Immigration Policy During the Holocaust, 1938–1945", *Yad Vashem Studies, XXI* (1991): 155–88; Rosa Perla Raicher, "Asilo en el Uruguay de refugiados judíos perseguidos por el nazismo", *Judaica Latinoamericana* (Jerusalem: Magnes Press and Amilat, 1988), pp. 68–78.

3 See the autobiography of Joseph Eskenazi Pernidji, *Das fogueiras da Inquisição as terras do Brasil* (Rio de Janeiro: Imago, 2002), pp. 191–207.

4 Margalit Bejarano, "Cuba as America's Back Door: The Case of Jewish Immigration, *Judaica Latinoamericana II* (Jerusalem: Magnes Press and Amilat, 1993), pp. 43–56; Alicia Gojman de Backal, "Inmigración de judíos polacos a México en el siglo XX", *Judaica Latinoamericana III* (Jerusalem: Magnes Press, 1997), pp. 45–72.

5 Victor A. Mirelman, "The Jews in Argentina (1890–1939), Assimilation and Particularism". Dissertation submitted for the degree of Doctor of Philosophy, Columbia University, New York, 1973, pp. 31–41; Haim Avni, *Emancipation and Jewish Education: A Century of Argentinian Jewry's Experience 1884–1984* (Jerusalem: The Zalman Shazar Center, 1985), pp. 29–50; 119–138.

6 Haim Avni, *Argentina y la historia de la immigración judía, 1810–1950* (Jerusalem: AMIA - Magnes Press, 1983).

7 On the Sephardim in Argentina see Margalit Bejerano, "El cementerio judío y la unidad comunitaria en la historia de los Sefaradim en Buenos Aires", *Michael*, VIII (1983): 24–43.

8 Haim Avni, "Jews in Latin America", *Judaica Latinoamericana* (Jerusalem: Magnes Press, 1988), pp. 9–11.

9 Margalit Bejarano, "The Land of Israel and Cuban Politics: The Role of the JNF in Preserving Jewish Identity under the Batista Dictatorship", *Judaica Latinamericana IV*, pp. 251–266.

10 Graciela Ben-Dror, *The Catholic and the Jews, Argentina 1933–1945* (in Hebrew) (Jerusalem: Zalman Shazar, 2000); Sandra McGee Deutsch and Ronald Dolkart, *The Argentinean Right* (Wilmington, Delaware: SR Books, 1993); Loris Zanatta, *Del estado liberal a la nación católica* (Buenos Aires: Universidad Nacional de Quilmes, 1996); Fortunato Malimacci, "Catholicisme et état militaire en Argentina 1930–1946". Dissertation submitted for the degree of Doctor of Philosophy, École des Hautes Etudes, Paris, 1988.

11 Graciela Ben-Dror. *La Iglesia católica ante el Holocausto. España y América Latina* (Madrid: Alianza Editorial, 2003), pp. 271–297; Rosa Perla Raicher, "Uruguayan Jewry", pp. 80–184.

12 Haim Avni, "State Antisemitismo in Argentina?", in Shmuel Almog, *Antisemitism Through the Ages*, (in Hebrew) (Jerusalem: The Zalman Shazar Center, 1983), pp 323–342.

13 Leonardo Senkman (ed.), *El antisemitismo en Argentina* (Buenos Aires: CEAL, 1989).

14 Adina Cimet Singer, "The Ashkenazi Jewish Community in Mexico. A dialogue among Ideologies", Dissertation submitted for the degree of Doctor of Philosophy, Columbia University, New York, 1992; Efraim Zadoff, "La disputa en torno al idioma nacional en los colegios judíos askenzíes de México a partir de la década de 1930", *Judaica Latinoamericana IV*, pp. 135–155.

15 Iosi (Jorge) Goldstein, "El movimiento Hebraísta en la Argentina (1948–1959)", in

Judaica Latinoamericana II (Jerusalem: Ed. Magnes Press, 1993), pp. 171–189; Efraim Zadoff, *Historia de la educación judía en Buenos Aires* (Buenos Aires: Mila, 1994), p. 33; Yossi J. Goldstein, "Coping Educationally with the Holocaust Period in Latin America", in *Holocaust and Education* (Jerusalem: Yad Vashem, 1999), pp. 23–33.

16 Silvia Schenkolewski-Kroll, "La conquista de las comunidades; El movimiento sionista y la comunidad ashkenazí de Buenos Aires (1935–1949), *Judaica Latinoamericana II* (Jerusalem: Magnes, 1993), pp. 191–202; Judit Bokser Misses, "El movimiento Nacional judío. El Sionismo en Mexico 1922–1947", Dissertation submitted for the degree of Doctor of Philosophy, Univesidad Nacional Autonoma de México, 1991.

17 S. Shenkolevski, *Judaica Latinoamericana IV*, pp. 183–212; Helena Lewin, "A construcao do 'diferente': O judeu nos arquivos secretos brasileiros", *Judaica Latinoamericana IV*, pp. 183–212; Avraham Milgram, "O 'milieu' judeo-comunista do Rio de Janeiro nos anos 30". Ibid., pp. 213–234; Moshe Nes-El, "Los judíos en la formación ideológica de los movimientos socialista y comunista en el Perú", *Judaica Latinoamericana III* (Jerusalem: Magnes, 1997), pp. 163–173; Rosa Perla Raicher, "Uruguayan Jewry", pp. 178–180, 244–251.

18 Yosi (Jorge) Goldstein, "El Estado de Israel, el Movimiento Sionista y la educación judía en Brasil, 1948–1955", in *Kivunim-Revista de Sionismo y Judaísmo*, 3 (Mayo 2000), 173–200; Jorge (Iosi) Goldstein, "*El Instituto Cultural Argentino-Israelí (I.C.A.I.): El proyecto y su implementación como nexo entre Israel y el Judaísmo argentino 1949–1953*", en *Ensayos sobre Judaísmo Latinoamericano* (Buenos Aires: Ed. Milá, 1990), pp. 125–147, Rosa Perla Raicher, "Uruguayan Jewry", pp. 238–244.

19 Silvia Shenkolevski, "Cambios en la relación de la Organizacion Sionista Mundial hacia la comunidad judia y el movimiento sionista en la Argentina hasta 1948", *Judaica Latinoamericana* (Jerusalem: Magnes-Amilat, 1988), pp. 149–166; Yossi (Jorge) Goldstein, "Comunidad voluntaria y educación privada: tendencias en el seno del judaísmo argentino entre 1990 y 1995", *Judaica Latinoamericana IV*, pp. 157–181.

20 Zionist Central Archives (ASC), Sessions of the Zionist Action Committee, Jerusalem, 5–15 May 1949, pp. 132–136, pp. 259–261 (in Hebrew).

21 Ibid.

22 About the 1930s and 1940s: in Brazil, see Jeffrey Lesser, *Welcoming the Undesirables, Brazil and the Jewish Question* (Berkeley: California University Press, 1995), pp. 118–177; in Uruguay, Rosa Perla Raicher, "Uruguayan Jewry"; in Argentina, Silvia Shenkolewski, op. cit.

23 About Argentina, one of the important pieces of research was done by Iosi (Jorge) Goldstein, "El periodismo judío en castellano en la Argentina 1948–1956. Sus posturas con respecto al sionismo e Israel", *Judaica Latinoamericana IV* (Jeruslaem: Magnes, 1997), pp. 307–311.

24 About the Uruguayan democracy, see Rama, G., *La democracia en Uruguay. Una Perspectiva de interpretación* (Montevideo: Arca, 1995) and about the possibilities of Jewish life and the Zionist movement see Rosa Perla Raicher and Haim Avni, *Historia Viva, Memorias del Uruguay y de Israel* (Jerusalén: Universidad de Jerusalén, 1989).

25 This tendency is very well described in a book dealing with the Youth movements of Mapai in Argentina, Shlomo Bar-Gil, Dror, *Gordonia and Hechalutz-Techezakna, 1934–1952* (To be published in Tel Aviv: Yad Tabenkin, 2006). I want to thank the author for giving me the possibility of reading his book before publication).

26 See for instance writings on *aliyah* as the only legitimate expression of Zionism in the Hashomer Hatzair publications at the Hashomer Hatzair Archives, Givat Haviva. About Uruguay, see Rosa Perla Raicher and Haim Avni, *Historia Viva, Memorias del Uruguay y de Israel*, op.cit.

27 *Mundo Israelita*, 9 December1950, ibid., 27 February 1954.

28 *Davar*, November-December, 1954; see the article of Iosi (Jorge) Goldstein, *Judaica Latinoamericana III*, p. 311–312; *La Luz*, 11 June 1948; Ibid, 21 December 1951.

29 See the several testimonies in Rosa Perla Raicher and Haim Avni, *Historia Viva, Memorias del Uruguay y de Israel*, op.cit.

30 See Raanan Rein, *Argentina , Israel y los judíos. Encuentros y desencuentros, mitos y realidades.* (Buenos Aires: Editorial Lumiere, 2001, pp. 87–100; 128–132.

31 *Rosa Perla Raicher*, Uruguay, la comunidad israelita y el pueblo judío (Montevideo: Universidad de la Republica y Universidad Hebrea de Jerusalem, 2003), pp. 192–222.

32 Raanan Rein, *Argentina , Israel y los judíos*, pp. 207–242.

14

The Role of Israel in French–Jewish Identity

Erik H. Cohen

French Jewry, Demographics and History

France is currently home to the second largest Jewish Diaspora community in the world, following only the United States. Slightly less than half a million Jews live in France, primarily in Paris and the surrounding suburbs, making Paris the fourth largest Diaspora Jewish population centre (World Jewish Congress 1998). Over 70 percent of French Jews today are of North African origin, making France the largest *Sephardi* Diaspora population in the world.

The Jews of France were the first European Jewish population to be granted political emancipation, following the French Revolution of 1789. This emancipation, however, was based on the Republican concept that individuals must not give loyalty to any entity other than the State. As stated by Count Stanislas de Clermont-Tonnerre to the French National Assembly in 1798, "To the Jews as individuals, everything; to the Jews as a nation, nothing." Public affiliation with religious or ethnic communities contradicts France's political culture of laity.

The Jews of France embraced and have continued to enjoy this political freedom, are well integrated and assimilated into French culture, and are strongly patriotic. However, a number of major events, which occurred in quick succession, inevitably had an impact upon the character of French Jewry and their attitudes towards their Jewish identity:

1. The betrayal of French Jewry by the Vichy government during World War II resulting in the deportation and death of almost a third of French Jewry and the destruction of all major French-Jewish institutions and leadership.
2. The immigration of a quarter of million Jews from France's former colonies in North Africa (Bensimon & Della Pergola 1986: 36).
3. The simultaneous immigration of millions of Muslims from the same North African former colonies.[1]

4 The emergence of a larger "crisis of identity" in French culture.
5 The establishment of the State of Israel in 1948 and the Six Day War of 1967.
6 The opportunity for Jews to freely come to Israel as tourists or immigrants.

It is this last item that I would like to address in this chapter, but it cannot be discussed in isolation of the others. The betrayal of the Vichy government raised questions about how fully, in fact, Jewish citizens were perceived as equal to other French citizens. The Jews who emigrated from North Africa, while somewhat acculturated from French institutions in their birth countries, nevertheless were and continue to be more religious, more traditional, and more openly Jewish than the established *Ashkenazi* Jewish population. The immigration of Muslims from North Africa has introduced another population not willing to discard their religious and cultural affiliations. It also has brought the larger Israeli–Arab conflict onto French soil, including attacks on Jews perpetrated by Muslim youth. In the wake of these waves of immigration from North Africa as well as from former colonies in the Caribbean, all of France (not only her Jewish population) is experiencing a crisis of identity and a re-assessment of Republican values in the face of an increasingly multi-cultural citizenship.

The threat to Israel posed by the Six Day War, and the pro-Arab stance adopted by the French government caused many French Jews to more publicly express their support of Israel. In May 1967, Jews held large demonstrations in support of Israel in France's major cities. These rallies, at which Israeli flags were flown, helped crystallize a new French–Jewish identity and gave birth to a sense of belonging to a national Jewish community. Over 1,000 French Jews came to volunteer in Israel during and immediately following the Six Day War. After the Six Day War, identification with Israel and pride in Israel were particularly strong among Diaspora Jews, and tourism to Israel greatly increased.[2] For example, participation in youth tours to Israel increased almost five-fold between 1967 and 1978 (Cohen and Cohen 2000). The role of the role of Israel in French Jewish identity, in the context of these other changes, will be the main subject of this chapter.

For the past two decades years I have conducted ongoing empirical research on the Jews of France in specific and international surveys comparing the identity of French–Jewish youth to that of Jews from other Diaspora countries. Based on this research, I can say that the place of the State of Israel in the identity of today's French Jews is important and unique, fulfilling a different role than it does for Jews in other parts of the world.

Israel in French–Jewish Identity

It may be said in general that Israel provides for Diaspora Jews the elements of identity which the surrounding cultures of their various countries of residence make difficult for them to access at home. The political culture of France makes it difficult for Jews (as well as other minorities) to establish meaningful and socially effective religious and cultural communities, which are distinct from the French national culture. The political culture of France makes it difficult for Jews to establish meaningful and socially effective communities. Jews are sometimes accused of being "communitarian"; the implication being that their loyalty lies with their particular community rather than with the Republic of France; in direct conflict with Republican values. If the label of communitarian is problematic for French Jews, the label "Zionist" has even more negative connotations. The French government's foreign policy has been tilted in favor of the Arab nations and against Israel for decades, and the media portrays Israel in a very negative light. For Jews, as a community, to publicly voice a pro-Israel stance sets them in opposition to national policy and again raises questions and accusations about dual loyalty regarding a particularly emotional and controversial subject (Hyman 1998: 201).

Based on my research, it is my theory that, given the difficulty of establishing a strong local community with religious, ethnic and nationalist ties, Israel functions as a substitute community for French Jews.

To empirically illustrate this theory, I will draw on the past research of my colleagues, in addition to my own study of French volunteers to Israel during the Yom Kippur War, a decade-long international study of participants in youth tours to Israel, a comprehensive survey of the heads of French-Jewish households conducted in 2002 with a follow-up in 2005, and a study of French professionals' attitudes towards *aliyah.*

Among adolescent participants in "Israel Experience" tours, the Jewish identity of French Jews was found to be strongly related to religious practice. However, in France's strictly secular political culture, religious practice is expected to be restricted to the private realm. In Israel, Jewish religious identity permeates the culture. Tourism to Israel is wide-spread and increasing among French Jews. Visits to Israel may fulfill a function in Jewish identity which, in the USA for example, is provided by local Jewish community centres. Israel, it seems, provides a locus for religious identity repressed at home.

Supporting this finding, 53 percent of the heads of Jewish households in France said that they infrequently or never participate in local Jewish community events. In contrast, 86 percent said they feel "very close" to Israel. Forty percent of those heads of households had visited Israel within the past few years (between 2002 and 2005). In fact, many French Jews have family in Israel and have made multiple visits. Research shows that almost 20 percent are considering moving to Israel (although only 4 percent said they are planning to do so soon). A survey of French-Jewish professionals found that logistical concerns such as employment, language and family ties are greater barriers to *aliyah* than ideological concerns.

Aliyah from France has doubled in recent years to approximately 2,500 per year. While this still represents a small percentage of French Jewry it indicates a subtle shift in French Jewish identity. French Jews are committed to Republican values and patriotic to France. However, the recent rise in anti-Semitism has caused many French Jews to question their future in their home country. Sixty-five percent said the situation for Jews in France has deteriorated, and a full third of French Jews surveyed in 2005 said that they do not see themselves living in France in the next several years. The majority of these are considering *aliyah* (Cohen 2002, 2005).

Nevertheless, most French Jews are not planning on relocating. For most, Israel functions as a substitute for something lacking in a home they don't intend leaving. In other words, Israel is a "surrogate community" for French Jews.

Israel as a Surrogate Community

Nisbet (1967) defined the characteristics of a community as including, "a high degree of personal intimacy, emotional depth, moral commitment, social cohesion and continuity in time". Visiting French Jews share each of these with the Jewish community in Israel except for continuity in time. Because a permanent local Jewish community in France is restricted from reaching its full potential by the surrounding culture, Israel serves as a sort of surrogate community for French Jews. This temporary participation in the Jewish community of Israel is similar to the creation of "temporary communities" such as summer camps and retreats, which has been has been noted as a means of preserving or fostering a sense of identity among a wide variety of religious, ethnic and cultural groups (Slater 1984; Williams 2002; Warner and Witter 1998; Keysar, Kosmin and Scheckner 2000; Kozinets 2002; Eichberg 2003; Siddiqui 2004).

In a study of the images of Israel held by participants in educational group tours, adolescent Jews from France had a view of Israel which balanced elements of spirituality, home, Zionism and pragmatism (Cohen 2003). This contrasted sharply with the images held by American Jews, who saw Israel almost exclusively as a spiritual pilgrimage site. In other words, French Jewish youth were far more likely to see Israel as a potential home. This difference between the two largest Diaspora populations may be understood by differences between both the Jewish educational systems in France and the US, and the tourism patterns among the two populations. In American Jewish schools, the religious role of Israel is emphasized (Chazan 2000), while in French Jewish schools, attention is also given to study of modern Israeli culture and language. In a market survey of the Israel Experience programme, it was found that 38.8 percent of French participants had previously been to Israel with their families, compared to 18.5 percent of American participants. The group tours generally have minimal interaction with Israeli society, with much of the time spent on buses with the group, shuttling between tourist sites and scheduled activities. Participants are thus more likely to see Israel as a vacation spot or a sort of spiritual retreat. In contrast, those coming with their families, particularly if Israeli relatives are visited, are more likely to see various facets of daily life in Israel.

Sub-populations of French Jews

It is important to recognize that the French Jewish population is not homogenous. The influx of Jews from North Africa in the 1950s — 1970s greatly changed the nature of the community. Similarly, the Sephardi population itself is composed of immigrants from Morocco, Algeria and Tunisia, plus their children and grandchildren who were born in France. Table 14.2 shows differences between these sub-populations along various indicators of "attachment to Israel".

Jews from North Africa are more likely to have close family in Israel. When the former French colonies became independent and the Jewish populations left en masse, emigration was split between Israel and France. Jews born in Morocco and Tunisia were more likely to have visited Israel multiple times than those born in either Algeria or in France. Algerian Jews are the least likely to be considering *aliyah*. Those born in

France were the least likely to wish they had been born in Israel, with those born in Tunisia the most likely.

Table 14.1 Attachment to Israel, by Nation of Birth

	France	*Morocco*	*Algeria*	*Tunisia*	*Others*	*Total*
Never visited Israel	29	12	25	16	20	23
Visited Israel three or more times	48	64	45	60	49	53
Have very close family in Israel	40	65	63	66	64	55
Considering aliyah (soon, later)	24	27	15	26	37	23
Would prefer to be born in Israel	39	50	51	62	32	47

"If You Could Be Born Again . . . ", An Indicator of Jewish Identity

In the following section, I would like to elaborate on a topic introduced in the last line of table 14.1: "would prefer to be born in Israel". Asking respondents to hypothetically choose a religious and national identity provides interesting insight into attitudes and may be used as an indicator of identity. This data is particularly important because it may be analyzed in the context of responses to the same question gathered from many populations over the course of several decades.

In Horowitz's study of 10,000 (mostly Jewish) volunteers to Israel following the Six Day War (1969, 1971), respondents were asked, "If you could be born again, would you prefer to be: Jewish in your home country, Jewish in the Diaspora, non-Jewish in your home country, non-Jewish in the Diaspora, Jewish in Israel, identity and place are not important?". The Horowitz study provides the first comparative data on this question from different Diaspora communities. It constitutes a baseline, against which new data may be compared and changes tracked.

This same question was asked in a number of subsequent studies I directed. In 1983 we interviewed some 250 French Jews who had volunteered in Israel during the Yom Kippur War (1973). The majority of interviewees were male, born in North Africa and were an average of 32-years old at the time of the interview (therefore 22 when they volunteered) (Cohen 1986). In 1984, we conducted a survey among more than 500 participants of the French-speaking Israel Experience programmes in the Youth and *Hechalutz* Department. More than 90 percent were born in France. On average, they were 18 years old and the majority was female. The third survey covers 5,117 participants of the Israel Experience programmes (1993–2000) and 485 participants of the *Taglit-birthright israel* programme (2003) from around the world. Finally, this question was included in the survey of heads of French-Jewish households in 2002. The following tables present the responses to this question in these surveys. Tables 14.2 and 14.3 compare Jews from various countries; Table 4 compares only French respondents from various studies.

Among all the populations and across the thirty-five years covered in these surveys, Jewish identity is strong. The highest level of ambivalence was found among the heads of French Jewish households, 19 percent of whom said that religion and place were not important to them. This population sample was the most "general". All of the other populations consisted of individuals who chose to participate in an educational tour or volunteer programme in Israel. Of these, a tiny minority (never more than 5 percent) wished to be non-Jews. The major difference, then, is between those who were content to be Jews in the Diaspora and those who wished they had been born in Israel.

Table 14.2 *If you could be born again; what would you choose to be?* The 1967 Volunteers According to their Country of Residence (Horowitz et al. 1969)

	USA	*Western Europe*	*United Kingdom*	*South Africa*	*South America*
Jew in Home Country	47	30	29	50	23
Jew in Israel	30	47	39	25	43
Jew in Whatever Country	5	5	10	5	12
Non-Jew	2	2	3	5	3
No Answer	16	16	19	15	19
Total	100	100	100	100	100

Table 14.3 *If you could be born again, what would you wish to be?* Jewish Youth from Diaspora Visiting Israel 1993–2003: By Continent

	North America	*Western Europe*	*South America*	*Eastern Europe*	*Total*
Jewish in Home Country	61	48	57	30	56
Jewish in Israel	26	37	27	41	30
Jewish in Another Country in the Diaspora	3	6	8	8	5
Non-Jewish in Home Country	1	1	0	1	1
Non-Jewish in Another Country in the Diaspora	0	0	0	1	0
Identity and Place are of No Importance	5	5	6	17	5
Other	3	2	2	1	3
Total	100	100	100	100	100

Given the wide range of countries and long time covered in these surveys, the data is relatively stable. Not surprisingly, we see that a somewhat higher percentage of those who volunteered in Israel in 1967 said that they wished they had been born in Israel. Volunteers from the USA and South Africa were more likely to say they would choose to be born again in their home countries than those from Europe or South America. Overall, participants in the Israel Experience tours over the past decade were more likely to wish to be born again in their own home country than in Israel. Those from Eastern Europe and, as we shall see, from France, were exceptions.

Table 14.4 presents the results of various surveys I have conducted over the last twenty years. The responses to this question reveal a remarkable recurrent trait of the Jewish community in France.

Table 14.4 If you could be born again, what would you wish to be? 1973 French Jewish Volunteers Interviewed in 1983 / French Israel Experience Participants in 1984 / French Israel Experience Participants in 1993–2003 / Heads of French–Jewish Households 2002

	1973 Jewish Volunteers Interviewed in 1983	*French–Israel Experience participants in 1984*	*French–Israel Experience participants 1993–2003*	*Heads of French–Jewish Households 2002*
Jew in France*	33	29	36	42
Jew in Israel	50	54	57	38
Non-Jew in Diaspora	0	0	0	0
Identity and Place are of No Importance	9	3	7	19
Other	7	8	0	1
No answer	1	5	0	0
Total	100	100	100	100

* Less than 2 percent of respondents specified that they would prefer to be Jews in a Diaspora country other than France

Of those who joined tours or programmes to Israel, at least half said they would have preferred to have been born as Israeli Jews. This percentage has increased over the past two decades. The percentage among the general Jewish population is somewhat lower, but is still quite high at 38 percent. It is particularly telling to note the graphic difference between the participants in Israel Experience tours from France and from other countries: 57 percent of the French participants said they wish they could have been born as Israeli Jews, by far the highest percentage in the world.

Summary

How can we understand this strong desire expressed by French Jews to be Israeli? First, we should stress that this question is hypothetical: it does not reflect an actual intention to become an Israeli citizen, and it bypasses practical considerations such as starting a new profession or moving far from family. Nevertheless, it gives insight into the central question of this article: the place of Israel in French–Jewish identity. Many French Jews, particularly young French Jews who have visited Israel, would prefer to be Israeli. Why?

I suggest that being born again as a Jew in Israel would resolve the contradictions inherent in the increasingly difficult socio-political situation in France. If French Jews express a strong identification with the Jewish community they risk being accused of being "communitarian". If they express solidarity with Israel, their loyalty to France may be called into question, particularly given the anti-Israel sentiment prevalent in France today. French Jews face social pressures and conflicts not felt (or less strongly felt) in other Diaspora countries. Their wish to be re-born in Israel may well express a desire to sidestep these difficulties.

Acknowledgements

Thanks to Allison Ofanansky for her editorial contribution in the preparation of this chapter.

Notes

1 As France does not keep statistics on its citizens' religious affiliation, there are no official records of the number of Muslims in France. Estimates range from as low as three million to as high as ten million. The French High Counsel on Immigration estimates between four and six million Muslims live in France (Haut Conseil à l'Intégration 2001). The Minister of the Interior Nicholas Sarkozy estimates between five and six million (Charles and Lahouri 2003). Zuhair Mahmood, director of the European Institute of Human Sciences and Danielle Hervieux-Léger, director of the Center for Interdisciplinary Religious Studies (Hervieux-Léger 2001; Religioscope 2002) estimate between five and seven million Muslims live in France. The vast majority are of North African origin.

2 Around this time international air travel became more widely available, facilitating the growth of Jewish tourism to Israel.

References

Bensimon, D. & Della Pergola, S., *La population juive de France : Socio-démographie et identité.* Jewish Population Studies No 17. (Paris-Jérusalem: The Institute of Contemporary Jewry, The Hebrew University of Jerusalem and Centre National de la Recherche Scientifique, 1986).

Charles, G. & Lahouri, B. (2003). "Les vrais chiffres". In *L'Express*, 4 December 2003. Viewed online 29 August 2005, at: <http://www.lexpress.fr/info/societe/ dossier/mosquees/ dossier.asp?ida=415633>.

Chazan, B., "Through a glass darkly: Israel in the mirror of American Jewish education". In: A Gal & A Gottschalk (eds), *Beyond Survival and Philanthropy: American Jewry and Israel* (Cincinnati, OH: Hebrew Union College Press, 2000).

Cohen, E. H., *Les volontaires juifs de France vers Israel durant la guerre de Kippour, Contribution à l'étude des relations Israel-Diaspora.* Dissertation submitted for the degree of Doctor of Philosophy (Paris: University de Nanterre, June 1986).

Cohen E. H., *Les Juifs de France: valeurs et identité* (Paris: Fonds Social Juif Unifié, 2002).

Cohen, E. H., "Images of Israel: A structural comparison along gender, ethnic, denominational and national lines". *Tourist Studies* 3, 3 (2003): 253–280.

Cohen E. H,. *Touristes Juifs de France en 2004* (Paris-Jérusalem: Alya et Meilleure Intégration, 2005).

Eichberg, H. (2003). "Playing and Displaying Identity: About Bodily Movement, Political Ideologies and the Question of Olympic Humanism". Paper presented at the Academy of Physical Education and Sport as contribution to the first Eurobaltic Academy of Sports Humanism, Gdansk, June 2003.

Haut Conseil à l'Intégration, *L'Islam dans la République* (Paris: La Documentation Française, 2001).

Hervieu-Léger, D. (2001). *L'état des religions en France, Analyses et réflexions, Archives du premier ministre.* Viewed online 29 August 2005 at: <www.archives.premier-ministre.gouv.fr>.

Horowitz, T., Cialic, M., and Hodara, J., *Volunteers for Israel In the Wake of the Six Day War: Their Motives and Work Careers* (Jerusalem: Henrietta Szold Institute, 1969) (in Hebrew).

Horowitz, T. et al., "Volunteers for Israel during the Six Day War: Their Motives and Work Careers". *Dispersion and Unity*, 13–14 (1971): 68–115.

Hyman, P., *The Jews of Modern France: Jewish Communities of the Modern World* (Berkeley: University of California Press, 1998).

Keysar, A., Kosmin, B., and Scheckner, J. (2000). *The Next Generation: Jewish Children and Adolescents*. Albany, NY: State University of New York Press.

Kozinets, Robert V. (2002). "Can consumers escape the market? Emancipatory illuminations from Burning Man". *Journal of Consumer Research*, 29: 20–38.

Nisbet, R. A., *The Sociological Tradition* (London: Heinemann Educational Books, 1967), p. 47.

Religioscope (2002). "Notre patrie , c'est la France". Interview with Zuhair Mahmood in *Religioscope*, 18 May 2002. Viewed online 29 August 2005 at: <http://www.religioscope.com/info/articles/015_islam_france_c.htm>.

Siddiqui, S. (2004). *Reward Your Kids with a Muslim Camp this Summer*. Viewed online 29 August 2005 at: <http://www.soundvision.com/info/misc/summer/sum.camp.asp>.

Slater, T., *The Temporary Community: Organized Camping for Urban Society* (Northampton, MA: Albatross Books, 1984).

Warner, S. and Witter, J. (eds), *Gatherings in Diaspora: Religious Communities and the New Immigration* (Philadelphia: Temple University Press, 1998).

Williams, B. (2002). *Theological Perspectives on the Temporary Community: Camping and the Church*. Wheaton College. Viewed online 29 August 2005 at: <http://www.cci.org.au/pdf/Christian-Camping-and-the-Church.pdf>.

World Jewish Congress. (1998). *The Jewish Population of the World*. Lerner Publication Company. Viewed online 25 August 2005 at: <http://www.jewishvirtuallibrary.org/jsource/Judaism/jewpop.html>.

15

Identity with Israel from Afar: The Australian Story

Suzanne D. Rutland

The history of Australian Jewry is relatively short. The first Jews arrived as convicts in 1788: Jews have been present from the beginnings of white settlement.

As a small community, Australian Jewry has struggled to maintain its Jewish identity for much of its history. However, the nature and structure of the community changed dramatically as a result of the impact of pre-and post-World War II refugee and survivor immigration. The survivors brought about a rebirth of Jewish life in Australia, radically changing every aspect of communal structure and institutions and bringing with them a strong commitment to Zionism.

Since 1960, the community has been further reinforced by migration of Jews from South Africa, the former Soviet Union, and Israel. Today the community numbers around 105,000, with around 50,000 in Melbourne, 40,000 in Sydney, 6,500 each in Perth, 3,500 in Brisbane, 3,000 on the Gold Coast and Queensland, and much smaller centres in Adelaide, Canberra and Hobart.[1] Identification with Israel is one of the key features of present day Australian Jewry.

Vibrancy of Australia Zionism in the Twenty-first Century

On any specific criteria, Australia ranks high in terms of Zionist endeavour and commitment. This includes *aliyah* rates, visits to Israel, the level of fund-raising, Zionist education and youth movements, and Australian Zionist leadership in Israel. In what many see as the post-Zionist era, Australian Jewry is one of the last bastions of traditional Zionism. The community maintains a plethora of Zionist organizations, all of which are affiliated with State Zionist Councils that act as coordinating bodies. They in turn are represented in the Zionist Federation of Australia (ZFA),[2] together with representatives of major federal organizations such as the United Israel Appeal and the Jewish National Fund. The Federation was the first communal federal body to be established at a national level in 1927. It has attracted strong leadership both in terms of its lay leaders and also its executive personnel, and it has developed an effective infrastructure within Australia. This is largely due to its stress on educational endeavours that in recent years have focused not only on the Zionist youth movements but also on the day schools. As a result, it is probably the only genuine Diaspora Zionist Federation left.

In 1992 John Goldlust conducted a major study of Melbourne Jewry. His survey revealed strong support for Israel through a number of different questions. In response to a question of how respondents would feel if Israel was in danger, 28 percent replied "as strong as if danger was to self" while more than half (58 percent) replied that they would feel "special alarm because it is Israel". Of the remaining respondents, 12 percent stated they would feel more concerned than if it was another country while only 2 percent replied that they would feel the "same as if any country was in danger".[3]

The strongest index of identification with Israel can be seen with those who would choose to live in Israel, if not living in Australia. Australian *aliyah* rates have been high compared to those of other western countries, with 10,000 Australian Jews, 10 percent of the community, making the commitment to *aliyah*.[4] While over half of the respondents in the Goldlust survey would choose to live in Israel, a much higher proportion had visited Israel at least once. Only a quarter (27 percent) of the respondents had never visited Israel; another quarter had visited Israel once; 26 percent had visited Israel between two to three times; and a further 22 percent had been there more than four times. Length of stay is also significant, and of all Australian Jews who had visited Israel, over half had spent more than two months there. The major reasons given for visiting Israel were as tourists (42 percent), and to visit family (41 percent). Eighteen percent of the respondents had been residents at one time in Israel. Most Australian Jews have strong ties with Israel, as 72 percent of respondents indicated that they had either close family or friends living there.[5]

Goldlust's survey found that a slightly higher proportion of the younger, Australian-born respondents had actually been to visit Israel when compared with the older age groups. This younger age group had participated in Israel-based programmes through school, Zionist youth movement programmes or the Australasian Union of Jewish Students (AUJS).[6] The AUJS has become a very significant body in organizing Israel programmes for university students, with between 200–280 participants each year. In recent years the community has been committed to providing some funding for these Israel programmes, which in the past year has culminated in funding for the *birthright israel* programmes. Thus, the major goal of *birthright israel* — that is, to ensure that all Jewish youth visit Israel at least once — has been part of the philosophy of Australian Jewry for many years. The high percentage of Australian Jews who have visited Israel is even more significant when the length of the flight and the costs of the journey are taken into account. A trip to Israel from Australia is a minimum flying time of 23 hours, and costs over Aus$2,000 (US$1200–1500). Even so, a significant percentage of the 18–39 age group had visited Israel more than once.

With its focus on the suffering of German Jewry during the late 1930s, Zionist fund-raising in Australia became "a pattern of normative community activity"[7]. Since 1948 fund-raising has remained the central focus for Australian Zionism through the two main agencies, *Keren Hayesod* (United Israel Appeal (UIA)) and *Keren Keyemet*

(Jewish National Fund (JNF)). The UIA conducts a major appeal annually, and usually brings a few key emissaries, mainly from Israel, to Australia to lead the appeal. The importance of the UIA in terms of Jewish identification and pride in Israel's achievements cannot be underestimated, with major appeals attracting audiences of up to 4,000 in Sydney and Melbourne, and over 1,000 in Perth. The JNF conducts its activities throughout the year with Blue Box and *Simcha* collections, and the promotion of specific projects. Recently, it has initiated two major annual events — Green Sunday associated with *Tu B'Shvat* to raise funds for the environment (with some of the funds also going towards tree planting in Australia), and a major appeal dinner in November to raise funds for specific Australian JNF projects in Israel.[8] In terms of overall monies raised for the Jewish Agency, the World Zionist Organization (WZO) in Israel, and UIA and JNF in Australia, raise the highest per capita and, after the USA, are the next best in gross collections, with the only possible "challengers" being Canada and Mexico. But in what is called "united" or "free" money Australian Jewry definitely raises the highest amounts after the USA.[9]

Zionist education and youth work have developed into a central part of Zionist endeavours. Since 1948 Jewish education has been supported "in order to unite the Diaspora with the State of Israel".[10] The Zionist youth movements, still largely based on the political ideologies pre-dating 1948 (*Betar*, *B'nei Akiva*, *Habonim Dror*, and *Hashomer Hatzair*) continue to play a significant role in education and facilitating *aliyah*.[11] Two new movements have emerged more recently — *Netzer*, the Reform Zionist Youth Movement, and *Hineni*. The development of *Hineni* is particularly interesting as this organization started as a synagogue youth group associated with the Central Synagogue, Sydney, in the 1970s. Over time it has developed a modern, religious Zionist ideology and in the 1990s was reconstituted as a Zionist youth movement with branches in Sydney and Melbourne. While *Hineni* is a religious movement it appeals to traditional young Jews who are not as strictly religious in their observance as *B'nei Akiva* members, who have moved much more towards the religious right in recent years. Thus, the *Hineni* ideology has more appeal to mainstream Australian Jewish youth as representing a combination of Jewish tradition and Zionism, which reflects the majority position of Australian Jewry. While world *B'nei Akiva* is apolitical, Australian BA leans strongly to the right, consistent with its sister movement in Israel, both of which feel a connection to the National Religious Party (NRP). On the other hand, *Hineni* is genuinely apolitical, although if anything its members lean to the left along *Meimad* lines.

As the youth movements grew, they received their own *shlichim*. The arrival of young Zionist emissaries from Israel dedicated to the Zionist cause played an important part in education, as well as helping to break down the barriers produced by Australia's isolation. Thanks to the lobbying of Federation president, Dr Ron Weiser, there are at present 11 *shlichim* in Australia, serving communities across the nation. They are involved in the running of regular weekly meetings and annual camps held in both the winter and summer at state and national levels.

The various youth movements are also combined in an umbrella organization, the Australian Zionist Youth Council, which alternates its headquarters between Melbourne and Sydney.[12] From its inception, *Machon L'Madrichei Hutz L'Aretz* (Institute for Jewish Leaders from Abroad) has been the most important training programme for the future leadership of Australian Jewry. In the mid 1990s, Shlomo

Gravitz, then head of the Youth and *HeChalutz* department of the Jewish Agency, noted that of the 770 participants in *Machon* each year, around 100 come from Australia. In recent years the number of leadership programmes has been extended and while numbers were low in 2001–2002 because of the Intifada, they are again on the rise.

Another form of identification with Israel is sport. Since 1950, when there was one lone Australian participant, tennis player Eliyahu Honig, Australia has been sending participants to the Maccabi Games. In 1997 at the 15th Maccabia, Australia sent its biggest contingent ever, with over 400 participants, only to be met with disaster. The bridge that had been built across the Yarkon River collapsed as the team was marching across it for the opening ceremony. Four participants died — Lilly Bennett, Elizabeth Sawicki, Greg Small, and Warren Zines — while a fifth, schoolgirl Sasha Elterman, has undergone a series of operations because of the effects of the pollution of the river on her lungs. The Australian team decided that, despite the tragedy, they would continue to participate. Since their return, Australian Maccabi leaders and the Federation have faced a frustrating battle with World Maccabi.[13] It took until 2004 for all outstanding issues relating to compensation to be resolved. Yet, despite this disaster, Australian Jewry's commitment to Israel has not weakened. President of the Federation, Dr Weiser, has been indefatigable in his fight for justice for the Maccabi victims, but he has in no way slackened his campaign for continued support of Israel.

Australian Zionists have also increased their presence in the Zionist leadership in Israel. In 1978, Robert Zablud was the first Australian national president to be elected to the World Zionist presidium. Then, in 1988, Mark Leibler was the first Zionist leader outside the United States to be elected to the executive of the WZO. Subsequently, ZFA presidents, first Ann Zablud and then Dr Ron Weiser, have been elected to the Jewish Agency's Board of Governors.[14] For a small community numbering only 105,000, this is clear recognition of its ongoing contribution to the Zionist endeavour. In 2004, Perth-born Greg Masel was appointed as the executive director of *Keren Hayesod* in Jerusalem.

Not only have Australian Zionists come to make a contribution to world leadership, but they have also played a key role in the general Australian Jewish leadership and, indeed, could be seen as dominating that leadership. Many of the presidents of the Executive Council of Australian Jewry (ECAJ) began their careers in the Zionist movement, particularly in Sydney. For example, Louis Klein was chairman of UIA before becoming president of the ECAJ, Nathan Jacobsen was president of both the ZFA and the ECAJ, and Diane Shteinman was very active in Women's International Zionist Organisation (WIZO) before becoming ECAJ president. Probably the most outstanding Australian Jewish leader on the world scene is Isi Leibler, who went on *aliyah* to Israel in 1995, whilst his brother who still lives in Australia was ZFA president and today heads the powerful Jewish lobby group, Australia Israel Jewish Affairs Council (AIJAC).

Reasons for Australian Jewish Support of Zionism

The Effects of the Holocaust

To understand Australian Jewry's strong attachment to Israel, the historical context must be borne in mind. While Australian Jews had strongly opposed Zionism until the 1930s, attitudes changed significantly with the events of the 1930s and the Holocaust. For example, Nazi racist theories led the journalist Eric Baume, himself an assimilated Jew, to declare as early as 1936 that:

> Hitler had given the Jews of every country in the world a startling lesson of what not to do.
> He has indicated that even in a violently anti-Semitic country it is better to be a Jew courageously than to avoid or seek to avoid the menace of anti-Semitism by the often attempted movement towards assimilation . . . The Jew who is ashamed of being a Jew has no place not only in the Jewish community but anywhere in the world . . .
> The answer to Hitler's challenge does not lie in wild talking or empty vain threats. The challenge to every Jew can only be answered by the thought of the Zionist movement.[15]

The mass influx of European immigrants into Australia between 1938 and 1961 brought an even stronger commitment to Zionism. As victims of anti-Semitism, they were keenly aware of the need for a Jewish homeland to provide a refuge from persecution. They also brought with them their own experience of involvement in European Zionist organizations.[16]

The Impact of the Arab–Israeli Wars

Any remaining suspicion of Zionism was overcome with the impact of the 1967 and 1973 wars between Israel and the Arabs. Throughout the Jewish world there was a spontaneous and immediate response to the 1967 crisis. The Australian Jewish community was no exception. In Melbourne, out of a community at the time of 34,000, 7,000 attended a public rally called at the outbreak of the fighting, while a further 2,500 attended a youth rally held in the same week.[17] Similarly, in Sydney, over 6,000 people crowded into the Central Synagogue and its surrounds, while in both cities hundreds of Jewish youth volunteered to go to Israel.[18] A 1967 study of Melbourne Jewry found that most people interviewed reacted with a sense of deep emotional upset, listening to the news much more often than usual and seeking social contacts with family and Jewish friends.[19] In addition, those Jews who were fairly assimilated into the general community or who were not active in communal organizations were, in the main, just as affected. These feelings were further reinforced by the Yom Kippur War of 1973.[20]

While feelings during the invasion of Lebanon in 1982 were more ambivalent, the Gulf War of 1990–1 had a direct impact on Australian Jews, who found themselves and their institutions under attack. In Sydney, during the period of the war and its immediate aftermath, five synagogues were attacked by arson. Similarly in Melbourne, Jewish communal buildings were attacked with graffiti and there was a bomb alert during one of the key rallies. To date, no one in Sydney has been arrested and charged with these attacks.[21]

The Growth of Multiculturalism

Another major factor in Zionist identification has been the growth of multiculturalism, which has resulted in a major transformation of Australian society. Until World War II, Australia's migration policy was 98 percent Anglo-Celtic. However, the threat of the Japanese invasion during World War II and Australia's vulnerability due to her small population led to a radical reassessment, with European migration being encouraged and a Department of Immigration being established in 1945. At first the government advocated Anglo-Saxon conformity from the newcomers, encouraging them to assimilate as quickly as possible. Gradually, political leaders became aware of the advantages of pluralism, which was fostered for the first time during the Labour leadership of Gough Whitlam.[22] In 1973, he established a Committee on Community Relations, chaired by a German Jewish refugee, Walter Lippmann of Melbourne. Its recommendations included the concept that:

> For migrants to feel secure in their adopted country, they need firstly to feel secure in their emotional attachment to the cultural values that influence their behaviour . . . Ethnic groups therefore should be seen to be a vital and integral part of the total community structure. They have a duty to preserve their own cultural heritage and an important role to play in the integration of their members into the total community.[23]

These attitudes were reinforced under Malcolm Fraser, who as a Liberal Prime Minister became a strong supporter of multiculturalism. Acknowledgement of different ethnic identities made support for Zionism acceptable within the Australian framework.

Jewish Day Schools and Zionist Education

The growth of Jewish day schools has also fostered Australian Zionism. In Melbourne, up to 75 percent of Jewish children attend Jewish schools, and in Sydney the figure is 62 percent. Most Jewish day schools in Australia foster support for Israel, particularly through informal education programmes. These include the Israel Study Tour (IST), which was introduced by Moriah College in Sydney in 1984, for Year Ten students (aged 15–16). Over the years IST has become an integral part of the Sydney Jewish high school programme, having a powerful impact on its participants. As an experiential education programme, it enabled Jewish Studies to come alive. Spending time in Israel is also very emotional for many students, especially when Israel is experienced, often for the first time, with their peers. The social factors are also very important. The students are away from home, usually for the first time, creating a sense of adventure and freedom.[24]

Another important development in the 1980s was the introduction of the Zionist Seminars, known was *mifgashim* (meetings), for Year 9 students of Jewish schools.[25] These seminars were introduced in 1985 and incorporated a variety of techniques such as values clarifications, films, role play and drama presentations.[26] As the Jewish press reported, "Israel was recreated in a northern Sydney suburb [Pennant Hills] for 140 Year Nine Masada and Moriah College students".[27] The programme was considered to be very beneficial and has become an ongoing part of the informal Jewish education programme of Jewish high schools in Australia.

The introduction of the Zionist seminars and IST reinforced the Counterpoint programme that had started for Years 10 and 11 in the 1970s. In 1981, Moriah principal Lionel Link advocated that a team of *madrichim* (youth leaders) from the Torah Department in Israel should be used instead of the Yeshiva University team from New York. He argued that using staff a team from Israel "will provide a much needed Israel overtone to the seminar".[28] Since that time, Israeli *teams madrichim* have been used for Jewish schools across Australia. The combination of Zionist Seminar in Year 9, Counterpoint in Year 10, IST at the end of Year 10, and Counterpoint in Year 11 has proved to be a very powerful combination.[29] These informal education programmes, reinforced for a large percentage of students with programmes in Israel after completing matriculation, have produced a younger generation with strong Israel identification.

Newer Immigrant Waves: Russians and South Africans

Holocaust survivors' pro-Israel orientation has been reinforced by the more recent waves of immigrants from South Africa, the former Soviet Union and Israel. When Russian Jews feel that Israel is under attack, they will come out to express their support. In April 2002, Sydney Jewry held one of the largest ever pro-Israel demonstrations seen in Australia, outside the Israeli consulate in the city. It was estimated that between 5,000 and 10,000 Jews and non-Jewish supporters attended the rally, with a very noticeable contingent of Russian Jews present.[30]

The situation with South African Jews is more complex. South African support of Zionism was strong, with 89 percent of respondents to the recent Jewish Agency survey donating to Israel.[31] The more established South African Jews in Perth are seen as particularly vital to Zionist activities in the community. However, overall, South Africans have tended to be more involved with *shul* (synagogue) and school, and less involved with the Jewish Board of Deputies and the Zionist organizations.

Israel as an "Insurance Policy"

In a recent interview, former chairman of UIA, Avraham Avi-hai, commented that in terms of Israel and the Diaspora, "there are two types of Jewish communities: those who believe that Israel needs them, such as American Jewry, and those who believe they need Israel. Australian Jewry fits into the latter category, as most Australian Jews, whether refugees, survivors or more recent migrants, are very aware of Israel's importance for them as a possible refuge". The issue of distance, with Australia being on "the edge of the Diaspora", reinforces this sense of need.[32]

The Growth of Terrorism and the Cycle of Violence

Until recently, anti-Semitism has not been a major issue in Australia and Australian Zionism. *Aliyah* has related resulted fromto a strong community sense of the need for a Jewish homeland, and of the importance of supporting Israel after the *Shoah*. As discussed above, during the First Gulf War of 1990–1991, many Jewish institutions were attacked. In the subsequent decade, the Jewish community's sense of insecurity has increased and they have felt the need to develop a systems of internal communal security, to levels which are not needed by any other religious or ethnic group in Australia. Since September 11, there has been a world-wide increase of anti-Semitic attacks on both individual Jews and Jewish communal institutions, and this has included Australian Jewry. Many commentators worldwide feel that the honeymoon that Jews experienced after the Holocaust, when anti-Semitism was condemned at a global level, is over.

The ongoing cycle of violence in Israel, with increasing condemnation of Israel by world powers and left-wing intellectuals in Australia, particularly on campus, has added to the sense of embattlement amongst the Jewish community. The impact, especially on Jewish university students, has been threefold. For some, it has intensified their Jewish and Israel commitment and activism; while others have been too afraid to speak out or take action. A third group have become disillusioned with Israeli policies, resulting in an alienation from the established Jewish community which tends to oppose open dissent with Israeli policies. It is difficult to estimate the size of the last "anti-Israel" group or its significance for the future of the community.

Since the outbreak of the Al-Aqsa Intifada in September 2000, the majority of Australian Jewry has regularly expressed its strong support for Israel.

The Australian Government's Support for the Jewish State

The story of the relationship between the Australian government and the Jewish state is a complex one, which has been recently analyzed by Dr Chanan Reich in a book entitled *An Ambiguous Relationship*. Reich has shown that successive Australian governments have not always totally supported every action of Israel.[33] Despite the ambiguities in the official relationships, and specific tensions over the years, the overall sense within Australian Jewry is that from the days of Dr Herbert Vere Evatt, Labour Minister for External Affairs, 1944 to 1949, to John Howard, Liberal Prime Minister in government since 1995, Australia has been extremely supportive of the Jewish state, whilst also advocating the two-state solution to the Palestinian problem.

Under the leadership of Dr Evatt, Australia is seen as having played a central role in the events leading up to the establishment of the State of Israel. Australia was one of the fifteen nations constituting the United Nations Special Committee on Palestine (UNSCOP), which recommended either partition or the creation of a unitary state. In the UNSCOP vote on these proposals, Australia abstained on Evatt's instructions. Following this, an Ad Hoc Committee on Palestine was formed, with all the member states of the UN represented. Dr Evatt, who had hoped to become chairman of the United Nations General Assembly but had been defeated by Dr Aranha of Brazil, was invited instead to chair the Ad Hoc Committee, which voted on the two proposals on 25 November 1947. While a majority of 25, including Australia, voted for, there were 13 against and 17 abstentions (including New Zealand and some South American countries). In the intervening four days before the crucial General Assembly crucial vote, New Zealand was lobbied to change its position[34] and Evatt requested the United Nations Secretary-General, Trygve Lie, to ask the United Nations Chairman, Aranha, to persuade the Latin American countries to support partition because, as he urged, "the choice now is between a complete washout and a positive solution".[35] A two-thirds majority for partition was required and each vote was vital. On 29 November,

33 member nations supported the proposal, including Australia, 13 opposed the proposal and nine abstained from casting a vote on Resolution 181, which would have created two states, Arab and Jewish, with Jerusalem under international control.

On Evatt's return to Australia he was given a tremendous ovation at a dinner organized by the Zionist Federation and attended by over 400 people. All speakers paid tribute to the key role he had played in the historic decision. Bishop Pilcher complimented Dr Evatt's "typically Australian feat of horsemanship in bringing home 57 refractory steeds".[36] When the USA sought to overturn the decision by proposing a trusteeship for Palestine in early 1948, Evatt strongly opposed the American change of front, insisting that, "the decision of a competent international conference should be accepted after there has been a full and fair debate, and a settlement has been reached".[37] Evatt also continued to be highly critical of British policy regarding Israel.[38] In 1948, when United Nations Mediator, Count Folke Bernadotte, recommended that the Negev be ceded to the Arabs and restrictions be imposed on Jewish immigration to Israel, Australia again strongly objected.[39]

On 15 May 1948, David Ben-Gurion declared Israel an independent state but the new country was immediately faced with a struggle to remain alive. The British government placed pressure on Australia not to recognise the new State immediately and diplomatic relations were only established on 29 January 1949, when Australia extended both *de facto* and *de jure* recognition, even though Britain only extended *de facto* recognition.[40] Evatt was chairman of the United Nations General Assembly when Israel was admitted as a member. In May 1949, Aubrey (Abba) S. Eban, Israel's representative to the United Nations acknowledged Evatt's key role in the UN.[41]

Since 1949, most official policy statements of Australian governments (both Liberal and Labour) on Australia–Israel relations have been based on the position developed by Evatt in the key period from 1947 to 1949.[42] The so-called Whitlam years (1972–1975) was the main period which deviated from this policy. When Labour leader, Gough Whitlam, was elected, he introduced what he called a more "even-handed policy" which was seen as highly controversial in the Jewish community.[43] When Liberal leader, Malcolm Fraser, became Prime Minister, he reverted to the more traditional stance on Israel and supported Australia participating in the multinational peace keeping force in the Sinai. The years of Robert J. Hawke's leadership (1983–1991) were more controversial, but Hawke's strong personal commitment to Israel was well known. When he had been selected as the first Sam Cohen Memorial Lecturer in 1971, and went to Israel, he had said he had "a general knowledge about Israel, but no particular interest". His visit was to completely change this for, from the moment of his arrival, "Hawke and Israel were *en rapport*".[44] Whilst the UN voting record of his government caused concern, the perception of Hawke as a true friend of Israel remained strong within the Jewish community.[45]

The UN resolution, "Zionism is Racism", passed in 1975, was one issue where the Australian government played a key role on a bipartisan basis. Under the effective leadership of Zionist Federation president, Mark Leibler, the community was able to influence the Australian federal parliament to pass a resolution in 1986 demanding that the UN rescind this motion. Australia's resolution became a model for other western countries, and with effective campaigning by the World Jewish Congress president, Edgar Bronfman, assisted by Australian Isi Leibler's contacts in the Far East and the Pacific, this resolution was rescinded by the UN General Assembly in 1993

— the only time this has occurred in the history of the UN. The key role played by Australian leadership, both general and Jewish, further reinforced Australian Zionist identity.

Under the Howard government, Australia has opposed anti-Israel resolutions at the United Nations. Australia has supported Israel's right to construct a security fence, whilst campaigning that the route be changed to run closer to the "green line". Thus, there is no conflict between the official government position and the Australian leadership of the Australian Jewish community, further reinforcing the Zionist endeavour.

Dissent with Israel

The official leadership of the Jewish community in Australia has taken a very strong position on the issue of public dissent with policies of the Israeli government by members of the Jewish community. The line that is generally taken within the community is that Jews living outside of Israel do not have the right to criticise actions of the Israeli government in public because they are not facing the security issues and military difficulties of Israel.

The problem of dissent has been more difficult during the periods of Likud governments, when left-wing members of the Jewish community have been highly critical of the Likud government. Conflict first emerged during the Lebanon war of 1982, when divisions also appeared within Israeli society for the first time. Groups such as Paths to Peace, and later, the Australian Jewish Democratic Society in Melbourne and the Women in Black, have supported the position of the Israeli left, such as *Shalom Achshav* (Peace Now) and have openly criticized Israeli policies (see chapter by Mendes). When the AJDS sought to affiliate with the Jewish Community Council of Victoria, its application in 1987 was at first rejected.[46] For a number of Jewish feminists, their struggle for "*tikun olam*" includes campaigning against what they see as Israeli oppression of the Palestinians.[47] Thus, to portray Australian Jewry as being in total support of Israel would be incorrect, but these left-wing dissenters only constitute a small minority of the community.

More recently, right-wing dissent in relation to the disengagement has also been evident (for example, with Dr Danny Lamm, president of the State Zionist Council of Victoria (SZCV)). Dr Lamm, who expressed his personal opposition to Ariel Sharon's policy, was previously president of Melbourne Mizrachi, the religious right modern Orthodox community that reflects the NRP. Furthermore, 33 *Chabad* rabbis published a signed full-page protest against the disengagement in the *Australian Jewish News*. On 7 August 2005 (one week prior to the official date of disengagement), a formal debate was organized by the SZCV, with the aim of providing the community with an opportunity to hear both sides of the issue. The SZCV stated that: "As the roof body of Zionist organizations in Victoria, the SZCV sees it as its fundamental role to allow for open discussion in the community on critical issues about Israel. Whilst the SZCV supports the official Israeli government of the day and its policies, it is aware of the diverse political views within the community".[48]

Thus, not only the Left but also the Right have "shattered the notion of automatic support for the Israeli government, which can no longer be guaranteed as a core feature of the Australian Jewish relationship with Israel". A survey conducted by

Danny Ben-Moshe showed that the younger generation of Australian Jews are not as unconditionally committed to Zionism and Israel as their parents were.[49]

A key issue is the teaching of the reality of Israel — including the Arab–Israeli Conflict — as opposed to what one researcher, David Bryfman, calls "mythical Israel" — an idealised version of Israeli history. Recent studies have demonstrated that most Jewish day schools take a very conservative approach to this issue, with only a minority choosing to broaden the syllabus to deal with the realities. This has occurred in a Year 11 elective course taught at Moriah College, but the decision to include criticisms of Israel led to a strong attack on the school from the Zionist leadership. Bryfman has argued that this neglect of the realities will have negative repercussions for Jewish day school graduates. He asks:

> The question that needs to be pondered by Jewish-Zionist educators is what type of education best serves the ultimate pedagogic desired outcomes for students. Will the teaching of a mythical Israel fill students with an affinity to the perfect Jewish state? Or, will teaching some of the harsher realities of Israel's past and present turn students away from wanting to identify with Israel?[50]

In answer to this question, Bryfman argues in support of teaching a broadened curriculum, including the arguments of the post-Zionists, on the basis that it will better prepare students to cope with anti-Zionism on campus. Ultimately, he says, a balanced presentation of the issues will enhance the students' Jewish identity, rather than the opposite. This issue has become more prominent since the start of the Al-Aqsa Intifada, with Jewish day school students becoming exposed to negative criticism of Israel and Zionism in the media.

Summary

Historian Bernard Hyams wrote of the apathy of Australian Jewry in the 1920s as hindering the development of Zionism in Australia. In the intervening period, the situation for Australian Jewry has changed dramatically. Due both to external factors, with post Holocaust and more recent waves of immigration, and internal factors, such as multiculturalism and Australian government policies, Australian Jewry strongly identifies with Zionism and at every level of commitment has one of the highest profiles of any Diaspora community. However, current research indicates that there is a greater questioning of this total support for Israel from the younger generation.

Notes

1 Most demographic information on Australian Jewry in this article is based on the government census carried out every five years — the last three being in 1991, 1996 and 2001 — combined with studies sponsored by the Jewish community. The two most recent community studies are: for Melbourne, John Goldlust's, *The Jews of Melbourne: A Community Profile* (Melbourne: Jewish Welfare Society Inc, 1993) with the support of the Jewish Welfare Society (now called Jewish Community Services); and for Sydney, Gary Eckstein's, *Sydney Jewish Community Demographic Profile* (Sydney: New South Wales Jewish Communal Appeal (JCA), May 1999). In 2004 the Jewish Community Council of Victoria produced a CD-ROM with the demographic profile of the Victorian Jewish Community based on the 2001 census. Other demographic studies include those undertaken by Professors W.D. Rubinstein and Sol Encel. There has been much debate about

the findings of these various demographers, largely because of significant under-enumeration; many Jews being reluctant to declare themselves "Jewish" on the census forms, thus making it difficult to draw definitive conclusions. There is significant debate over the reasons for under-enumeration. Some argue that it is a result of the large percentage of Holocaust survivors being reluctant to declare themselves as "Jewish" on a government form, whilst others argue that under-enumeration is a result of the younger, more assimilated Jews not being interested in registering themselves as "Jewish". The 2001 census put the Jewish population of Australia at 84,000, but communal sources estimate that there are around 105,000 Jews. The 20 percent used to allow for the under-enumeration factor has been verified by checking the census data with communal statistics for funerals and *barmitzvahs*.

2 The Zionist Federation was created in 1927. A detailed history was published to mark its seventieth anniversary in 1997. See Bernard Hyams, *The History of the Australian Zionist Movement* (South Caulfield, Melbourne: Zionist Federation of Australia, 1998). See also Eliyahu Honig, *Zionism in Australia, 1920–1939, The Formative Years* (Sydney: Mandelbaum Publishing, Series in Judaica, No 7, 1997).

3 Goldlust, *The Jews of Melbourne*, p. 157.

4 It is difficult to estimate the exact number of Australians who have made *aliyah*. In 1967–1968 more than 400 Australians made *aliyah*. The highest level of Australian *aliyah* was in the 1970s; during the 1980s the level, while still impressive, was 50 percent of the 1970s level; and there was a slight increase in the 1990s. Since the outbreak of the Al-Aqsa Intifada in 2000, *aliyah* figures have stood at only around 100 a year. Frank Stein, who runs the Zionist Federation of Australia's Israel office, believes that the rough number of around 10,000 having made *aliyah* since 1948 is correct — that is, 10 percent of the total estimated Australian Jewish population of 105,000 in 2005. An Association of Australian *Olim* was established in the 1970s. Australians have enjoyed dual citizenship except for a period in the mid-1980s when the citizenship law was changed. Following protests from the Jewish community, dual citizenship was restored for Australian citizens who have settled in Israel. See Hyams, *The History of the Australian Zionist Movement*, pp. 153–4.

5 Ibid., p. 155.

6 Ibid., pp. 156–7.

7 Honig, *Zionism in Australia, 1920–1939*, pp. 101–2.

8 In addition, there are a number of specific Zionist organizations such as Youth *Aliyah*, *Magen David Adom* (Israeli Red Cross), Friends of Hebrew University, Friends of the Technion, Friends of Tel Aviv University and Friends of Bar Ilan. WIZO supports fund-raising activities and Zionist education, and has a substantial membership involving many women in Zionist work, while the National Council of Jewish Women devotes significant time to raising funds for its Israel projects. The Australia–Israel Chamber of Commerce and Industry, with branches in Melbourne and Sydney, assists in the development of trade between the two countries.

9 Suzanne D. Rutland, *Jewish Life Down Under: The Flowering of Australian Jewry* (Jerusalem: Institute of the World Jewish Congress, Policy Study No 21, 2001), p. 22.

10 P.Y. Medding, *From Assimilation to Group Survival: A Political and Sociological Study of an Australian Jewish Community* (Melbourne: Cheshire, 1968), p. 139.

11 The first Zionist youth movement, *Shomrim*, was established in Sydney in 1939 with its membership almost totally consisting of young people who had arrived as refugees immediately before the war. The *Habonim* youth movement emerged for younger age groups, being founded in Melbourne in 1940 by a group of twenty Polish youths who came to Australia under the Welfare Guardian Scheme. The movement then spread to Sydney, Brisbane and Perth during the war and today continues to be very active, being known as *Habonim-Dror*. After the war, movements representing the other Zionist ideologies were founded in Australia, including *Betar* and *B'nei Akiva* and *Hashomer Hatzair*, which func-

tions only in Melbourne. In the 1960s, *Netzer*, the international Zionist youth movement of Reform Judaism, was founded in Australia, and it has experienced significant growth, particularly in the last decade. The newest and most interesting Zionist youth movement in Australia is *Hineni*, based on modern Orthodox religious ideology. Commencing in 1975 as a local synagogue youth group connected with Central Synagogue in Sydney, in recent years it has spread to become a national movement. Unlike the other Zionist youth movements, *Hineni* did not develop in association with overseas movements, but has emerged to meet local needs. Its philosophy is more reflective of attitudes within Australian Jewish youth and this helps to explain its rapid growth. State Zionist Council of New South Wales Annual Report, February 2000, pp. 43–6.

12 In 1968, total Zionist youth movement membership was 2,600, three times the size of 1948. Hyams, *The History of the Australian Zionist Movement*, p. 161.

13 NSW Maccabi Report, State Zionist Council of New South Wales Biennial Conference, February 2000, p. 57.

14 Hyams, *The History of the Australian Zionist Movement*, p. 171.

15 Israel Horowitz (ed.), *The Dawn and the Rebirth of Palestine* (pamphlet) (Sydney: Jewish National Fund, 1936).

16 Suzanne D. Rutland, *Edge of the Diaspora: Two Centuries of Jewish Settlement in Australia* (Sydney: Brandl & Schlesinger, 1997), p. 303.

17 Ronald Taft, "The Impact of the Middle East Crisis of June 1967 on Melbourne Jewry: An Empirical Study", *The Jewish Journal of Sociology*, 9: 2 (1967), p. 261.

18 Suzanne D. Rutland, *Seventy-Five Years: The History of a Jewish Newspaper* (Sydney: Australian Jewish Historical Society, 1970), p. 94.

19 Taft, op. cit., pp. 250–1.

20 Ronald Taft and Geulah Solomon, "The Melbourne Jewish Community and the Middle East War of 1973", *The Jewish Journal of Sociology*, 16: 1 (1974), p. 58.

21 Suzanne D. Rutland, "The Jewish Experience", in Goot, M. and Tiffen, R. (eds), *Australia's Gulf War* (Melbourne: Melbourne University Press, 1992), pp. 82–96.

22 Janis Wilton and Richard Bosworth, *Old Worlds and New Australia: the post-war migrant experience* (Melbourne, Victoria: Penguin Australia, 1984), p. 34.

23 Written communication from Walter M. Lippmann, Melbourne, July 1987.

24 Interview with Morrie Finberg, Vice-principal of Moriah College Sydney, 11 July 2002.

25 *Australian Jewish Times*, 30 May 1985.

26 Minutes of Moriah College Board of Directors, 25 June 1985.

27 *Australian Jewish Times*, 13 June 1985.

28 Principal's Report to the Board of Directors, Moriah College, 19 March 1981.

29 Suzanne D. Rutland, "*If you will it, it is no dream*": *The Moriah Story* (Sydney: Playright Publishers, 2003).

30 Email correspondence with Dr Ron Weiser, 22 April 2004.

31 Rutland and Gariano, *Survey of Jews in the Diaspora* (A report commissioned by the Jewish Agency Research and Strategic Planning Unit and Department for Jewish Zionist Education) (unpublished).

32 Interview with Avraham Avi-hai, Jersualem, 26 December 2005. Avraham Avi-hai served as chairman of *Keren Hayesod* for ten years from 1978 to 1989.

33 There have been a number of scholars who have written on Evatt's contribution. Key works include: Howard Adelman, "Australia and the Birth of Israel: Midwife or Abortionist", *The Australian Journal of Politics and History*, 38: 3 (1992), 354–74; Rodney Gouttman, "First Principles: H.V. Evatt and the Jewish Homeland", in W.D. Rubinstein (ed.), *Jews in the Sixth Continent* (Sydney: Allen & Unwin, 1987); Chanan Reich, *Australia and Israel: An Ambiguous Relationship* (Melbourne: Melbourne University Press, 2002); and Alan Renouf "Let Justice be Done: The Foreign Policy of Dr H.V. Evatt", Dissertation submitted for the degree of Doctor of Philosophy, Department of History, University of Sydney, 1983.

This thesis was published in book form in the same year as it was submitted.

34 Max Freilich, *Zion in our time: Memoirs of an Australian Zionist* (Sydney: Morgan Publications, 1967), pp. 196–7.

35 Kylie Tennant, *Evatt: Politics and Justice* (Sydney: Angus & Robertson Pty Ltd., 1970), p. 219.

36 *Sydney Jewish News*, 26 December 1947.

37 Ibid., 9 April 1948.

38 As both Chanan Reich and Leanne Piggott have shown, the British sought to bypass Evatt and to not maintain a full exchange of information because of Evatt's pro-Zionist stance. See Rreich, *An Ambiguous Relationship* An Ambigous relationship and Leanne Piggott, "An Ideal Betrayed: Australia, Britain and the Palestinian Question", Dissertation submitted for the degree of Doctor of Philosophy Ph.D. thesis, Department of History, Faculty of Arts, University of Sydney, 2002.

39 Reich, *An Ambiguous Relationship*, p. 25.

40 Reich, *An Ambiguous Relationship*, p. 28.

41 Aubrey S. Eban, Israel Mission to the United States, to H.V. Evatt, 18 May 1949, copy in Box E17, ECAJ Correspondence. Files, 1948–1494, Archive of Australian Judaica, Fisher Library, University of Sydney.

42 Gouttman, "First Principles", p. 262.

43 This was a period when the left-wing Australian Union of Students (AUS) mounted a strong anti-Israel campaign on campus. Many Jewish students were mobilised by this to become politically active. In this period, the Australia–Israel Publications (AIP) was formed in August 1974 with Sam Lipski and later Michael Danby running the office. In 1977 they began publishing the *Australia/Israel Review*. When Sam Lipski stepped down in 1982, Dr Colin Rubenstein was appointed as chair of the editorial committee, a position he has retained. In the mid-1990s AIP was restructured and renamed the AIJAC (Australia Israel Jewish Affairs Council. See Hyams, *The Australian Zionist Movement*, pp. 137–8.

44 Blanche D'Alpuget, *Robert J. Hawke: A Biography* (East Melbourne: Schwartz in conjunction with Landsdowne Press, 1982), p. 246.

45 There were a number of occasions when the Zionist leadership criticized the Hawke government's policy on Israel. For example, in April 1989, Peter Wilensky (himself Jewish), Australia's ambassador to the UN, condemned Israel's decision to restrict Muslim entry to the Al-Aqsa Mosque, in a highly critical statement. The Jewish community wrote to the Minister for Foreign Affairs, Gareth Evans, stating that the "statement contained some of the most prejudiced assertions against Israel ever made by an official Australian representative". Hyams, *The Australian Zionist Movement*, p. 142.

46 For a detailed discussion on the AJDS see Philip Mendes, "Australian Jewish Dissent on Israel: A History of the Australian Jewish Democratic Society", *Australian Jewish Historical Society*, 1, 15 (1999): 117–38, and Part 2, 15 (2000): 459–74.

47 Barbara Bloch and Eva Cox, "Mending the World from the Margins: Jewish Women and Australian Feminism", in Geoffrey Brahm Levey and Philip Mendes, *Jews in Australian Politics* (Brighton & Portland: Sussex Academic Press, 2004).

48 "Disengagement Debate. Sunday 7 August 2005, State Zionist Council of Victoria, Melbourne Australia". Transcript viewed online at: <http://www.j-net.com.au/szcvic/szcvic-200508.html>.

49 Danny Ben-Moshe, "The End of Unconditional Love: The Future of Zionism in Australian Jewish life", in *New Under the Sun: Jewish Life in Australia* (Melbourne: Black Inc, 2006).

50 David Bryfman, "The Current state of Israel Education for Jewish High School students in NSW", Master of Education Thesis, Monash University, Melbourne 2001, p. 14.

16

Israel in the Identity of American Jews

Robert Wexler

Academic discussions regarding the significance of Israel for American Jews regularly assume that, all things being equal, Israel has had, and even should have, a strong claim on the interest and affections of Jewry's largest Diaspora community. Contemporary treatments of this subject are regularly given provocative titles hinting at the gradual unraveling of the relationship between the State of Israel and the Jews of the United States. Chaim I. Waxman questioned the commitment of American Jews in "Weakening Ties: American Jewish Baby-Boomers and Israel".[1] In 2001, Steven Rosenthal authored *Irreconcilable Differences: The Waning of the American Jewish Love Affair with Israel.*[2] In the same year, Jerold S. Auerbach contributed *Are We One? Jewish Identity in the United States and Israel.*[3]

American Jewish enthusiasm for Israel is not always easy to gauge. Should it be measured by the volume or success of the pro-Israel activity of organizations such as American Israel Public Affairs Committee (AIPAC), the American Jewish Committee (AJC) and the Anti-Defamation League (ADL)? Is it best reflected by the level of donations American Jews make to their local federations and Israel-based charities? Is it directly related to the frequency of visits by American Jews to Israel? Can it be inferred by Jewish voting patterns in American elections? What does the survey data tell us about American Jewish attitudes toward Israel?

Perhaps we would do well to consider a more fundamental question: Are American Jewish attitudes toward Israel a direct reflection of the role Israel plays in the substance of their Jewish identity? In other words, how deeply is an affinity for Israel and a commitment to its survival ingrained in the self-perception of American Jews and how is it expressed in practical terms?

The data collected by the decennial National Jewish Population Survey (NJPS) and the annual surveys conducted by the AJC provide valuable information on this topic, even if they do not directly address all of the more specific questions just raised.

American Jewish Attitudes toward Israel

According to the 2000 NJPS survey, American Jews maintain a moderately high sense of connection to Israel. When asked whether they feel emotionally attached to Israel, the results indicated the following positive responses:

Table 16.1 Levels of emotional attachment to Israel

Overall	*63%*
By Age:	
35–44	56%
45–54	64%
55–64	68%[4]

Source: NJPS 2000.

The NJPS survey also revealed significantly lower emotional attachment to Israel among those under 30 when compared to the results cited above.[5] Still, it is possible that this younger cohort's connection to Israel may yet increase as their world view changes with maturity and the accompanying assumption of adult responsibilities.

These results indicate that attachment to Israel diminishes with the age of the respondent. However, when asked whether US and Israeli Jews share a common "Jewish" destiny, the positive responses were as follows:

Table 16.2 Belief that US and Israeli Jews share a common "Jewish" destiny

Overall	72%
By Age:	
35–44	72%
45–54	71%
55–64	75%[6]

Source: NJPS 2000.

Whereas the sense of shared destiny seems to transcend age groups, the depth of emotional attachment to Israel does not. One could argue that, regardless of their personal attachment to Israel, adult Jews of all ages assume that their own future and security as Jews are closely intertwined with the fate of modern Israel. Remoteness from the events leading to Israel's founding in 1948 and the difficulties of Israeli–Palestinian relations may cause some younger Jews to feel more emotionally distant from Israel. Nevertheless, the recent (historically speaking) experience of the Holocaust coupled with the persistence of (perceived) anti-Semitism may lead them to conclude that the non-Jewish world still views Jews monolithically and that one common fate does, therefore, unite all Jews.

Perceptions of Israel

Similar results were found with regard to two additional questions examined by the NJPS survey. One query measures the familiarity of the respondent with the "social and political situation in Israel", while the other asks for a response to the statement, "Israel is the spiritual centre of the Jewish people". The results by age are as follows:

Table 16.3 Familiarity with the social and political situation in Israel and regard for Israel as the spiritual centre of the Jewish people

	Familiarity with social and political situation in Israel		*Israel is the spiritual centre of the Jewish people*	
	Very familiar	*Very or Somewhat familiar*[a]	*Strongly agree*	*Strongly or Somewhat agree*[b]
18–34	31	84	60	87
35–49	37	88	54	84
50–64	36	90	58	85
65+	46	92	57	82[7]

[a] This represents a combined total of two response categories: "Very familiar" and "Somewhat familiar."

[b] This represents a combined total of two response categories: "Strongly agree" and "Somewhat agree."

Source: NJPS 2000.

Although the familiarity of American Jews with the social and political situation in Israel does vary somewhat with age, the numbers are quite high in every cohort. Even the youngest group of Jews claims to be at least somewhat conversant with the current state of affairs in Israel. On the surface, this might indicate at least a strong intellectual interest in modern Israel, even if that interest does not automatically translate into an emotional attachment. The significance of this finding, however, depends upon how the respondents interpreted the question. It is likely that the question was understood to refer to the ongoing Arab–Israeli conflict rather than to a more in-depth knowledge of Israel society and politics. Given that this particular conflict is well covered by the American and international press, it is not surprising to discover that a highly educated group of (Jewish) Americans claims to be knowledgeable on this subject.

An additional factor in enhancing American Jewish familiarity with Israel might also be the influence of the Israel advocacy organizations. Although only a minority of Jews participates actively in these organizations, a far greater number of them are touched by the publications and pronouncements of these groups. We might also anticipate that the "Israel" presented by these advocacy groups projects a more positive image than the one portrayed in the mainstream media.

These assumptions regarding the sources of information about Israel are reinforced by the fact that only a relatively small number of American Jews have actually visited Israel. According to the 2000 NJPS survey, approximately 35 percent have visited Israel at least once, and only 20 percent have visited more than once.[8]

Nevertheless, as we have seen, a much higher percentage of American Jewish assert a familiarity with Israeli society and politics. Clearly, the information that most Jews claim to have does not come from experiencing the Jewish state directly.

The results of the question regarding the status of Israel as the "spiritual centre of the Jewish people" may also provide scant insight into the connection of American Jews to the Jewish state. The results vary little with age and, to the extent they do vary, the data defy explanation. Perhaps American Jews simply accept the centrality of Israel for Judaism as a learned fact rather than a matter of personal opinion. Informed non-Jews might well provide the same response when posed the same question. Individual Jews can affirm the spiritual significance of Israel for Judaism in general without drawing any particular implications for their own Jewish identities.

The Impact of Affiliation with the Jewish Community

A more faithful predictor of Israel attachment for the individual Jew is the level of his or her personal affiliation with the Jewish community. The 2000 NJPS survey indicates that highly affiliated Jews are much more likely to express an attachment to Israel and to endorse the concept of a shared fate than the unaffiliated.

Table 16.4 Communal affiliation and attachment to Israel

	Emotionally Attached to Israel	*U.S. and Israeli Jews Share Destiny*
Overall	63%	72%
Level of Affiliation:		
Highly Affiliated	85%	81%
Moderately Affiliated	74%	76%
Unaffiliated	48%	62%[9]

Source: NJPS 2000.

These results should not immediately be construed as demonstrating that an affiliation with the Jewish community automatically begets a closer sense of connection to Israel. Since highly affiliated Jews routinely tend to score much higher on almost all measures of Jewish connection than the unaffiliated,[10] it is not surprising that they also show a stronger affinity for Israel and a sense of shared destiny. Israel, it seems, is one among a variety of features that define the Jewish identity of the affiliated respondents.

The responses regarding familiarity with the situation in Israel and recognition of Israel's spiritual centrality did not differ greatly when measured by varying levels of Jewish affiliation. Even the unaffiliated claim to know at least something about modern Israel, and more than 80 percent of them affirm the spiritual importance of the country for Jews and Judaism.

Understanding Generational Shifts in Attitudes toward Israel

Although it appears that an emotional distancing from Israel has occurred among the younger cohort of Jews, the reasons for this growing disinterest are less obvious. Opinion in this regard can be divided into two schools: those who emphasize the changing perceptions of Israel in the world at large, and those who relate the changes to the continued Americanization of the Jewish community. Of course, these two views are not mutually exclusive and, taken together, may account for much of the generational shift in attitudes toward the Jewish state.

The argument based on changing perceptions of Israel assumes that the enduring image of Israel among older Jews was shaped primarily by "positive" historical events such as the odds-defying establishment of the state in 1948, Israel's miraculous victory in the Six Day War, the almost disastrous Yom Kippur War, and the heroic Entebbe rescue in 1976. The younger generation, on the other hand, has experienced the ill-fated 1982 Israeli invasion of Lebanon, the expansion of Jewish settlements on the West Bank in the 1980s, 1990s and 2000s, and two Intifadas beginning in 1987 and again in 2000. This type of analysis underlies the approach of Ardie Geldman. who identifies four stages in the evolving relationship between American Jews and Israel:

1 1948–1967: Indifference (after a short-lived activism during the War for Independence).
2 1967–1977: Avid Identification (in the wake of the 1967 war).
3 1977–1992: Criticism (spurred by the election of right-leaning Menachem Begin as Prime Minister).
4 1992–Present: Split (the Oslo Accords and their aftermath created a split in the American Jewish community between those who strongly favored a peace process and those who either opposed the process or urged great caution).[11]

Equally plausible, however, is the assumption that each succeeding generation of American Jews feels more "American" and, therefore, less attached to others outside of the United States, even if those "others" are fellow Jews. The logic of this position is bolstered by another important finding in the NJPS 2000 survey relating to the establishment of friendships outside the Jewish community. The question posed to those surveyed was whether half or more of their close friends were Jewish. The affirmative results were as follows:

Table 16.5 Respondents of whose close friends half or more are Jewish

Overall 52%	
By Age:	
35–44	45%
45–54	53%
55–64	59%

Source: NJPS 2000.

Clearly, younger Jews (under 44) are more likely to have non-Jewish friends than their older counterparts. This trend is even greater when we look at young Jewish adults between the ages of 18–24. Only 36 percent of this population reports that half or more of their closest friends are Jewish. This figure rises to 39 percent among those between the ages of 25–29. This phenomenon is the result of a gradual process of American Jewish assimilation and greater acceptability.

The large majority of American Jews are descendants of immigrants from Eastern and Central Europe who arrived in the United States toward the end of the nineteenth and the beginning of the twentieth century. In the countries of their birth, these Jews were understood to be a distinct minority within the majority culture. Jews born in Poland did not generally view themselves as Polish nor were they regarded as such by ethnic Poles. The same was true in Russia and the Ukraine. Only in Western and Central Europe, and only in the late nineteenth and early twentieth century did large segments of the Jewish population allow themselves to identify with the majority population.

An immigrant's gradual identification with his host country is a process. Some elements of assimilation can be almost immediate while others may take some time. The speed of this process is also dependent on the extent to which the immigrant group is accepted by the majority population.

The in-marriage rates of Jews in the early decades of the twentieth century testify to the fact that assimilation into the larger culture, although rapid, was not complete. As a result of the social revolution of the 1960s, however, Jews became more acceptable to non-Jews as marriage partners, and the rate of Jewish intermarriage began to accelerate.

Friendship, and even more so marriage, requires trust and a high level of affinity for the other. For Jews, as affinity with and acceptability by the "other" (that is, American non-Jews) grew, the sense of identification with their traditional ethnic group waned. The first few generations of American Jews internalized some of their parents' and grandparents' perspectives on the hostility of the non-Jewish world, particularly since they lived in an America that often excluded Jews from some aspects of its economic, cultural and social life. But recent generations forged their social relationships based not on the past experience of their ethnic group, but rather on the post-1960s realities and values of American society.

Given this pattern of greater integration into American life, it is not surprising that emotional attachment to Israel has declined among younger Jews. Maintaining the traditional sense of a Jewish peoplehood that transcends borders becomes less important when one feels more accepted by non-Jewish Americans.

Zionism in the United States

From the very inception of Zionism in the United States, the unique experience of American Jews brought its own particular twist to support for the Jewish state. The Zionism of Israel's founders assumed that the maintenance of a creative and secure Jewish life was impossible anywhere in the world except in a fully Jewish state. Unlike their eastern European forebears, American Jews did not feel vulnerable to the capriciousness of the governments under which they lived. They came to consider themselves as Jewish Americans and not just as Jews who happen to live in the United States. In this regard, America's Jews are also distinct from many of the other contemporary Diaspora communities.

In *Irreconcilable Differences*, Rosenthal analyzes the singular character of American Zionism as it developed at the end of the nineteenth and beginning of the twentieth century:

> Zionism raised the specter of dual loyalties and appeared to threaten the Jews' position in their homeland. As a result, during the first years of the twentieth century the American Zionist movement developed very slowly. The impetus to its growth was not domestic anti-Semitism but American Jews' identification with the plight of their Eastern European brethren. The anti-Semitism that fueled American Zionism was mostly secondhand, and American Jews joined the fledgling Zionist movement as a possible solution to the persecutions in Poland and Russia.[12]

For American Jewish life, the late nineteenth and early twentieth century was a period of transition from a community dominated by Jews from Central Europe (and in particular, Germany) to a community populated primarily by Jews of Eastern European ancestry. In general, Jews from Poland and Russia became the most devoted adherents of the Zionist cause, both in Europe and in the United States. Those who emigrated to the United States were concerned about the plight of those left behind. Nevertheless, the Zionism they espoused did not include plans for their own relocation to Palestine, but rather the hope that they could help establish a refuge for those who remained in Europe.

Not surprisingly, those most opposed to the concept of Zionism were often the American Jews of German origin. Their own ties to Europe had weakened, and their assimilation into American life was progressing rapidly. As leaders of Reform Judaism, they insisted that the movement distance itself from any support for the creation of a Jewish state. In the now famous Pittsburgh Platform of 1885, they made the following declaration:

> We recognize, in the modern era of universal culture of heart and intellect, the approaching of the realization of Israel's great Messianic hope for the establishment of the kingdom of truth, justice, and peace among all men. We consider ourselves no longer a nation, but a religious community, and therefore expect neither a return to Palestine, nor a sacrificial worship under the sons of Aaron, nor the restoration of any of the laws concerning the Jewish state.[13]

With the destruction of European Jewry during World War II, the focus of American Zionist ambitions changed to one of rescuing the survivors of the Holocaust. Once the state was established in 1948, new opportunities for rescuing endangered Jewish communities presented themselves. During the 1950s and extending into the 1960s, Israel systematically brought Jews to Israel from the Moslem-dominated societies of the Middle East. That having been accomplished, the emphasis began to shift to the USSR and the rescue of Soviet Jews. More recently, relocation efforts have focused on the Jews of Ethiopia. The organized American Jewish community has been a consistent, active partner in facilitating the emigration of these Jews and in financing their resettlement.

Yet despite this pattern of generosity, and with the exception of those years in which Israel was actively engaged in a war with its neighbors, official giving to Israel through the United Jewish Appeal (UJA) and its surrogates has declined steadily from 1948 to the present when adjusted for inflation. For example, the United Jewish Communities (UJC) reports that its contribution to Israel in 1950 was $101,954,000, representing 63 percent of the total giving to the UJA, the United Israel Appeal (UIA) and the Jewish Federations. In 2004, that figure stood at $199,700,000 and represented only 23 percent of total giving.[14] If we adjust the 2004 figure for inflation, we find that the support of Israel from these sources has declined by 75 percent.

As early as 1948, Marshall Sklare and Benjamin Ringer demonstrated that 90 percent of the American Jewish community supported the United States' decision to recognize the new State of Israel. Expressions of support grew to 96 percent when American Jews were asked to agree or disagree with the following statement: "Even if the United States does not help the Jews in Palestine, the Jewish people should help them."[15]

Sklare and Ringer also concluded that commitment to Jewish life had virtually no effect on the general pro-Israel political stance of American Jews, but they did detect a clear correlation between the level of overall Jewish commitment and the intensity of personal involvement with the new state.[16] As we have already seen, this relationship between a broad commitment to Jewish life and a more specific, emotional commitment to Israel still persists.

How We Measure American Jewish Attitudes

The analysis of survey data on the American Jewish community is often based on comparisons both external and internal to the community itself. The external view examines how the Jewish community compares with other ethnic and religious groupings in the United States. The internal view, on the other hand, either contrasts current soundings of American Jews with those conducted in the past or measures one Jewish subgroup against another. The decision whether to focus on external or internal comparisons may, at times, seem motivated more by communal ideology than by the requirements of sociological study. So, for example, data on Jewish political inclinations is most often compared with the leanings of other religious groups as a means of highlighting Jewish liberalism. Data on intermarriage rates among American Jews, however, is more often contrasted with these same internal rates as reflected in earlier surveys in order to emphasize the trend toward assimilation. Nevertheless, one could just as easily focus on the difference in intermarriage rates between Jews and other ethnic groups who have had a comparable longevity on American shores.

A similar argument can be made for examining the data on American Jewish attitudes toward Israel. We rarely ask the question of how these attitudes compare with other American ethnic groups who also possess a homeland. Of course, the case of American Jews is unique in that, for most of them, the Jewish homeland is primarily symbolic rather than the actual home of their recent forebears. Rather than lament any potential erosion in the American Jewish–Israel relationship, we may well ask why such a large number of American Jews — many of whose families have been in the United States for three, four and even five generations — still express such a relatively high level of attachment to a state in which neither they, nor their grandparents nor even their great grandparents were born.

Understanding the Role of Anti-Semitism in Attachment to Israel

Perhaps the explanation for this unusual phenomenon may be found in another rather dramatic statistic that regularly emerges from studies of the American Jewish community. In the 2004 American Jewish Committee survey, respondents were asked, "Do you think that anti-Semitism in the United States is currently a very serious problem, somewhat of a problem, or not a problem at all?" The responses were distributed as follows:

Table 16.6 Levels of concern about anti-Semitism

Very serious problem	27%
Somewhat of a problem	67%
Not a problem at all	6%
Not sure	0%[17]

Source: Annual Survey of American Jewish Opinion, American Jewish Committee, 2004.

Respondents were also asked, "Looking ahead over the next several years, do you think that anti-Semitism in the United States will increase greatly, increase somewhat, remain the same, decrease somewhat, or decrease greatly?" The responses had the following distribution:

Table 16.7 The future of anti-Semitism

Increase greatly	9%
Increase somewhat	33%
Remain the same	45%
Decrease somewhat	9%
Decrease greatly	2%
Not sure	3%[18]

Source: Annual Survey of American Jewish Opinion, American Jewish Committee, 2004.

This data emphasizes the extent to which American Jews remain very sensitive to the presence of anti-Semitism. Only 6 percent of Jews believe that anti-Semitism is not a problem in the United States while 94 percent express some level of concern. Furthermore, only 11 percent are convinced that the situation is likely to improve.

This high level of concern among American Jews may be better understood in light of the findings of Gary Tobin and Sid Groeneman in their study of anti-Semitic attitudes within American society. Among their various conclusions, Tobin and Groeneman note that, "The introduction of evidence from previous surveys suggests that anti-Jewish sentiment in the U.S. might have increased at least in the short-term."[19] Furthermore, they found that anti-Semitic attitudes were more prevalent among younger Americans than among the so-called "baby boomers".[20] This contradicts the oft-held assumption that anti-Semitism in America diminishes with each succeeding age cohort.

The long Jewish sojourn in the United States appears to be fraught with some level of insecurity. Consciously or unconsciously, American Jews are conflicted about their place in American society. American Jews intermarry at a fairly high rate and increasingly count non-Jews among their closest friends; yet, at the same time, they are not very optimistic about the anti-Semitic attitudes of non-Jews in general. Perceived anti-Semitism in the U.S. may not be enough to prompt Jews to uproot themselves and move to a Jewish homeland, nor may it be enough to inspire a strong emotional connection to Israel, but it may work to sustain their continued political and charitable support of Israel.

American Jews are also keenly aware of the recent growth of anti-Semitism in Europe. France, in particular, has seen an increase in attacks against Jewish persons and property. The Jewish Agency for Israel (JAFI) has also reported a percentage increase in the number of Jews emigrating to Israel from France, although the absolute numbers still remain low. The specter of resurgent anti-Semitism in Europe, while geographically distant, can be expected to influence the attitudes of Jews in the United States.

The Future of the American Jewish Relationship with Israel

Recognizing the complex and nuanced relationship of the current American Jewish relationship to Israel, Steven M. Cohen concludes that American Jews may be divided into three levels of connection:

1. those who are indifferent or even hostile to Israel;
2. those who are pro-Israel, but not intensely so;
3. those whose commitment to Israel is quite passionate.[21]

This typology is consistent with the data, but it could be used equally well if we substitute "Judaism" for "Israel" in each of the categories.

Regarding the future, however, it is difficult not to conclude with Cohen that, "One can make a convincing case that American Jewish attachment in the next five years will erode; alternatively, an equally convincing argument contends that it will hold steady."[22]

However, even if the argument for erosion proves correct, it is unlikely that the impact of this emotional distancing will be discernible in the near future. In practical terms, public support for Israel in the Jewish community is expressed through the matrix of organizations established either primarily or partially for this purpose. These organizations are routinely sustained by a very committed minority, and there is no reason to posit a "sea change" in the attitudes of this highly motivated group.

Notes

1 In Alon Gal, *Envisioning Israel* (Detroit: Wayne State University Press, 1996), pp. 374–396.

2 Steven Rosenthal, *Irreconcilable Differences: The Waning of the American Jewish Love Affair with Israel* (Hanover, NH: Brandeis University Press/University Press of New England, 2001.)

3 Jerold S. Auerbach, *Are We One? Jewish Identity in the United States and Israel* (New Brunswick, NJ: Rutgers University Press, 2001.)

4 *National Jewish Population Survey 2000–1: Strength, Challenge and Diversity in the American Jewish Population* (New York: United Jewish Communities, 2003), p. 12.

5 *National Jewish Population Survey 2000–1: Jewish Adults Ages 18–29* (New York: United Jewish Communities, 2004), p. 23.

6 *National Jewish Population Survey 2000–1: Strength, Challenge and Diversity in the American Jewish Population* (New York: United Jewish Communities, 2003), p. 12.

7 Jonathon Ament, *Israel Connections and American Jews* (New York: United Jewish Communities, 2005), p. 13.

8 *National Jewish Population Survey 2000–1: Strength, Challenge and Diversity in the American Jewish Population* (New York: United Jewish Communities, 2003), p. 12.

9 *National Jewish Population Survey 2000–1: Strength, Challenge and Diversity in the American Jewish Population*, p. 12.

10 *National Jewish Population Survey 2000–1: Strength, Challenge and Diversity in the American Jewish Population*, p. 12.

11 Ardie Geldman and Steven Bayme, "The Growing Gap Between American Jews and Israel: Two Views", *Journal of Jewish Communal Service* 78, 1 (2001): 32–40.

12 Steven T. Rosenthal, *Irreconcilable Differences: The waning of the American Jewish love affairs with Israel* (Hanover, NH: Brandeis University Press/University Press of New England, 2001), p. 9.

13 Central Conference of American Rabbis, viewed online 12 October 2005: <http://data.ccarnet.org/platforms/pittsburgh.html>.

14 Jewish Virtual Library, viewed online 12 October 2005: <http://www. jewishvirtuallibrary.org/jsource/ US-Israel/ujatab.html>.

15 Marshall Sklare and Benjamin B. Ringer, "A Study of Jewish Attitudes Toward the State of Israel", in *The Jews: Social Patterns of an American Group* (Glencoe, IL: Free Press, 1966), p. 442.

16 Ibid.

17 "2004 Annual Survey of American Jewish Opinion", American Jewish Committee, viewed online 12 October 2005:<http://www.ajc.org/site /apps/nl/content3.asp?c=ijITI2PHKoG&b=846741&ct=1051473>.

18 Ibid.

19 Gary A. Tobin and Sid Groeneman, *Anti-Semitic Beliefs in the United States* (San Francisco: Institute for Jewish & Community Research, 2003), p. 29.

20 Ibid.

21 Cohen, Steven M., "American Jews and Israel", in David M. Gordis and Yoav Ben-Horin (eds), *Jewish Identity in America* (Los Angeles: Susan and David Wilstein Institute of Jewish Policy Studies, University of Judaism, 1990), p. 121.

22 Ibid.

17

South African Zionism and Jewish Identity

Milton Shain and Richard Mendelsohn

The Zionist ideal gained special traction in Lithuania — the seedbed of South African Jewry — and was transported southwards by the emigrants in the late nineteenth century. Once in South Africa, Zionism gained a rapid and relatively easy communal ascendancy.[1] Beginning in earnest with the *Chovevei Zion* (Lovers of Zion) founded in Johannesburg in 1896, Zionist societies proliferated in town and countryside. Initiatives were undertaken to establish a South African Zionist Federation (SAZF) in Johannesburg in 1898, a year after the historic first Zionist Congress in Basel, Switzerland. As in "*der heim*", most Lithuanian Jews in South Africa — unlike some of the local Anglo-Jewish establishment — enthusiastically supported Herzl's vision of a Jewish national renaissance.

Within a decade there were over sixty Zionist societies in South Africa. In 1905 they met together for the first South African Zionist conference. Men monopolized the leadership positions, although women were equally enthusiastic supporters of the cause. Beyond advocacy, Zionist societies, with their well attended meetings, picnics and bazaars, fulfilled a broader function, providing a convivial social milieu for many. The Young Israel societies which proliferated in the 1910s and 1920s played a similar social role.

Unlike their counterparts in Europe and the United States, Zionists in South Africa were not seriously challenged by anti-Zionist ideological rivals. The socialist Bundists and the religious conservatives of the *Agudat Yisrael*, so powerful in Eastern Europe, were never as influential in South Africa.[2] And by the time the Reform movement arrived in the 1930s, its historic opposition to Zionism had mutated into a greater acceptance of Jewish nationalism.[3] Even the early disdain of some members of the Jewish establishment in England for Zionism, echoed in Cape Town's "mother congregation" led by the Reverend Alfred P. Bender, dissipated in the wake of the Balfour Declaration of 1917. By the end of the First World War, in the wake of the British promise of a Jewish "national home", Bender had shifted his stance towards that of his illustrious rabbinical colleagues such as Rabbis J. H. Hertz and J. L. Landau who, like most South African rabbis and ministers, had supported Zionism from the start.

Zionism as an ideology was aided in South Africa by the absence of pressure to discard an ethnic distinctiveness and particularism. In the early twentieth century, Afrikaans- and English-speakers still saw themselves as separate races. Assimilatory impulses were muted in a country struggling to define "South Africanness":[4] a country in which the white population was a minority, of which minority the Jews never comprised more than 4.7 percent. Most importantly, Zionism or Jewish nationalism was met with empathy and approval at the highest level. Prime Minister Jan Smuts, for example, subscribed to an ardent "gentile Zionism", while in the 1920s his political rivals, the Afrikaner Nationalists, publicly aligned their own national struggle with that of the Jews. Zionism was not seen as incompatible with loyalty to South Africa. Jan H. Hofmeyr, a future deputy prime minister, put this succinctly at a mass meeting in Johannesburg in 1920: "One could love one's mother as well as one's father . . . " In this supportive environment Zionism was to become the civil religion of South African Jewry.

Zionist commitment grew through the 1930s, reinforced by a burgeoning combination of foreign and domestic anti-Semitism, evident at home both in far-right Afrikaner movements such as the Greyshirts and within the mainstream opposition National Party.[5] In the late 1930s the National Party raised the "Jewish Question" and opposed South Africa's entry into World War II. This hostility lent Zionism an immediacy and an urgency which saw the growth of Zionist youth movements including *Habonim*, and the more leftist *Hashomer Hatzair*, founded in 1930 and 1936 respectively. By the end of the decade over 21,000 South African Jews (out of about 95,000) were "shekel holders", only 2,000 less than in Britain, with a community three times the size.

The 1930s also saw an ideological struggle between Left and Right within the Zionist movement, prompted at least in part by three visits to South Africa by Vladimir Jabotinsky, the Revisionist firebrand. His passionate advocacy of Jewish statehood resonated powerfully within an increasingly bourgeois Jewish community where socialist Zionism had only limited appeal. The Revisionist upsurge, stirred by Jabotinsky's oratory and organizational efforts, gave South African Jewry an international profile it otherwise lacked. And yet, despite Jabotinsky's best efforts, Revisionism did not conquer the community. Many opposed politicising Zionism, while others idealized socialist pioneering in Palestine, with a few of these preparing for *aliyah* on *hachsharah* (training) farms near Johannesburg in the 1940s. For the great majority, however, *aliyah* was not an attractive option. South African Zionism was at this point still largely vicarious. It was, nevertheless, deeply and widely felt as an ideology, especially in the wake of the Holocaust, where over 90 percent of Lithuanian Jews — the kinsmen of the community — perished.[6]

Although the National Party's victory in 1948 was greeted with great apprehension by South African Jews, fears were allayed when a delegation from the South African Jewish Board of Deputies (hereafter the Board of Deputies) visited Prime Minister D. F. Malan to discuss Jewish concerns about their place in Nationalist-ruled South Africa. They were assured that the "Jewish Question" would be laid to rest and, as a practical measure of the new government's goodwill, it permitted South African

Jewry to send material aid and manpower to support the fledgling Jewish state's war effort. In May 1948 South Africa officially recognized Israel. Four years later, Malan became the first head of government to visit the Jewish state.

Eight hundred young South African Jews volunteered for service in Israel's armed forces during the War of Independence as part of *Machal*, the "Volunteers from Abroad" programme.[7] These numbers were exceeded only by the number of volunteers from the much larger Jewish communities of the United States and Great Britain. This level of enthusiasm and support was indicative of the power of the Zionist idea for South African Jews. Of the 800 volunteers, about 300 remained and settled in Israel.

Zionist commitment was further reinforced by the development of an intricate "cradle to matric" Jewish education system, including Jewish day schools. The guiding formula, devised in the mid-1940s, was that Jewish education would be based on a "national-traditional" approach, a compromise between the requirements of religion and of secular Zionism.[8] Reinforced by the horrors of the Holocaust and Israel's ongoing security challenges, Zionism remained unquestioned as an ideology. In the early 1960s, some questions of Jewish loyalty towards South Africa were raised in the Afrikaans press when Israel supported the African bloc at the United Nations and condemned apartheid. This did nothing to undermine Zionist fervour. Only a few Jews on the radical Left questioned the basic assumptions of Jewish nationalism and instead devoted their political energies to the struggle against white minority rule.

By this time Zionism had become a key component of South African Jewish identity alongside a diluted religiosity, defined as "non-observant Orthodox".[9] This ethnic identity was also informed in large part by a shared past; including memories of the Holocaust and anti-Semitism in the 1930s and early 1940s. In the decade after the creation of Israel, South African Jews contributed more per capita to Israel than Jews anywhere else. Through these years Zionist organizations flourished. Branches of the *Bnoth Zion* (Daughters of Zion) attracted record numbers of women, while the Women's Zionist Organization had a membership of almost 17,000 in 1967. The Zionist youth movements — *Habonim, Betar, B'nei Akiva* and a waning *Hashomer Hatzair* — successfully recruited over 40 percent of all Jewish youngsters between the ages of 10 to 18. By 1969, these organizations boasted 8,535 members, providing a safe alternative focus for youthful idealism at a time when political protest was dangerous.

Anxieties about the future stability of a racially-polarized society added a peculiarly South African dimension to local support for Zionism: Israel was seen by some as a place of refuge if needed. But the general enthusiasm went much deeper than simple expediency, with deep roots going back to the *shtetl*. The overwhelming majority of Jews felt a deep sentimental attachment to Israel, and were willing contributors to the Jewish state. This enthusiastic commitment was reinforced by the palpable success of the young Jewish state. But it did not lead to mass *aliyah* in pursuit of the Zionist ideal. South African Jews by and large were content to remain at home, though there was a steady if limited stream of emigration to Israel: approximately 100 annually in the 1950s, increasing to almost 300 in the 1960s.

The Six Day War of June 1967 demonstrated the depths of South African Jewry's attachment to Israel. In the tense weeks before hostilities, offers of assistance began to arrive at the offices of the SAZF and the Board of Deputies. Funding and a programme for volunteers were arranged. Some 1,800 individuals applied for the programme, with an initial contingent of 782 volunteers setting out two days after the outbreak of war.[10]

In relative terms the South African group was the largest of any Diaspora Jewish community. Few South African Jews remained uninvolved in the war. Moreover, the ruling National Party showed great sympathy for the beleaguered Jewish state, ending any lingering bitterness from the memories of the 1930s and early 1940s when it had opposed war against Hitler's Germany and from the early 1960s when it had cut funds to Israel because of the Jewish state's anti-Apartheid position.

The forging of close ties — including scientific, military and technological cooperation — between Pretoria and Jerusalem from the mid-1970s [11] made Zionism even more comfortable for South African Jews, though a substantial number were acutely embarrassed by Israel's intimacy with the Apartheid state.

Young Jews in particular — especially the high proportion who attended university — were troubled. They were confronted at the Universities of Cape Town and of the Witwatersrand by Muslim and Black organizations which condemned Israel and associated Zionism with Apartheid. While vigorously defending the Jewish state, some were uneasy at the apparent similarities between the two "pariah" states, especially with regard to the unresolved question of the West Bank.[12] On the whole however, most Jews supported Israel uncritically, though a few were disquieted by Israel's incursion into Lebanon in 1982 and by its tough response to the Intifada which broke out in 1987.

These concerns did not erode the vitality of Zionist youth activities which continued to flourish, albeit without the same level of ideological fervour and sophistication as in the 1950s and 1960s. The annual youth summer camps at the sea remained immensely popular, as much, if not more, for their social than for their educational activities. Significantly, however, the emerging phenomenon, notable particularly from the early 1980s in Johannesburg, the largest Jewish centre, diluted some of the Zionist passion. On the whole, however, rising religiosity has not undermined positive sentiment.

Township uprisings, states of emergency, international sanctions and a faltering economy preoccupied Jews, as they did all whites, in the 1970s and 1980s, reinforcing the notion of Israel as a safe haven. Between 1970 and 1991, close to 40,000 Jews — one third of the Jewish population — emigrated. In the 1970s, about 38 percent of these chose Israel as a destination, with this number declining to 23 percent in the 1980s.[13] Throughout this period Jewish identity remained strong, with out-marriage relatively low (at less than 10 percent). In part, this low rate was a function of ethnic obsessions in a deeply stratified plural society.[14]

The ushering in of dramatic political changes in 1990 following President F. W. de Klerk's 2 February speech, in which he announced that Nelson Mandela would be released from prison and that South African society would be normalized, was met with some anxiety by South African Jews — as indeed by all whites.[15] But Jews had their own specific fears, particularly the prospects for Zionist activity in the "new South Africa" and the country's future relationship with Israel. The strongest black group, the African National Congress (ANC) had long maintained close ties with the Palestine Liberation Organization (PLO).

The community's worst imaginings were seemingly realized a fortnight after

Mandela's release when he hugged PLO leader, Yasser Arafat, at a meeting in Lusaka in Zambia. Matters were not helped when Mandela peremptorily dismissed anticipated Jewish criticism of this embrace with the words: "Too bad". In the wake of his comments, mass meetings were held in Cape Town and Johannesburg, where communal leaders, including Chief Rabbi Cyril Harris, sought to assuage Jewish anxieties and promised that the Board of Deputies would closely monitor developments.

Equilibrium was rapidly regained and Jews by and large adapted to the new realities. The ANC-led government made it clear that it accepted Israel's right to exist within secure borders alongside a Palestinian state. Jews continued to retain a strong sense of identity, and loyalty to the Zionist cause remained strong. In a national survey conducted in 1998, 54 percent indicated a "strong attachment" and 33 percent a "moderate attachment" to Israel. Only one percent expressed negative feelings towards Israel. Similar surveys in the United States and England found 69 percent and 80 percent respectively could be categorized as "strongly" or "moderately" attached to Israel. This survey also revealed that a majority of South African Jews felt Israel was the victim of bias in the South African media. Most significantly, 79 percent of respondents in the survey had visited Israel at least once, as opposed to 78 percent in Britain and 37 percent in the United States. Just over eight in ten of South African Jews indicated that they had close friends or family in Israel.[16]

The Jewish state has thus played an important part in the identity of South African Jews. Deep attachments to Israel are evident in Israeli Independence Day events (which continue to draw large numbers of Jews), in the Jewish day school curriculum and in Zionist summer camps. More significantly, the commitment to Israel has by and large been reinforced by a burgeoning anti-Zionism, as a certain defensiveness consolidates attachments to Israel.

Anti-Zionist public discourse is driven largely by South African Muslims who number about 750,000, or 1.7 percent of the total South African population. Tempers fluctuate as the political temperatures rise and fall in the Middle East. *Al-Quds* (Jerusalem Day) is regularly commemorated, usually with incendiary rhetoric, while radical protestors frequently march on the Israeli and American embassies and consulates, burning flags and chanting "Death to Israel" and "One Zionist, One Bullet", the latter a play on an Africanist liberation slogan.

The anti-Zionist mood reached its apogee during the World Conference Against Racism in Durban in 2001, which coincided with the Second Intifada. Israel was lambasted as an Apartheid state and Zionist delegates were effectively drowned out. This was "anti-Semitism in the guise of anti-Zionism", claimed Marlene Bethlehem, national president of the Board of Deputies. But far from eroding Jewish attachments to Israel, the "hate fest" consolidated the hold of Zionism on the community.

The Durban conference also raised serious questions for South African Jewish leaders, who increasingly questioned the government's self-declared policy of even-handedness in the Middle East. These fears were confirmed shortly after the Durban conference when a Jew and one-time hero of "the struggle", Ronnie Kasrils, the Minister of Water Affairs and Forestry in the ANC government, launched a forceful attack on Israel during a special Middle East debate in the National Assembly. All blame was heaped on Israel for the political impasse between Jews and Palestinians. Kasrils' text became the basis of a "Declaration of Conscience on the

Israeli–Palestinian Conflict" which was signed by 284 South African Jews under the title of "Not in my Name".

The fact that so few Jews signed the petition, and the powerful defensive response in the media by individual Jews and Jewish representatives — including a counter petition that attracted 13,000 Jewish signatures — revealed the depth of the Zionist commitment of South African Jewry. This was again confirmed in a national survey conducted in 2005. As with the 1998 survey, this survey revealed close bonds between South African Jews and the centrality of the Jewish state in South African Jewish identity. Seventy-eight percent of those surveyed indicated that they had close friends or relatives living in Israel, and eighty-three percent had visited Israel, with fifty-five percent of those in the last ten years. However, there are indications that those aged between eighteen and twenty-four have an attachment to Israel marginally below that of the older generation. Attachments nonetheless remain strong.[17]

The "new South Africa", self-defined as a "rainbow nation", has not dissipated Jewish identity. Indeed there are indications that with the celebration of multiculturalism and diversity in the "new South Africa", Jews enjoy a sense of confidence and a determination to maintain an ethnic particularism which in no way undermines loyalty to the new post-Apartheid order. The assimilatory impulses — to the extent that they exist — in forging a broader "South Africanness" have not had any measurable impact on Jewish identity, despite a growing sense of well being in South Africa expressed in the recent national survey.

Notes

1 For the emergence and rise of Zionism in South Africa, see Gideon Shimoni, *Jews and Zionsim:The South African Experience 1910–1967* (Cape Town: Oxford University Press, 1980).

2 For the early Left, see Evangelos A. Mantzaris, *Labour Struggles in South Africa: The Forgotten Pages 1903–1921* (Windhoek Namibia: Collective Resources Publications, 1995).

3 Reform Jews never made up more than 17 percent of affiliated Jews in South Africa.

4 See George Calpin, *There are no South Africans* (London: Nelson, 1941), which reflected on the absence of a genuine sense of common nationhood.

5 See Patrick J. Furlong, *Between Crown and Swastika. The Impact of the Radical Right on the Afrikaner Nationalist Movement in the Fascist Era* (Johannesburg: Witwatersrand University Press, 1991).

6 See Milton Shain, "South Africa" in David Wyman (ed.), *The World Reacts to the Holocaust* (Baltimore: Johns Hopkins University Press, 1998).

7 See Henry Katzew, *South Africa's 800. The Story of South African Volunteers in Israel's War of Birth* (No place of publication provided, nor publisher, 2003).

8 See M.E. Katz, "The History of Jewish Education in South Africa, 1841–1980", unpublished Ph.D. dissertation, University of Cape Town, 1980.

9 See Jocelyn Hellig, "Religious Expression" in Marcus Arkin (ed.), *South African Jewry* (Cape Town: Oxford University Press, 1984).

10 See Milton Shain, "Consolidating the Consolidated: The Impact of the Six-Day War on South African Jewry" in Eli Lederhendler (ed.), *The Six-Day War and World Jewry* (Bethesda: University Press of Maryland, 2000).

11 See Naomi Chazan, "The Fallacies of Pragmatism. Israeli Foreign Policy Towards South Africa", in *African Affairs*, 82, 327 (1983).

12 See Gideon Shimoni, *Community and Conscience. The Jews in Apartheid South Africa*

(Hanover, NH and Cape Town: University Press of New England for Brandeis University Press and David Philip, 2003).

13 Allie A. Dubb, *The Jewish Population of South Africa. The 1991 Sociodemographic Survey* (Cape Town: Jewish Publications South Africa, Kaplan Centre, University of Cape Town, 1994), pp. 12–13. Of the emigrants to Israel, 21 percent returned to South Africa and almost 10 percent moved to another country. South Africa also attracted some 9,000 *yordim* from Israel. The majority of Jewish emigrants from South Africa preferred English-speaking countries to Israel.

14 See Sally Frankental and Milton Shain, "The open ghetto: Growing up Jewish in South Africa" in Pam Reynolds and Sandra Burman, *Growing up in a divided society: the contexts of childhood in South Africa* (Johannesburg: Ravan Press, 1986).

15 For the first decade after De Klerk's speech see Milton Shain, "South African Jewry: Emigrating? At Risk? Or Restructuring the Jewish Future?" in Sol Encel and Leslie Stein (eds), *Continuity, Commitment, and Survival. Jewish Communities in the Diaspora* (Westport, Connecticut: Praeger, 2003).

16 Barry A Kosmin, Jacqueline Goldberg, Milton Shain and Shirley Bruk, *Jews and the "New South Africa": Highlights of the 1998 National Survey of South African Jews* (London: Institute for Jewish Policy Research, and the Isaac and Jessie Kaplan Centre for Jewish Studies, 1999).

17 Shirley Bruk, *The Jews of South Africa 2005* – Report on a Research Study, Kaplan Centre for Jewish Studies, University of Cape Town, 2006.

18

The Place of Israel — Symbolic and Real — in the Life of Russian-Soviet Jewry

Larissa Remennick

The place of Israel among the forces shaping the identity and lifestyle of Jews in the former Soviet Union (FSU) and contemporary Russia, Ukraine and other post-Soviet states, has been both rather central and controversial. The emergence of the Jewish state as a major focus of international politics after World War II had multiple repercussions for Soviet Jewry, living as they did under a constant shadow of institutional and social anti-Semitism. Subjects of an omnipotent state, Soviet Jews could not stay indifferent to the official anti-Zionist and anti-Israeli political agenda that was in place from the late 1950s until the Glasnost reforms of the late 1980s. On the other hand, official anti-Israeli propaganda has always bred contempt and resistance in a large fraction of Soviet Jewry, strengthening a relationship to the Jewish State as their spiritual anchor and potential homeland, albeit mostly a symbolic one. From the 1970s on, Jewish emigration to Israel became a pivotal item on the Soviet foreign policy agenda, while for tens of thousands of Soviet Jews Israel suddenly became an actual immigration destination and a new homeland. In this chapter, I will first outline the main features of the social history and identity formation among Soviet Jews, emphasizing the place of Israel in their national consciousness. I will then focus on the two major waves of Soviet Jewish emigration to Israel, and finally I will depict Israeli influences on the Jewish community life in post-communist Russia and Ukraine.[1]

Russian-Soviet Jewry in the Second Half of the Twentieth Century: A Social Portrait

Estimates of the size of the Jewish population of Russia and FSU vary, depending on the chosen definition of the Jews. Religious Jewish organizations in the FSU, and their foreign sponsors, are usually interested in the "core Jews", that is, those born of two Jewish parents or at least of Jewish mothers. Their numbers in the USSR and successor states have consistently dropped from one census to the next, from 2,279 million in 1959, to 1,480 million in 1989, 544 thousand in 1999, and an estimated 400 thousand in 2002. By 2002, the majority of the remaining Jews (233,600) lived in Russia (vs. 551,000 in 1989), while less than 90,000 remained in Ukraine, and all the other former republics together hosted about 55,000 core Jews (Tolts 2003, 2004). At the same time, The Jewish Agency (*Sochnut*) that brokers and manages immigration to Israel, bases its count on the entitlement for *aliyah* and Israeli citizenship in a way that also embraces half and quarter Jews (with only one Jewish parent or grandparent), with their immediate families.

Counted in this way, the enlarged Jewish population of Russia may exceed half a million, and, for the whole FSU, ranges between 800,000 and 1.2 million. The World Jewish Congress and other international Jewish organizations usually prefer to cite the upper-limit figures to facilitate their fund-raising for Jewish causes in the FSU.

The demographic decline of Soviet and post-Soviet Jewry is explained by four major factors: mixed marriage, low fertility, advanced age composition, and an intense emigration process. Mark Tolts estimated that between 1989 and 2002, the core Jewish population of Russia has dropped by 55 percent; about 42 percent of this decrease reflected negative vital balance (that is, excess of deaths over births) and 58 percent was due to emigration. In 1994, 63 percent of Jewish men and 44 percent of Jewish women in Russia were married to non-Jews, compared to 51 percent and 33 percent, respectively, in 1979. Among Ukrainian Jewry, the percentages of out-married men and women in 1996 were 82 percent and 74 percent, respectively; the same was true of Jews in Latvia (86 percent and 83 percent). No data on out-marriage are available for the early 2000s, but these numbers have definitely climbed. The greater tendency to out-marriage among Jewish men partially reflects the lack of Jewish brides in the major Russian cities where great numbers of young Jewish men had migrated earlier. As a result, among Soviet / Russian half-Jews, the share of those with Jewish fathers (who are not recognized as Jews in Orthodox Judaism) significantly exceeds those with Jewish mothers. Between 1988 and 1995, the percentage of children born to Jewish mothers and non-Jewish fathers, out of all children born to Jewish mothers, rose from 58 to 69 percent, and by the early 2000s has probably exceeded 80 percent (Tolts 2003, 2004).

In contrast to their forefathers, and their counterparts in Israel and some Diaspora countries, Soviet Jews have typically had fewer children than the surrounding majority. During post-communist years their fertility rates dropped even lower: from 1.5 children in the late 1980s to 0.8 in 1994, compared to 1.9 and 1.25, respectively, in the general population of Russia. Besides low fertility norms in Russia and the modest living standards of most citizens, Jews limited their offspring to one or two children due to a strong emphasis on the quality of their upbringing and great parental investment in each child. Reflecting many decades of low fertility combined with high life expectancy among the Jews, their age pyramid was inverted, pointing to the rapid ageing of the Jewish population in Russia. By the mid-1990s, death rates among Russian Jews surpassed birth rates by 27 units, leading to a steady decline of their numbers. Similar trends have occurred in other successor states. The Jewish population of the FSU is the oldest one among all Diaspora Jewish communities: the mean age of a Russian Jew today approaches 60.

Let me now look at the social context behind the facts of Soviet Jewish demography and the forces that shaped Russian-Jewish identity during the last decades of the twentieth century. Being Jewish had never been a matter of choice for Soviet Jews. Since the mid-1930s, the internal passports of all Soviet citizens had had an explicit record of their ethnic origin (*nationality*, in the Soviet lore), singling out the Jews as carriers of a special "social disability". At the age of 16 everyone was ascribed the ethnicity of one's parents; those born of mixed marriage could choose either ethnic title. Among the youths, who could choose between their Jewish and non-Jewish affiliation, about 90 percent registered as Russians, Ukrainians, etc., in order to avoid a negative label that could hinder their future education and career prospects (Nosenko 2004). By the mid-1990s, only 6 percent of these youths chose to register as Jews (Tolts 2003), suggesting that the popularity of Jewishness did not increase in the post-Soviet era. Beside the overt statement of their *nationality* in the passport and most other documents, Jews were easily recognizable by their non-Slavic last names and typical patronymics such as *Izrailevich* or *Abramovich*, as well as their physiognomic features and some aspects of their speech and demeanor. Thus, Jews were visible in the midst of the Slavic majority, regardless of what their documents said.

During the first two post-revolutionary decades, Jews became a privileged minority group, as the young Republic of peasants and workers needed their relatively high professional and administrative skills, as well their political loyalty. As Yuri Slezkine shows in his book (2004), Russian Jews had a long and soaring affair with Communism as ideology and political regime, which ultimately entailed rather destructive results both for them and for the country. By the late 1930s the regime had recruited and trained enough cadres from the ranks of Russians and other Slavs, and the ubiquitous presence of Jews in high-ranking posts in the Party apparatus, government, and secret services was rapidly reduced via relentless cleansing campaigns (Zeltser 2004). Ever since, the rising and falling tides of anti-Semitic plots and campaigns, masterminded in the Kremlin and conducted by the KGB in concert with the central Party press, have served as a mechanism for controlling Jewish social mobility and ethnic representation (Pincus 1988, Friedgut, 1989; Gitelman, 1999).

The price Jews had to pay for their unprecedented social mobility under state socialism was the virtual destruction of Jewish culture (Altshuler 1987, 1998). By the early 1950s, the system of Jewish schools and cultural institutions has been almost completely destroyed, as were synagogues and *yeshivas*. The majority of Jewish educated professionals and civil servants who grew up in the large Soviet cities did not speak any Yiddish and knew little about Jewish traditions. Some outposts of the *Ashkenazi* Jewish lifestyle still remained in the provincial towns (former *shtetls*) of the Pale of Settlement in parts of the Ukraine, Belorussia, Moldavia, and the Baltic states, but they were also fading away as the carriers of tradition grew older and died. Reflecting forced secularization over 70 years of Soviet power, Jews became an ethnic minority rather than a religious denomination. Jewish affiliation became defined by purely bureaucratic means — parental ethnicity and registration in civil papers — and lost any direct connection with Judaic faith or religious practice. In fact, Jews were the most Russified of all ethnic minorities: in the last Soviet Census of 1989, about 90 percent of the Jews named Russian as their native language, compared to 30–60 percent among other ethnic groups (Remennick 1998). By the late 1970s, Jews became the most urbanized and educated minority in the USSR: over 98 percent of them lived in the cities and over 60 percent held academic degrees, working mainly in science, technology, education, medicine, culture and media-related jobs. Given their propensity for higher education, Jews competed with the Russians and other "titular nations" for positions in the public service and various professions, and often won the competition whenever merit rather than a "nomenclature principle" was at work. On top of this, they were virtually the only minority group entitled for emigration, automatically rendering them untrustworthy, if not outright traitors.

The official stance towards Israel has always been a potent lever, often used by the Soviet regime to control its Jewish citizens. The formation of the Jewish state in 1948, backed up by Stalin's government, was a pivotal event in the formation of their national consciousness and "Jewish pride". Yet, soon enough, Stalin's hopes for unopposed Soviet influence on Israel's political makeup dwindled and relations between the USSR and Israel soured. During the Cold War, the Soviet propaganda machine persistently attacked Zionism as an imperialistic movement and Israel as an American outpost in the Middle East, while simultaneously increasing its military and economic support of the hostile Arab nations. This reversal of the official course meant that support for Israel now meant disloyalty to the Soviet State. Many Soviet Jews were caught in this conflict of allegiance, which grew more intense as the political and military challenge posed to Israel by the Arab states was aggravated by the approaching 1967 Six Day War. The weeks preceding the war had a strong impact on Soviet Jewry, as Israel's very existence was at stake, and many Jews felt an upsurge of Jewish solidarity, realizing that Israel's very presence had a tangible impact on their own lives. Suddenly, the Jewish Homeland they never saw attained a value; that of a dream facing destruction (Ro'i 2003). Jews from across the USSR and from all walks of life were glued to foreign radio stations (especially Kol Israel), picking up bits and pieces of unbiased information about the War. As the threat not only passed but was transformed into a major victory, their anxiety turned into joy and pride. Moreover, since Arab armies were actively supported by the Soviet military and used Soviet-made weapons, many Jews felt alienation from the state they were living in, exacerbating the above-mentioned loyalty conflict. In the words of Yaakov Ro'i, "the Six Day War was in many ways a watershed, and those Jews who consciously made a choice in Israel's favor, realized that they have reached a point of no return" (p. 16). In the wake of the Six Day War, Soviet anti-Zionist propaganda soared and retained its high pitch until the Yom Kippur War of 1973. Like elsewhere in the Jewish world, Russian Jews perceived the latter war with mixed feelings of grievance and pride, and for many it ultimately influenced their decisions about emigration to Israel or to the West.

When researchers coming from the Anglo-Jewish world and raised in the "cultural Judaism" of the contemporary Diaspora first tackle the issue of Russian Jewish identity, they are shocked by the apparent absence of its recognized pillars — knowledge of Jewish history and holidays, keeping some household and cooking traditions, the imperative to marry other Jews, religious rites of passage and Jewish education for children, knowledge of Jewish languages, and identification with Israel. These components of the international Jewish canon were obscure or foreign for most Soviet Jews, and are even less relevant for those who remain in the FSU today (Nosenko

2004; Ryvkina 2005). In a survey of 1,000 Jews of Moscow, Kiev and Minsk (Brym and Ryvkina 1994), the most salient factors of respondents' perceived Jewish identity (in decreasing order) were exposure to Jewish culture while growing up; plans to emigrate; parents' and spouse's "passport nationality"; experience and/or fear of anti-Semitism; and city size. Among those self-identifying as core Jews, only 12 percent celebrated high Jewish holidays or tried to pass Jewish traditions on to their children; 8 percent participated in Jewish organizations, and 4 percent regularly read the Jewish press. Only 14 percent expressed interest in religion, and among these, more leaned towards Russian Orthodoxy than Judaism. In the authors' view, Russian Jewish identity manifests as both elastic and pragmatic, that is, coming to the fore only when it serves a purpose (that is, emigration) and subdued for the rest of the time. Most of the building blocks of Soviet Jewish identity were imposed by state policies or came in reaction to discrimination and humiliation. In a more recent survey among Russian and Ukrainian Jews (Cherviakov et al. 2003), the majority believed that key features of their Jewish identity were "being proud of your nationality", "defend[ing] Jewish dignity", and "remember[ing] the Holocaust". Holocaust memories form perhaps the main common denominator between the Soviet and other Diaspora Jews, while Israeli themes have become less salient during post-communist times. Yet, this conclusion is challenged by some other data showing that, as a result of mass resettlement of Russian Jews to Israel, for many remaining Jews the human links with Israel have become more salient than its symbolic representations.

Israel as Chief Emigration Destination: The 1970s and 1990s Waves of Russian Aliyah

Many Soviet Jews harbored dreams of leaving the Socialist paradise, especially after the end of World War II and the shock of the Holocaust (over one half of the Jews living in the USSR before the war had been exterminated). For many years, these dreams were a dangerous diversion and could hardly be voiced, even between friends and relatives. Jews who had close relatives in Israel, the US and capitalist Europe (and many did) had to conceal their existence, and avoided corresponding with them; having relatives abroad was a serious liability. There is little doubt that the very possibility of emigration, or even playing with this idea, became one of the main axes of the Soviet Jewish identity throughout the last three decades of Socialism.

Two historic events were involved in the upsurge of emigration motivation among Russian Jews: the upsurge of Zionist sentiments after the Six Day War, and the anti-Zionist ideological backlash and the rising tide of anti-Semitism in the wake of these events; and the ruthless destruction by the Soviets of the Czech uprising in 1968. The last hopes for political and economic liberalization, still lingering after the short-lived Thaw,[2] were gone now and many of the more active and self-conscious Jews realized that they, and especially their children, had no future in this country. Another potent "push" factor came in the form of severe restrictions for Jews in higher education. The tacit quotas for Jewish applicants to universities were re-introduced by the Soviets (emulating the tsarist practice) soon after Israel's 1967 victory and the ensuing anti-Zionist backlash. After the early 1970s, when Jews started to emigrate in significant numbers, most prestigious schools virtually closed their doors to Jewish candidates as they were seen as potential émigrés. This campaign, signaling the red light to social mobility for the next Jewish generation, greatly boosted moral readiness for emigration (Altshuler 1987).

The first real chance to leave presented itself with the beginning of the détente and concomitant warming of East-West relations in the early 1970s. For decades, Jewish emigration has been a political bargaining chip in Soviet politics, making ordinary Jewish citizens hostages of the give-and-take deals between the Kremlin and the White House, and, later on, in the contested interests of American Jewry and the Israeli government (Gitelman 1999; Lazin 2005).

Between 1971 and 1977, most Jewish émigrés finally got their exit permits and Israeli visas, and left the USSR. After 1977, the process slowed down and came to a halt in 1979–1980, after the Soviet invasion of Afghanistan. Those who applied for emigration in the 1970s and early 1980s and were refused exit visas (either because of their alleged exposure to state secrets or for no clear reason), became so-called *refuseniks* (*otkazniki* in Russian), and were stuck without jobs and income as social pariahs. Their survival hinged on mutual support, and thus dense social networks that included running free Hebrew and English classes, lending money, distributing and Western aid packages were formed by *refuseniks* over the course of the 1980s. The social groups formed by *refuseniks* were fertile ground for the clandestine Soviet Zionist movement of the 1980s; they were also intertwined with other streams of political dissidence and their leaders experienced harsh KGB persecution and imprisonment. Yet, at the same time, hunger strikes, sit-ins, and street demonstrations organized by desperate *refuseniks* gave international visibility to the "plight of Soviet Jewry" and increased the political pressure on the Soviet government from the West (Pincus 1988; Gitelman 1999). By the early 1980s, over 22,000 Soviet Jews had found themselves living in an economic, legal, and political limbo — for years at a time. The growing stream of letters, literature, and other alternative information sources from abroad (with mostly good news about life after emigration), the support of Western and Israeli Jewry, and hopes for the inevitable re-opening of emigration opportunities helped Soviet Jews to live through the final trying years of the Soviet regime, which were marked by material privations and new anti-Semitic campaigns inspired by the 1982 Lebanon war (Friedgut 1989).

The social composition of the Jews who were leaving the USSR during the 1970s was rather mixed. The first category included Jewry from the Soviet periphery — the Baltic republics, western Ukraine and Moldavia that had been included in the USSR only in 1939–40 and had thus experienced less "sovietization" and secularization than the central cities. Jews living in the western parts of the USSR, especially in smaller towns, were much more Jewish in the traditional sense, had strong Zionist orientations, and even some active Zionist cells. Georgian Jewry and smaller groups of Tats and Mountain Jews from the Caucasus were of similar ilk. When the Kremlin first signaled to local authorities to let the Jews out, emigration procedures were made expedient, and by the mid-1970s the majority of these pioneers found themselves in Israel. The majority of these emigrants had average Soviet educational attainment and belonged to the varied ranks of clerical and technical workers, teachers, white-collar service and trade occupations. After the Jackson-Vanik amendment of 1974 that made US–Soviet trade relations conditional upon the right to emigrate (reserved only for the Jews), the emigration movement received a new impetus, and now began involving the Jews of Moscow, Leningrad and other major cities as well (Gitelman 1999). Those who ventured out at this time were mainly educated professionals and intellectuals seeking freedom and economic prosperity rather than wishing to join the on-going Israeli battleground. Some of them were Zionists (and went to Israel), but the majority were merely disillusioned refugees from State Socialism. Additional discouragement from making *aliyah* had to do with the shock and losses of the Yom Kippur War of 1973 and the bitter realization that Israel was destined to fight for its existence for many years ahead.

Thus Israeli invitations and visas became mere tokens along the exit routes of Soviet Jews. After the mid-1970s, increasing numbers of those who arrived at the transit camps in Vienna opted to continue for the West, mainly the USA, and then proceeded to Rome to wait for US visas. By 1979, over 85 percent of the potential repatriates to Israel "dropped out", in Israeli terms, and "defected" to the West. This "violation of the initial intent" (that is, exiting on Israeli visas but not actually going there) was one of the pretexts used by the Soviet authorities to explain the virtual stoppage of emigration by the early 1980s (Friedgut 1989; Lazin 2005). The Israeli government was very angry at the US Jewish organizations — the Hebrew Immigrant Aid Society (HIAS) and the Jewish Distribution Committee (JDC) — that had allegedly lured Russian Jews to America by offering them generous financial aid. The same scenario (the US–Israeli "trade" for Jewish souls) was reproduced later, after the inception of the mass Jewish exodus in 1989 (Dominitz 1997).

After the dead-zone period of the early 1980s, the first winds of change blew after Gorbachev declared his Perestroika and Glasnost plans in 1985–86, with the following renewal of the emigration movement in 1987–88. The *refuseniks* and other Jews who had been prepared to leave were the first ones to apply for exit visas. After the demise of the USSR in 1991, the procedures for exiting the country were liberalized and émigrés could retain their former citizenship. The iron curtain fell and, sure enough, tens of thousands of former Soviets soon lined up at Western embassies seeking better fortunes abroad. The country was rapidly changing, and new opportunities appeared for industrious and talented people, along with new risks and stresses. The liberal reforms of the first half of the 1990s engendered severe economic polarization of the population whereby the majority sank into poverty. Yet many Jews rapidly learned how to swim in the surging waters of the new market economy and readily entered the entrepreneurial world; their material wealth and lifestyles significantly improved. As always in times of turmoil, anti-Semitism, rising from the grass-roots rather than sponsored by the government, was a corollary of pluralism and democratic freedoms. Once again, Jews were reminded that they had always been a foreign element in this country and would be better off leaving it for good (Friedgut 1989).

Throughout the 1990s the decision to leave was shaped by a constellation of factors: the realities of "jungle capitalism" in the FSU; employment and career prospects in Russia vs. abroad; fear of anti-Semitism; age; health; and the wish to join family members already living abroad. The social costs of emigration became much lower, exit procedures became easier, and rituals of exclusion and punishment at work vanished along with the rest of communist ideology. Potential émigrés were looked upon with envy rather than disdain now. In addition, many urban residents had privatized their apartments by 1992–93 and could sell them at market prices, making initial resources for their resettlement abroad. In any event, the emigration decisions of

Russian Jews in the 1990s were driven by pragmatic rather than ideological considerations, that is, the careful weighing of the gains and losses in the FSU *vis-à-vis* those of possible destinations abroad.

Then the second crucial decision was had to be made: where to go? Israel and the U.S. had been the chief options during the 1970 and late 1980s; in 1989 alone 38,395 Soviet Jews hadve entered the US as refugees and another 30,000 or more had applications pending. Yet the special status of Soviet Jews in the US refugee programme was discontinued, and from the early 1990s on, their emigration to the US sharply decreased. In Europe, only Germany received Soviet Jews after 1991, but many Jews had strong anti-German attitudes in the wake of the war with the Nazis and the Holocaust. For many others, though, the possibility of living in the heart of "civilized Europe" and the generous welfare policy of the German state had been very enticing. Many mixed families opted for Germany as it did not inquire into their Jewish "purity". Australia and Canada screened the applicants by age, health and "human capital" rather than ethnicity, and their immigration programmes were generally small-scale. Throughout the 1990s and early 2000s, Israel was the only country receiving all Jewish émigrés without any screening. The checks into Jewish "purity" were relaxed over time as the demographic potential for ex-Soviet *aliyah* was running out. Meantime the *Sochnut* continued its nation-wide campaigns aimed at recruiting post-Soviet Jews (mainly of mixed origin) for *aliyah*. Yet Israel was not an attractive destination for many pragmatically disposed Russian Jews: a small country in the Middle East with few jobs, a hot climate, a difficult language, and an on-going military conflict with its neighbors. For many parents who had saved their sons from being drafted into the Soviet Army and possible participation in the Chechen war, mandatory military service in Israel was another strong deterrent. This is not to say that Zionist sentiments were completely missing among Soviet Jews planning emigration, but they were certainly less common than in the early 1970s wave.

While Russian Jews were contemplating emigration, covert political struggle about their fate and destination was ongoing between the two interest lobbies: the Israeli government and its Zionist arm *Sochnut* versus American Jewish organizations and their lobbyists in the White House. As a result of their efforts to lift the restrictions, the refugee quotas for ex-Soviet Jews were once again increased after 1992, and almost 157,000 were resettled in the US before the end of 1996 (HIAS 1997). The Israeli government observed the continuing influx of Russian and Ukrainian Jews into the US with growing frustration. In the words of a high-ranking Israeli official, Yehuda Dominitz (1997: 121), "The start of the Soviet Jewish exodus to Israel was considered an historic opportunity to increase the Jewish population of Israel, build the nation and strengthen Israel's social fabric and cultural foundations. *To forfeit such an opportunity by letting tens of thousands of Jews opt for other countries of migration would be unforgivable.*" (my emphasis). Thus Russian Jews were treated once again as a tool for reaching the macro-level political and ideological goals of state power holders, rather than as individuals seeking better lives and making independent decisions. American Jewry seemed split on this issue, with Zionist circles believing that artificial direction of the wave of migrant Jews to Israel was necessary and morally justified, while a liberal lobby insisted on freedom of movement for those leaving the FSU. Both sides realized that the US would be a destination of choice for the majority of the new migrants. The Israelis remembered only too well the dropout of Russian Jews in

Vienna during the late 1970s, and made sure that this transit camp was closed in 1990. Soon after reopening the Israeli embassy in Moscow, Israel established direct flights to Tel Aviv from several major cities. Both applications and issuance of visas to the US (on a case-by-case basis rather than on automatic grounds) moved directly to the American Embassy in Moscow, eliminating the need to use Israeli visas for the transit. This ensured that the process of emigration to Israel was fast-tracked, while emigration to the Western countries for ex-Soviets became as protracted as for other international applicants.

As a result of this restructuring of the policies of the main hosting countries, Israeli authorities could proudly report that from 1989 to 1993, almost twice as many Soviet Jews made *aliyah* to Israel than moved to the West (close to half a million and 250,000, respectively). The *aliyah* movement enjoyed record years in 1990 and 1991: over 183,000 and 147,000 new immigrants, respectively, arrived in Israel in just two years (33 percent of the total size of the 1990s wave). After 1993–94 the emigration drive of the Jews diminished in line with the improving economy in Russia and the relaxation of anti-Jewish sentiments. The pull to Israel was further diminished by discouraging news from friends and relatives about the hardships of adjustment there: the lack of jobs for professionals; the challenge of learning Hebrew; housing shortages; and a broad cultural gap between Russian and Israeli Jews. Together, these changes curtailed the stream of migrants to Israel by 300 percent. During the mid-1990s, between 68 and 50 thousand Jews were registered annually as Russian *olim* (Hebrew for new immigrants), with a similar number leaving for various Western destinations (mainly the US and Germany). A brief upsurge in immigration to Israel occurred in 1999 — over 67,000, vs. 46,000 in the previous year — in response to the 1998 financial crisis in Russia, after which many Jews lost their savings and small businesses. This is a strong indication of the dominance of "push factors" in the *aliyah* movement of former Soviet Jews, and the perceived image of Israel as a shelter country. In the new millennium, the flow of new immigrants to Israel slowed to some 34,000 in 2001, and then to slightly over 10,000 in 2004. Since 2002, more ex-Soviet Jews have emigrated annually to Germany than made *aliyah* to Israel, and the numbers of ex-Soviet Jews coming to the US as refugees dropped to less than 5,000 per year.

The social composition of the immigrants to Israel has significantly evolved over the 17 years since the inception of the Great *Aliyah*, as it is called in Israel. The first *olim* to move this time were of the top professional echelon from the capitals and other big cities, many of whom missed their train to the US after 1989 but felt compelled to leave Russia, fearing chaos and violence. In 1989–90, 34 percent of the *olim* came from Moscow alone. By 1993 this had dropped to 17 percent; the respective figures for the Jews of St. Petersburg were 28 percent and 12 percent. The share of immigrants from smaller provincial cities grew respectively from 54 percent in 1989 to 71 percent in 1993, and reached 95 percent in 2001. Over time, less *olim* came from Russia and more from the Ukraine, Belarussia, Central Asia, and the Caucasus. As was mentioned above, the size and location of the city of origin strongly correlates with the "human capital" of Soviet Jews; the professional elite usually coming from Moscow, St Petersburg and a few other major industrial and academic centres. Thus the percentage of *olim* with higher education in 2002 dropped to 35 percent, vs. 72 percent in 1990. Many experts believe that, compared to those who migrated to North America and Europe, Israel has accommodated the older, less healthy, and less professionally fit portion of ex-Soviet Jewry — mainly due to its unselective immigration policy towards any carrier of Jewish ancestry. Yet, after an initial period of material privations and cultural shock, most Russian Jews have found their place in the complex social structure of Israeli society (see Part II in Remennick 2006).

Jewish Life after State Socialism: The Role of Israel in the Jewish Revival

By the early 2000s, the Jewish emigration flow had dried up to a trickle of 30–40 thousand annually to all destinations, with Israel the least popular among them. Jews who have remained in the FSU are either too old to move, or too assimilated and rather well adjusted. In her 2005 book *Jewish Lives in Russia: Recent Dynamics* sociologist Rosalina Ryvkina compared two waves (1995 and 2004) in her survey of a sample of 1,000 Jewish households in four large Russian cities, including Moscow. (About half of the sample participated in both surveys, with the other half of the sample recruited in 2004). Her discussion of Israel's role in the lives of her respondents mainly revolves around emigration plans and ties with relatives and friends living in Israel. Ryvkina reports, for example, that 23 percent of respondents in 2004 had close relatives in Israel and 65 percent had some family there; about 80 percent had "significant others" with whom they kept in touch (family or friends) — (the broader categories are inclusive of the narrower ones and are not meant to add up to 100 percent). Visits to Israel were reported by 41 percent (including 18 percent who had two or more visits and 15 percent spending three months or more in Israel). Thus a significant fraction of Russian Jews have a first-hand knowledge of Israel and maintain personal links with Russian Israelis. Ryvkina suggests that ties between Russian Jews and their friends and relatives in Israel are closer, more intense and regular than the ties Russian Jews have with any other country of Jewish emigration (for example, US, Canada, or Germany).

At the same time, about 70 percent of respondents in 2004 believed that all or most of those Jews who had not left already would stay in Russia (vs. 30 percent in the 1995 sample). Only 6 percent of respondents in 2004 (vs. 15 percent in 1995) agreed with the statement that all Jews should eventually go to Israel, and 0 percent (vs. 3 percent in 1995) believed that this would actually happen with Russian Jews. The lack of interest in making *aliyah* reflected the first-hand knowledge of many respondents (via their Israeli contacts and visits) about the difficulties of integration in Israel. Only 8 percent of the sample believed that their life in Israel would be an improvement over their current lives in Russia (vs.16 percent in 1995) and only 9 percent said that Israel would be a better place for their children, while the majority believed that Russia (37 percent) or other countries (26 percent) would promise them a better future. Only 23 percent said that Israel offers good or decent conditions for Russian immigrants' accommodation, while 62 percent believed that conditions were poor or did not know. The respondents who estimated their personal prospects in Israel more positively belonged to either a younger age group (18–29) or to those of retirement age (65+), while middle-aged respondents were pessimistic about their chances to find good jobs and prosper. When asked about the prospects of peace in Israel, 41 percent did not believe that Arab–Israeli conflict can be solved in the visible future and another 23 percent assumed that it can be solved after a decade or more. Interest in Israeli politics was found mainly amongst older generations of Russian Jews, who closely follow current events in the media, call their relatives after acts of terror, etc. Jews with stronger Jewish identity (for example, having two Jewish parents vs. one) expressed stronger feelings towards Israel and had more contact with their close ones living there. In summary, this survey indicates that most Russian Jews no longer connect their personal future with Israel, although many enjoy personal ties and visits to this country, and express solidarity with Israeli causes generally. Thus, Russian Jews' attitude towards Israel resembles the attitude found in parts of North American Jewry and in other Diaspora countries.

There is only sparse data available on the role of Israel in the Jewish education and community participation of younger Jewish generations. Some recent surveys (Chlenov 1997; Cherviakov et al. 2003; Ryvkina 2005) indicate that the fraction of Jews involved in Jewish community life in any form (subscriptions to Jewish press, attendance of synagogues and community events, taking Hebrew classes, participation in actions and fund-raising on behalf of Israel) varies between 5 and 15 percent (depending on the sample). What's more, those actively involved with the Jewish community and interested in Israel tend eventually to embark on *aliyah* and thus stop contributing to local Jewish life. Although about 100 Jewish schools have opened since the early 1990s across Russia, only a fraction of Jewish children (between 10 and 20 percent) attend them as their main day school. These schools are usually funded by *Chabad*, or Israeli and American Jewish organizations, and offer good physical resources (for example, free lunch, textbooks, busing). Because of this, Jewish schools increasingly attract parents with poor economic backgrounds, who are not necessarily Jewish. As these schools devote a larger chunk of their schedule to Jewish subjects, they often lag behind good regular schools in the sciences, math, languages, and other core disciplines deemed as central by educated Jewish parents. Secular (or cultural) Jewish schools in large Russian cities can only survive with external funding, and only if their curriculum is not "too Jewish", that is, compatible with the national standards, thus allowing their graduates to bid for higher education (Krichevsky 2005). The involvement of younger Jews (usually of mixed descent) with Israel mainly occurs via *Sochnut* programmes for study in Israel targeting high school students (such as NAALE 16 and SELA). These programmes assume that after two to three years of academic study in Israel, most visitors will make *aliyah* and eventually lead their parents to join them (in Hebrew, the acronym NAALE means *youth migrating before parents*). Typically, no short-term visits to Israel are offered to Russian youth by *birthright israel* nor by other *Sochnut* programmes run in the US and other western countries. Policy-wise, the focus is on direct brokerage of *aliyah* for young Russian Jews, rather than a symbolic "rite of passage" to Jewishness (Bardach 2005).

After the fall of communism, Russia experienced a true religious revival, allowing different faiths to bloom and proselytize. Jewish religious organizations, *Chabad* being the most visible and active among them, now compete for the hearts and minds of the remaining Russian Jews. While both the Russian Orthodox Church and several Judaic denominations welcomed those leaning towards organized religion, many Russians with religious tendencies chose the predominant and familiar Christian faith (Deutsch Kornblatt 2003). Those interested in Orthodox Judaism went to religious schools and joined the synagogues for a short while, only to realize that true Jewish life is hardly possible in Russia; eventually most of these Jews left for Israel or the US. Liberal Judaic confessions (Reform and Conservative) are not strongly represented in the Soviet successor states, and Orthodox Judaism is too dogmatic and obsolete for most former Soviets. Political power games between various rabbinical officials (for example, the chronic conflict between the two Chief Rabbis of Russia — Adolf Shaevich representing the old Soviet/Russian version of religious Judaism and Berl Lazar appointed as a leader of "New Russian Jewry" from *Chabad*'s global headquarters in New York), the aggressive proselytism of Hassidic organizations, their cozy relationship with the Kremlin and flashy demonstrations of alleged philo-Semitism by the current power holders (for example, Chanukah celebration in the Kremlin Palace) have further repelled many from joining any Jewish activities. There is not enough indigenous grassroots initiative and drive to let Jewish causes thrive in Russia; many articles in the 2003 volume *Jewish Life after the USSR* edited by Gitelman et al., as well as my own recent visits to Moscow and conversations with a few remaining Jewish relatives and friends — all attest to this sad conclusion. David Shneer's upbeat depiction of the "Jewish revival" in Moscow (Shneer 2005) reflects the author's outsider stance, his highly selective sources (he interviewed mainly Jewish activists), and a certain naiveté in interpretation. Of course the signs of Jewish presence are much more visible to a foreigner's eye in today's Russian cities than they were during Soviet times, but this impression is superficial. The remaining Jews are largely of mixed origin and/or well assimilated and consider Russian cultural traditions, with their built-in Orthodox Christian streak, their own (Nosenko 2004). Having no long-term cultural and demographic basis in Russia and other Slavic countries, the Judaic "boom" is probably short-lived. It will eventually dissolve, along with its corollary social and financial aid programmes sponsored from the West that, indeed, helped many Jews survive the hard times of post-communist transition. Those ethnic Jews who chose Russia not only as their cultural anchor but as their homeland are not likely to ever coalesce into a Jewish community or profess the Jewish faith.

The Ties between FSU and Israel in the Open World: Transnationalism and the New Jewish Diaspora

New forms of connection between Russia and Israel are emerging in the open society, marked by transnational activities and lifestyles. With their emigration, Russian Jews discovered freedom of movement, unthinkable in Soviet times. As already noted, many immigrants revisit their cities of origin in the FSU and their relatives and friends in the West as often as their modest incomes allow. About one third of all post-1989 *olim* keep Russian or Ukrainian passports and do not need visas; some also have apartments or country cottages to stay in. It should be noted that after the economic and political freefall of the 1990s, living standards and consumer markets in Russia and Ukraine have significantly improved. There is a thriving business culture and the winds of opportunity blow strong in the vast former Soviet territories. For creative and sociable individuals, especially those endowed with some capital and business skills, the sky is ostensibly the limit in Moscow. The thriving culture of restaurants, clubs, and discos fits any taste and wallet; the city is increasingly cosmopolitan and diverse. The level of street anti-Semitism is much lower today than it was in the early post-

Soviet years, and institutional anti-Semitism has all but vanished, judging by the visibility of Jewish politicians and businessmen.

Given that many immigrants still have dense social networks in large Russian cities, and thrive in the familiar language and culture, the idea of return is very appealing. After a number of shuttle visits, some *olim* may decide to return to Russia or alternatively, to live in both countries (Feldman 2003). The Jewish organizations in Moscow estimate that the number of returnees who live and work in the city is around 35,000, and their number is growing. At the same time, the statistical bureau of the Russian Federation reported that only about 14,000 immigrants who returned to all Russian cities from Israel have registered as permanent residents between 1997 and 2003 (Shapiro 2005). Russian Jews who have lived in Israel and returned to Moscow have established various cultural and entertainment venues for their own ilk in Moscow, such as Israeli club *Darkon* ("passport" in Hebrew) which is frequented by young programmers and IT designers who speak a mix of Russian and Hebrew. Restaurants serving Israeli and Middle Eastern food, stores selling Israeli musical records and DVDs, and other businesses owned by Russian Israelis in Moscow, St. Petersburg and Kiev serve as a mirror image of the Russian stores in Tel Aviv, Haifa, and other Israeli cities. Everything Israeli is no longer clandestine but, on the contrary, rather trendy, so Russian Jews who can speak Hebrew enjoy a high status in Moscow's inner crowd.

The option of keeping two homes is more practical for the retired immigrants not tied to workplaces in either country; some of them continue to collect their modest pensions in both countries, spending winters in Israel and summers in Russia. The Israeli old-age benefit payment of some US$300 per month is still two to three times higher than an average Moscow pension, and these combined incomes allow older Jews to live more comfortably in their home cities. Another category of returnees is that of the entrepreneurs whose ventures draw on supplies or partnerships in Russia and Ukraine. Speaking with some of the more successful *olim* business people, I heard a repeated complaint that growing "Russian" businesses are stifled and limited in Israel by local protectionism and nepotism; for outsiders and novices there is simply no access to low-interest bank loans, prestigious premises, and lucrative contracts. For some others, the internal Israeli market is just too small. Frustrated by these barriers, some businessmen have moved their operations to a more dangerous, but familiar Russian capitalist jungle. Yet another category of returnees includes high-tech specialists, especially in IT and programming, who could gain higher incomes and better contracts than in Israel in the booming Russian high-tech industry. Yet, for most returnees, this comeback is not final, but rather, another stage in their cosmopolitan life cycle. Although "double return migrants" spend most of their time in Moscow or St. Petersburg (two main hubs of return), they never sever their ties with Israel; many keep apartments in Israel and often visit their parents and friends there.

Throughout the last decade the policy-makers and demographers have tried to measure the extent of out-migration of former Soviet *olim* from Israel. In 2004, the number of Russian Jews who left Israel and did not return for at least one year stood at 58,400. Juxtaposed with the 908,200 immigrants from the FSU who resettled in Israel between 1990 and 2001, this means that out-migrants form around 6 percent of the total. This is a much lower level of exit compared to other immigrants to Israel from developed countries (for example, 25 percent among North American Jews, 18 percent among Argentinean Jews, and 16 percent among the French Jews). The majority of ex-Soviet Jews who left Israel moved to Canada and the US, with some also leaving for Russia, Ukraine or European countries. As all of these people keep Israeli passports and some of them will possibly return or come for prolonged visits, it is technically difficult to measure the fraction of final out-migrants (*yordim*, that is, going down, in the Hebrew lore). In any case, the absolute majority of the post-1989 Russian immigrants have remained in Israel, despite all the political turmoil, security problems, and economic ups and downs (Remennick 2006).

To conclude, Israel has been part of Jewish lives in Russia continuously, but in different ways over the years. During Soviet times, Israel and *aliyah* were symbols of dissent with the oppressive regime and a call for freedom, fueling the will to persevere and promising a better future for the children. The Israeli wars of 1967 and 1973 served as building blocks for the dormant Jewish identity among many Soviet citizens. When the iron curtain showed its first cracks in the early 1970s, many émigrés with a stronger Jewish identity made *aliyah*, while many others sought their fortunes in the US. With the renewal of the emigration movement in the late 1980s and throughout the 1990s, 1.6 million Jews and their family members left the FSU, and over 60 percent found themselves in Israel due to changes in the global immigration context. The establishment of a thriving isle of Russian Jewish life in Israel has reinforced cultural and social links between the two countries, made possible by open borders and the transnational lifestyles of many Russian Israelis. Thus, tangible images of the real Israel — via its cultural products, food, and the sounds of Hebrew in the streets — have entered the lives of Moscow, St. Petersburg, Kiev and other major Russian and Ukrainian cities, influencing local Jews and non-Jews alike.

Notes

1. More detailed discussion of the evolution of the Russian Jewish identity during Soviet and post-Soviet times can be found in Part 1 of my book *Russian Jews on Three Continents: Identity, Integration, and Conflict* (Transaction Publishers, 2007).
2. The short period of political liberalization of the Soviet regime a few years after Stalin's death (late 1950s–early 1960s), which ended with the ascent to power of Leonid Brezhnev in 1964.

References

Altshuler, Mordecai, *Soviet Jewry Since the Second World War: Population and Social Structure* (Westport, CT: Greenwood Press, 1987).

Altshuler, Mordechai, *Soviet Jewry on the Eve of the Holocaust: A Social and_Demographic Profile* (Jerusalem: Center for Research on East European Jewry, The Hebrew University of Jerusalem, and *Yad Vashem* — The Holocaust Martyrs' and Heroes' Remembrance Authority, 1998), Chapters 2–4.

Bardach, Rebecca, "Israel: A Country of Immigration". In *World Migration 2005: Costs and Benefits of International Migration* (Geneva: International Organization for Migration, 2005).

Brym, Robert J. (with the assistance of Rosalina Ryvkina), *The Jews of Moscow, Kiev and Minsk: Identity, Antisemitism, Emigration* (New York, NY: New York University Press, 1994).

Cherviakov, Valeriy, Gitelman, Zvi, and Shapiro, Vladimir (2003). "*E Pluribus Unum?* Post-Soviet Jewish Identities and Their Implications for Communal Reconstruction". In Gitelman, Zvi et al. (eds), *Jewish Life After the USSR* (Bloomington: Indiana University Press, 2003).

Chiswick, Barry R., "Soviet Jews in the United States: Language and Labor Market

Adjustments Revisited". In N. Lewin-Epstein et al. (eds), *Russian Jews on Three Continents: Migration and Resettlement* (London: Frank Cass, 1997), pp. 233–260..
Chlenov, Mikhail, "Jewish Community and Identity in the Former Soviet Union". In *Jews of the Former Soviet Union: Yesterday, Today, and Tomorrow*, Conference Proceedings. (New York: The American Jewish Committee, 1997), pp. 11–16.
Deutsch Kornblatt, Judith, "Jewish Converts to Orthodoxy in Russia in Recent Decades". In Gitelman, Zvi et al. (eds), *Jewish Life After the USSR* (Bloomington: Indiana University Press, 2003), pp. 209–223.
Dominitz, Yehuda, "Israel's Immigration Policy and the Dropout Phenomenon". In N. Lewin-Epstein, Y. Ro'i and P. Ritterband (eds), *Russian Jews on Three Continents. Migration and Resettlement* (London, UK & Portland, OR: Frank Cass, 1997), pp. 113–127.
Feldman, Eliezer, *Russkii Izrail': Mezhdu Dvuh Polusov* (translates as "Israel: Between the Two Poles"). (Moscow: Market DS, 2003.) (In Russian.)
Friedgut, Theodore H., "Passing Eclipse: The Exodus Movement of the 1980s".
In R.O. Freedman (ed.), *Soviet Jewry in the 1980s. The Politics of Anti-Semitism and Emigration and the Dynamics of Resettlement* (Durham: Duke University Press, 1989), pp. 3–25.
Gitelman, Zvi, "Soviet Jews: Creating a Cause and a Movement". In M. Friedman and A. D. Chernin (eds), *A Second Exodus. The American Movement to Free Soviet Jews* (Hanover & London: Brandeis University Press, 1999), pp. 84–93.
Gitelman, Zvi, "Thinking About Being Jewish in Russia and Ukraine". In Z. Gitelman, M. Glanz and M.Goldman (eds), *Jewish Life After the USSR* (Bloomington: Indiana University Press, 2003), pp. 49–60.
Krichevsky, Lev, "Teaching for the Future. Leaders of Jewish Schools in Ex-USSR Hope to Attract Masses. *Evreiskaya Gazeta* (Moscow Jewish paper), 12 June 2005.
Lazin, Fred A., *The Struggle of Soviet Jewry in American Politics: Israel Versus American Jewish Establishment* (New York, NY: Lexington Books, 2005).
Nosenko, Elena E. "Byt' ili chuvstvovat'? Osnovnye aspekty formirovaniya evreiskoi samo-identifikatsii u potomkov smeshannykh brakov v sovremennoi Rossii". (Translates as "To Be or to Feel Jewish? The Expressions of Jewish Identity among Offspring of Mixed Marriage in Contemporary Russia".) (Moscow: Institute of Oriental Studies, Russian Academy of Sciences, 2004). (In Russian.)
Pincus, Benjamin, *The Jews of the Soviet Union. The History of a National Minority* (New York, NY: Cambridge University Press, 1988).
Remennick, Larissa, "Identity Quest among Russian Jews of the 1990s: Before and After Emigration". In E. Krausz and G. Tulea (eds), *Jewish Survival: The Identity Problem at the Close of the 20th Century* (New Brunswick, NJ: Transaction Publishers, 1998), pp. 241–258.
Remennick, Larissa, *Russian Jews on Three Continents: Identity, Integration, and Conflict* (New Brunswick, NJ: Transaction Publishers, 2006).
Ro'i, Yaakov, "Religion, Israel, and the Development of Soviet Jewry's National Consciousness, 1967–1991". In Z. Gitelman, M. Glanz and M. Goldman (eds), *Jewish Life After the USSR* (Bloomington: Indiana University Press, 2003), pp. 13–26.
Ryvkina, Rosalina, *Kak Zhivut Yevrei v Rossii?: Sociologicheskii Analiz Peremen.* [Translates as "How Do Jews Live in Russia?: Sociological Analysis of Changes" (Moscow: Dom Yevreiskoi Knigi, 2005).
Shapiro, Inna (2005). "*Reverse Immigration to Russia Falls by 20%*". Viewed online 3 January 2005 at: <www.haaretz.com>.
Slezkine, Yuri, *The Jewish Century* (Princeton, NJ: Princeton University Press, 2004).
Shneer, David, "'They Aren't Stuck Here, They Live Here': Moscow Jews and Russian Jewish Life". In D. Shneer and C. Aviv *New Jews: The End of the Jewish Diaspora* (New York, NY: New York University Press, 2005).
Tolts, Mark, "Demography of the Jews in the Former Soviet Union: Yesterday and Today". In

Zvi Gitelman (ed.), *Jewish Life After the USSR,* Bloomington: Indiana University Press (2003), pp. 173–208.

Tolts, Mark, "The Post-Soviet Jewish Population in Russia and the World", *Jews in Russia and Eastern Europe* (a publication of the Hebrew University of Jerusalem), 1, 52 (2004): 37–63.

Zeltser, Arkadii, "Jews in the Upper Ranks of the NKVD, 1934–1941". *Jews in Russia and Eastern Europe* (a publication of the Hebrew University of Jerusalem), 1, 52 (2004): 64–91.

Conclusion
Israel in Diaspora Jewish Identity

A PERPECTIVE FROM ISRAEL

What Does It All Mean

Gabriel Sheffer

World Jewry, like most ethno-national-religious diasporas, is experiencing major changes. Even unbiased sensitive observers of the Jewish phenomenon have realized and argued that these changes are in fact fundamental transformations. Most authors of the chapters in this volume have quite obviously, but unfortunately not emphatically enough, noticed these changes. These writers argue that the changes or transformations are both reflected in and affecting Israel's position in the identity of world Jewry, and in Israel's various roles in the entire Jewish nation, as perceived by Diaspora Jews.

Before dealing with the reasons for these changes and their above mentioned impacts, two basic aspects characterizing Jewry, which are very frequently forgotten in analyses of the position of World Jewry, should be emphasized. First, it goes almost without saying that Israel's position in the minds and feelings of Diaspora Jews is determined by separate developments in both the Diaspora and Israel. The second significant aspect, which only few stress, but again is expressed in some of the chapters in this volume (see for example, Gordis and Livni in this volume), is that, like other ethno-national-religious diasporas, World Jewry, including Israel, is not a homogeneous entity by any means. The entire nation and each of its constituent parts are split in regard to most issues — identity, identification, Israel's position and desired role, Diaspora relations with Israel, the needed support for Israel, the organization of the Diaspora entities and the entire World Jewry, and the preferable strategies and activities. These two very basic and important aspects should be taken into consideration in any in-depth analysis of the Jewish Diaspora–Israeli case.

It is true that the demographic development and changes in the geographical locations that have occurred and are occurring in World Jewry are not the most essential factors determining the place of Israel in the minds and feelings of Diaspora Jews.

However, these factors contribute to the cognitive and conceptual, as well as individual and collective psychological and behavioural transformations. These demographic and geographic changes include the following factors:

1 the fast diminishing number of living Jews who escaped the Holocaust, or lived during that horrible period, which according to certain chapters on both general issues and on particular Jewish entities, have had an impact on the Diaspora's connection to Israel, and its corollary role of younger Jews who have been influenced by other trends (see for example, Rynhold in this volume);
2 the fact that in the not too distant future the largest Jewish concentration in the world may be in Israel;
3 the social, political and economic implications of the need to organize and reorganize new Jewish entities as a result of migration, population movements within one hostland and demographic changes;
4 the improving or worsening cultural, social, political and economic situation of Jews in their homelands;
5 the impacts of globalization and glocalization; etc.

While all these developments do really occur and have impact on World Jewry and its relations with Israel, it should also be noted that the fear, which is expressed by many Israelis and Diaspora Jews, that the Jewish nation will disappear as a result of the substantial drop in natural growth (the annual rate now is 0.06 percent), growing assimilation, or full integration is exaggerated.

In this respect, all those who study the past and current situation of World Jewry as a unique phenomenon and make predictions about its future, should consider the growing literature on other ethno-national diasporas. It is pretty clear that, although some of the historically older and established diasporas are losing some members through assimilation and lack of willingness to participate in diasporic organizations and activities, their cores are far from disappearing. Moreover, dormant diasporas are being revived, and second and third generations of members of new and incipient diasporas maintain their identity, affiliation and active membership within these diasporas (see for example, Braziel and Mannur 2003; Sheffer 2003).

In any case, an important factor affecting Israel's position in the entire Jewish nation — not so much in the hearts but rather in the minds of Diaspora Jews — is the percentage of *core Jews* (those whose identity, affiliation and identification is clearly Jewish, which means also a strong connection to the homeland, whether on the basis of religious beliefs or on the basis of secular ideational, or ideological views, or ethno-national feelings) and the percentage of *peripheral Jews* (those of Jewish origins, but who do not identify as such and whose emotional and practical contacts with Israel are also far from being continuous or close). These percentages differ from one hostland to another — thus, in Russia core Jews constitute 89 percent of the entire entity, in the US 74 percent, with similar percentages in other Jewish centres. These percentages are changing as a result of intermarriage, assimilation, full integration and lack of concern about identity and affiliation. These factors certainly influence the attitudes toward Israel and the actual contact with it, as evidenced by rates of immigration, remittances, investment and visits. (On visits to Israel issue see Mittelberg in this volume.)

If we proceed to further examine the effect of the demographic and geographic impacts on the Diaspora and its relations with Israel, we find, as briefly mentioned before, that 90 percent of World Jewry permanently live in 2 percent of the states that enjoy the highest degree of "human development" (on this conception and term see the United Nations' *Millennium Development Goals*, 2003). While most Diaspora Jews permanently live in the highest rated hostlands, Israel is now rated only twenty-second on that list of developed countries. As a result of this sad, ongoing drop in Israel's position, and as will be argued below, due to additional substantial factors, Israel's image is becoming damaged, especially in the eyes of Diaspora Jews. There is no doubt that this development influences Israel's position in the mentality, feelings and actual deeds of many Diaspora Jews, especially younger and non-affiliated Jews.

Moreover, in most hostlands Jews live mainly in cities or towns, most obtain secondary and higher education, and they make their living being employed by technical enterprises (including high-tech), businesses and academia, all professions that require a high degree of individual specialization and dedication (this does not mean that there are no Jews with a lesser degree of education and affluence). However, by dint of this situation, many of these persons will be more critical about many aspects of Jewish life in general and Israel in particular. Among other things, these individuals place on the Jewish agenda very tough questions about Israel's centrality in World Jewry.

Certainly no less important, and probably more momentous than the previous factors, are the major changes in the patterns of identity and identification of Diaspora Jews. These changes should be attributed partly to the demographic and geographic developments mentioned earlier, and partly to the cultural, social and political developments in host countries and the global environment. As noted by some of the authors in this volume, in this respect even the Jewish core is becoming less homogeneous and more diversified in comparison to its previous situation, from the aftermath of World War II until the 1980s.

Here let me add a few words about the general issue of Jewish identity. According to the approach that argues the Jewish Diaspora is an ethno-national-religious organized trans-state entity (Sheffer 2003) its identity is based on a combination of primordial, mythical–psychological and instrumental elements. This characterization is based on the integrative theoretical approach concerning ethnicity and nationalism in general, and diasporas in particular (see, for example, Kelass 1991). Hence, despite the demographic and geographic changes in World Jewry, due to the loyalty of core members to their identity, as defined above, and to an extent because of hostility that is occasionally directed at Jews in their hostlands, pessimism about the continuity of World Jewry is exaggerated. However, this does not mean that Jewish and Israeli leaders should rest assured. Again, as some of the contributors to this volume have mentioned, there is much to do to ensure Jewish continuity, especially concerning Jews who regard themselves as core members and maintain emotional and rational connections to Israel.

Under the influence of continued globalization and the more liberal atmosphere in most democratic host countries, and despite ups and downs in anti-Semitism (see Ben-Moshe in this volume), the scope of the shared beliefs and values that characterized the Jews from World War II until the 1980s is diminishing. Thus, nowadays the previous dominant conception that Jewry is primarily a religious community is diminishing too. In fact, the identity and identification of more Jews is based on their ethno-national-communal views and sentiments. That is, the identity and identification are based on general cultural principles rather then predominantly on the "pure" religious elements in Jewish culture. Partly this shift is also caused by a marked change from feelings and cognition based mainly on communal values and solidarity to more individual and individualistic values. Through what is called "contagion" this trend is of course enhanced by the impact of cultural globalization, glocalization, liberalization and other similar fashions (DellaPergola 2005).

As noted by three contributors to this volume, it is true that in the US the order of connectedness to Israel is as follows: because of their religious beliefs Ultra-Orthodox and Orthodox Jews are most connected, and then in a descending order are the Conservatives, Reconstructionists, Reformist and finally Secular Jews (Waxman; Gordis; Livni in this volume). However, the fact is that the Orthodox and Conservative Jews are far from being the majority of the Jewish entity in the US or of other Jewish communities worldwide. Thus, the actual favourable, as well as more negative attitudes, of the majority of Jews towards Israel are not a result of the religious Ultra-Orthodox or Orthodox factor. The sources of these attitudes should be sought in other aspects of Jewish existence today (Cohen 1998; Shain 2002).

Therefore, a significant aspect that should be seriously reviewed is the situation of one of the more noteworthy social factors — the Jewish family. The cultural, attitudinal and emotional factors, which are enhanced by the tendency toward greater integration in host countries, pose significant dilemmas and difficulties for the family institution. There is no question that the family, which used to be one of the main socializing instruments in Jewry, is losing its predominant role. The family used to pass on Jewish identity and commitment to it to the younger generations. Now the failing family institution creates ambiguity in the identity of grown ups and younger Jews following in their footsteps. The almost expected consequences are the growth of the number of peripheral Jews who demonstrate greater ambiguity in their identity and identification with the entire nation in general, and Israel in particular. These changes further diminish the readiness of many core and peripheral members to actively get involved in-communal activities and thus also in activities for Israel.

This is closely related to and enhanced by the growing criticisms — made especially by younger Jews — of most of the existing traditional organizations that are, for all intents and purposes, led and run by professionals who are identified with Israeli interests. This phenomenon creates additional alienation towards Israel. This happens fairly constantly except during periods of great threats to Israel. Mostly under such circumstances the support for Israel increases.

As noted above, identity and identification are the most significant elements that determine active membership in Jewish entities and the nature of the relations between Diaspora Jews and Israel. In this context it should be added that it is a fact that most core and peripheral Jews in the Diaspora do not regard themselves as living in *Galut* (Exile). Most of these Jews feel and think that they are permanent residents in their hostlands as a result of their own rational choices, or in fewer cases, as a result of inertia. This is quite different from the perceptions of most Israelis who still regard Diaspora Jews as living in *Galut*. This unfounded perception of many Israelis, including politicians and bureaucrats involved in Israeli–Diaspora relations, is reflected in their statements and actions. On the other hand, these feelings and views are not shared by many Diaspora Jews. The result is that there is self-assurance about living in hostlands, which is strengthened by social and political legitimisation granted to the Jews by many host societies and governments, to continue to live in these countries. Hence there is no widespread urge to return to Israel. This self assurance is shared by both Jews and Israelis living outside Israel — the *yordim* (Gold and Bruce 1996; Gold in this volume). To an extent, after the late Yitzhak Rabin withdrew from his negative attitude concerning the Israelis and Jews permanently living in the Diaspora, more, but certainly not all, Israelis and even Israeli politicians began to accept and legitimize the Diaspora and stress the need to keep contacts and close relations with it.

These factors influence the main strategies of Jewish entities in the Diaspora concerning the need to ensure their own continuity, strength and revival. The other side of this coin is that to facilitate the attainment of their local needs they tend to limit the scope of their relations with Israel, including donations, political involvement, visits, etc.

Again, probably of even greater significance in this context, Israel is seen, at present, through the eyes of many Diaspora Jews, neither as a very inspiring nor innovative cultural entity. Israel is regarded by many Diaspora Jews as a mediocre state. Some of its scientists may get the Nobel Prize, but on the whole neither its cultural nor scientific achievements are very impressive. Consequently, few Diaspora Jews view Israel as a source of inspiration or target of full identification. Moreover, many Diaspora Jews have realized that the revival and continuity of Jewish culture in the Diaspora does not depend on the knowledge of Hebrew, or on Israeli cultural achievements. Since various leaders in the Diaspora, especially in the US, France and Russia, know that Jewish culture is very important for their continuity, they are trying to enhance the knowledge and understanding of general Jewish culture, but not necessarily according to Israeli interpretations. Since leaders and activists in the Diaspora maintain that Israel would not be able to fulfill this cultural mission, the educational programmes and syllabi are prepared in the local languages by intellectuals and experts in the Diaspora.

Another problem facing many Jewish Diasporic entities concerns the positions and roles of some of their organizations, especially those who have special and close relations with Israel. Despite the significant role that some of these venerable organizations have fulfilled and are fulfilling, there is a marked decrease in their legitimacy in the eyes of Diaspora Jews and the respect shown to them by these Jews. Veteran organizations especially are criticized and accused on the grounds of their ideology, their goals, the directions of their activities, their undemocratic management, and that, in fact, they are led by a cadre of professionals rather than by lay leaders. Such allegations are made chiefly by the younger and more liberal members of Jewish communities, whose numbers in most democratic hostlands are increasing.

The problem has become serious because of the close relations, connections and coordination that such organizations maintain with Israel, its government, the Jewish Agency and other related organizations. It is pretty well known that Israel has tried to influence the activities of such organizations (not only of the American Israeli Public Affairs Committee (AIPAC), and now an adverse reaction can be easily identified.

In the final analysis, more recently Diaspora Jews and their organizations are formulating their policies and making their decisions autonomously. These decisions concern, among other things, their positions regarding assimilation, mixed marriages, and full and partial integration in their hostlands. A careful examination of these policies and decisions would show that Diaspora Jews are less interested in Israeli affairs than before. Consequently, as noted before, since the 1980s, the decline in donations transferred to Israel, the reduced number of visits to Israel, and even public criticism of Israeli governments regarding relations with the Palestinians — as well as the intensified debates concerning identity issues such as: "Who is a Jew"? "The Right of Return", "Separation of State and Religion" and so on — are reflecting the negative reactions to what is happening these days in Israeli society and politics.

All these issues and developments raise the basic question of "centre" and "periphery" in World Jewry. Actually, this question is not new. In fact, it was raised in the early 1980s, after the problematic Israeli conduct of the 1973 War. More Diaspora Jews than not think that Israel is not the essential or most significant centre. This is from the viewpoint of Israel's great attitudinal and actual difficulties in generating cultural innovation, and ensuring spiritual continuity and physical security to Jewish communities abroad. This applies mainly to the three largest and most active diasporic entities — the US, France and Russia. In each of these communities, there is an increasing demand that equal positions be attributed to Israel and all other Jewish communities. There is a wish among Diaspora Jews to create a semi-federal structure for World Jewry. However, this does not mean that a semi-federal structure should be governed by a ruling institution, and particularly not one that would be dominated by Israel, as proposed, for instance, by the Israeli President Katzav. I suggest that if any such institute were to be eventually formed, it should be responsible for advising and coordinating joint matters, but not dominated by Israel or any single Jewish Diasporic community.

The fact that the Diaspora's connection to Israel has become far more problematic — to a great extent due to the fact that more Jews have doubts about Israel's centrality — is well demonstrated by local and general events organized by individuals and organizations in the Diaspora. By the same token it is enough to follow fund-raising campaigns, visit the growing number of Jewish museums, and examine the political and diplomatic support that is extended to Israel (see for example Rynhold; Seliktar in this volume), to understand that in addition to their efforts to ensure continuity of their communities, more Jews are interested in what is going on in the entire Jewish nation worldwide, rather than specifically in Israel.

On the level of their interests and activities in host countries, Diaspora Jews are giving considerable attention to questions such as: immigration, migration, relations with other ethnic minorities and diasporic entities, ethnic integration, changes in identity and identification, cultural hybridization, the attainment and maintenance of civil and political rights, cooperation with the hostland's society and government, and related issues concerning their individual and collective continuity.

This situation is clearly reflected in a survey conducted toward the end of 2002 for the Department of Jewish-Zionist Education of the Jewish Agency on American Jews' views and positions *vis-à-vis* Israel. In this survey 31 percent answered that they are "very strongly connected to Israel", 41 percent said that they are "somewhat connected", 8 percent answered that they are "not connected" and 20 percent said that they are "strongly not connected". Only 11 percent of American Jews answered that their connections to and involvement in Israeli affairs has increased as a result of the Second Intifada. According to those who conducted the survey, only that percentage of American Jews who had said that they are "very strongly connected" (31 percent) also truly care about Israel and are ready to invest various efforts on its behalf. And these constitute a minority in the entire American Jewish entity (*Ha'aretz* 2003b). There are various indications that smaller and smaller proportions of Diasporic entities truly care about Israel and are ready to invest various efforts on its behalf, with the probable exception of certain segments of the Canadian, Australian, South African and French entities that still show devotion toward Israel (Cohen; Goldberg; Mendelsohn and Shain; Rutland in this volume, but cf. Ben Moshe 2006b).

In conclusion, it seems that such surveys demonstrate the true and actual situation concerning the place of Israel in the identity and identification of the majority of Diaspora Jews.

What can be done? Some of the contributors to this volume have suggested certain strategies and tactics to change this quite "natural" situation (it is "natural" since the same happens in other ethno-national trans-state entities) of the Jewish Diaspora. Here I would focus on what Israel should do. As a first step to change the situation, Israeli politicians, bureaucrats and people at large should become aware of the actual situation in the Diaspora. This is really needed because of the great ignorance about the Diaspora among too many Israelis, especially the younger ones. Second, all these people should change their Israelo-centric inherent orientation, which alienates many Diaspora Jews. They may then realize that the Diaspora is equal to Israel and treat it as such, which in turn may change the attitudes of Diaspora Jews and prevent even greater alienation from Israel. And most importantly, Israeli politicians and activists must try to repair the inherent cultural, societal and political weaknesses which are so characteristic of Israel at the beginning of the twenty-first century and which estrange so many Diaspora Jews.

References

Ben Moshe, D., "Israel, Anti-Semitism and Anti-Zionism", in this volume.
Ben Moshe, D., "The End of Unconditional Love: The Future of Zionism in Australian Jewish Life". In *New Under the Sun: Jewish Life in Australia* (Melbourne: Black Inc, 2006b).
Braziel, J., and Mannur, A., *Theorizing Diaspora* (Oxford: Blackwell Publishing, 2003).
Cohen, E., "France", in this volume.
Cohen, R., *Global Diasporas* (London: UCL, 1997).
DellaPergola, S., *Alternative Futures of the Jewish People: Annual Assessment* (Jerusalem: The Jewish People Planning Institute, 2005).
Gold, S., "Israelis in the Diaspora", in this volume.
Gold, S. and Bruce, P., "Israelis in the US". In *The Jewish Yearbook 1996* (New York, NY: The American Jewish Committee, 1996).
Goldberg, D., "Canada", in this volume.
Gordis, D., "Conservative Jewry and Israel", in this volume.
Ha'aretz, 30 January 2003.
Kelass, J., *The Politics of Nationalism and Ethnicity* (New York, NY: St. Martin's Press, 1991).
Livni, M., "Reform Jewry and Israel", in this volume.
Mendelsohn, R. and Shain, M., "South Africa", in this volume.
Millennium Development Goals, 2003, United Nations Development Programme, available online at: <http://hdr.undp.org/reports/global/2003>.
Mendes, P., "The Jewish Left: Dissenters, Israel and the Peace Process", in this volume.

Mittelberg, D., "Jewish Continuity and Israel Visits", in this volume.
Rutland, S., "Australia", in this volume.
Ryhnhold, J., "Israeli Foreign and Defence Policy and Diaspora Jewish Identity", in this volume.
Seliktar, O"., Jewish Public Opinion and the Peace Process", in this volume.
Shain, Y., "Jewish Kinship at a Crossroads: Lessons for Homelands and Diasporas". In *Political Science Quarterly*, 117, 2 (2002).
Sheffer, G., *Diaspora Politics: At Home Abroad* (Cambridge: Cambridge University Press, 2003).
Waxman, C., "Orthodox Communities and Israel", in this volume.

A PERSPECTIVE FROM THE DIASPORA

Jewish Vulnerability and Critical Barometers

Steven Bayme

As the essays in this volume neared completion, President Moshe Katzav of Israel announced plans for a World Jewish Forum to be convened at periodic intervals to deliberate challenges confronting the Jewish People globally.[1] Katzav's announcement, at least symbolically, presupposed the mutual interdependence between Jews everywhere and, in sharp contrast with prior Israeli presidential pronouncements, affirmed the reality of Diaspora Jewry as valued asset for the Jewish people.

Whether the projected World Jewish Forum will, in fact, realize its aspirations for ongoing Israel–Diaspora dialogue and exchange, only time will tell. In the interim, the significance of Israel for Diaspora Jewish identity cannot be minimized any more than the real tensions between Israel and Diaspora Jewry may be overlooked. Some years ago the late Charles Liebman and Steven M. Cohen argued, in *Two Worlds of Judaism*, that the core bases of Jewish identity in Israel and the Diaspora are fundamentally different. Israeli Jewish identity focused on the collectivity of Jewish peoplehood and the particularistic concerns of Jews. By contrast, Jewish identity in America, at least, the single largest Jewish population in the world, focused more on personal and existential needs, for example, spirituality, than on the collectivity of the Jews as a people. Similarly, American Jews focus considerable energy and emphasis upon universalistic concerns, at times from a Jewish perspective, at times not, in pronounced contrast to Israeli emphases on particularism.

Nonetheless, Liebman and Cohen argued, concern for Israel represents the glue tying the Jewish people together. At a time of widespread assimilation and erosion of Diaspora Jewish identity, Israel remains one of the few areas of consensus as a Jewish cause with a claim upon Jewish communal commitments and resources even if one might part company or quarrel with one or another aspect of Israeli society. Israel, in short, continues to energize the Jewish people and bring Jews out in vast numbers to express their Judaic commitments. Notwithstanding their title, both authors concluded that there were "hardly two Judaisms".[2]

In this context, Israel and Diaspora Jewry do enjoy a synergistic relationship in which each side brings positive assets to the Jewish table, and each side may benefit from the other's input and presence. Diaspora Jews need to internalize the concept of common peoplehood and tie their personal existential narratives to the broader narrative of the collective Jewish people. Individualistic "journeys" become Jewish only insofar as they are connected to the broader Jewish whole. For example, the Jewish calendar suggests that what makes a Passover Seder a Jewish event is that Jews around the world are all commemorating the Exodus at that moment as a foundation of Jewish peoplehood. This emphasis upon the collective emanating from Israel stands in sharp contrast to currents of personalism so prevalent in America.[3] For example, in recent years, some have touted the fact that on *Rosh Ha-Shonah* the *shofar* may be heard over the Internet rather than in the *Beit Knesset*, or, literally, the "assembly of Jews". In other words, the very idea of sounding the *shofar* at the beginning of the New Year represents a rallying cry to the Jewish people to be done in the company of Jews rather than through impersonal or remote instruments such as the Internet.

By the same token, the Diaspora focus upon Judaism may in turn enrich Israeli Jewish identity. Increasingly Diaspora Jews are seeking to define their identity through religious frameworks, and Diaspora Jewish leaders have repeatedly noted that only a religious revival among Jews may preserve future Jewish identity and continuity in the Diaspora.[4] By contrast, their Israeli counterparts do not agree and often dismiss religion as a source of conflict, or even of immoral behaviour, looking elsewhere for Judaic enrichment. The quest for personal and existential meaning that lies at the root of Diaspora Jewish identity is very different from, but can also complement well, the commitment to the Jewish collective so characteristic of Jewish identity in Israel.[5]

More generally, the birth of Israel in 1948 irrevocably altered the meaning and map of Jewish peoplehood in the contemporary world. First, it signaled the return of the Jews to sovereignty and statehood after 2,000 years of statelessness. Secondly, Israel as a Jewish state marked a shift of paradigm in Jewish peoplehood — both geographically and demographically. The birth of Israel initiated a reversal of the 2,600-year old pattern of a numerical ascendancy of the Diaspora Jewish population over that of the Jewish homeland. Within the next 50 years, for the first time since the Babylonian exile, a majority of the Jewish people will reside in the Jewish homeland rather than in the Diaspora. Current demographic projections suggest that almost half of Jewish children under age 14 reside in Israel and by 2020 nearly 60 percent will do so.[6] More broadly, Israel's existence coupled with the well-known threats to that existence has propelled much of the agenda of the Jewish people for the past 50 years.

During the Oslo years, the agenda of Israel–Diaspora relations itself underwent a series of profound shocks. Early in his tenure the late Prime Minister Yitzhak Rabin dismissed the importance of the American Israel Public Affairs Committee (AIPAC) claiming that Israel as a sovereign state had no need for intermediaries with the United States government. In 1994, then-President Ezer Weizman convened a world-wide gathering of Jewish leaders to discuss the Jewish future but concluded by stating that Israel needed Diaspora Jewry only for purposes of *aliyah*. Finance Minister Avraham Shochat dismissed the significance of Israel Bonds, claiming that Israel could do better by borrowing on the open markets. Perhaps most shockingly, Deputy Foreign

Minister Yossi Beilin trivialized the significance of Diaspora Jewish economic support for Israel, claiming that Israel could take care of its own needs and that the monies would be better spent on advancing Jewish education in the Diaspora. That Beilin chose the international conclave of the Women's International Zionist Organization (WIZO) as the venue for such a message only compounded the shock and dismay of Diaspora Jewish leaders.[7]

Underlying these shocks was the perception that the Oslo process was irreversible, peace between Israel and her neighbors lay within reach, and that, while the process will by no means be smooth, it will culminate in a secure Israel no longer dependent either politically or economically on Diaspora largesse. Given these assumptions, many at the time sought to recalibrate the Israel–Diaspora relationship. These efforts were by no means without value. One notes especially the importance of the *birthright israel* programme, which was born during those years. However, the collapse of the Oslo process at Camp David in July 2000, as several contributors note, "resecuritized" the Israel–Diaspora relationship. Israel once again mattered to Diaspora Jewry because of threats to her existence. These threats, in turn, were understood properly as threats to the Jewish people as a whole.

For one thing, anti-Semitism now returned to Europe in virulent forms. That the return of anti-Semitism occurred in otherwise liberal democratic societies, many of which had emphasized heavily the teaching of the Holocaust, was especially shocking. The irony of anti-Semitism returning to places that had maximized Holocaust education challenged the assumptions of Jewish leaders that knowledge of the Holocaust constituted the best preventative for anti-Semitism. Moreover, this "new" anti-Semitism was clearly related to anti-Zionism. Frequently, it de-legitimated Israel as a Jewish state. One critical source of this anti-Semitism was a growing and younger Muslim population in Europe, for whom anti-Americanism and anti-Israelism were closely linked, especially in the context of the Iraq war. Anti-Zionist rhetoric (for example, that of Hamas) often failed to distinguish between Jew and Zionist, and the claim to be against the "occupation" rarely disclosed that Hamas' consistent refusal to recognize the legitimacy of Israel as a nation-state in effect connoted that in the eyes of Hamas every inch of Israel — both within and beyond the "Green line" — constituted "occupied Islamic territory". Even if one might distinguish theoretically between anti-Semitism and anti-Zionism, in practice these phenomena coalesced and, in so doing, made the importance of countering efforts to de-legitimize Israel as a Jewish state all the more imperative for the Diaspora communal agenda.

Needless to say, this "resecuritization" of the Israel–Diaspora relations agenda affects the Jewish identity of Diaspora Jewry. Surveys indicate that among Diaspora Jews memory of the Holocaust continues to trump all other barometers of Jewish identity. In other words, the age-old fears of Jews are today triggered by threats to Israel's existence. Although the Jewish condition internationally today is nowhere near as precarious as in the 1930s, memories of the Holocaust, coupled with the resurgence of anti-Semitism and anti-Zionism, to say nothing of terrorism, enhance Jewish anxieties and vulnerabilities. In turn, for many Diaspora Jews the definition of what is a Jew all too often becomes translated as someone who is vulnerable by dint of his or her membership in the Jewish people. Courses on the Holocaust, for example, attract greater numbers of Jewish college students today than virtually any other area of academic Jewish studies, with the possible exception of Hebrew-language courses.[8]

Beyond the relationship of Jewish identity to Jewish vulnerability, Israel's role in Diaspora Jewish identity may in fact be receding. At one extreme are intellectuals who claim embarrassment to themselves as Jews at Israel's actions and policies. For example, Professor Tony Judt of New York University claims that Israel as a Jewish state causes him discomfort as an American.[9]

To be sure, Judt may be exceptional, and certainly his call for a bi-national state today evokes few echoes among his intellectual peers, to say nothing of the mass base of Diaspora Jewry. More significantly, however, observers do note sustained distancing between Israel and Diaspora Jewry over a period of decades. To be sure, each Diaspora community is different, with greater or lesser attachment to Israel. However, certainly in America the distancing has been documented. To some extent it is generational. Those who remember May 1967 as a bonding experience between Israel and American Jewry in all likelihood have greater attachment to Israel as a Jewish state. Younger American Jews, by contrast, who lack such defining moments, feel greater distance from Israel and are less likely to report that Israel remains central to their identity as Jews.[10]

More profoundly, however, distancing from Israel cannot be understood apart from distancing from Jewish matters generally. Herein lies the strong connection between the agenda of Israel–Diaspora relations and that of Jewish continuity. Those most committed to Judaism are most likely to be committed to Israel. Secular Jewish identity, so prevalent in Israel, evokes few echoes among American Jews. Rather, those who are not identifying with religious frameworks are least likely to be attached to Israel. Religion for many, as at least one sociologist has noted, may be the way of practicing one's ethnicity in America today (shades of Mordecai Kaplan!). For others, as noted, attachment to Israel is age-related. Still other Jews remain woefully ignorant concerning the most elementary facts of Israeli society. Fewer than 40 percent of American Jews could even identify 1967 as the year in which Israel gained possession of the West Bank. In each of these cases, one cannot minimize the importance of assimilation in America. As assimilation proceeds unimpeded, one of its most critical expressions is indifference to Israel as a Jewish state.

Another critical barometer of the distancing is travel to Israel. To be sure, other Diaspora Jewish communities report higher rates of visitation to Israel. American Jews do poorly by comparison. Less than 40 percent of American Jews have actually visited Israel. Repeat visits are particularly significant as an indication of degree of attachment — that is, caring enough about Israel to visit a second time. Although 57 percent of Orthodox Jews have been to Israel on repeat visits, less than a fifth of Conservative Jews have done so, and ever fewer Reform Jews. Some attribute this fall-off to the poor treatment accorded to Conservative and Reform rabbis in Israel. However, while both sets of rabbis are treated with equal disdain, Conservative Jews do score significantly higher on visitations.[11]

The *birthright israel* programme represents an attempt to reverse this pattern. In principle, *birthright* represented a critical statement of the role of Israel in contemporary Jewish identity. By labeling a visit to Israel the "birthright" of every Jew, the architects of the programme were articulating how the fact of Israel as a Jewish state irrevocably altered the meaning of membership in the Jewish people for Jews everywhere. More tangibly, *birthright* signaled Israel's responsibility for maintaining Jewish life in the Diaspora and insuring its future continuity. Lastly, the programme signaled a change in philanthropic norms in which leading funders defined Jewish continuity as the critical priority for their philanthropic activity.

Whether the programme will, in fact, realize its objectives can be measured only over the long term. Preliminary indications certainly are favorable. Over 100,000 participants have visited Israel on an organized mission by dint of the programme. These young people have had a real-time Jewish experience bringing Israel into their personal lives.[12] The Jewish Agency has announced a follow-up programme of full-time study in Israel for longer periods. Beyond the increase in numbers and the attraction the programme holds for its participants, long-term impact can be measured only via sustained longitudinal studies. In the interim, *birthright* has overcome great initial skepticism and has occupied an important niche on the Jewish communal programme agenda.

What, then, of the future? Several conclusions appear probable, although by no means inevitable. First, the role Israel plays in contemporary Diaspora Jewish identity cannot be separated from the problem of assimilation and Jewish continuity in the Diaspora. Attachment to Israel will very much be a function of attachment to Judaism. This accounts for American Orthodox exceptionalism in the degree of attachment to Israel and, by contrast, the relative weakness of attachment among Reform Jews. Orthodox attachment, to be sure, was challenged by the Gaza disengagement, and, in all likelihood, will only be further challenged by future dismantling of West Bank settlements.[13] Nonetheless, Israel is so deeply bound up with the warp and woof of contemporary Orthodox Judaism that, notwithstanding some glitches, it appears safe to presume continued Orthodox intensity of attachment to Israel. The best indicator of such attachment remains the popularity of post-high school one-year study programmes for Orthodox students in Israeli *yeshivot*, which have become normative for Orthodox day school graduates prior to entering college.

Secondly, the need for political support for Israel in the Diaspora, often dismissed as irrelevant or as an anachronism in the sunny 1990s, appears ever more pressing today and for the foreseeable future. Support for Israel remains a key source of cohesion for many Diaspora Jews. To be sure, there are and always will be dissenting voices, including those who claim that Diaspora support for Israel inhibits rather than advances the cause of peace in the region. Yet that continued political engagement by Diaspora Jewry benefits Israel strategically by creating a reservoir of diplomatic support for her abroad. It also provides a challenging agenda for Diaspora Jewry, strengthening ties both to Israel and to the Jewish people worldwide. Israeli leadership correctly fears that a diminished Diaspora will connote weakened support for Israel. Conversely, however, a Diaspora bound to Israel will, in all likelihood, be a Diaspora strengthened in its Jewish identity and Judaic commitments.

Lastly, those concerned with enhancing the image of Israel among young people today, especially university students, must understand that the relative absence of outspoken political support for Israel on university campuses does not necessarily emanate from a hostile or pro-Palestinian climate on campus so much as from widespread indifference toward and ignorance about Israel's role in the modern Jewish experience, the meaning of a democratic Jewish state, and, of course, the history of the Arab–Israeli conflict. When Jewish students do not care about being Jewish, they cease to care about Israel's safety and security. In that sense, a strong Jewish education that counters indifference and instills love of the Jewish people and appreciation of Jewish history, will, in the long term, strengthen the Israel–Diaspora relationship, the place of Israel in the identity of Diaspora Jews and provide the best antidote to contemporary anti-Zionism and anti-Semitism.

Notes

1 *Jerusalem Post*, 19 March 2006.
2 Charles S. Liebman and Steven M. Cohen, *Two Worlds of Judaism* (New Haven and London: Yale University Press, 1990), chapter 7.
3 On personalism and individualism in American Jewish identity, see Steven M. Cohen and Arnold M. Eisen, *The Jew Within* (Bloomington: Indiana University Press, 2000), esp. chapter 8. See also Charles S. Liebman, "Post War American Jewry: From Ethnic to Privitized Judaism", in Elliott Abrams and David G. Dalin (eds), *Secularism, Spirituality, and the Future of American Jewry* (Washington, DC: Ethics and Public Policy Center, 1999), pp. 7–17.
4 See, for example, Arthur Hertzberg, *The Jews in America* (New York: Simon and Schuster, 1989), pp. 386–388.
5 Bernard Susser and Charles S. Liebman, *Choosing Survival* (New York and Oxford: Oxford University Press, 1999), chapters 8–9.
6 Sergio Della Pergola et al., "Projecting the Jewish Future: Population Projections, 2000–2080", *American Jewish Year Book*, vol. 100 (2000), pp. 124–127.
7 Steven M. Cohen and Charles S. Liebman, "Israel and American Jewry in the 21st Century", in Allon Gal and Alfred Gottschalk (eds), *Beyond Survival and Philanthropy* (Cincinnati: Hebrew Union College Press, 2000), p. 4. See especially Yossi Beilin, *The Death of the American Uncle* (in Hebrew) (Tel Aviv: Yedioth Aharonoth Books and Chemed Books, 1999), pp. 118–122. For responses to Beilin, see "Roundtable on Yossi Beilin's The Death of the American Uncle", *Israel Studies* 5: 1(Spring, 2000).
8 *2005 Annual Survey of American Jewish Opinion* (New York, NY: American Jewish Committee, 2005), Question 28, p. 7. For a review of studies documenting the centrality of Holocaust remembrance to the Jewish identity of young American Jews, see Jacob Ukeles et al., *Young Jewish Adults in the United States Today* (New York, NY: American Jewish Committee, 2006).
9 Tony Judt, "Israel: The Alternative", *New York Review of Books*, 50:16 (23 October 2003).
10 Steven M. Cohen, "Younger Adults Clearly Less Engaged with Israel than Their Elders: New Evidence from a Recent National Survey of American Jews", unpublished paper (kindly sent to me by the author). See also Steven T. Rosenthal, *Irreconcilable Differences?* (Hanover and London: Brandeis University Press, 2001), pp. 170–171 for review of survey data trends over two decades. The dissonance here between the emphasis upon the Holocaust and the Jewish identity of younger adults and the relative weakness of attachment to Israel is especially striking. See Ukeles et al., *Young Jewish Adults in the United States Today* (New York, NY: American Jewish Committee, 2006).
11 *2005 Annual Survey of American Jewish Opinion*, American Jewish Committee, Table 6.
12 Leonard Saxe et al., *A Mega Experiment in Jewish Education: The Impact of birthright israel* (Waltham: Cohen Center for Modern Jewish Studies, Brandeis University, 2002), pp. 17–22.
13 Steven Bayme, "Can Religious Zionism Survive?", *New York Jewish Week*, 21 October 2005.

Glossary

Agudat Yisrael – A non-Zionist Israeli political party which represents a number of Chassidic groups in Israel. It originated in Europe in the early part of the Twentieth Century and represented Chassidic Jews to the British authorities during the British Mandate of Palestine (1917–1948).

Ahad Ha-Am – Pen name of Asher Ginzberg (1856–1927) the foremost advocate of cultural Zionism and a fierce critic of the founder of political Zionism Theodore Herzl. Ha'am's concepts of Hebrew culture had a definitive influence on the objectives of early Jewish settlement in Palestine. He called for Israel to be a spiritual centre for the Diaspora.

Ahavat haaretz – Love of the land of Israel, a traditional Zionist value.

Aliyah – Literally means "ascent" in Hebrew, but is the term for emigrating to the State of Israel or the pre-State Yishuv.

Al HaNisim – A prayer which praises God for delivering the Jewish People from the Greeks at the time of the Maccabees. It is inserted into the daily prayers during the festival of Chanukah.

Am Yisrael Chai – Meaning "The people of Israel shall live" in Hebrew, this is a popular religious song which is also expressed as a political statement of Jewish defiance against threats to destroy the Jewish People.

Amidah – A core Jewish prayer said during the three daily services. The word *Amidah* literally means standing, because the prayer is recited while standing.

Amona – An Israeli settlement, on a hill overlooking the long established Jewish settlement of Ofra in Samaria on the West Bank. Amona was founded in 1997 and inhabited by young people originally from neighbouring Ofra. Amona is usually categorized as an outpost since it has never been fully approved by an Israeli government.

Ashkenazi / Ashkenazim – The term that describes Jews who are descended from East European Jewish ancestors and follow European Jewish tradition.

Ba'al Teshuvah – The Hebrew term referring to a person who has repented and become religious.

Bar mitzvah – According to Jewish law, when Jewish children reach the age of maturity (12 years for girls – Bat Mitzvah – 13 years for boys) they become responsible for their actions, a boy is said to become Bar Mitzvah and a girl Bat Mitzvah. Bar Mitzvahs are recognised through the ritual of the boy reading from the Torah (bible) in synagogue for the first time. Today, the emphasis of many bar mitzvahs is on the celebratory party that often has limited religious meaning.

Beit Knesset – Literally means "House of Assembly," but is the Hebrew term for a synagogue.

Betar – The Revisionist Zionist youth movement founded in 1923 in Riga, Latvia, by Ze'ev Jabotinsky. A right-wing organisation that favoured military militancy and opposed socialism, Betar members fought against the British during the Mandate, and in the creation of Israel. Betar was the ideological forerunner of the Israeli political party Herut which later evolved into Likud. Betar continues to exist as a youth movement across the world and in Israel.

Betselem – The Israeli Information Center for Human Rights in the Occupied Territories which was established in 1989 by a group of prominent academics, attorneys, journalists, and Knesset members. It aims to document and educate the Israeli public and policymakers about human rights violations in the Occupied Territories.

Birthright Program – Taglit-Birthright provides one free educational trip to Israel for Jewish young adults ages 18 to 26. Sponsored by the Government of Israel, local Jewish communities around the world and leading Jewish philanthropists, Taglit-Birthright Israel is a major response to the assimilation of Diaspora Jewry.

Birkhat Kohanim – Blessings of the High Priests at the time of the Temple. Today descendents of the Kohanim perform specific blessings in synagogues.

Bitzur – A unit of the Mossad Israeli secret service organisation that is focussed on the security of Diaspora Jewry and assisting their release from countries of oppression, such as the former Soviet Union. The unit tracks and maps anti-Semitic incidents.

Bnei Akiva – A religious Zionist youth movement founded in Palestine in the 1920s, Its ethos is *Torah V' avodah* (religion and work), and is predicated on a belief in the Land of Israel, the People of Israel and the Torah of Israel. In Israel Bnei Akiva is a right-wing movement identified with the Religious Kibbutz Movement and the National Religious Party.

Camp Ramah – An organization that began in 1947 which organises Zionist oriented Jewish summer camps throughout the United States, Canada, and Israel.

Chabad – The Chassidic Lubavitch movement. Founded in 1772 by Rabbi Schneur Zalman of Liadi, Chabad promotes the mystical and traditional Judaism while using modern methods and technology for educational purposes. Unlike other Chassidic groups Chabad maintains an active outreach program to interact with non-chassidic Jews to get them to observe Jewish ritual.

Chalutzim – The Hebrew word for "pioneers", often used to describe those who settled new parts of the Yishuv and State of Israel. These pioneers were at the vanguard of the Zionist enterprise and settlers in the West Bank consider themselves continuing the pioneering tradition.

Chutzpah – The Hebrew and Yiddish word for audacity. In Hebrew, *chutzpah* is used indignantly, to describe someone who has out-stepped the boundaries of accepted polite behaviour for selfish reasons, while in English *chutzpah* can be spoken in admiration of non-conformist but gutsy audacity.

Clal Yisrael – In Hebrew means the entire community of Israel, another term for the People of Israel.

Columbus Platform – A declaration issued by a conference of U.S. Reform rabbis meeting in Columbus, Ohio, in 1937. It supported the use of traditional ceremonies, the use of Hebrew in the liturgy and reemphasized the idea of the Jewish people. This was a dramatic revision of the Reform principles as stated in the Pittsburgh Platform (1885).

Conservative Judaism – A stream of Judaism located between Reform and Orthodox Jewry. Like Orthodoxy, Conservative Judaism accepts the written Jewish law, but differs from Orthodoxy in that they believe the oral (Rabbinic) law can evolve to meet the needs of the Jewish people in varying circumstances. The name Conservative derives from the idea that the movement would be necessary to conserve Jewish traditions in the U.S., a culture in which Reform and Orthodoxy were not believed to be viable. There is a nascent Conservative movement in Israel known as *Masorti* which means "traditional".

Dreyfus trial – The "Dreyfus Affair" was a political scandal which divided France during the 1890s and early 1900s. It involved the wrongful conviction for treason of a French Jewish artillery officer, Captain Alfred Dreyfus, and the political and judicial scandal that followed until his full rehabilitation. Theodore Herzl, the founder of Zionism, witnessed the French public's reaction to the conviction of this assimilated French Jew and this strongly influenced Herzl's thoughts on the acceptance of Jews in Europe and was a seminal moment in his development on Zionism and the need for Jews to have a state of their own.

Emet Ve-Emunah – The Hebrew for "truth and faith", a phrase from the evening prayer service.

Emunah – A modern Orthodox Zionist women's organization which promotes religious Zionist ideals through a range of activities.

Eretz Israel – The Land of Israel.

Etrogim – A citrus fruit of the orange and lemon family. It is one of the Four Species used in a prayer the Jewish holiday of *Sukkot* (Tabernacles).

First Aliyah – Between 1882 and 1903, approximately 35,000 Jews immigrated to Palestine which was then a province of the Ottoman Empire. Many of these Jews belonged to early Zionist movements Hibbat Zion and Bilu. They came primarily from Eastern Europe with a smaller number arriving from Yemen. Many established agricultural communities.

Galut – The Hebrew for "exile", *galut* was traditionally used to refer to Jews outside of Israel. However, negatively meaning a forced exile, the term is no longer widely used and instead "Diaspora" is used to describe the free choice with which Jews live outside of Israel.

Garin Arava – A *garin* is a collective group that settles in a particular area. The Arava is a desert area in the South of Israel indicating where this group will live.

Gush Emunim – Literally meaning "Block of the Faithful" this is the name of a right wing religious political lobby group that arose in the aftermath of the Six-Day War in 1967. Formally established as an organization in 1974, it encouraged Jewish settlement in the biblical areas of Judea and Samaria Israel took control of in the 1967 in the belief that this was part of an ongoing redemptive process.

Gush Etzion – A group of Israeli settlements in the northern Judea region of the West Bank which are commuter suburbs to Jerusalem. Gush Etzion was held by Jewish forces prior to Statehood but were lost to Jordan in the War of Independence before being retaken by Israel in 1967.

Habonim Dror – A Socialist-Zionist youth movement in Israel and the Diaspora formed by the merger in 1982 of the classical Zionist youth movements Habonim and Dror.

Hachsharah – The *Hachsharah* (preparation) movement provided intellectual and physical training, especially in physical labour, such as farming, for pioneers (*chalutzim*), for settlement in Palestine. The term is currently used to mean preparation for a particular activity in Israel.

Hadassah – A Women's Zionist Organization in the Diaspora that run educational programs and engage in fundraising for Israel.

Haftarah – Reading from The Prophets read in the synagogue.

Hagshama – Literally meaning "fulfilment" in Hebrew, it is the name of a current department in the World Zionist Organisation which instils and nurtures Zionist identity in 18 to 30 year olds in the Diaspora.

Halakha – The collective corpus of Jewish religious law, including the written biblical law and the oral law from the Talmud.

Hanukkah – Also known as the Festival of Lights, this religious holiday is observed in Jewish homes by the kindling of lights on each of the festival's eight nights, one on the first night, two on the second night and so on. According to the Talmud, following the victory of the Maccabees over the Seleucid Empire, there was only enough consecrated olive oil to fuel the eternal flame in the Temple for one day. Miraculously, the oil burned for eight days – which was the length of time it took to press, prepare and consecrate new oil. *Hanukkah* commemorates the miracle of the oil and Jewish survival.

Hasbara – A Hebrew noun that literally means "explanation", the term is used to describe disseminating information &/or propaganda about Israel. It is effectively public relations activities to explain Israeli government policies.

Haskalah – The nineteenth century Jewish Enlightenment movement which sought to disseminate secular European culture among Jews in the belief that it was compatible with Judaism and would lead to Jewish emancipation in Europe. Haskalah marked the beginning of the wider engagement of European Jews with the secular world, resulting, ultimately, in the first Jewish political movements and the struggle for Jewish emancipation.

HaShomer – A Zionist-socialist youth movement founded in 1913 in Galicia and was also the name of the group's political party in the Yishuv during the pre-1948 British Mandate of Palestine.

Hatikvah – "Our Hope", the Israeli national anthem written by the Galician-Jewish poet Naphtali Herz Imber in Zloczow (Ukraine) in 1878. In 1897, at the First Zionist Congress, it was adopted as the anthem of Zionism.

Hassidic – Hassidic Judaism is an ultra-Orthodox Jewish religious movement which originated in Eastern Europe in the 18th century, founded by Rabbi Israel Ben Eliezer, also known as the Ba'al Shem Tov.

Haredi – A person who follows Hassidic Judaism and leads a strictly ultra-Orthodox lifestyle.

Iggun – A Jewish woman unable to obtain a get, a document of divorce from he husband and therefore cannot remarry.

Kabbalat Shabbat – The prayer service said to usher in the Sabbath.

Kehilah – Community.

Kedushah – Holiness; a fundamental concept of Judaism. *Kedushah* is fundamental to God's nature, and the Jewish people are to imitate God by also being holy.

Kesher – Meaning "Connection" in Hebrew, Project Kesher, founded in 1989, is the largest Jewish women's organization in the CIS and one of the fastest growing women's advocacy and human rights organizations in the region.

Kibbutz/im – An Israeli collective community inspired by socialist Zionist ideology. Since the 1980s most *kibbutzim* have incorporated capitalist systems in their operations, such as differential wages and private ownership.

Kibbutznik – A person who lives on a Kibbutz.

Kippah – Skullcap worn by Jews.

Kosher – Food in accordance with Jewish dietary laws. Key principles are:

Animals must be mammals which chew their cud and have cloven hoofs.

Fish must have fins and scales

Meat and milk cannot be served in the same meal, or cooked using the same dishes or utensils. Observant Jews have separate dishes for meat and milk.

Kosher slaughter requires all animals (and birds) to be slaughtered by a trained individual (a s*hochet*) using a special method of slaughter. Blood must be thoroughly removed from all meat.

Likud – A centre-right political party in Israel. The Likud's roots are in Zeev Jabotinsky's pre-State Betar youth movement which became the Herut political party.

Lirot – Israeli currency prior to the currently used shekel.

Lubavitcher – A member of the Lubavitch movement; a follower of Chabad Hassidism – *see* Chabad.

Machal/Machalnakim – The Hebrew acronym for *Machalniks – Mitnadvei Chutz L'Aretz* which means military volunteers from outside Israel. In 1948, approximately 3,500 overseas volunteers came from about 40 different countries to fight for the nascent State of Israel during the 1948 War for Independence. Most were World War II veterans and included Jews and non-Jews, men and women.

Machers – Colloquially refers to leaders or equivalent to VIP (very important person).

Machsom Watch – Meaning "Checkpoint Watch" in Hebrew, this is an organisation of Israeli women who monitor Palestinian human-rights at Israeli checkpoints from the West Bank and Gaza into Israel.

Madrich – A leader, often of youth groups, and is often an informal educator whose tools are discussion and games, not formal book-learning. It is similar to being a scout or guide leader or summer camp councillors in the USA.

Masorti – Literally meaning "traditional", it is the Hebrew name for Conservative Judaism.

Matzah –A flat, crispy, cracker-like bread made of plain flour and water, which is not allowed to ferment or rise before it is baked. Matzah is the traditional substitute for bread during Passover. According to the Torah, when the Israelites were leaving Ancient Egypt, they had no time to wait until their bread rose, so they baked it before it had a chance to rise, and the result was *matzah* (Exodus 12:39).

Maskil – Literally someone who is sensible, wise, insightful or prudent, but Maskilim were followers of the Haskala movement – *see* Haskala.

Meimad – A small politically left-leaning religious Zionist political party in Israel, founded in 1999 allied with the Israeli Labour Party which embraces the values of many social democratic parties.

Midrash – A Hebrew word referring to a method of exegesis of a Biblical text. The term *midrash* also can refer to a compilation of Midrashic teachings, in the form of legal, exegetical or homiletically commentaries on the Jewish Bible.

Minhag – An accepted tradition or group of traditions in Judaism.

Mitzvot – A word used in Judaism to refer to (a) the commandments, of which there are 613, given in the *Torah* (the first five books of the Hebrew Bible) or (b) any Jewish law at all.

Mizrahim – Jews descended from the Jewish communities of the Middle East.

Modern Orthodox – A stream of Orthodox Judaism which believes observance of Jewish law is compatible with living a modern lifestyle. Unlike Charedi Jews, modern Orthodox wear modern clothing and complete secular studies and engage in a wide range of secular employment.

Moledet – A small right-wing political party in Israel that advocates the voluntary transfer of the Palestinian population from the West Bank and the Gaza Strip.

Moshav – A cooperative agricultural community of individual farms pioneered by the Labour Zionists during the Second Aliyah. Many moshavs today are no longer farms but are residential communities.

(The) Mossad – The Israeli intelligence agency responsible for intelligence collection, counter-terrorism, and covert action.

Musaf – Prayers said on the Sabbath and Jewish holidays.

Na'amat – A Hebrew acronym for "Movement of Working Women and Volunteers," whose aim is to enhance the quality of life for women, children and families in Israel, the U.S. and around the world.

Nativ – Means path in Hebrew and is the name of a year program in Israel for future leaders of the Conservative movement.

Nebech – A descriptive phrase for someone who is to be pitied, from Yiddish but also used in modern Hebrew.

Neturei Karta – A small extreme right wing sect of Haredi (Ultra-Orthodox) Jews who reject all forms of Zionism and actively oppose the existence of the State of Israel.

Netzer/ Netzer Olami – Netzer is the acronym for the Reform Zionist youth movement, established in 1980, which is the youth arm of the World Union for Progressive Judaism. Netzer operates across the Diaspora, and in Israel. Netzer Olami is the name of the world movement based in Jerusalem.

Olim – The Hebrew term for Jews who immigrate to Israel. *Olim* often receive financial assistance from the Israeli government and other agencies.

Sabra – The word used to describe a native-born Israeli. It comes from the Hebrew name of a prickly pear found in Israel, which is prickly on the outside but soft in the middle, thus said to depict the Israel character.

Satmar Hassidic sect – A movement of Orthodox Haredi Jews originating from the Hungarian town of Szatmárnémeti (now Satu Mare, Romania).

Second Aliyah (socialists) – Between 1904 and 1914, 40,000 Jews emigrated to Palestine, mainly from Russia following pogroms and outbreaks of anti-Semitism. Many of these migrants were infused with socialist ideals and were set on establishing Jewish settlement in Palestine along socialist lines. They established the first kibbutz, Degania, in 1909 and formed self defense organizations, such as *Hashomer*, to counter Arab hostility and bandits. During this period, some of the underpinnings of an independent nation-state arose: the national language of Hebrew was revived; newspapers and literature written in Hebrew were published; and political parties and workers organizations were established. The first area in what became the city of Tel Aviv was established at this time.

Seder Tu B'Shvat – A kabbalistic way to celebrate the religious holiday of *Tu B'Shvat*, the festival which celebrate the new year for trees, through various symbolic offerings of the seven species of the Land of Israel.

Sephardi – Jews of Arabic and Persian backgrounds, from other Muslim countries and in South East Asia such as India. Sephardi is a term which distinguishes them from Ashkenazi Jews who are of European origin.

Shabbat – The Sabbath or weekly day of rest observed, from sundown on Friday until nightfall on Saturday.

Shabat chol hamo'ed. A Shabbat that occurs during a Jewish holiday.

Shabbetai Zvi – A 17th century false messiah.

Shaliach/Shlicha/Shlichim/Shlichut – The Hebrew word(s) for an Israeli emissary who works in an educational and leadership capacity about Israel in Jewish organisations around the world. Chabad-Lubavitch who are not centred in Israel use the term *shluchim*, which translates to "the ones who are sent", to describe their religious emissaries. *Shlichut* is the period of service served overseas.

Shlilat Hagalut – Meaning "negation of the Diaspora" in Hebrew, this reflects a classical Zionist belief that all Jews should go to live in Israel.

Shofar – A ram's horn blown in synagogue on Judaism's high holy days of Rosh Hashanah and Yom Kippur.

Shtadlanut/Shtadlans – A *shtadlan*, also known as the court Jew, was an intercessor who represented interests of the local Jewish community (such as of a town's ghetto), and worked as a "lobbyist" pleading for the safety of Jews with the outside authorities of Medieval Europe. *Shtadlans* is the Hebrew plural of *Shtadlan*.

Shnat – The name of 10-month leadership and educational program in Israel for senior diaspora members of the socialist Zionist youth movement Habonim.

Shoah – The Hebrew term for the Holocaust.

Shtetl – A small town/village with a large Jewish population in pre-Holocaust Central and Eastern Europe. The concept of shtetl culture is used as a metaphor for the traditional way of life of 19th-century Eastern European Jews.

Shuls – A Yiddish but commonly used term by Ashkenazi Jews for a synagogue.

Siddur – The Jewish prayer book.

Siddur Sim Shalom – The first comprehensive and official Siddur for the Conservative movement.

Simcha – A happy occasion, such as a wedding.

Sochnut – The Jewish Agency for Israel. Incorporating the World Zionist Organization it is the world body that coordinates the partnership between Israel and the Diaspora. Governed by a Congress with delegates from Israel and the Diaspora it runs a wide range of programs in Israel and the Diaspora.

Tavnit nof moladeto – The Notion that Israelis are 'shaped by the stature of Israel's landscapes' .

Tefillah – Prayer.

Tehilim – The Book of Psalms whose principal author was King David.

'***Tikkun olam***' – A Hebrew phrase that translates to "repairing the world" — often used to explain the Jewish concept of social justice. Some religious Jews believe that acts of *tikkun olam* will either trigger or fulfil the prophesied coming of the messiah.

Torat chaim – Living a religious life according to the Torah.

Tu B'Shvat – A minor Jewish holiday (meaning there are no restrictions on working), *Tu Bishvat* is the "new year of the trees".

Ultra-Orthodox – *see* Haredi.

WIZO – Women's International Zionist Organization, operating in Israel and the Diaspora dedicated to the advancement of the status of women. Founded in 1920 it raises funds for women's welfare projects it runs in Israel.

Yad Vashem – The Israeli Holocaust Museum in Jerusalem, formerly "The Holocaust Martyrs' and Heroes' Remembrance Authority", established in 1953 by an act of the Israeli Knesset. Yad Vashem is entrusted with documenting the history of the Jewish people during the Holocaust period, preserving the memory and story of each of the six million victims, and imparting the legacy of the Holocaust for generations to come through its archives, library, school, museums and recognition of the Righteous Among the Nations.

Yahrtzeit – The annual anniversary of the day of death of a relative which is comemmorated through the lighting of a candle.

Yedid Nefesh– A song sung on the Sabbath.

Yerida – Literally meaning "to go down" it is a somewhat derogatory term used to describe emigration by Jews from Israel. It is the opposite action of immigration by Jews to Israel which is *aliyah* meaning "ascent".

Yeshiva – A religious seminary.

Yishuv – The Jewish community and Zionist settlement in Palestine prior to the establishment of the State of Israel in 1948.

Yom Ha'atzmaut – Israeli Independence Day.

Yom Hazikaron – Israel's National Memorial Day for the Fallen and the Victims of Terror.

Yom Kippur – The Day of Atonement, the holiest day in the Jewish calendar. A day of fasting, it is observed by the majority of secular Jews who may not otherwise adhere to religious practice.

Contributors

Caryn Aviv teaches in the Core Curriculum and the Center for Judaic Studies at the University of Denver. Her research focuses on global Jewish identities, gender and sexuality, and Israel Studies. Dr Aviv is co-author of *Queer Jews* (Routledge 2002), *New Jews: The End of the Jewish Diaspora* (2005), and *American Queer: Now and Then* (2006). Her current research is entitled "Peace Camps: Gender, National Identity and Middle East Conflict Resolution Programs for Youth". She also co-founded Jewish Mosaic: The National Center for Sexual and Gender Diversity.

Amiram Barkat is a *Ha'aretz* reporter. He also writes a weekly column for the op-ed section of the English edition of *Ha'aretz*. His reportage covers Jewish communities around the world, focusing on such issues as Jewish identity, Jewish organizations, anti-Semitism and immigration to and from Israel. Born in 1973, Barkat grew up in Jerusalem, serving in the Israel Defence Forces Spokesman unit. Before joining *Ha'aretz* in 2002, he was with the newspaper *Kol Ha'ir* for four years, having worked and specialized in Commercial Law.

Steven Bayme serves as Director of the Contemporary Jewish Life Department of the American Jewish Committee, and of the Institute on American Jewish–Israeli Relations. He is also Visiting Associate Professor of History at the Jewish Theological Seminary of America. He has taught previously at Yeshiva University, Hebrew Union College, and Queens College. His recent publications include *Understanding Jewish History: Texts and Commentary* (1997) and a volume of essays titled *Jewish Arguments and Counter-Arguments: Essays and Addresses* (2002).

Avi Beker is the Head of the Diplomacy and Jewish Policy Program at the School of Government and Policy at Tel Aviv University. He is the former Secretary-General of the World Jewish Congress and was active in campaigns and negotiations with many foreign governments. He received his Ph.D. at the Graduate Center of the City University of New York and was a member of the Israeli mission to the UN. He has published books and articles on international relations, arms control and the UN, and Israeli and world Jewish affairs.

Graciela Ben Dror is the Director of "Moreshet", the Mordechai Anilevich Memorial and a Lecturer in the Department of Jewish History at the University of Haifa. Dr Ben Dror is also a Researcher at the Stephen Roth Institute for the Study of Contemporary Antisemitism and Racism at Tel Aviv University. She was born in Montevideo, Uruguay and came to Israel in 1969, living since then on Kibbutz Ramot

Menashe. She received her BA and MA from the University of Haifa, and her Ph.D. from the Hebrew University of Jersusalem, at the Institute of Contemporary Judaism. Her publications include: *La Iglesia católica ante el Holocausto. España y América Latina, 1933–1945* (2003) and *Católicos, Nazis y judíos. La Iglesia Argentina en tiempos del Tercer Reich, 1933–1945* (2003).

Danny Ben-Moshe is an Associate Professor and Director of the Institute for Community Ethnicity and Policy Alternatives and Associate Professor at Victoria University in Melbourne, Australia. He has an undergraduate degree from the School of Oriental and African Studies at the University of London and a Ph.D. from the University of Melbourne. Danny has worked for a range of Jewish organizations including as director of the Israel office of the British Israel Public Affairs Centre and as the executive director of the Australia/New Zealand B'nai Brith Anti-Defamation Commission. He has published widely on Israel–Diaspora relations, Israeli politics, Jewish identity and anti-Semitism. He is the co-producer and co-director of the documentary film *The Buchenwald Ball.*

Jean-Yves Camus is a political scientist and associate fellow at IRIS (Institut de Relations Internationales et Stratégiques) in Paris. He is a member of the Task Force on Antisemitism, the European Jewish Congress, and is an expert for the Council of Europe. He is a graduate of the Institut d'Etudes Politiques de Paris, and the author of *Le Monde Juif* (with Annie-Paule Derczansky, 2001). He has also written several other books on racism, anti-Semitism and the Extreme Right.

Erik H. Cohen teaches at the School of Education, Bar Ilan University. His research interests include cross-cultural studies, tourism, youth culture, education, research methodology, and data analysis. Dr Cohen has widely published articles and chapters in these fields. He has also published three books: *L'Etude et l'éducation juive en France* (1991), *Entre la France et Israël: la jeunesse juive* (with Maurice Ifergan, 2005), *Israel Experience: Educational and Policy Analysis* (with Eynath Cohen, in 2000, in Hebrew).

Eliezer Don-Yehiya is Professor of Political Science at Bar-Ilan University and Director of the Argov Center for the Study of Israel and the Jewish People at Bar-Ilan University. He has published many books and articles on Israeli and Jewish politics, and on State and Religion in Israel. His books include: *Civil Religion in Israel* (1983); *Religion and Politics in Israel* (1984) (both co-authored with Charles Liebman); *Religion and Political Accommodation in Israel* (1999); and *Israel and Diaspora Jewry: Ideological and Political Perspectives* (co-edited with Charles Liebman, 1991).

Jonathan Freedland is an award-winning journalist and broadcaster. He writes weekly columns in *The Guardian* and the *London Evening Standard*, as well as a monthly piece for *The Jewish Chronicle*. He also presents BBC Radio 4's contemporary history series, *The Long View*. He worked for four years *as The Guardian*'s Washington Correspondent, and has written for a variety of US publications, including the *New York Times*, *Los Angeles Times* and *Newsweek*. Among other publications his latest book is *Jacob's Gift* — a memoir telling the stories of three generations of his own family as well as exploring wider and urgent questions of identity and belonging.

Steven J. Gold is a professor of sociology at Michigan State University. Having served as chair of the International Migration Section of the American Sociological Association, he is co-editor of *Immigration Research for a New Century: Multidisciplinary Perspectives* (2000, with Rubén G. Rumbaut and Nancy Foner); and is the author *of Refugee Communities: A Comparative Field Study* (1992); *From the Worker's State to the Golden State* (1995); *Ethnic Economies* (with Ivan Light, 2000); and *The Israeli Diaspora* (2002).

David H. Goldberg is Director of Research and Education for the Canada-Israel Committee (Toronto). His Ph.D. in political science is from McGill University, with a Specialized MA in international affairs from Carleton University. His publications include *The Domestic Battleground: Canada and the Arab–Israeli Conflict* (edited, with David Taras, 1989), *Foreign Policy and Ethnic Interest Groups* (1990), *The Decline of the Soviet Union and the Transformation of the Middle East* (edited, with Paul Marantz, 1994), *Political Dictionary of Israel* (with Bernard Reich, 2000), and *Historical Dictionary of Israel* (with Bernard Reich, forthcoming).

Daniel Gordis is Vice President of the Mandel Foundation, Israel, and Director of the Mandel Leadership Institute in Jerusalem. Prior to his family's making *aliyah* in 1999, Dr. Gordis served as Vice President for Public Affairs and Community Outreach at the University of Judaism in Los Angeles. He is the author of several books, including *God Was Not in the Fire: The Search for a Spiritual Judaism* (1995, 1997), and *If a Place Can Make You Cry: Dispatches from an Anxious State* (2002). He resides with his wife and three children in Jerusalem.

Lisa D. Grant is Associate Professor of Jewish Education at the Hebrew Union College–Jewish Institute of Religion, New York. She holds a Ph.D. in Jewish Education from the Jewish Theological Seminary. Her research and teaching interests include adult Jewish learning, the professional development of Jewish educators, and the role Israel plays in American Jewish life. Her publications have appeared in a range of academic journals and teaching guides. She is the lead author of *A Journey of Heart and Mind: Transformative Learning in Adulthood* (with Diane Schuster, Meredith Woocher, and Steven M. Cohen 2004).

Reuven Hammer received his rabbinic ordination from the Jewish Theological Seminary of America and earned a doctorate there in theology. He also has a Ph.D. in Education from Northwestern University. After serving as a congregational rabbi for fifteen years he moved to Israel in 1973. He has served as director and dean of the Jewish Theological Seminary's Israel programme, as founding director of the Seminary of Judaic Studies (now the Schechter Institute) and as professor of rabbinic literature. In 2002 he was elected President of the International Rabbinical Assembly. He is the author of several books on prayer, *midrash* and Jerusalem. A founder of the Masorti Movement in Israel, he is currently the head of its Rabbinical Court.

Rona Hart is the head of the Community Research Unit of the Board of Deputies of British Jews, and a post-doctoral fellow at the School of Education, Tel Aviv University. Primarily a policy researcher, Dr Hart is currently engaged with several research projects, including a follow-up study of the Israeli community in Britain; a study from a Jewish perspective on interfaith relations in Britain, a survey on synagogue membership in the UK, research on Jewish schools and the choice of school among London Jews, a study on the demographic patterns of the Jewish population in Britain, and more.

Alan Hoffmann has dedicated his professional life to promoting Jewish education, and in February 2000 he became the Director General of the Education Department of the Jewish Agency in Israel. Under his leadership, this department is playing a critical role in developing and launching new initiatives to intensify the connection of young Jews to Israel, and promoting Jewish education across the globe. He is leading the Jewish Agency's Education Department towards its mission of intensifying the unique and multi-dimensional significance of Israel in connecting the next generation of Jews to their heritage, people and homeland.

Avi Katzman is an author, journalist, editor and culture critic. He contributes to *Ha'aretz*, a daily newspaper and broadcasts his talk-show at Kol Israel, the Israeli public radio station. He has edited over 100 books on Israeli and Jewish history and culture, by Yeshayahu Leibowitz, Amos Oz and Tom Segev, among others. Mr Katzman teaches at the Hebrew University and at the Mandel Leadership Institute, Jerusalem, and lectures on Israeli and Jewish culture around the country. Currently he is writing on the history of public controversies in Israel.

Scott Lasensky is a Senior Research Associate at the Center for Conflict Analysis and Prevention at the United States Institute of Peace, and an Adjunct Assistant Professor of Government at Georgetown University. He received the Yitzhak Rabin Shimon Peres Peace Award (Ph.D. category) from Tel Aviv University in 1999.

Neil Lazarus is Israel's leading consultant and keynote speaker on Israel advocacy or *Hasbara*. He has helped train a new generation of Israeli diplomats, as well as Jewish community and student leaders. His extensive client list includes The Israeli Ministry of Foreign Affairs, The Israeli Ministry of Tourism, Keshet Television, The World Bank, Harvard University Extension Courses in Israel, Hillel, Hadassah, *birthright israel* and The Jewish Agency of Israel. Born in Britain, he received his first degree in Political Science at the University of Wales. Neil immigrated to Israel in 1988 and soon after received his Masters Degree at the Hebrew University of Jerusalem.

Michael Livni was born in Vienna in 1935, growing up in Vancouver, Canada where he graduated with an MD. In 1963 he made *aliyah* to Kibbutz Gesher Haziv. Over the past 30 years, he has been involved with Reform Zionism—as a *shaliach* (emissary) to the movement in North America, and later as a coordinator of the Israeli Reform youth movement—and settled on the Reform Kibbutz, Lotan in 1986. From 1989–92 he directed the World Zionist Organization's Department of Jewish Education and Culture. His book, *Reform Zionism: An Educator's Perspective* appeared in 1999. During the last decade, Livni has developed educational and ecological tourism on Kibbutz Lotan.

Michael Marmur has been the Dean of the Hebrew Union College in Jerusalem since 1998. After his ordination from the Israel Rabbinic Program at HUC, he served at the Leo Baeck Education Center in Haifa for six years before being appointed Dean of the College back in Jerusalem. Michael was born in London and came to Israel in 1984. He holds a BA in Modern History from the University of Oxford, an MA in Jewish History from the Hebrew University, and a Ph.D. from the Hebrew University in Modern Jewish Thought.

Richard Mendelsohn heads the Department of History at the University of Cape Town. His research interests lie in South African Jewish history and in "film and history". He is the author of *Sammy Marks: 'The Uncrowned King of the Transvaal,* a biography of the pioneering South African Jewish industrial and mining entrepreneur (1991) and is co-editor, with Milton Shain, of *Memories, Realities and Dreams: Aspects of the South African Jewish Experience* (2002).

Philip Mendes is Senior Lecturer in Social Policy and Community Development in the Department of Social Work at Monash University, Melbourne, and has published widely on welfare politics and the welfare state, illicit drugs, young people leaving state care, Israeli/Palestinian politics, and Jews and the Left. Dr Mendes is the author or co-author of five books including *The New Left, the Jews and the Vietnam War, 1965–72* (1993), *Jews and Australian Politics* (2004), and *Inside the Welfare Lobby: A History of the Australian Council of Social Service* (2006). He is currently preparing a second edition of *Australia's Welfare Wars* (2003) for publication in 2007.

David Mittelberg is Head of the Department of Sociology at Oranim, The Academic College of Education, Tivon, Israel, where he is also Head of the Center of the Study of the Jewish People. Dr Mittelberg also serves as a Senior Research Fellow at the Institute for Kibbutz Research at Haifa University, Israel, where he formerly served as its Director. He is the author of *The Israel Connection and American Jews* (1999) and *Strangers in Paradise: The Israeli Kibbutz Experience* (1988). He has published articles on ethnicity, migration, gender, tourism, kibbutz education and the sociology of American Jewry.

Françoise Ouzan is an Associate Professor at the University of Reims Champagne-Ardenne and Associate Researcher at the French Research Center of Jerusalem (CRFJ, CNRS). She is a senior researcher at the Diaspora Research Center at the University of Tel Aviv, and conducts research on immigration and Jewish identity. Her publications include *Ces Juifs dont l'Amérique ne voulait pas, 1945–1950* (1995), *Histoire des Américains juifs de 1654 à nos jours, de la marge à l'influence* (Bruxelles, Éditions Complexe, 2007) and *De la mémoire de la Shoah dans le monde juif* (co-edited with Dan Michman, forthcoming).

Larissa Remennick is Professor of Sociology at Bar-Ilan University, Israel. She was born and educated in Moscow, Russia, and immigrated to Israel in 1991. Her research interests are quite diverse and include the sociology of ethnicity, immigration and social integration in general, and specifically among former Soviet Jewry. Her most recent book *Russian Jews on Three Continents: Identity, Integration, and Conflict* (2006) offers a comparative study of acculturation and social insertion among Russian-speaking Jews who migrated to Israel, US, Canada and Germany after the fall of communism.

Suzanne D. Rutland (MA (Hons), Ph.D., Dip Ed) is Associate Professor and Chair of the Department of Hebrew, Biblical and Jewish Studies at the University of Sydney. Sydney-born, Suzanne has published widely on Australian Jewish history. Her latest book is *The Jews in Australia* (2005). With Professor Sol Encel, she has received a major government grant to study "The Political Sociology of Australian Jewry". She has held numerous leadership positions, including being immediate past president of the Australian Jewish Historical Society.

Jonathan Rynhold is a lecturer in the Department of Politics, and a Research Associate at the BESA Centre for Strategic Studies, at Bar-Ilan University, Israel. His research interests include analysis of the role of culture in Israeli foreign policy. In this vein, he has published numerous articles, including "Deconstructing Unilateral Disengagement: Identity and Security in Israel" (Israel Studies Forum 2004); "Religion, Postmodernisation and Israeli Approaches to the Palestinians" (*Terrorism and Political Violence* 2005). Dr Rynhold has also co-edited a book on the 2003 Israeli elections entitled *Israel at the Polls* (2003).

Naama Sabar holds the Joanne and Haime Constantiner Chair for Jewish Education at Tel Aviv University. Her fields of specialization are Jewish education, curriculum development, and qualitative research methods — in particular, ethics in qualitative research. She has written over 100 refereed articles and chapters in books, as well as several books in Hebrew and in English, among them *Kibbutzniks in the Diaspora* (2000). Professor Sabar is the recipient of the Tel Aviv Award for Research in Education for the year 2005.

Ofira Seliktar has recently retired from teaching political science at Temple University and Gratz College, Philadelphia, USA. She is now an Associated Scholar at the Middle East Center at the University of Pennsylvania, and a Visiting Professor at the National Security Studies Program at Tel Aviv University. Seliktar has published extensively on the Middle East conflict, Israel and American Jews. She is the author of seven books and dozens of articles on these subjects, including *Divided We Stand: American Jews, Israel and the Peace Process* (2002). She is currently writing a new book on the Oslo peace process.

Zohar Segev is a Lecturer at the Department of Jewish History, University of Haifa, Israel, and teaches courses on American Jewish history and Zionist history. Dr Zegev has written widely about American Zionism. These writings include: "The Jewish State in Abba Hillel Silver's Overall World View" (forthcoming); "American Zionists' Place in Israel after the Establishment of the State: Involved Partners or Outside Supporters" (forthcoming); and his book, *From Ethnic Politicians to*

National Leaders: American Zionist Leadership, the Holocaust and the Establishment of Israel.

Milton Shain teaches Modern Jewish History and is Professor and Director of the Isaac and Jessie Kaplan Centre for Jewish Studies and Research at the University of Cape Town. He has written and edited several books on South African Jewish history and the history of anti-Semitism. These include: *Jewry and Cape Society. The Origins and Activities of the Jewish Board of Deputies for the Cape Colony* (1983), *The Roots of Antisemitism in South Africa* (1994), *Antisemitism* (1998), and *Jewries at the Frontier: Accommodation, Identity and Conflict* (co-edited with Sander L Gilman, 1999). He has also co-edited *Israel: Culture Religion and Society, 1948–1998* (with Stuart A Cohen, 2000) and *Memories, Realities and Dreams. Aspects of the South African Jewish Experience* (with Richard Mendelsohn, 2002). His latest edited book was *Opposing Voices: Liberalism and Opposition in South Africa Today* (2006).

Alice Shalvi was born in Germany in 1926, and educated in England (MA in English Literature, Cambridge University, Diploma in Social Work, London School of Economics). In 1949, she immigrated to Israel and began teaching in the English Department of the Hebrew University of Jerusalem, from which she retired in 1990. From 1975 to 1990 she served as principal of the Pelech Experimental Religious High School for Girls in Jerusalem. From 1984 to 2001 she was the founding chairwoman of the Israel Women's Network. More recently she has been connected with the Schechter Institute of Jewish Studies in Jerusalem.

Gabriel (Gabi) Sheffer is Professor of the Political Science Department at The Hebrew University of Jerusalem. His research focuses on security policymaking networks in democratic states, and ethnic politics, with special emphasis on ethno-national diaspora politics, Israeli politics and the Israeli–Arab conflicts. He has published many books and articles on all these subjects, including: *Modern Diasporas in International Politics* (1986), *Middle Eastern Minorities and Diasporas* (co-edited with Moshe Maoz, 2002), *Diaspora Politics: At Home Abroad* (2003); *Who Governs the Jewish Nation? Israel–Diaspora Relations* (2006, in Hebrew, with an English version forthcoming).

Colin Shindler is a lecturer in Israeli and Modern Jewish Studies and the chairman of the Centre for Jewish Studies at the School of Oriental and African Studies at the University of London. He was an editor for the *Jewish Quarterly* from 1985 to 1994, and then for *Judaism Today* from 1995 to 2000. His most recent book, *The Triumph of Military Zionism: Nationalism and the Origins of the Israeli Right* was published in 2006.

David B. Starr serves as Dean of the Me'ah programme of adult Jewish learning at Hebrew College, where he teaches Jewish history. Dr Starr received his doctorate in history and Jewish Studies from Columbia University. He holds rabbinic ordination from the Jewish Theological Seminary. He has been rabbinic advisor at Harvard Radcliffe Hillel, and taught at Brandeis University. He is currently writing a biography of Solomon Schechter.

Elana Maryles Sztokman is an educator, researcher, writer and activist specializing in Judaism, gender, and education. She received a doctorate in education from Hebrew University in Jerusalem, and has worked in a variety of positions in Jewish education in New York, Australia, and Israel. She currently teaches education and gender at the Bar Ilan Institute of Gender Studies, and the Efrata Religious Teacher Training College, works as Managing Editor of the *Jewish Educational Leadership Journal* of the Lookstein Center, and consults to Jewish schools and communal institutions on issues of gender and Jewish education.

Gabriel Trajtenberg is a sociologist at the University of Buenos Aires, FLACSO and Gothemburg University, and was a National Researcher between 1989–92. He has been a lecturer at Buenos Aires University, Belgrano University, Lujan University and San Andres University. From 1988 to 1997 Mr Trajtenberg was a very active member of the Argentinean ecological movement, the Swedish environmental federation and President of Green Cross Argentina. From 1995 until 2002, he worked as a project director of various programmes of the American Joint Distribution Committee (JDC) in Latin America. Since 2002 he has been the Executive Director of Hillel Argentina and is also their Latin American Supervisor.

Chaim I. Waxman is Professor Emeritus of Sociology and Jewish Studies at Rutgers, The State University of New Jersey, USA. He now serves as Senior Fellow at the Jewish People Policy Planning Institute in Jerusalem. He holds an MA and Ph.D. from New School for Social Research, as well as a Masters of Hebrew Literature from Yeshiva University. Professor Waxman specializes in the sociology of religion and ethnicity, with particular focus on Jews in the United States and in Israel. His publications include *The Stigma of Poverty: A Critique of Poverty Theories and Policies* (1977; second edn. 1983) and *America's Jews in Transition* (1983).

Dov Waxman is an assistant professor in the Political Science Department at Baruch College of the City University of New York. His research concerns the impact of identity politics in international relations. He is the author of *The Pursuit of Peace and the Crisis of Israeli Identity: Defending / Defining the Nation* (2006). His articles and reviews have appeared in *The Middle East Quarterly*, *Current History*, *World Policy Journal*, *The Washington Quarterly*, *Commentary*, *Israel Affairs*, and *Israel Studies Forum*, among others.

Robert Wexler has been president of the University of Judaism in Los Angeles since 1992 where he also serves as the Colen Distinguished Lecturer in Bible. He received his doctorate from UCLA in the Literature of the Ancient Near East, his MBA degree from Baruch College in New York, and ordination from the Jewish Theological Seminary of America. Dr Wexler lectures frequently on a variety of topics related to contemporary Jewish life.

Index